THE
POLITICAL IDEAS OF HAROLD J. LASKI

THE
POLITICAL
IDEAS OF Harold J. Laski

HERBERT A. DEANE

ARCHON BOOKS · 1972

Library of Congress Cataloging in Publication Data

Deane, Herbert Andrew, 1921–
   The political ideas of Harold J. Laski.

   Originally presented as the author's thesis,
Columbia University.
   Bibliography: p. 346-359
   1. Laski, Harold Joseph, 1893-1950. I. Title.
[JC257.L4D4 1972]   320.5'0924   70-179574
ISBN 0-208-01234-6

CLARKE F. ANSLEY AWARD

This study was selected by a committee
of the FACULTY OF POLITICAL SCIENCE, Columbia University,
to receive the Clarke F. Ansley Award for 1953.

To
MY MOTHER
and to
THE MEMORY OF MY FATHER

Acknowledgments

To Mrs. Frida Laski and to Professor Laski's chief publishers, The Viking Press, Inc., in the United States and George Allen & Unwin, Ltd., in Great Britain, the author is grateful for their generous permission to quote extensively from his works. A list of his works, including the thirty titles in the Abbreviations, with complete publication data, appears in the Bibliography.

The author is also grateful to the following publishers for permission to quote: Harcourt, Brace & Company, Inc., for Laski's *The Foundations of Sovereignty and Other Essays;* Harper & Brothers, for *The American Presidency, The Dangers of Obedience and Other Essays,* the 1930 edition of *Liberty in the Modern State,* and *The Strategy of Freedom,* all by Laski; J. B. Lippincott Company, for Laski's *Politics;* and Oxford University Press, for *Communism* and *Political Thought in England: From Locke to Bentham,* both by Laski, *An Autobiography,* by R. G. Collingwood, and *The Modern State,* by R. M. MacIver.

HERBERT A. DEANE

Preface

THIS book belongs to all those who, by their writing, teaching, or conversation, have contributed to my education during the last thirty years. Above all, it belongs to my teachers—especially to the late Franz L. Neumann, who was my principal guide and critic at every stage in the preparation of this study of Harold Laski. With characteristic generosity he made available to me his amazing store of knowledge, his keen powers of analysis, and his deep concern for the problems of political theory. As a result of his careful comments and criticisms, much of the original manuscript was revised. It is unspeakably difficult to face the fact that this great teacher and devoted friend will no longer be one of the leaders of the intellectual life of Columbia University.

My gratitude to Robert M. MacIver, whose wise counsel and criticism have saved me from many errors in analysis and evaluation, is far greater than my ability to express it.

I am indebted to all those who helped to make my year in England so pleasant and profitable, and particularly to those who generously gave me their time to discuss Laski and his work. I am especially grateful to Frida Laski and to her daughter, Diana Matthewson, for their kindness and assistance.

Among my many debts to Columbia University, it is a great pleasure to acknowledge the Henry Evans Traveling Fellowship, which permitted me to begin my graduate studies at Harvard University in 1946–1947, and the William Bayard Cutting Traveling Fellowship, which allowed me to spend the academic year 1950–1951 in England.

My friends John Eaves, Jr., Julian H. Franklin, James Gutmann, Moses Hadas, John P. Plamenatz, Norman Rosenberg, John B. Stewart, Lionel Trilling, and David B. Truman have read parts of the manuscript and have generously given me their advice and criticism. While I am deeply grateful to all who have helped me, I take full responsibility for whatever errors and omissions may still remain

in the book. I also wish to thank Elinor G. Truman and the staff of
Columbia University Press for assistance in the preparation of the
manuscript for publication.

HERBERT A. DEANE

Columbia University
in the City of New York
October 1954

Contents

Abbreviations

The following abbreviations have been used throughout this work in footnote references to Laski's major publications:

AD	*The American Democracy*
AMS	*Authority in the Modern State*
C	*Communism*
CAC	*The Crisis and the Constitution*
CM	*Communist Manifesto; Socialist Landmark*
CTS	*"The Crisis in the Theory of the State"*
DBG	*The Danger of Being a Gentleman and Other Essays*
DC	*Democracy in Crisis*
DO	*The Dangers of Obedience and Other Essays*
DOT	*The Dilemma of Our Times*
FRC	*Faith, Reason, and Civilization*
FS	*The Foundations of Sovereignty and Other Essays*
GP	*A Grammar of Politics*
KM	*Karl Marx: An Essay*
LMS	*Liberty in the Modern State*
LPC	*The Labour Party and the Constitution*
MT	*Marx and Today*
P	*Politics*
PGE	*Parliamentary Government in England*
PTE	*Political Thought in England: From Locke to Bentham*
REL	*The Rise of European Liberalism*
ROC	*Reflections on the Constitution*
ROM	*The Rights of Man*
RR	*Reflections on the Revolution of Our Time*
SLP	*Studies in Law and Politics*
SOF	*The Strategy of Freedom*
SPS	*Studies in the Problem of Sovereignty*
STP	*The State in Theory and Practice*
TU	*Trade Unions in the New Society*
WDWG	*Where Do We Go from Here?*

THE
POLITICAL IDEAS OF HAROLD J. LASKI

Introduction

FROM 1914 until his death in 1950, Harold J. Laski wrote a vast number of books, pamphlets, and articles dealing with the most crucial political issues of our time—the nature of the modern state and its relationships to individuals and groups, liberty and equality, sovereignty and obedience, and the doctrines of democracy, socialism, Communism, and Fascism. At successive stages of his career he was an ardent proponent of pluralism, Fabianism, and, finally, Marxist socialism. Both in England and the United States his writings reached an audience far larger than that of the ordinary professor of political science, and he exercised a strong influence upon intellectuals on the Continent and in the countries of Asia and Africa. Particularly in the 1930's were his writings a powerful force in molding political opinion, especially among students and young people. He was also an extremely successful and stimulating teacher; from 1920 to 1950 he taught politics and political theory to thousands of students at the London School of Economics and Political Science and at many other universities in England as well as America. To many of these students, and especially to those who came from foreign countries to study politics, the London School and Laski were virtually synonymous terms.

His name was also closely associated with the British Labor Party, since he was for many years a member of its Executive Committee and was the Chairman of the Committee when the Party came to power in 1945. Some foreigners tended to think that Laski was the real leader of the Labor Party and that, because of his great knowledge and intellectual power, he was able to guide the actions of the official leaders, Attlee, Morrison, and Bevin. Finally, he achieved wide fame because of his close friendship with some of the great figures of the century, such as Justice Holmes and Justice Frankfurter in the United States and Lord Haldane and all the leading personalities of the Labor Party in England.

This combination of roles—political philosopher, teacher, publicist, party leader, public speaker, and confidential adviser to statesmen and politicians—gave Laski unmatched opportunities to achieve political insight and understanding. The only role in the world of politics which he did not play was that of holding high office; by his repeated refusals to stand for one of the "safe" Labor seats in the House of Commons, he deliberately chose not to become a legislator or a minister.[1] His activities were so numerous and varied that they would have quickly exhausted any ordinary man. By a prodigious effort of will he managed for many years to carry on all these tasks and, at the same time, found the time to engage in extensive correspondence with a number of close friends. In view of his physical frailty it is not surprising that the crushing burden of work that he carried led to his death at the age of fifty-six. The question naturally comes to mind: Did he use his energies wisely, or should he have limited his activities to teaching and writing? Before any attempt is made to answer this question, however, his career and his works must be examined.

Harold Laski was born on June 30, 1893, the second son of Nathan and Sarah Laski. His father, a prosperous cotton shipper and a leader of the Jewish community in the city of Manchester, saw to it that the family maintained the strict canons of orthodox Judaism. Laski was an extraordinarily precocious child, who became a prize pupil at the Manchester Grammar School, then directed by John Lewis Paton. In July, 1910, there was published in the *Westminster Review* an article by Laski entitled "On the Scope of Eugenics." This essay called forth a letter of congratulation from Sir Francis Galton; the elderly scientist was amazed and delighted when he met Laski, who was then only seventeen years old. He left school in December, 1910, after having won a history exhibition at New College, Oxford, and for

---

[1] As early as November, 1921, he writes to Justice Holmes that he has refused four different requests to stand for Parliament at the next election. See *Holmes-Laski Letters, 1916–1935,* ed. by Mark DeWolfe Howe (2 vols., Cambridge: Harvard University Press, 1953), I, 382 (Nov. 23, 1921). In March, 1923, he writes that he has turned down an offer to stand for a seat where the Labor majority is ten thousand, *ibid.,* I, 488–89 (March 29, 1923). Late in 1923 he notes that MacDonald offered him a cabinet post if he would fight an election, *ibid.,* I, 570 (Dec. 13, 1923). In 1929 he writes that MacDonald wanted him to go to the House of Lords as a debater for the Labor Party, *ibid.,* II, 1153 (June 4, 1929).

the next six months he studied eugenics with Karl Pearson at University College in London.

In the summer of 1911, he went off to Scotland to marry Frida Kerry, whom he had first met late in 1909. The revelation of his marriage to a Gentile was a great shock to his orthodox family, who insisted that the young couple must be separated during Laski's three years at Oxford from 1911 to 1914. After a year of reading science at Oxford, Laski shifted to history; he studied under H. A. L. Fisher and Ernest Barker and was greatly influenced by the writings of the late F. W. Maitland. Although he was a member of the Fabian Society at Oxford, his principal political activity seems to have centered about the suffragette movement, in which his wife was intensely interested. While working in support of this cause, the young couple became the close friends of H. W. Nevinson and George Lansbury, then editor of the *Daily Herald*.

In June, 1914, Laski won his First Class and the Beit Essay Prize. Immediately thereafter, he accepted an invitation from Lansbury to work on the *Herald* during the summer months. He wrote articles dealing with Ireland and constitutional problems from the point of view of the trade unions, which constituted the main audience for the *Herald*'s syndicalist message. When the war began, Laski's attempt to enlist failed when he was rejected on medical grounds. He then accepted an invitation to lecture in history at McGill University in Montreal, and in September, 1914, he and his wife sailed for Canada.

It is interesting to note that the political movements which made the deepest impression on Laski in his undergraduate days, and to which he constantly referred in his early books and articles, were the women's suffrage movement, the growing radicalism and the approach to syndicalism of some of the trade unions, and the alliance between Ulster and a section of the Conservative Party to sabotage the Liberals' Home Rule legislation for Ireland. These phenomena of the prewar period, which George Dangerfield has called the era of "the strange death of Liberal England," [2] shared certain common characteristics; all three movements were rooted in a violent and

[2] George Dangerfield, *The Strange Death of Liberal England* (New York: Harrison Smith and Robert Haas, 1935).

irrational outburst against the spirit of Victorian liberalism. Good form, reasonable discussion and compromise, respect for constitutional procedures, the conviction that women were dependent and "spiritual" creatures, the belief in gradual and inevitable progress—all the sacred principles of the nineteenth century were openly rejected by the more violent suffragettes, by the radical trade unionists, and by the Tories who attempted to revive the powers of the House of Lords and to use force to prevent Ulster from being incorporated into a united Ireland. It almost seems as though nineteenth-century respectability and orderliness had become so great a strain upon the emotions and feelings of a number of men and women that they struck out wildly and blindly to destroy the Liberal world that was suffocating them.

George Orwell has commented: "From the whole decade before 1914, there seems to breathe forth a smell of the more vulgar, un-grown-up kinds of luxury, a smell of brilliantine and crème de menthe and soft-centered chocolates—an atmosphere, as it were, of eating everlasting strawberry ices on green lawns to the tune of the Eton Boating Song." [3] It was in this world that Laski grew up and passed his formative years in school and college, and against this atmosphere that he became a rebel. Conscious from his youth that his Jewishness set him apart from the main stream of his society, he felt a strong impulse to become the ally of all those whose want, ignorance, and misery were hidden behind the placid façade of the Victorian era and who could therefore be ignored by the successful and contented. He felt the need to dedicate his life to the search for a new world view which would absorb the highest ideals of traditional Judaism and Christianity and bring understanding and release to all men everywhere.[4] The causes and the movements to which he was attracted in the years before 1914 were all expressions of a reaction against the self-assurance, the materialism, and the willingness to compromise which marked the leaders of the society. These leaders were amazed and baffled by the emotional force with which both suffragettes and some union leaders pressed uncompromisingly

[3] George Orwell, "Such, Such Were the Joys," *Partisan Review*, XIX (Sept.–Oct., 1952), 533.

[4] See the account of Laski's unpublished essay on the Jewish problem, "The Chosen People," which was written before he was twenty, in Kingsley Martin, *Harold Laski* (New York: The Viking Press, 1953), pp. 14–18.

towards their "unrealistic" goals, and by their willingness to reject the accepted order if it could not accommodate their demands for justice and for freedom of self-expression.

Another commentator, in his discussion of the years preceding the outbreak of the war, notes:

Once more the human mind grew restless, revolted against the accepted standards of the day and searched for an ideal of justice, like many previous generations. The sources of this restlessness were many. Science began to become doubtful about itself and the certainty of scientific facts. Youth rebelled against the self-satisfaction of the bourgeoisie, against cities, money worship, and the flatness of modern life. Social reformers and socialists attacked the social inequalities hidden under legal formalism, and the authority worship of positivists.[5]

Thousands of these young rebels in England and France were killed during the four years of massacre in the trenches. Is it wholly implausible to assume that much of the inertia and apathy of English and French life between the two wars was the result of this heavy loss of youthful idealism and vigor? Through the accident of medical unfitness for military service Laski was saved from this destruction and allowed to continue his education and development in the comparatively sheltered atmosphere of North America. When he returned to England in 1920, he was one of a handful of young men who were eager to effect sweeping reforms and to build a new and more just society on the ruins of that nineteenth-century England which the war had completely destroyed.

I have outlined the main events of Laski's life up to 1914. Now, turning to his published writings on political, social, and economic issues, I shall follow his career down to his death in 1950. There is little of personal biography in the pages that follow. That task must be left to those who knew Harold Laski intimately and who have access to his personal papers. I will have little to say about Laski the teacher or Laski the friend and counselor, who gave himself unsparingly to all who came to him for help and advice. It is, in a sense, unfortunate that these two phases of his career must be ignored, since it is undoubtedly true that he was at the height of his powers in his discussions, lectures, and arguments with his students.

[5] W. Friedmann, *Legal Theory* (2d ed., London: Stevens and Sons, Ltd., 1949), p. 62.

Perhaps his most attractive quality was demonstrated in the interest and help which he gave so lavishly to young people and to all the "underdogs" who found their way to his door. But the task here is a different one. I shall endeavor to present his main ideas on a series of central problems of modern politics and to discover the significant changes that occurred in his teachings through the years.

In attempting to organize the materials for this work, I have found that it was essential to treat Laski's ideas chronologically rather than topically, since the connections between his views on different subjects in a particular period are closer than the links between his discussions of the same theme or problem at different times. Part One of the text deals with his ideas in the "pluralist" period that began with his earliest writings on politics in 1914. It is difficult to make a clear demarcation between this first phase and the following period, which I have labeled "Fabianism" or "socialized Benthamism." I have selected 1925 as the beginning of the second period since that was the year when Laski published *A Grammar of Politics,* his first major work after his return to England in 1920. The next important shift in his position occurred at about the time of the formation of the MacDonald National Government in 1931. He outlined his new approach to politics in *Democracy in Crisis,* published in 1933. In Part Three of this work I have, therefore, considered his Marxist writings on the state from 1932 to 1939. Part Four surveys the war years, 1940 to 1945, and Part Five deals with the postwar period. In each of the first four parts I have organized the material under the same general headings in order to show the significant changes in his ideas.

This attempt to set forth Laski's political ideas and the major changes in his views has made it necessary to include a large number of quotations from his works. It has seemed wise to allow him to speak, as far as possible, in his own words so that the shades of meaning and the subtle changes in his position might not be obscured by another's efforts at summary and paraphrase.

I shall also examine the reasons which impelled him to adopt a particular position or to revise or abandon it. To do this, a certain amount of attention must be paid to the details of his life and of his activities and to the influence exerted upon him by other writers and by external events. In addition, I shall endeavor to analyze and criticize his theories in terms of their logical consistency, their range of applicability, and their power to explain the political facts and developments with which he was dealing. Whenever I move from statements of his views to commentary and criticism of them, I shall attempt to make the transition clear to the reader. On occasion I may be tempted to outline an alternative answer to a problem raised by Laski, but I shall try to limit such expositions of my own views so that they do not interfere with the central purpose of this work. In the final chapter I shall seek to assess Laski's significance as a political thinker and to measure his actual accomplishments against the potentialities which he demonstrated. Throughout the discussion I shall aim to present his views as clearly and as accurately as possible, and I hope to be unsparingly critical without being guilty of malice or triviality. If he were alive today, he would certainly not object to the dissents and the criticisms, for he was always delighted—though usually unconvinced—when his students or younger colleagues disagreed with him and attempted to demonstrate how mistaken his views were.

Part One

1914-1924

1

The Nature of the State and Political Power

LASKI's earliest political writings are a constant polemic against what he terms "mystic monism" [1] in political thought—the conception that the state is to political theory what the Absolute is to metaphysics, that it is mysteriously One above all other human groupings, and that, because of its superior position and higher purpose, it is entitled to the undivided allegiance of each of its citizens. Laski believes that the main prop of this monistic theory of the state is the concept of state sovereignty, elaborated by Bodin and Hobbes in the sixteenth and seventeenth centuries and given modern form in John Austin's definition of the legal sovereign as the "determinate human superior, not in a habit of obedience to a like superior," who receives "habitual obedience from the bulk of a given society." [2] He therefore attempts to destroy the monistic view by concentrating his critical fire on the concept of sovereignty.

Following Figgis's analysis,[3] Laski argues that with the breakup of feudalism and the rise of the modern state, the state assumed for itself the *plenitudo potestatis* that medieval Popes and their apologists had claimed for the Papacy. The state was trying to counter the claims of older feudal loyalties and, more important, it was endeavoring to answer, on their own ground of "right," theories—whether Protestant or Catholic—that insisted on the right to disobey the state in the name of conscience and thereby threatened to destroy the social fabric in an unending series of civil and religious wars. The state therefore claimed for its ruler or rulers an absolute right to the com-

[1] *Studies in the Problem of Sovereignty* (New Haven: Yale University Press, 1917), hereinafter cited as SPS, p. 3; see also "The Personality of the State," *The Nation*, CI (July 22, 1915), 115.
[2] John Austin, *Lectures on Jurisprudence* (2d ed., London: John Murray, 1861), p. 170.
[3] See J. N. Figgis, *The Divine Right of Kings* (2d ed., Cambridge: Cambridge University Press, 1914) and *Studies of Political Thought from Gerson to Grotius* (2d ed., Cambridge: Cambridge University Press, 1916).

plete obedience of all individuals and groups within the society. When, in the eighteenth and nineteenth centuries, the magic of monarchy faded, the theory of state sovereignty was buttressed by the new notion of popular sovereignty; Rousseau argued that the state as the embodiment of the general will had absolute power over the individual's actions and beliefs and over all groups and associations in the society. In England Bentham and Austin set forth the theory of the legal omnicompetence and sovereignty of the state's will as expressed by Parliament, while in Germany Hegel and some of his disciples maintained that since the state is the highest manifestation of Reason its will has moral pre-eminence over the wills of individuals or inferior social groups. For Laski, the result of this whole process of magnifying the authority of the state has been "the implicit acceptance of a certain grim Hegelianism which has swept us unprotestingly on into the vortex of a great All which is more than ourselves. . . . So the State has become a kind of modern Baal to which the citizen must bow a heedless knee." [4]

Laski's attack on the concept of sovereignty is double-barreled. He insists, first, that if we look at the modern state in its relations with its citizens we find nothing that resembles Austinian sovereignty. He believes that this conclusion follows from the obvious fact that citizens do not always obey the commands of the state, that when the state comes into conflict with a church or a trade union the latter sometimes wins the obedience of its members. Defenders of the traditional theory retort, of course, that the fact that men do not always obey the law does not constitute a refutation of the Austinian theory. The theory does not assume that obedience is perfect; if it were, there would be no need for courts and police. Nor does the theory assume that disobedience is ethically wrong or immoral; it simply asserts that it is illegal. Laski himself seems to recognize this when he says, "Legally, no one can deny that there exists in every state some organ whose authority is unlimited. But that legality is no more than a fiction of logic." [5] He maintains that while Parliament may be the legal sovereign in Great Britain, there are, in fact, many things that it cannot do. His conclusion is that the idea of parlia-

[4] SPS, p. 208.

[5] *The Foundations of Sovereignty and Other Essays* (New York: Harcourt, Brace and Co., 1921), hereinafter cited as FS, p. 236.

mentary sovereignty and the view that law is the command of the sovereign are so absurd as to be useless as working hypotheses in any adequate political theory. This criticism rests on a blurring of the distinction between sovereignty as a legal and as a political concept; Laski's attack demonstrates only that the Austinian analysis does not constitute an adequate political theory since it overstresses the legal aspect of the state and pays insufficient attention to the social and political forces that determine the content of law and shape the manner of its application to specific cases.[6]

His second criticism is that the idea of the sovereignty of the state is ethically indefensible. "The Austinian theory of sovereignty," he argues, "ungenial enough even in its abstract presentation, would as a fact breed simple servility were it capable of practical application."[7] The repeated surrender of the judgment of the individual's conscience, necessarily involved in unquestioning obedience to the dictates of the state, stunts the development of each citizen's personality and moral stature. Laski here seems to be confusing the Austinian concept, which makes no assumption about the moral rightness of legal imperatives or about the immorality of disobeying the law, with the argument of those idealists, such as Hegel, Treitschke, or Bosanquet, who argue that the moral supremacy of the state over individuals and groups gives it the right to the obedience of its citizens.

To add to this confusion, Laski fails to distinguish between his two lines of attack on the traditional concept of sovereignty—its inadequacy as a description and explanation of the processes by which political power is exerted in any community and its indefensibility on moral grounds. Sometimes he argues that there is no such thing as political sovereignty;[8] at other moments he defines the sovereignty of the state as the degree of consent that its actions can win from its citizens and objects to the orthodox theory because it ignores this factor of consent in its equation of law with the sovereign's fiat.[9] In the latter case, his argument seems to be that no government is in fact sovereign and that the state cannot and should not be regarded,

---

[6] See Francis W. Coker, "Pluralistic Theories and the Attack upon State Sovereignty," in Charles E. Merriam and H. E. Barnes, eds., *A History of Political Theories— Recent Times* (New York: Macmillan Co., 1924), p. 110.

[7] SPS, p. 273.　　　　　　　　　　　　[8] See FS, p. 230.

[9] See SPS, pp. 14 and 262; FS, p. 244; and *Authority in the Modern State* (New Haven: Yale University Press, 1919), hereinafter cited as AMS, p. 165.

a priori, as sovereign since its sovereignty rests on the consent of each of its members. The sovereignty of the state thus becomes an "ideal limit," approached as the extent of popular consent to a given state action approaches universality, but, given the inevitable diversity in the beliefs and judgments of the members of a society, never actually attained.[10] Even if we agree that this is what Laski means by "sovereignty," we may conclude that he should have abandoned the term altogether in his own exposition; he succeeds only in bewildering his reader by both attacking the concept and seeking to retain it with an altered meaning.

Laski's redefinition of state sovereignty obviously implies a clear demarcation between state and society and between state and government. He criticizes idealists such as Bosanquet for their identification of state and society; the identification ignores the fact that there are social relationships which are as primary as the individual's relationship to the state and that these relationships cannot be expressed through the state. We must, he says, reaffirm the old truth that "the allegiance of man to the state is secondary to his allegiance to what he may conceive his duty to society as a whole." [11] He also condemns the idealists for their failure to make a clear differentiation between state and government. Idealism, he argues, "asserted, and with justice, that right and truth ought to prevail; but its actual result, in the hands of its chief exponents, was to identify right and truth merely with the decisions of the governmental authority legally competent to make them." [12] He maintains that the state is always divided into the government, the small number of men who exert power, and the subjects, the great mass of citizens who, for the most part, acquiesce in the decisions that are made. In his eagerness to discredit the traditional state theory, Laski virtually scraps the distinction between state and government that he emphasizes so strongly in his criticism of the idealists; what we term state action is, in actual fact, action by government. The policy of the government becomes state action only after it has been carefully scrutinized by the citizens and generally accepted by them as a fulfillment of the state's pur-

[10] See SPS, p. 206.   [11] AMS, p. 122.
[12] *The State in the New Social Order*, Fabian Tract No. 200 (London: The Fabian Society, 1922), p. 8.

pose.[13] In view of the inertia and passive acquiescence of the average citizen, there is very little, if any, genuine state action in our society.

Laski continues: "We lend to government the authority of the state upon the basis of a conviction that its will is a will effecting the purpose for which the state was founded. The state, we broadly say, exists to promote the good life, however variously defined; and we give government the power to act for the promotion of that life." [14] This statement implies an acceptance of a broad view of the nature and purpose of the state that is not compatible with his attack upon the state. Further, he attempts to combine with this view of the state's function a radically individualistic theory of obedience, [15] in which he holds that only the individual can judge whether a given act of government does serve the end for which the state exists and so is indeed a state act. This is his solution to what he calls the real problem of democratic government—the discovery of the means whereby the interest of the people as a whole may secure supremacy over the interest of any special portion of the community and, in particular, over the self-interest of the rulers.

In Laski's strong distrust of political power and of those who wield it, we can hear echoes of Lord Acton's famous dictum on the corrupting effects of power. His desire to prevent the force of the state from being concentrated at any single point within it leads him to attack the idea of the state's sovereignty; [16] he wants to see power split up, divided, set against itself, and thrown widespread among men by various devices of decentralization, and he wants to be certain that the civil, economic, and social rights of individuals and groups are ensured against the encroachments of those who exercise power. What, we may ask, is the motive that leads him to emphasize the dangers inherent in political power, particularly when it is concentrated? Why does he place so much stress on the divergence of interests between rulers and subjects? And, finally, what lies behind his extended polemic against state sovereignty? We cannot answer these questions simply by referring to the influence of the ideas of Gierke, transmitted to Laski by Figgis and Maitland. The fundamental problem remains—why did he find these ideas, rather than

---

[13] See AMS, p. 30; FS, p. 136; and SPS, p. 14.
[14] AMS, p. 28.   [15] See below, chap. 2.   [16] See AMS, p. 120.

others, attractive and persuasive? Nor is it sufficient to refer to the
reaction against the idealist theory of the state that occurred in England after the outbreak of war in 1914. Laski's antistatism is not a
simple reflection of the view that saw in the nationalism, imperialism,
and militarism of Imperial Germany the fruits of a Hegelian overemphasis on the majesty of the state and the moral pre-eminence of
its commands.[17]

We must remember the thesis that Laski constantly reiterates—
although, in theory, a state may exist to secure the highest life for its
members, in actuality the good maintained is that of a certain section
and not that of the community as a whole.[18] Normally the will that
gets registered is the will of those who operate the machine of government. And since government is, for the most part, in the hands of
those who wield economic power, it is clear that political power is
the handmaid of economic power.[19] Laski assures us: "It is today
a commonplace that the real source of authority in any state is with
the holders of economic power. The will that is effective is their will;
the commands that are obeyed are their commands."[20] The motive
underlying his attack on the concept of state sovereignty is laid bare
when he states that the theory "assumes that the government is fully
representative of the community without taking account of the way
in which the characteristics of the economic system inevitably per-

[17] But note his statement that nineteenth-century Germany "etherealized the principles of Machiavelli, and erected them into an ethical system. Hegel gave to them a
philosophic, and Treitschke a quasi-historical justification." "A Philosophy Embattled," *The Dial*, LXII (Feb. 8, 1917), 96.

[18] See SPS, p. 15.

[19] See his comment: "No political democracy can be real that is not as well the
reflection of an economic democracy; for the business of government is so largely
industrial in nature as inevitably to be profoundly affected by the views and purposes
of those who hold the keys of economic power. That does not necessarily mean that
government is consciously perverted to the ends of any class within the state. . . . But
when power is actually exerted by any section of the community, it is only natural that
it should look upon its characteristic views as the equivalent of social good." AMS,
p. 38. See also *Holmes-Laski Letters, 1916–1935,* ed. by Mark DeWolfe Howe (2 vols.,
Cambridge: Harvard University Press, 1953), I, 76 (April 5, 1917).

[20] FS, p. 62. See also his statement: "Those who hold power will inevitably feel
that the definition of good is the maintenance, in some fashion, of the *status quo*. . . .
The business of government has, for the most part, been confided to the middle class;
and the results have largely reflected the aptitudes and purposes of that class." *Ibid.,*
p. 63.

verts [*sic*] the governmental purpose to narrow and special ends." [21]
The state that Laski seeks to discredit is, he argues,

in reality the reflexion of what a dominant group or class in a community
believes to be political good. And, in the main, it is reasonably clear that
political good is today for the most part defined in economic terms. It
mirrors within itself, that is to say, the economic structure of society. It is
relatively unimportant in what fashion we organise the institutions of the
state. Practically they will reflect the prevailing economic system; practically also, they will protect it.[22]

The power of the contemporary state is thus predominantly used
to promote the interests of the capitalist class and to hinder the interests of labor. "For the social order of the modern state is not a
labour order but a capitalist, and upon the broad truth of Harrington's hypothesis it must follow that the main power is capitalist also.
That will imply a refusal on labour's part to accept the authority of
the state as final save where it is satisfied with its purposes." [23] Laski
makes it very clear that his fundamental objection is to the capitalist
state, and not the sovereign state, when he says: "No one would object to a strong state if guarantees could be had that its strength
would be used for the fulfilment of its theoretic purposes." [24] To
endow the state with omnicompetence and sovereignty is to leave
it at the mercy of any group powerful enough to exploit it, that is,
the small group that wields economic power. "The only way out of
such an impasse," Laski concludes, "is the neutralisation of the state;
and it cannot be neutralised save by the division of the power that is
today concentrated in its hands." [25] It may be observed that this interpretation of Laski's attack upon the state enables us to link his
early pluralistic writings with the radically different views that he
later advocated. For, on the basis of his early thesis, it is clear that
if the labor movement should cease to be a minority group struggling
against the power of a hostile behemoth and if the social order could
be transformed from a capitalist to a labor order, there would be no
hindrance to the fulfillment by the state of its theoretic purposes and,

[21] *Ibid.*, Preface, p. vi.   [22] AMS, p. 81.

[23] *Ibid.*, p. 88; see also "Democracy at the Crossroads," *Yale Review*, n.s., IX (July,
1920), 797.

[24] AMS, p. 374.   [25] *Ibid.*, p. 385.

consequently, no reason for objecting to a strong, or even a sovereign, state.

It is significant that Laski cites Harrington rather than Marx when he argues that political power is the handmaid of economic power. At this stage he is critical, as we shall see, of Marx's economics and theory of history.[26] Indeed, he is suspicious of all dogmatic and simple theories of history and politics; his temper is rationalistic, but it is also marked by scepticism of final truths and by a consistently pragmatic and realistic bias. Telling us that "an admission of vast complexity is the beginning of wisdom in political philosophy," [27] he warns that "the price we pay for militant certitude in social affairs is always the establishment of a despotism." [28] He criticizes traditional political thought for its concentration on *staatslehre* at the expense of *politik,* for its oversimple assumptions about human nature, and for its penchant for deductive reasoning. He says: "The simple *a priori* premises of Hobbes or Locke, the intriguing mysticism of Rousseau's general will, eloquence about the initiative of men and its translation into terms of private property, are no longer suited to a world that has seen its foundations in flame because to its good intentions an adequate knowledge was not joined. What we need . . . is the sober and scientific study of the conditions of social organization." [29] Repeatedly he calls for a new inductive political philosophy, centered less on political principles than on administrative functions, and based on a realistic social psychology that will do more justice to the complex character of human personality and motivation than does the psychology of Aristotle or Machiavelli or Hobbes. The new political theory, seeking an institutional structure that will offer opportunities for the creative expression of the diverse impulses of men more adequate than those provided by the sovereign state, must be grounded in a satisfactory knowledge of the motives and desires of men.

Each man must be encouraged to realize his own personality, while the state must be so organized as to give scope to the individual's sense

[26] See below, chap. 3, section 2.

[27] "Democracy at the Crossroads," *Yale Review*, n.s., IX (July, 1920), 803.

[28] "Lenin and Mussolini," *Foreign Affairs*, II (Sept., 1923), 54; see also "The Temper of the Present Time," *The New Republic*, XXI (Feb. 18, 1920), 335–38.

[29] "Democracy at the Crossroads," *Yale Review*, n.s., IX (July, 1920), 802–03. See also *Holmes-Laski Letters*, I, 15 and 105 (Sept. 6, 1916 and Oct. 21, 1917).

of spontaneity and his creative impulses, thereby fostering the emergence of a wide diversity in the desires, attitudes, and values of its citizens.[30] Since he is primarily concerned with the preservation and promotion of individuality and spontaneity, Laski rejects order and unity as final values.[31]

All that men are willing to sacrifice to society is the lowest and not the highest common factor of their intimate beliefs. For they are not simply members of a herd; they are something more. They are individuals who are interested passionately in themselves as an end, and no social philosophy can be adequate which neglects that egocentric element.[32]

He frequently cites William James's dictum that "we live in a multiverse and not a universe"; as James endeavored to expel the demons of absolutism and monism from philosophy, so Laski aims to drive them from the precincts of political thought.

His choice of the term "pluralist" to describe his new political theory is testimony to the influence that the pluralist and instrumentalist currents in American thought exerted on him during his stay in North America from 1914 to 1920. In the pluralistic and pragmatic philosophies of James and Dewey he found a point of view that was extremely congenial to his own opposition to idealism and monism and to his conviction, which marks him as heir to the utilitarian tradition of Bentham and the Mills, that the state is to be judged in the light of its actual contributions to the well-being of its citizens. His pluralist theory, which insists that the state, in common with every other association, must prove itself by what it achieves rather than by the methods it uses or the purposes it claims to serve, is, he says, what Dewey calls "consistently experimentalist" in form and content.[33] "It does not try to work out with tedious elaboration the respective spheres of State or group or individual. It leaves that to the test of the event. It predicates no certainty because history, I

---

[30] See SPS, pp. 24–25 and 235–37; AMS, p. 279; and FS, p. 86.

[31] See the statement: "however valuable may be the benefits of order, they are useless so long as they stifle the spontaneity of the human mind." AMS, p. 320.

[32] *Ibid.*, p. 177.

[33] See SPS, p. 23; AMS, pp. 68–69, 177, and 375; "Democracy at the Crossroads," *Yale Review*, n.s., IX (July, 1920), 803; *The State in the New Social Order*, p. 15; and the Introduction to Léon Duguit, *Law in the Modern State*, tr. by Frida and Harold Laski (New York: B. W. Huebsch, 1919), p. xxxiii.

think fortunately, does not repeat itself." [34] The test of the validity
of state action is thus a pragmatic test—how successful is it in achieving its purpose, the promotion of the good life for its citizens? "Political good," he asserts, "refuses the swaddling-clothes of finality
and becomes a shifting conception. It can not be hegelianised into
a permanent compromise. It asks the validation of men and actions
in terms of historical experience." [35] Viewed in this instrumentalist
fashion, the sovereign state becomes what Duguit calls "a great public
service corporation," no more than the greatest of public utilities. Like
every such institution, it is to be judged by the adequacy of the service that it renders to its public.

Typical of Laski's pragmatic approach to politics is his analysis of
the law as an instrument for satisfying social needs, as opposed to a
formal theory of law as a self-contained logical system.[36] This sociological and pragmatic approach to law, though it derives immediately
from the new jurisprudence of Duguit, Pound, and Justice Holmes,
is clearly compatible with the tradition of British utilitarianism. Laski
maintains, for example, that the only valid explanation of the doctrine
of vicarious liability, by which the employer is held responsible for
his servant's torts even if he is himself without fault, is that "in a
social distribution of profit and loss, the balance of least disturbance
seems thereby best to be obtained." [37] This sociological view of the
function of law is also the basis for his insistence that the doctrine of
vicarious liability must be made applicable to corporations and unincorporated associations as well as to individuals, and that, in general,
the law should apply to group action the same canons of judgment
that it uses in dealing with the actions of individuals. Echoing
Holmes's reminder that the life of the law is not logic but experience,
Laski says: "We have to search for the mechanisms of our law in life
as it actually is, rather than fit the life we live to *a priori* rules of rigid
legal system." [38] He concludes: "We come once more to an age of
collective endeavor. We begin the re-interpretation of law in the terms
of our collective needs. . . . It is our business to set law to the rhythm
of modern life. It is the harmonization of warring interests with

---

[34] SPS, p. 23.   [35] AMS, p. 166.
[36] See FS, pp. 260–61, 272–73, and 284.
[37] *Ibid.*, p. 261; see the entire article, "The Basis of Vicarious Liability," *ibid.*,
pp. 252–91.
[38] *Ibid.*, p. 261.

which we are concerned. How to evolve from a seeming conflict the social gain it is the endeavor of law to promote—this is the problem by which we are confronted." [39]

What are the essential features of the pluralist view of the state that Laski proposes to substitute for the "outmoded" monistic theory of state sovereignty? He tells us that just as the essence of James's philosophic pluralism was his insistence that things are "with" one another in many ways, but that there is no Absolute, nothing which includes everything or dominates everything, so the core of his political pluralism is the proposition that the parts of the state are as real and as self-sufficient as the whole and that the state is "distributive" and not "collective." [40] The state is only one of the many forms of human association; there is no fundamental difference between its nature and the nature of any other association, such as a baseball club.[41] The state is not to be eliminated as it is in anarchism or in some varieties of pluralism,[42] but Laski denies that it is inherently entitled to primacy over other groups. "It is not necessarily any more in harmony with the end of society than a church or a trade-union or a freemasons' lodge." [43] The state has only that pre-eminence—and no more—to which on a particular occasion of conflict of its will with the will of another group, its possibly superior moral claim may entitle it.[44] As we have already noted, the sovereignty of the state, for Laski, is merely its ability to get its commands accepted by its members; it does not, therefore, differ from the power of a church or a trade union, for their power, too, is a function of the degree to which their commands are accepted by their members.[45]

Laski's pluralism is an extremely individualistic doctrine; men belong to many groups, including the state, and "a competition for allegiance is continuously possible. . . . Whether we will or no, we are bundles of hyphens. When the centers of linkage conflict a choice

[39] *Ibid.,* p. 291.   [40] See SPS, pp. 9–10; FS, p. 169.

[41] See "The Personality of the State," *The Nation,* CI (July 22, 1915), 116; see also his statement: "The state is an organized group actuated by a particular idea, and men belong to it because they believe in the goodness of that idea." *Ibid.*

[42] See, e.g., G. D. H. Cole, *Guild Socialism Re-stated* (London: L. Parsons, 1920), p. 124: "Coordination is inevitably coercive unless it is self-coordination, and it must therefore be accomplished by the common action of the various bodies which require coordination."

[43] AMS, p. 65.   [44] See SPS, p. 19.

[45] *Ibid.,* p. 270.

must be made." [46] The theory leaves to the individual the decision whether in a particular conflict he will give his allegiance to the state or to the church or the union. At a later point we shall have to give detailed consideration to this theory of obedience.[47] Here we need only note Laski's thesis that since society is essentially federal in nature, it is impossible and unwise to attempt to confine sovereignty to the state or to any of the coordinate groups that constitute society; "the paramount character of the state is *ipso facto* denied." [48] Power no longer needs to be concentrated at a given point in the social structure; as a good pragmatist, Laski argues that it can and should go where it can be most wisely and effectively utilized for social purposes. In every society we confront a wide variety of functional and territorial interests. The pluralistic state will abandon the vain attempt of the monistic state to apply uniform and equal solutions to things neither uniform nor equal; it will be a federal state in which sovereignty will be distributed among the various functional groups and associations as well as the geographical subdivisions of the society.[49] Whereas the structure of the sovereign state is hierarchical, that of the pluralistic state will consist in "a series of co-ordinate groups the purposes of which may well be antithetic." [50]

There are serious difficulties and confusions in Laski's pluralism. How, for instance, can anyone who insists, as he does, on a sharp distinction between state and society refer to the associations of men —their clubs, churches, and trade unions—as parts of the *state* that are as real and primary as the whole? Even if we explain away this difficulty as a mere verbal slip, we are left with the major problem —the nature of the relationship between the state, even the pluralistic state, and these other associations. The latter, he tells us, "are, it may be, in relations with the state, a part of it; but one with it they are not. They refuse the reduction to unity." [51] Assuredly, but is it not also obvious that the state is essentially different from a group such as a baseball club? All the members of the society are members of the state, state membership is compulsory in a manner that differs significantly even from the union membership of a worker employed in a "closed shop," and the state has a monopoly of the exercise of

[46] FS, pp. 169–70.
[47] See below, chap. 2.
[48] AMS, p. 74.
[49] See FS, Preface, p. viii.
[50] AMS, p. 84.
[51] FS, p. 169.

final coercive power in the society. These peculiar characteristics of the state, taken together with its function of regulating the relationships and, particularly, the conflicts among other social groups, imply that in case of a conflict, for example, between the state and a trade union, there is some prima-facie reason for the individual to give greater weight to his allegiance to the more inclusive group.

If we are to take literally Laski's theory of the "polyarchism" of coordinate groups in the pluralistic state, the state will have no power to regulate the actions of other associations or their relationships. Unless we assume a natural law of harmony among social groups—and Laski never explicitly makes or defends this assumption —we are faced with a succession of struggles between competing groups and interests in the course of which social order and peace will be destroyed. And the outcome of each such clash between opposing interests is likely to depend far more on the naked power that the various groups can muster than on rational decisions of individuals about the superiority of the moral claim of the state to that of a group, or of one group over another. This pluralistic ideal of a society made up of free and "coordinate" groups engaged in eternal conflict and, it is hoped, compromise, with no one group enjoying primacy over the others, reminds us of Pope Gelasius I's Doctrine of the Two Swords, wherein the Church and the Empire were described as two coordinate and cooperating institutions ordained by God for the proper governance of human society. We know how often this Gelasian attempt at a compromise between the claims of temporal and sacerdotal jurisdiction broke down; the unstable equilibrium of two coordinate powers tended to resolve itself into an assertion of the primacy of the imperial power in the writings of a Dante or a Marsiglio, or into a claim of *plenitudo potestatis* for the Papacy in the *Dictatus Papae* of Gregory VII or in Boniface VIII's *Unam sanctam*. The vastly more complicated equilibrium of the multi-group pluralistic state would doubtless be even more difficult to maintain. The anarchy that would result if group conflicts were uncontrolled by the state might well lead the federation of trade unions, the association of employers' groups, or some other powerful social or economic organization to make a bid to assume supreme coercive power in the society.

Laski claims that his destruction of the sovereign state and his

proposal to place all associations, including the state, on an equal
footing follow as necessary conclusions from the doctrine of the real
personality of groups, developed by Gierke and promulgated in England by Maitland and Figgis.[52] Gierke maintained, in opposition to
the fiction and concession theories, that the group is a real entity
with a life, a consciousness, and a will of its own; the group is a real
person whose existence is independent of the state and the law—
groups are born and exist before they are recognized by the law and
they cannot be created or destroyed by legal fiat. In their legal theories
Gierke and Maitland stressed the fact that organized groups are in
fact "persons" with rights and duties whether or not the state has
endowed them with legal personalities, and they called for a more
realistic treatment of groups by the law. It should be noted that
Gierke did not argue, as does Laski, that acceptance of the theory of
the real personality of groups necessarily involves the denial of the
state's sovereignty. The state, he says, is sovereign where general interests demanding the exertion of power for their maintenance are
concerned. The will of the state is the sovereign general will and
the state is the highest *Machtverband*.[53]

Figgis used Gierke's theory of group personality to defend the freedom of the church as a corporate body in the modern state. Contending against all forms of Erastianism and insisting that the
church's corporate freedom must be recognized to the end that she
may fulfill her divine mission, Figgis denied that the church was a
mere creature of the state. Indeed he claimed that it was a *societas
perfecta,* a society no less perfect in form and constitution than the
state. He did not deny, however, that the state had a distinctive function and a superior authority as an agency of coordination of the

---

[52] Otto von Gierke, *Das deutsche Genossenschaftsrecht* (3 vols., Berlin: Weidmann,
1868–1913). F. W. Maitland translated a part of Vol. III of this work as *Political
Theories of the Middle Age* (Cambridge: Cambridge University Press, 1900); see his
Introduction to this translation. See also H. A. L. Fisher, ed., *The Collected Papers
of Frederic William Maitland* (3 vols., Cambridge: Cambridge University Press, 1911),
especially "Moral Personality and Legal Personality" (1903), III, 304–20. For the
views of Figgis, see *The Divine Right of Kings, Studies of Political Thought from
Gerson to Grotius,* and *Churches in the Modern State* (London: Longmans, Green
and Co., 1914).

[53] See "Die Grundbegriffe des Staatsrechts und die neuesten Staatsrechtstheorien,"
Zeitschrift für die gesammte Staatswissenschaft, XXX (1874), as cited and discussed
by Francis W. Coker, "Pluralistic Theories and the Attack upon State Sovereignty,"
in Merriam and Barnes, eds., *A History of Political Theories—Recent Times.*

various groups in society; he concedes that "it is largely to regulate such groups and to ensure that they do not outstep the bounds of justice that the coercive force of the State exists."[54] Figgis described the state as a *communitas communitatum,* akin to the medieval empire; he believed that he had solved the knotty problem of the proper relationship between the state as the organ of coordination and the corporate persons within its territory by the dictum that the state should leave the church free from control where the church's actions concerned only its own affairs, while it might regulate those acts of the church that impinged on persons outside the group. This attempted compromise, analogous to J. S. Mill's attempt to demarcate the area of individual liberty by making a distinction between the self- and other-regarding actions of individuals, is no more satisfactory than Mill's principle, for it leaves unsolved the basic problem—who is to decide when the activities of the church cease to be of concern to itself alone and begin to affect persons outside the group. Moreover, as Barker has pointed out,[55] the theory of the state as a *communitas communitatum* implies that there is an ascending hierarchy of groups and that there is an ultimate group, the state, which serves to regulate the less extensive groups; it also suggests that in a crucial situation the broadest group commands—or should command—the highest loyalty. Whatever the value of the concept may be, its implications seem to be distinctly unfavorable to pluralism; they point, rather, to a monistic view of the state, and it is surprising that Laski should borrow from Figgis the phrase *communitas communitatum* as a description of the pluralistic state that he advocates.[56]

In his early works Laski applies Figgis's ideas in a series of historical studies of great conflicts between the state and various churches.[57] In these essays he displays his sympathy with the anti-Erastians and their "tremendous and brilliant plea for ecclesiastical freedom that is clearly born from the passionate sense of a corporate

[54] J. N. Figgis, *Churches in the Modern State,* p. 49.

[55] See Ernest Barker, "The Discredited State," *Political Quarterly,* No. 5 (Feb., 1915), pp. 101–21.

[56] See SPS, p. 274; and "Democracy at the Crossroads," *Yale Review,* n.s., IX (July, 1920), 796.

[57] See SPS, where he discusses the secession from the Established Church of Scotland in 1843, the Oxford Movement in the 1830's and 1840's, the Roman Catholic revival in nineteenth-century England, and Bismarck's Kulturkampf; and AMS, where he presents a long essay on Lamennais, pp. 189–280.

church." [58] He rejects the lawyers' concession theory of corporate personality and derides the legal fiction that the unincorporated association, often clad in the legal garment of the trust, has no personality.[59] Following Gierke and Maitland, he says: "Societies are persons as men are persons. They have . . . their ethos, character, nature, identity. They are born to live within the pale of human fellowship." [60] "It is purely arbitrary," he argues, "to urge that personality must be so finite as to be distinctive only of the living, single man." [61] He seems unaware that this ascription to the group of a real personality, as distinct from a legal personality, and the acceptance, as a consequence, of the concepts of group mind and group will lead to difficulties as great as or greater than those involved in the lawyers' concession theory or their interpretation of the corporation as a *persona ficta*. As Barker asks,[62] what is the nature of this transcendent group will or group mind that is distinct from the wills or minds of the members of the group, and where is it located? Further, as MacIver has observed,[63] it is a logical error to seek to interpret the unity of a whole, such as a state or a society or a voluntary association, as though it were exactly correspondent to the unity of each of its components, that is, the unity of a person.

In any event, the theories of Gierke and Figgis demonstrate that the acceptance of the idea of the real personality of groups does not necessarily lead to the rejection of the traditional theory of the sovereignty of the monistic state. It may even be argued that the doctrine is more compatible with the orthodox view of the state, especially in its idealist form, than it is with Laski's projected pluralism. For, as he concedes, if we view other groups and associations as real persons whose personality is the result of collective action, we are forced to admit that the state, too, is a real personality, with a will

---

[58] SPS, p. 94.   [59] See FS, pp. 139–45; and AMS, p. 84.
[60] SPS, p. 208.   [61] FS, p. 157.

[62] Barker, "The Discredited State," *Political Quarterly,* No. 5 (Feb., 1915).

[63] See Robert M. MacIver, *The Modern State* (London: Oxford University Press, 1926), p. 452: "A grove of trees is not a tree, nor a colony of animals itself an animal. . . . The very thing we are seeking after, the social nexus, disappears if we identify the relationship with the nature of the objects to be related. We want to know how minds are related, and we are told that the system of relationships is itself a mind. . . . No unity of like elements can possibly be described as equivalent in structure to that of its own elements."

and a mind of its own.[64] "States," he says, "are persons as men are persons. . . . They are born to live a life in the fellowship of nations as men are born to live in the fellowship of men. They are subject to the rules of conduct which the process of human experience has developed. They may be wrong as men and women are wrong; then they must be so judged." [65] Even if we waive the vexing question— can or should a state be held to exactly the same rules of conduct that are applied to individuals—it is apparent that other conclusions, less pleasing to Laski and far less consonant with his views of the nature of the state, also follow from this admission that the state is a person with a will and a mind of its own. Like other persons it must be viewed as an end in itself, existing in its own right, concerned with its own welfare, and entitled to strive for its greatest possible self-fulfillment. This conception of the state, which is a part of the idealist theory that Laski has rejected, implies that the state has an intrinsic value and a goal or purpose beyond the purposes of its citizens. It cannot be reconciled with his utilitarian view of the state as a public-service corporation.

Although Laski undertakes a number of historical studies of church-state conflicts, he is not personally interested, as was Figgis, in the right of a particular church to lead its corporate existence free from state control. He is, rather, concerned with what he takes to be the essence of such anti-Erastian movements as Tractarianism—"the plea of the corporate body which is distinct from the State to a separate and free existence." [66] This essential principle of the doctrine of the real personality of groups he applies to the association whose role in modern society he believes to be crucial and whose independence from state interference he is anxious to protect—the trade union.[67] Since, as we shall see, he believes that labor regards the trade union as "the single cell from which an entirely new industrial order is to be evolved," [68] he tends to read "trade union" wherever Figgis wrote "church." Indeed, in discussing the problem of the personality of associations, he asserts: "Nothing has brought into more striking prominence the significance for practical life of this controversy than

---

[64] See "The Personality of the State," *The Nation,* CI (July 22, 1915), 115–17.
[65] "The Apotheosis of the State," *The New Republic,* VII (July 22, 1916), 303.
[66] SPS, p. 108.   [67] See AMS, p. 83; SPS, p. 270; and FS, pp. 77–78.
[68] AMS, p. 87.

the questions raised in the last decade and a half by trade-union activity." [69] Readers of his later works may be amazed to find the Laski of 1916 defending the principles of the Taff-Vale decision,[70] which he later describes as a vicious attack upon the unions by the capitalist interests in control of the state. In 1916 he agrees with the Court's judgment that the union may be held responsible for the tortious acts of its agents, since this finding accords with his view that the union is a real person endowed with a group will; we must, he maintains, "treat the personality of our group persons as real and apply the fact of that reality throughout the whole realm of law." [71] On the other hand, he regards the decision in the Osborne case [72] as a reactionary step because the Court there held that a union's support, as a group, of the Labor Party was illegal because the action was political and not industrial in its scope. His comparison between the Osborne case and the Gorham judgment of 1850 shows how completely he has assimilated his studies of the churches' struggles for freedom to his concern with the efforts of the trade unions to secure recognition of their corporate integrity and autonomy: "The experience of the Privy Council as an ecclesiastical tribunal might herein have given a lesson to the House of Lords. There was it sternly demonstrated that the corporation of the English Church—a corporation in fact if not in law—will not tolerate the definition of its doctrine by an alien body. The sovereignty of theory is reduced by the event to an abstraction that is simply ludicrous. It may well be urged that any similar interference with the life of trade unions will result in a not dissimilar history." [73]

Finally, we must survey briefly Laski's proposals for translating his pluralistic conception of the state into political institutions. Centralized authority, he asserts repeatedly, is baffled by the range and complexity of the tasks it has assumed; it seeks to apply wide generalizations that are usually irrelevant to specific situations, and it stifles experiment and variety. Thus control from a single center necessarily becomes narrow, despotic, and overformal in character.[74] His remedy is a large measure of decentralization of power. The federalism that he advocates is to be functional as well as territorial; the

[69] FS, p. 165.

[71] FS, p. 168.

[73] FS, p. 166

[70] 1901, A.C. 426; see FS, p. 165.

[72] 1910, A.C. 87; see FS, pp. 165–66.

[74] See AMS, pp. 75–81.

state must recognize that individuals tend increasingly to look to private groups and, particularly, to economic associations such as trade unions and professional societies for the promotion of their interests and the satisfaction of their needs. These professional and industrial associations are becoming self-governing and sovereign in the sense that the rules they draw up and impose on their members are recognized by the state as the authoritative answers to the problems they have to meet.[75] His criticism is that "on the one hand, no real effort has been made to relate that economic federalism to the categories of the political structure, and, on the other, within each function there is no adequate representative system." [76] The failure to give these functional associations a legitimate place in the structure of government has meant that they have had to exert their power by such indirect methods as lobbying, informal access to department heads and civil servants, and politically motivated strikes. The only solution to this problem, according to Laski, is to make these economic groups, especially the trade unions, politically real, that is, responsible, by giving them definite social functions to perform and the powers necessary to carry on those functions.

While Laski stresses functional decentralization rather than territorial devolution of power, since he believes that geographical areas no longer coincide with the foci of men's major interests and problems, he is prepared to defend territorial federalism as found in the United States on the ground that it is more consonant with political facts than the theory of the unitary state. He criticizes those American progressives who argue that state governments and local opinions must be overridden by Federal power if progress is to be made. The passage in which Laski emerges as an ardent "states-righter" is worth quoting if only for comparison with his later views. He asks whether

America will not gain more from the slow self-struggle of New York to intelligence, than from the irritating imposition from without of a belief to which it has not been converted. I can not avoid the emphatic opinion

---

[75] See *ibid.*, pp. 384–85. Laski argues, e.g., that even though the state retains formal control by enacting into law a medical code drafted by the medical association, it is clear that the substance of authority has passed from the state to the technically competent professional group.

[76] FS, p. 91. He notes: "What we have to do is rather to make our political system mirror the sectional economic interests within itself and try to work out a harmony therein." *Holmes-Laski Letters*, I, 76 (April 5, 1917).

that in this, as in other matters, nature is not saltatory. Politically we probably gain more from the slow, and often painful erosion of prejudice by education, than when we attempt its elimination by more drastic methods. It is, of course, annoying for those of us who consider we have found the truth; but if we are to have democratic government we must bear with the inconveniences of democracy. . . . I am a frank medievalist in this regard. It seems to me admirable that a country which, in certain aspects, is one, should yet adapt its governance to suit the severalty which is no less characteristic of other aspects. In a democracy, the surest guaranty of civic responsibility seems to lie in the gift of genuine functions of government no less to the parts than to the whole. . . . Only thus can we prevent Washington from degenerating into Dublin Castle. In the end, maybe, the ways of attainment will be as different as the objects at which they aim; but the good of the universe is manifold and not single. We are as travellers breasting a hill, and we reach its summit by a thousand devious paths.[77]

Laski does not advocate a federal structure for England; the country is so much an economic unit that a measure of decentralization is the most that can be hoped for. Indeed in his discussion of English local government, he not only advocates greater use of the grant-in-aid, a technique whose use increases the control of the central authority over local bodies, but argues that what is needed is not so much new powers for the local authorities as the requirement by the central government that they meet higher standards of attainment in carrying out their present functions.[78] These suggestions hardly seem to be leading us to a pluralistic state in which sovereignty will be partitioned and the present hierarchical state structure destroyed. Even if we ignore these details and concentrate on Laski's general proposals for decentralization, it is difficult to see how his program of devolving certain governmental functions and powers to inferior territorial and functional units bears any adequate relationship to his idea of a pluralistic society in which the state is no longer sovereign over other groups. The example of the United States shows that a federal structure is compatible with the existence of a state possessing legal sov-

[77] SPS, pp. 282–85; see this entire essay, "Sovereignty and Centralisation." See also his defense of American federalism against the criticisms of eager reformers and his opposition to the Child Labor Amendment, *Holmes-Laski Letters,* I, 721 (March 14, 1925).

[78] See FS, pp. 46–47 and 57–59.

ereignty. Even in a federal state, and, therefore, a fortiori, in a decentralized state, there are areas of action in which the central government is supreme, and the powers of the constituent states or local units of government are subject to the overriding authority of the central government or of the constitutional instrument that defines the proper spheres of the various governmental units.

Laski's concrete proposals for changes in the British political structure would leave the government at Westminster the all-important financial weapon of control, the grant-in-aid, and the responsibility for defining the scope of the functions and powers of local authorities and for determining and enforcing minimum standards of accomplishment in such fields as housing and education. His suggestions for decentralization on functional lines [79] indicate that the central government would not only determine the powers to be granted to the industrial and professional associations, but also retain the power to alter the range of subjects to be dealt with by such bodies, together with the authority to override any action taken by them. Under such conditions the authority of the state would be greater than that of any other group or association, and it would still retain its principal functions—regulation of the relationships among the various groups in the society and their members and control of certain aspects of the relationships between each association and its members. The institutional changes that Laski proposes would not result in the creation of his ideal pluralistic state; the state would still possess legal sovereignty, hierarchical structure would not be replaced by a series of "coordinate groups," and the parts of the state would in no sense be as "primary" and as "self-sufficing" as the whole.

[79] See below, chap. 3, section 1.

Obedience, Liberty, and Equality

1. THE PROBLEM OF OBEDIENCE

THE PROBLEM of the basis of obedience to authority is one of the oldest and most fundamental issues in political thought. When we look at any state, past or present, democratic or authoritarian, we see a few men exercising the functions of political rule over the vast majority of the population, and securing obedience from them. Remembering Hobbes's remark that men do not exhibit great natural differences in strength, we are driven to wonder how this rule of the few over the many can be maintained. The classic problem of obedience is really two separate questions—what are the psychological and sociological factors that actually impel men to obey the law, and why and to what extent should they obey their rulers? The answer one gives to the question of fact may well influence one's response to the ethical problem, but the failure to distinguish clearly between the two aspects of the problem has often confused and weakened the attempts to set forth a theory of obedience.[1] To the question, why should men obey the state and what are the limits of that obedience?—various answers have been given in the course of history; obedience has been said to be ordained by the will of God, by the laws of nature and of reason, or by the obligations assumed in a social or political contract. The problem of why, in fact, men do obey has received less attention, but the two main answers to the question have been that their obedience is based on their fear of the punishment that is the consequence of not obeying, and the utilitarian argument that they obey because they recognize that the well-being and security of each man depend upon the acceptance by all of the state's commands.

Men have never been satisfied with the view that political power justifies itself by its mere existence. Especially in the period after Rousseau men have insisted, as Laski notes, "that the fundamental

[1] Robert M. MacIver has always insisted that this distinction be clearly made.

problem in politics is not the description or maintenance of the organs of authority but the inquiry into their legitimacy." [2] Since Laski's main concern is to deny the state's title to absolute obedience to its commands, the problem of obedience is, for him, a crucial issue. He views modern society as an arena in which the state and many other groups are engaged in struggle; the wills of these groups necessarily differ, and often no "general will" emerges from the conflict, and no ultimate reconciliation of the competing interests is possible. He sometimes argues that the will of the state is no more than a competitor with the wills of other groups and that, in advance of a trial of strength, we have no way of determining which of these wills is the superior.[3] At other times, he indicates that the will of the state is formed by the struggle that takes place among the competing wills of other social groups; the law of the state is regarded as the result of a successful effort to harmonize or compromise the conflicting interests of other groups.[4] He refuses, however, to accept the implication of this view—that the law is entitled to a superior status—and insists that law, as the expression of the state's will, has, and should have, no pre-eminence over the expression of the will of any other group in society. He states: "Whenever in a state a group of persons large enough to make its presence felt demands the recognition of certain claims, it will not recognise a law which attempts defiance of them; nor will it accept the authority by which that law is enforced." [5]

His pragmatic definition of a law is that it is simply a rule of convenience whose goodness consists in its consequences. This definition is in accord with his general belief that "right conduct, the conduct, that is to say, which men ought to perform is that which will be attended by the best possible consequences." [6] The first difficulty we encounter here is the circularity of this definition of "the good" or "the right"; the use of the words "the best possible consequences" in the *definiens* leaves us exactly where we were when the analysis began. Moreover, even if we presume that we have an independent standard for measuring the "goodness" of the results of an action, Laski's simple pragmatic formulation fails to provide a standard by which

[2] AMS, p. 224.   [3] See SPS, p. 270.

[4] See AMS, p. 67; and FS, p. 291.   [5] AMS, p. 44.

[6] "The Means and the End," review of *Political Ideals* by C. Delisle Burns, *The New Republic*, IV (Sept. 4, 1915), 133.

to judge between the various courses of action that are possible in a given situation. In practice the formulation would seem to equate the right with the more powerful and the successful. Thus Laski tells us that we can say that America was right in rebelling in 1776 and that the South was wrong in 1861 because we now know that the first revolution succeeded while the latter failed; but we cannot in 1916 say whether the revolution in Ireland is right or wrong since the struggle is not yet finished.[7]

With specific reference to obedience to the law, we can say that a law is good and should be obeyed only if and when it has triumphed in a trial of strength against the expressed wills of other groups, that is, if and when it has already been obeyed. Social groups frequently find themselves in conflict, and there is a constant competition for the allegiance of those who are members of more than one group. The group will that emerges triumphant from this Darwinian struggle is, by definition, the will that is to be called good. The state gets its commands obeyed when it can and to the extent that it can; while it may emerge victorious from a given struggle with a church or a trade union, that group or another one may, on the morrow, return to the fray with greater strength and force the state to beat a hasty and undignified retreat.[8]

To this "realistic" view of the problem of obedience in modern society Laski inconsistently joins a radically individualistic and "idealistic" theory of obedience. He approves Newman's principle: "Man should do that which he deems morally right, and the only obedience he can render is the obedience consonant with his ethical standards." [9] He applies this general theory specifically to the state as follows:

The only ground for state-success is where the purpose of the state is morally superior to that of its opponent. The only ground upon which the individual can give or be asked his support from the state is from the

---

[7] "The Apotheosis of the State," *The New Republic*, VII (July 22, 1916), 303–04.

[8] This "Darwinian" attitude towards group conflict may be a reflection of his early interest in the field of eugenics. In 1916 we find him still advocating improvement of the human stock as more important than changes in the environment. He writes: "I am a Darwinian . . . again and again we are given proof that only the inbred qualities of men really count, and that you spread those by selecting them for survival, and not by building Polytechnics or starting settlements in the slums." *Holmes-Laski Letters, 1916–1935*, ed. by Mark DeWolfe Howe (2 vols., Cambridge: Harvard University Press, 1953), I, 17 (Sept. 9, 1916).

[9] SPS, p. 206.

conviction that what it is aiming at is, in each particular action, good. We deny, that is to say, that the general end of the ideal state colours the policy of a given act of a special state. And that denial involves from each member of the state continuous scrutiny of its purpose and method.[10]

In other words, each citizen must examine the purpose of every action of the state in order to determine whether it is "morally superior" to other purposes; he should obey the state only if he is convinced that the aim of a given state act is good, that is, consonant with his ethical standards. Laski makes no attempt to demonstrate how this approach to the problem of obedience, which requires the individual to submit competing purposes to an ethical evaluation, is to be combined with his pragmatic belief that it is not possible to determine, before the conclusion of the struggle, which of the competing group wills is superior.

Moreover, the chasm cannot be bridged by saying that Laski the pragmatist is speaking of what is while Laski the individualist and idealist is discussing what should be and what may some day actually be. He does not regard as undesirable or evil the unceasing conflict among group wills; on the contrary, his constant complaint is that most men render unthinking obedience to the will of the state and are awed into an unquestioning acceptance of its sovereignty. Apathy of the citizens in the face of governmental wrongdoing and injustice, indifference to the actions of the state, the passive concurrence of the masses in decisions on great events—these are the actual conditions that lead him to declare: "The slavery of inertia is a weed that grows everywhere in wanton luxuriance; and we are, above all, concerned to make provision against its intrusion."[11] His moral prescription against this evil is to insist "that the mind of each man, in all the aspects conferred upon him by his character as a social and a solitary being, pass judgment upon the state; and we ask for his condemnation of its policy where he feels it in conflict with the right."[12]

Since each individual is pre-eminently a moral being, the greatest contribution he can make to the state is the full exercise of his moral faculties. "Every government is a *de facto* government except insofar as the rightness of its effort makes it *de jure*. A man has, above all, to be true to himself; for, once the fatal step is taken of humbling

---

[10] AMS, pp. 45-46.   [11] *Ibid.*, p. 122; see also pp. 121 and 387.
[12] *Ibid.*, pp. 121-22.

himself, against his inner promptings, before the demands of authority the way to acquiescence is easy." [13] The state, like any other group, is entitled to a man's allegiance when its act is in accordance with its end; but the individual alone can judge whether a given state act is an adequate fulfillment of its purpose, the promotion of the good life. If his conscience tells him that a given act does not advance the state's purpose, he must refuse to accept it; indeed, he is obliged to register his active dissent from the decision of authority. "To acquiesce in its sin, to judge of it by criteria other than those of individual action, is to place authority before truth." [14] To deny the voice of conscience, to bow to the contrary dictates of authority— political, ecclesiastical, or economic—is the ultimate sin; for obedience to authority, unless it springs from individual conviction, denies the essence of the human spirit, man's character as a free and responsible moral agent. The individual may attempt to temporize between the demands of his conscience and those of authority; but, in the end, he will discover what Lamennais realized at a certain point in his relations with the Papacy—"that, in any final examination, he must take for truth and right conduct that which his conscience told him he might identify with truth and right conduct." [15] No matter how severe the penalties for disobeying the dictates of authority and even though his disobedience should "break the heart of the world," at some point a man must take his stand and say with Luther, *"Ich kann nicht anders."* Laski concludes that, faced with the commands of the political authority, "an individual may decide on a course which enables justice to be done even though the state perish in the doing of it." [16]

Laski's thesis is political Protestantism with a vengeance, and it is not surprising that he refers repeatedly to the words of Luther, Lamennais, Tyrrell, Döllinger, and other great rebels against the claims of the leaders of the Roman Catholic Church to absolute and infallible authority. While he urges that right and truth must prevail over the demands of authority, he neither attempts to specify the meanings of "right" or "truth" nor gives any indication of the circumstances in which resistance or rebellion is justified. Nor is this an omission on Laski's part; central to his intensely individualistic

[13] *Ibid.*, p. 58.   [14] SPS, p. 209.
[15] AMS, p. 254.   [16] *Ibid.*, p. 316.

position is the belief that "the discovery of right is, on all fundamental questions, a search, upon which the separate members of the state must individually engage." [17] In the last analysis loyalty is "in every case a matter of the private judgment of each of us." [18] He concludes: "The law may resolve, and attach sanctions to its resolution; but the decision that is made takes place, if it is a real decision, separately in the mind of each member of the state." [19]

This radically individualistic solution of the problem of obedience is only one instance, albeit the most important, of the marked strain of individualism in Laski's early thinking. He repeatedly states that for him the only final values are the individual, his spontaneity and freedom of expression, and his unfettered moral and intellectual development. He seems to have been unaware of the possibilities of conflict between this stress on the individual and his emphasis on the personality and organic nature of social groups; at any rate he makes no attempt to harmonize the two views. When he is discussing social groups and their relationships with the state, the individual is lost to view; he insists that, for the most part, the average man thinks and acts as a member of some group or fellowship.[20] When, on the other hand, he turns to the individual's relation to the state, particularly in the context of the moral problem of obedience, he pays little attention to associations of men and maintains that his pluralism is an individualistic theory of the state. He tells us that "however organic be the community in which we live, man is a solitary no less than a social being, and his ideal world is at bottom interstitial. However much he acts in common, he wishes also to act alone; however much he thinks as a member of the herd, he will wish also to think as a lonely wanderer. It is, perhaps, an antinomy; but it is one which no theory of the State dare afford to neglect." [21] For Laski the final argument in favor of democratic and limited government is the need to preserve these areas of individual freedom of thought and action from encroachments by those who wield power.

Laski's ultra-Protestant theory of obedience is, for all its nobility, a doctrine fraught with great danger. Since it gives the state no

---

[17] *Ibid.*, p. 122.   [18] *Ibid.*, p. 275.

[19] Laski's Introduction to *A Defence of Liberty against Tyrants,* a translation of the *Vindiciae contra tyrannos* by Hubert Languet (London: G. Bell and Sons, Ltd., 1924), p. 56.

[20] See FS, p. 67.   [21] SPS, pp. 264-65.

greater claim to men's allegiance than any other social group, it would tend to produce anarchy if put into practice in a modern society made up of a variety of competing groups. Furthermore, the theory elevates this state of anarchy to the level of a moral imperative by urging each citizen to disobey a governmental order unless he is convinced that the moral worth of the government's decision is greater than the appeal made to his conscience by the contradictory demand of another group. By isolating the problem of obeying a particular command of the state from the general context of the nature and value of law-abidingness, Laski ignores the fact that in a given case it may be better to obey a command of which one does not approve than to disrupt the entire fabric of allegiance to the state. Moreover, his thesis is seriously weakened by its reliance on the individual's capacity for an uninterrupted and ever-wise exercise of the faculty of moral judgment. If we reject the notion that the voice of the individual's conscience is always right, we cannot accept the conclusion that each man must be allowed to act in accordance with his own view of right or justice even though the heavens may fall or the state may perish in the process.

If a moralist were to insist that each man must, in his daily life, scrutinize every proposed action in the light of moral principles, we would reply that he was ignoring the importance of the distinction between those human situations in which the exercise of deliberate evaluation and conscious choice is proper and necessary and the more common situations in which the social wisdom accumulated in conventions and routine is an adequate guide to action. The obvious result of attempting to exercise indiscriminate moral discrimination—if it were not quite impracticable—would be a paralysis of the moral will; since anything might be done and everything would have to be weighed, nothing could, in fact, be accomplished. Similarly, the individual who attempted to carry out Laski's principles of political obedience would discover that his constant scrutiny of the actions of government, together with the never-ending process of weighing the moral claims of each act against competing demands, left him with a vast backlog of unmade political decisions and no time or energy to devote to the other necessary or pleasant activities of life.

After the last three decades of experience of tyrants' efforts to crush by manipulation and terror the independence of individuals and groups, most of us will readily admit that there are, for each man and for every group of men, situations in which obedience to the dictates of political authority should be refused. Few will argue that resistance to the Nazis was unjustified, or, to take a more remote example, that Antigone should have submitted to Creon's decree that her brother be left unburied.[22] We agree that when a man feels that his entire scheme of values, the set of moral principles by which he is endeavoring to live, is being invaded and endangered by the actions of his rulers, he must, like Antigone, refuse to admit the state's title to obedience. Heedless of the scorn of opponents, the apathy of the indifferent, and the entire apparatus of coercion and punishment of which the state disposes, he must join with other individuals of like mind in a struggle against the state. At this point he can and must say with Luther, "God helping me, I can do no other." This view —that government, and particularly democratic government, should be obeyed unless its actions seem to the individual to constitute a serious attack upon his moral code—differs sharply from Laski's thesis that government should be obeyed only when its action seems to the individual to be morally right. Laski takes the marginal case as the norm and enshrines rebellion as a value in itself, while the view here advocated looks on disobedience and rebellion as the court of last appeal in a democratic society, to be resorted to only in the rare marginal situation. A Laskian state, kept in constant tension and alarm because of the possibility of individual and group disobedience for trivial as well as grave reasons, would be a state verging on anarchy. The usual consequences of a period of anarchy are a widespread demand for security and order, and the emergence of a new political authority that endeavors to reimpose order by strong measures designed to eliminate or curb the power of the warring factions. Thus our last state is worse than our first; the overemphasis on individual and group autonomy leads to a reaction in the course of which authority, from being despised, comes to be venerated, while the freedom of men and their groups is sharply curtailed.

Laski admits that his theory involves the possibility of anarchy, but argues that he is merely recognizing the fact "that at times in the history of a state there may well come a point where the main-

---

[22] See MacIver's Preface to Robert M. MacIver, ed., *Conflict of Loyalties* (New York: Harper and Bros., 1952), pp. 1–6.

tenance of order seems to some group of men worthless as an end
compared to achieving, by other than constitutional means, some
good deemed greater than peace." [23] He concludes: "The one thing
of which we may be certain is that no state which has acted with
uprightness need fear the transition from criticism to revolt." [24]
"Revolution," he argues, "never comes from the effort of chance con-
spirators or malevolent ideas. It is the outcome always of wrongs that
have become too intolerable to be borne." [25] These statements, even
if they are historically accurate, are not an adequate defense against
the charge that his theory of obedience would lead to anarchy if it
were put into practice. He gives us no definition of "right" or "uprightness," and he can give us none, since he insists that only the individual is entitled to make the judgment that a given act is "right."
Even if a government has acted with what it considers to be the greatest possible "uprightness" and even if the majority of its citizens agree
with it, that action is, in terms of Laski's theory, not right for the
individuals or groups who do not admit its rightness; thus neither
the government nor the majority has any moral right to ask for the
obedience of the recalcitrant minority.

Laski also argues that peace and the maintenance of order are
neither the highest human values nor the final end of the state. "The
supreme interest of the state is in justice, and it does not necessarily
follow that justice and order are in perfect correlation." [26] The orthodox theory of the sovereign state, by its beatification of order and its
failure to inquire into the purposes for which order is maintained,
places itself at the disposal of the capitalist group which now dominates the life of the state.[27] We note that his discussion of obedience
and order leaves out the vital consideration that the maintenance of
general peace and order is the basic task of government. When peace
and security are absent from a society for a considerable period of
time, men realize that social order alone makes it possible for them
to pursue or enjoy the other goods of life. Laski's disparagement
of the value of order, like his general attack on sovereignty, must be
understood in the light of his hostility to the capitalist order which

[23] AMS, pp. 53–54.
[24] "The Apotheosis of the State," *The New Republic,* VII (July 22, 1916), 304.
[25] *The State in the New Social Order,* Fabian Tract No. 200 (London: The Fabian
Society, 1922), p. 6.
[26] AMS, p. 385.   [27] See FS, pp. 28–29.

the state supports and his chosen role as defender of a new labor order. "There are times," he declares, "when the business of law is not the maintenance of an old equilibrium but the creation of a new one. It is to that task that our efforts must today be directed." [28] In place of a frank avowal of the goal of social and political reconstruction and a clear statement and defense of the values in terms of which he regards a labor order as preferable to a capitalist order, he elaborates a confused and complex ideological apparatus to defend the interests of labor against a hostile state—a moralistic theory of obedience, not grounded upon a consistent and examined ethical theory, and difficult to reconcile with his pragmatic view of group conflict. He maintains that order must be sacrificed to the demands of justice, but he attempts no inquiry into the nature either of "justice" or of the means by which it is to be attained.

2. LIBERTY, EQUALITY, AND NATURAL RIGHTS

Laski bases his entire discussion of liberty, equality, and natural rights upon a broad and idealistic theory of the purpose for which the state exists, which is hardly compatible with his antistatism and anti-idealism. "We start," he says, "from the theoretic purpose we admit in the state. It aims at the development of the fullest capacities for good possessed by its members. That implies at once liberty and equality." [29] This view of the purpose to be pursued by the state goes beyond the thesis of those idealists who argue that the state exists to promote the conditions of the good life rather than the good life itself. Laski makes no attempt to deal with the patent contradictions between this formulation of the aim of the state and his attacks on the state's claim to a position of pre-eminence among social groups. If, as he frequently asserts, the good that men seek is manifold and varied and if other social groups "live a life of their own and exist to support purposes that the state itself fails to fulfil," [30] he cannot logically hold that it is the function of the state to promote the self-realization of its individual members, unless he is willing to accept the idealist's identification of state and society. Moreover, he offers

[28] AMS, p. 379.   [29] FS, p. 88.   [30] AMS, p. 84.

no definition or analysis of the nature of "the good" that the state should promote. His statement of the purpose of the state is a meaningless abstraction, which is not only useless as a criterion for judging state actions but also contradicts the major elements of his pluralistic theory.

When Laski returned to England in 1920, the postwar boom had given way to depression, and unemployment was mounting steadily. The Lloyd George Coalition Government, which had won a large majority in the "snap election" of December, 1918, made no serious effort to deal with unemployment or with the strikes in critical industries such as coal mining. Increasingly Laski's attention turned to economic problems and to the need for political action in order to solve those problems. At this time he states that "the dominant purpose of the contemporary State is to secure for the least of its members a certain minimum standard of civilized life and to secure the conditions which guarantee that standard." [31] This "basic minimum" must be guaranteed to each man by the state in order that his citizenship may be possible. In particular, the state must guarantee general equality of educational opportunity. "For," Laski says, "if the object of the state is to enrich the social heritage through the enlargement of individual personality, then individual personality must be given that power of adequate expression which comes through knowledge to make its needs known." [32]

Laski asserts that his conception of the state's purpose implies both liberty and equality. What does he mean by these concepts and what does he conceive their relationship to be? Rejecting as inadequate the view that liberty means the absence of restraint, he defines it as "the positive and equal opportunity of self-realisation." [33] He applauds T. H. Green's definition of freedom as "a positive power of doing or enjoying something worth doing or enjoying, and that, too, something that we do or enjoy in common with others." [34] He also

---

[31] "The Civil Service and Parliament," in *The Development of the Civil Service; Lectures Delivered before the Society of Civil Servants, 1920–1921* (London: P. S. King and Son, Ltd., 1922), p. 23.

[32] *The State in the New Social Order*, p. 13.

[33] AMS, p. 37; see also *Political Thought in England: From Locke to Bentham,* Home University Library of Modern Knowledge No. 103 (New York: Henry Holt and Co., 1920), hereinafter cited as PTE, p. 309.

[34] Quoted in AMS, p. 55.

pays tribute to Acton's conception of liberty as "the assurance that every man shall be protected in doing what he believes his duty against the influence of authority and majority, custom and opinion."[35] The major weakness in Laski's discussion is his failure to undertake a rigorous analysis of the concept of freedom and of its relationship to his other ideas. His tendency towards an unreflective eclecticism leads him to adopt a vague notion of freedom in which are combined both Acton's emphasis on the importance of freedom of individual thought and opinion and Green's stress on the shared activities of men in pursuit of a rationally defined good. Though the Actonian element is more compatible with Laski's thesis that the individual's conscience should be the arbiter of conflicting claims upon his loyalty, he tends, in practice, to place the emphasis upon the expression of men's creative impulses in group activities.

While defining liberty as the positive opportunity for self-realization, he is unable to implement the definition by analyzing the nature of the self which is the goal of the process of realization. Since he is unwilling to accept the idealist's identification of reality and reason, he cannot assert that the process of self-realization is one in which the individual's behavior is increasingly determined by rational factors. His basic difficulty arises from the fact that he is using the idealist's formula after having rejected the entire substratum upon which that formula rests. He is thus forced to the position that liberty consists in the opportunity to express any of men's "creative impulses"; in the attempt to avoid the difficulties involved in specifying the "real self" or "the good," he goes to the other extreme of giving carte blanche to all "creative impulses," without recognizing that some of these impulses may be antisocial or immoral and that their expressions in the actions of a number of individuals may conflict. At moments he shifts to a historical analysis and maintains that the concrete meaning of liberty will vary from age to age: "Each generation will have certain things it prizes as supremely good and will demand that these, above all, should be free."[36] At another time he argues that "in each age the substance of liberty will be found in what the dominating forces of that age most greatly want."[37] Here again we see that the individual, who is supposed to be the focus of Laski's concern, sometimes seems to be swallowed up in the larger

[35] Quoted, *ibid*. [36] AMS, p. 54. [37] PTE, p. 312.

struggles between competing groups and forces; it is small comfort for the person whose ideas and actions are not in accord with those of the majority to be told that the substance of his liberty is to be found in what the dominating forces of the age "most greatly want." The real point that Laski wishes to make in his discussion of liberty is that in the present hierarchically organized economic and political order opportunities for creative self-expression are denied to all but a small group of men. Liberty, in the sense of free play for the creative impulses of men and a high degree of individual diversity, "is incompatible with the present system of property; for its result is a concentration of power which makes the political personality of the average citizen ineffective for any serious purpose." [38]

Liberty thus implies equality; liberty and equality are not in conflict nor even separate, but are "different facets of the same ideal." [39] Laski argues that we must recognize that liberty "is impossible save upon the basis of the acceptance of certain minimal standards *which can get accepted only through collective effort*." [40] He insists that to proclaim that men are born equal is not to proclaim that they are born identical, and he defines equality as the expression of "an opportunity for the full development of personality." [41] If, with Laski, we define liberty as "the positive and equal opportunity for self-realization," [42] it is obvious that liberty and equality are, as he says, neither contradictory nor separate. Indeed since they are identical, there can be no problem of how or to what extent they are or can be related; this is surely the neatest, if not the most satisfactory, solution ever devised for a perennial problem in political philosophy.

For Laski, the most significant fact in the modern world is men's increasing desire for the reduction of the disparities and inequalities of social and economic life; the main effort of our age is "in a direction which challenges the legal rights established by prescription in the name of an equality for which our institutions are unsuited." [43] Every citizen who is prepared to work must be assured by collective action of at least a minimum of material well-being. Justice, he says,

38 FS, Preface, p. ix.   39 *Ibid.*, p. 87.
40 PTE, p. 309; italics mine.   41 AMS, p. 182.
42 PTE, p. 309.
43 FS, p. 29; see also "Democracy at the Crossroads," *Yale Review*, n.s., IX (July, 1920), 803.

implies equality where human beings are equal in their needs; but he fails to tell us what these needs are or to what extent they are, in fact, equal in all men. He maintains that his call for equality does not necessarily involve the abolition of private property, but agrees that it does mean "spiking its guns." [44] The enjoyment of property rights must be made conditional upon the performance of useful service, and what Laski calls "the payment of a monopoly-rent to ability" is to be allowed only "when we can be certain that a social need can be satisfied in no other fashion." [45]

Laski ignores the fact that these proposals for controls over the distribution of property and for a guarantee of a minimum income to every citizen imply a continuous regulation of the workings of the economic system that plays havoc with his plans for eliminating the paramount power of the state. Nor will he admit that, unless we assume that our resources can satisfy all possible desires, the drive towards equality must be accompanied by certain restrictions on the liberties of some individuals and groups, even if, at the same time, it means an increase in the liberties of other sections of the society. Laski's program for equality would obviously curtail the liberties of those who realize their creative impulses by accumulating wealth or amassing control over property. Even if we dismiss these activities as unworthy of the title of opportunities for self-realization, how are we to deal, for example, with a group of skilled workmen who, having achieved through organization and superior skill a wage level higher than the proposed national minimum, object to collective action designed to assure that minimum to every citizen, particularly if this policy means that they must pay higher taxes? Will they not argue that their opportunities for self-realization have been reduced? Clearly the relationship between liberty and equality—or, rather, between liberties and equalities—is far more complicated than Laski's simple identification assumes. While liberty and equality are not simple contradictories, they are not the same thing. In the actual situations that we confront, we may be forced to curtail some liberties of some people in order to achieve wider equality of opportunity, and we will have to impose certain restrictions on one group in order to safeguard or promote certain freedoms for another group. When we

[44] *The State in the New Social Order*, p. 14.   [45] *Ibid.;* see also p. 10.

attempt to deal with these problems, we will not find Laski's oversimple formulations of the concepts of liberty and equality and of
their interrelation particularly useful.

In view of his hostile attitude toward the state and political power,
it is not surprising that Laski expresses sympathy with the natural-
right theorists, such as Locke, who suppressed the idea of sovereignty and attempted to limit political power by postulating the
existence of certain rights that were anterior to the state and had to
be safeguarded against its interference. He argues that the essential
truth of the natural-law theory can be redeemed from its major
error—the view that the principles of natural law are fixed and un-
changeable—if, with Stammler, we regard the ideal of natural law
as continually changing in content.[46] Since the natural rights of individuals and groups are the armor evolved to protect their vital interests, their content will change as conditions change. The modern
theory of natural law, he argues, "does not lay down any eternal or
immutable laws of human conduct; it simply urges that the research
of reason cannot help reaching conclusions which are valid so long
as the conditions they resume obtain. Such a generalisation must be
the necessary basis of all political action." [47]

He begins his analysis of natural rights by considering the purpose for which the state exists—the development of its members'
fullest capacities for good. The individual has a right to expect the
state to fulfill its purposes, that, is, to make it possible for him to
attain certain goods; the precise nature of these goods and the level
of expectation will change in the course of historical development.
Laski states: "When the realisation of these hopes is keenly enough
felt to be essential to the realisation of the purpose of the state we
have a political right. It is a right natural in the sense that the given
conditions of society at the particular time require its recognition.
It is not justified on grounds of history. It is not justified on grounds
of any abstract or absolute ethic." [48] The vagueness of this argument,
which verges perilously close to sermonizing, is not eliminated by his
alternative formulation of natural rights as "the fundamental no-

[46] See AMS, p. 64.

[47] Introduction to Léon Duguit, *Law in the Modern State,* tr. by Frida and Harold
Laski (New York: B. W. Huebsch, 1919), p. xxviii.

[48] AMS, p. 43.

tions of each age," which must be placed "beyond the temptations of malicious enterprise," [49] that is, beyond the reach of the power of government. His thesis appears to be that a right is a demand or a need of an individual or group that must be satisfied if the purpose of the state is to be fulfilled, and that "if, in a given condition of society, power is so exerted as to refuse the recognition of that right, resistance is bound to be encountered." [50]

If rights are demands that the state does not dare to refuse since their rejection will lead the individuals or groups concerned to resist authority, how are we to draw up a catalogue of such rights, even at a given stage of historical development? If, as Laski suggests, we begin with the state's purpose, it is difficult to deduce therefrom any concrete right whose realization is essential, since the goal—the development of the citizens' highest capacities for good—is too abstract and vague to allow us to designate as means any specific set of essential conditions. If, on the other hand, accepting his definition of natural rights as "the demands for the fulfilment of certain conditions without which an important fragment of the state ceases to feel loyalty to its institutions," [51] we attempt to begin the analysis by asking what are "the fundamental notions of each age" whose denial by the political authority will cause men to resist, we are forced to conclude that, in advance of a given act of resistance, we cannot state these rights in concrete terms. Laski rejects the idea of an absolute ethic from which certain specific rights might be deduced; as we have seen, he sets up the moral judgment of the individual as the sole standard for justifying resistance to authority. The conclusion to be drawn from his thesis would seem to be that if an individual believes that a governmental act denies a certain demand whose satisfaction he considers essential to the maintenance of his loyalty to the state, he will offer resistance to the government and, thereby, will demonstrate that the demand in question is a natural right. Since, however, no one else has any warrant for anticipating the results of the individual's moral deliberations, we cannot state in advance that the demand constitutes a natural right.

In attempting to overcome these obstacles to the elaboration of a list of natural rights, Laski occasionally falls back on a historical

[49] *Ibid.*, p. 65.   [50] *Ibid.*, p. 43.
[51] Introduction to *A Defence of Liberty Against Tyrants*, p. 56.

explanation of such rights, in spite of his original statement that they are not to be justified on grounds of history. He tells us, for example, that when we speak today of natural rights, we mean that the human needs whose satisfaction history has demonstrated to be essential must be put beyond the control of any organ of the state.[52] The difficulties, however, of a theory of natural rights which is rooted in the appeal to the universal judgment of historical experience are no less serious than they are obvious. If men who live today in our own society differ in their views of those human needs whose satisfaction is essential, we can hardly expect that there will be general agreement among them or, a fortiori, among men of other eras and other societies, about the judgment of past ages upon this question. Furthermore, a theory of natural rights based upon the appeal to historical experience can give no warrant for changes in the content of rights. The past cannot be called upon to validate new demands or new claims to rights; tradition offers little or no support for most of the rights listed by Laski as the conditions that are necessary to the fulfillment of the duties of citizenship—free speech, a living wage, an adequate education, a proper amount of leisure, and the power to combine for social effort.[53]

The pitfalls and problems concealed in terms like "proper," "adequate," and "living" are serious; in fact most of the real issues in political action involve efforts to define these vague and elusive concepts. It is difficult to see the value of attempting to impose a theory of natural rights upon the processes of politics, particularly if one is unwilling or unable to subscribe to a set of fundamental and universally applicable moral axioms. The a priori moral judgments are needed not only to give a foundation for the natural rights proclaimed, but also to infuse into them some specific content. In view of the fact that, since the beginning of the modern era, there has been in Western civilization no general acceptance of a fixed hierarchy of values, the elaboration of a theory of natural rights seems to be an impossible and an unrewarding venture. We can argue that freedom of opinion, of religion, and of association, or the more recent "right to work" must be preserved and promoted because they constitute values that we, as individuals or groups, hold to be supremely im-

---

[52] See AMS, pp. 101–02.
[53] See FS, pp. 245–46. See also *Holmes-Laski Letters*, I, 116–17 (Dec. 8, 1917).

portant, or because they are the necessary conditions for the attainment of our values. But we do well to realize that there is nothing "natural" or metaphysically "given" about these rights or freedoms; like all the other components of what we call "civilization," they are essentially artificial. Men, who have slowly and painfully wrested these principles of rational and ethical conduct from the great ocean of the "natural" forces that shape human behavior, have constantly to build and rebuild dikes to protect these small islands in the sea of unreason. It follows that these rights will be maintained only as long as, and to the extent that, we believe the values that they enshrine to be so transcendently important that we are willing to struggle to maintain them. Such beliefs on the part of a group of men and the actions that result therefrom are the only final safeguards of their rights and freedoms.

Laski argues that a Bill of Rights is supremely important now that state activity is increasing so rapidly, and that only by judicial control in terms of natural rights will the path of administration become also the path of justice.[54] But mechanical devices should not be confused with the reality that lies beneath and sustains them. It is important to remember that for sixty years the provisions of the Bill of Rights of the American Constitution were completely fictitious guarantees for virtually all Negro citizens. Even today there is for these citizens a large gap between constitutional promise and administrative and judicial performance. Nor did the Bill of Rights serve as a shield to protect the rights of American citizens of Japanese ancestry during the Second World War; in the face of widespread fear of the Nisei and antagonism towards them and an even more widespread indifference to their fate, the constitutional guarantees remained largely empty promises. The clearest proof of the inadequacy of merely formal or constitutional guarantees of civil or political rights is offered by the elaborate and eloquent catalogues of rights inserted into the constitutions of the new "people's democratic republics" of Eastern Europe.

Judicial control over administrative or legislative action may, in some circumstances, be a useful device for the protection of individual and group freedoms. On rare occasions a courageous judge has defied an angry and aroused public opinion by upholding the constitutional

[54] See AMS, pp. 101–02.

guarantees of the liberties of unpopular individuals or groups. But Americans, remembering that in the period from the 1870's to the 1930's the courts frequently used the constitutional guarantees of "due process of law" to restrict the rights and freedoms of the many, will not be tempted to regard the device of judicial control of administration or judicial review of legislation as an infallible safeguard of their rights or liberties.

3

Economic and Political Change

1. POLITICS AND ECONOMICS

IN A SURVEY of his life and beliefs published in 1939, Laski states: "I have, I suppose, been a socialist in some degree ever since the last years of my schooldays." [1] While it is difficult to determine the sources of this socialist faith, which he calls "the central conviction of my life," [2] we can note that he records the influence exerted upon him while he was a schoolboy in Manchester by "a great schoolmaster who made us feel the sickness of an acquisitive society," [3] by the books he read, especially those of the Webbs, and by a speech in which Keir Hardie described the labor struggles of the Scottish miners. He also mentions his work as a student at Oxford during the years from 1911 to 1914 in the Fabian Society and in propaganda for women's suffrage.

In addition, Laski refers to his belief in socialism as "the outcome of a Jewish upbringing, the sense it conferred of being treated differently from other people and for no obviously assignable cause." [4] At the same time, he notes, "I cannot even remember a period in which either ritual or dogma had meaning for me." [5] His sense that he was alienated from the main stream of English life because of his family's religious beliefs, although he did not share them, and his feeling that the treatment that he received at the hands of society was rationally indefensible were no doubt sharpened by his experiences at Oxford, which, he says, first made him aware of the intensity of class division in England. It is difficult to avoid the conclusion that Laski's strong feeling that his Jewish background was

[1] "Harold J. Laski," in Clifton Fadiman, ed., *I Believe: The Personal Philosophies of Certain Eminent Men and Women of Our Time* (New York: Simon and Schuster, 1939), p. 139.
[2] *Ibid.*
[3] *Ibid.*
[4] *Ibid.*
[5] *Ibid.*, p. 148.

the reason why, in spite of his marked intellectual distinction and precocity, he was treated unfairly is a fundamental factor in his life-long sympathy with all who were discriminated against and disadvantaged, his constant passion for justice for all men, and his eloquent denunciations of inequality and injustice.

From 1914 to 1916 Laski was a lecturer in history at McGill University in Montreal, Canada; during this period he made a speech attacking Lloyd George's policy of "bitter-endism" that led to urgent demands for his dismissal. More important, however, in Laski's evolution as a socialist was the famous Boston police strike of 1919, which occurred during his stay at Harvard University. He tells us that as soon as the strike began, President Lowell offered the services of the University to the city; Laski, on the other hand, found out and said that the strike "was the outcome of long-accumulated grievances met without sympathy or insight." [6] This statement led to an investigation of Laski by the Overseers of Harvard University; their decision was that he was not to be dismissed, but the experience, and President Lowell's warning that a teacher limited his utility when he spoke on matters of current controversy, were undoubtedly factors in Laski's decision in 1920 to leave Harvard and the United States and to return home to accept a post at the London School of Economics and Political Science. More significant were the conclusions that Laski drew from the Harvard experience; he learned, he says, that "the university scene in America was vitally related to the social environment. One could speculate freely, but one must not question the basic assumptions of the system." [7] The Boston police strike and strikes such as those at Ludlow and Lowell deepened his socialist faith by demonstrating "how the vast machinery of the state is used to crush any movement that questions the authority of those who own economic power." [8]

Writing in 1939, he sums up the main lessons he learned during his first stay in America:

I saw there, more nakedly than I had seen in Europe, the significance of the struggle between capital and labor. . . . I came back from America convinced that liberty has no meaning save in the context of equality, and I had begun to understand that equality, also, has no meaning unless the instruments of production are socially owned. But I was still academic enough in experience to believe that this could be proved on rational

[6] *Ibid.*, pp. 141–42.   [7] *Ibid.*, p. 141.   [8] *Ibid.*, p. 142.

grounds, and that its proof would be sufficient to win acceptance for it as a principle of social organization.[9]

He notes that his early socialism "was above all the outcome of a sense of the injustice of things as they were. It had not become an insight into the processes of history." [10]

Laski's early socialism, rooted in his passionate sense of the injustices caused by existing institutions, bears a much closer kinship to the beliefs of those whom Marx called "Utopian Socialists" than to the theories of Marx and Engels. The parallels between the views of Laski and those of Proudhon are particularly striking; both of them regard society as basically federal and pluralistic, rather than hierarchical, in nature, and both are flatly opposed to the sovereign centralized state, the state which Marx wanted the proletariat to take over. For both Laski and Proudhon the central focus of attention is the freedom of the individual in all phases of human activity and particularly in his daily labor, rather than his freedom in the narrowly political sphere. Laski is deeply sympathetic to the contempt for political action demonstrated by large numbers of French workers, the idealistic and revolutionary character of their trade-union movement, and the drive towards administrative syndicalism among the civil servants.[11] He specifically notes the Proudhonian basis of these French movements as well as his own preference for the socialism of Proudhon over that of Marx: "Proudhon has displaced Marx as the guiding genius of French labour; and it is above all his federalism that is the source of the new inspiration." [12] He argues that the significance of this desertion of Marx in favor of Proudhon lies in the fact that the latter "sought in a federalist organisation of society the ·clue to freedom. He understood, as Marx never understood, that the root of the industrial problem lies less in an indignant sense of exploitation than in an eagerness to share in the determination of working conditions." [13]

[9] *Ibid.*, pp. 142–43.   [10] *Ibid.*, p. 143.

[11] See "Administrative Syndicalism in France," AMS, Chapter V, pp. 321–87.

[12] AMS, p. 114. Speaking of Proudhon, he says: "He seems to me to have anticipated most of Karl Marx and to have said it better." *Holmes-Laski Letters, 1916–1935*, ed. by Mark DeWolfe Howe (2 vols., Cambridge: Harvard University Press, 1953), I, 82 (April 29, 1917).

[13] Introduction to Léon Duguit, *Law in the Modern State*, tr. by Frida and Harold Laski (New York: B. W. Huebsch, 1919), pp. xiii–xiv; see also "Democracy at the Crossroads," *Yale Review*, n.s., IX (July, 1920), 795–96.

In the realm of labor strategy Laski's Proudhonian attitude, which is closely related to his pluralist view of the state, emerges clearly in his insistence that the attention of the workers ought to be concentrated on the workshop and factory rather than on the ballot box and Parliament. It is relatively unimportant how we organize the institutions of the state, for "the fundamental truth remains that the simple weapons of politics are alone powerless to effect any basic redistribution of economic strength." [14] While the state's primary interest is in uninterrupted industrial service and, as a result, in getting the trade-union member back to work when he is on strike, the worker is aiming at a fundamental redistribution of the economic power now held by the small group of owners. In contrast to the "social liberals" and the Fabians, who believe that the power of the workers in a political democracy can and should be used to achieve social and economic reforms, "the worker sees in the productive process a lever that will react upon the state itself. True political democracy is, as he realises, the offspring of true industrial democracy." [15]

When, in this period, Laski speaks of "industrial democracy," he attaches a literal meaning to the phrase; he means the determination by the workers of the methods to be employed at each stage of the process of production, the choice of foremen and leaders, and the settlement of tasks, hours, and wages.[16] The goal of labor is the substitution of cooperative endeavor for hierarchical control in industry; as we have already noted, the trade union is regarded as the single cell from which an entirely new industrial order is to be evolved. Of the trade unions Laski says: "The root of the future democracy is in them and not in Parliament." [17] In a rudimentary fashion the union movement is already assuming the typical characteristics of a state; it has organs of reasoned government, an increasingly influential view of life, a deep concern for its members' spiritual freedom, and a hold on their loyalty as great as or greater

---

[14] AMS, p. 82.   [15] *Ibid.*, p. 86.

[16] See *ibid.*, p. 87; see also his comment in 1918 that the Russian Revolution "seems to demonstrate that the worker is able to secure the actual process of production by democratic methods." "The Literature of Reconstruction," *The Bookman*, XLVIII (Oct., 1918), 218.

[17] "Parliament and Revolution," review of *Parliament and Revolution* by J. Ramsay MacDonald, *The New Republic*, XXII (May 19, 1920), 384.

than that of the state. He concludes that "as it becomes every day more obvious that the hold of the business theory of life upon the state is weakening, so does it also become more clear that the trade unions will become the categories into which the structure of capitalism will be absorbed." [18]

Existing political institutions, developed to meet the needs of the economically secure middle class in the era prior to the Industrial Revolution, are utterly inadequate to the problems of a complex industrial society and to the needs of the workers. Legislative bodies, political executives, and political parties of the traditional type have declined in power and prestige, while the state, in its efforts to deal with modern problems, is increasingly driven to bureaucratic domination and overcentralization. The most dangerous sign of this *malaise de la démocratie,* more apparent in France than in England, is the fact that the average citizen is increasingly less interested in the political process, except at moments of crisis or abnormal excitement; he demands certain results but does not greatly care about the methods by which they are attained.[19] More and more, decisions are made by a small number of men in each society, while the vast majority of citizens are becoming simply *des administrés.* Laski argues that the socialized liberalism which, since 1906, has been the dominant viewpoint in English political life is an attempt to discover the minimum changes that must be made if the present social order is to be maintained, rather than a genuine effort towards that complete reconstruction of the social order which is essential. Moreover, this liberalism involves the creation and administration of various schemes for social reform by political leaders and experts; like Plato's guardians, they are presumed to know what is really good for the people and how that good can be accomplished. To this trend Laski is violently antagonistic: "Social legislation has the incurable habit of tending towards paternalism; and paternalism, however wide be the basis of consent upon which it is erected, is the subtlest form of poison to the democratic state." [20]

Although Laski often argues that the main danger of this socialized

[18] "Democracy at the Crossroads," *Yale Review,* n.s., IX (July, 1920), 792.

[19] See FS, pp. 38 and 226. Laski often expresses doubts about the universal validity of democracy; see *Holmes-Laski Letters,* I, 42 and 540–41 (Dec. 16, 1916 and Sept. 16, 1923).

[20] FS, p. 43; see also PTE, p. 308.

liberalism is that it has produced political apathy and a concentration on purely materialistic improvements among the masses, he frequently reverses his stand and asserts that "the worker" is dissatisfied with the accomplishments of the state in spite of the large volume of social legislation intended to improve his lot. Laski's description of the sources of the worker's discontent often seems to reflect his own fears and his quasi-syndicalist ideals more closely than it sums up the attitudes of the average worker. The basis for the modern democratic discontent, he tells us, is the fact that the

liberty and equality implied in the modern state are purely theoretic in character. The industrial worker has the suffrage; but he is caught in the ramifications of a system which deprives its use of any fundamental meaning. . . . He sees that democracy in politics does not in the least imply democracy in industry and, since the better portion of his life is spent in earning his daily bread, it is to the latter that he has turned. He has found the state useless for the purpose he had in view, and that is why he must refuse to accept it as in any fundamental sense the representative of the community. The economic federalism that exists largely results from his effort to conquer through industrial action what he has failed to gain from political. The labor movement has been his real training-ground in politics.[21]

Laski argues that such phenomena as the publication in 1912 of *The Miners' Next Step,* the popularity of the guild socialist movement and of its organ, "The New Age," and the interest of trade unionists in the writings of G. D. H. Cole and Bertrand Russell are clear indications that the tradition of English syndicalism is far from dead. In 1919 he writes that the Labor Party seemed to the workers

hardly more instinct with hope than the traditional political forces of the country. It was in workshop and factory that the new ideas were being forged. They showed a striking renaissance of that attitude which, as in Owen and Thompson and Hodgskin, believed that the diversion of labour power into political rather than into economic fields was mistaken. . . . It [labor] had realised that the basis of its ideal must be the conquest of economic power. It was upon that mission that it had embarked.[22]

Again in 1920 we find Laski ascribing his broadly syndicalist outlook to "labor"; the worker's ideal is that his "economic subserviency to

[21] FS, pp. 76–77.   [22] AMS, pp. 111–12.

a process of which he is to-day so largely ignorant will be replaced by an intelligent co-operation in the varied details of the productive process." [23] In his opposition to the proposals of Fabians such as Sidney Webb for extension of governmental control over economic affairs and for government ownership and operation of vital industries, Laski also assumes a coincidence between his beliefs and those of "the workers." Webb's views are rejected, he says, because "they leave the worker face to face with government; and there is little reason to suppose that a civil service is more merciful or efficient than the present system." [24] Fabianism, Marxism, and Liberal social reformism seek to improve the standard of life of the masses by governmental action; this paternalistic attitude, which ignores the Aristotelian conception of citizenship as the capacity to rule not less than to be ruled in turn, is totally inadequate because it fails to breed self-respect among individual citizens. Laski asserts: "All save the older socialists have come to see in the simple solution of government control an implication of contingent bureaucracy at no time more inviting than the capitalist system." [25]

His sharpest criticisms, however, are reserved for the Marxists or Fabians who advocate the nationalization of basic industries as the solution of contemporary problems; he flatly maintains that "no real attempt is anywhere made at the democratization of any industry owned, or operated, by the agencies of the state." [26] He warns that the evils implied in a regime of state management of industry are

hardly less great than those of the present system. For to surrender to government officials not merely political but also industrial administration is to create a bureaucracy more powerful than the world has ever seen. It is to apotheosise the potent vices of a government department. It is to make certain a kind of paternalism which, perhaps above all other systems, would prevent the advent of the kind of individual freedom we desire.[27]

Even if nationalization improves the material conditions of the workers' lives, it must be rejected since the concomitant centralization of control "would mean the transference of all power to a class of guardians within the state whose main object even more than today

[23] "Democracy at the Crossroads," *Yale Review*, n.s., IX (July, 1920), 791.
[24] *Ibid.*, p. 800.   [25] *Ibid.*, pp. 795–96.
[26] FS, p. 83.   [27] AMS, p. 95.

would, at all costs, be the maintenance of regularity of supply." [28]

In view of Laski's violent antipathy to the idea of nationalization, it may be interesting to examine briefly his comments on the specific problem of nationalizing the coal mines. In 1919 Lord Haldane gave evidence before the Royal Commission on the Coal Mines, headed by Sir John Sankey, which was considering the miners' demand that the mines be nationalized. Haldane's testimony was published as a pamphlet, entitled *The Problem of Nationalization*,[29] to which Laski and R. H. Tawney contributed an introduction. The Commission's Report recommended that the industry be managed, under a Minister of Mines, by councils at the mine, district, and national levels, each council to be made up of representatives of consumers, technical experts, the miners, and the commercial side of the industry. The experts were to be not merely specialists in engineering, accounting, or medicine, but also men whose training as administrators along the lines suggested by Lord Haldane would enable them to see the general problems of the pit, the district, or the entire industry. Laski and Tawney argue that if, as Haldane maintains, such qualities as a capacity for fellowship and a sense of cooperation in creative endeavor can be developed by training in administration, there is no reason to expect in government-controlled industry that inertia and soullessness which it is customary to charge against it.

These statements, as well as the approval given by Laski and Tawney to the rather limited degree of workers' participation in the government of the coal industry proposed in the Sankey Report, are far removed from the ideal of workers' control of the industrial process and the denunciations of government control or operation of industry which Laski was constantly repeating in his other writings at this time. It is strange that after his violent denunciations of paternalistic control by a new class of guardians he should place so much emphasis on the role of the new group of trained administrators in the work of the various control councils. The ghosts of Owen and Hodgskin would certainly be disturbed by the prophecy of Laski and Tawney that a government-controlled industry, organized in the manner

---

[28] *Ibid.*

[29] Richard B. H. Haldane, 1st Viscount Haldane, *The Problem of Nationalization*, with an introduction by R. H. Tawney and H. J. Laski (London: George Allen and Unwin, Ltd.; Labour Publishing Co., Ltd., May, 1921).

suggested by Lord Haldane and the Sankey Report, will be able to develop "a discipline not less rigid, a spirit every whit as eager, and co-operation as fully intense" [30] as those manifested by the Army and Navy. One can only speculate about a good syndicalist's reaction to. their concluding comment: "As professions the Army and Navy are poorly paid; yet they attract into their service ability and energy as great as any other career can show. That is the example the coal industry must follow." [31]

This example of the proposed organization of the coal-mining industry sharply outlines the basic dilemma faced by anyone who attempts to give a practical and institutional expression to the ideals of the theory of economic federalism—the release of the individual's creative impulses, and the organization of the process of work by voluntary cooperation among individuals and groups rather than by hierarchical control and autocratic discipline. The strength of the Proudhonian and guild-socialist analyses lies in their description of the psychological and sociological effects of the bureaucratic and hierarchical pattern of organization that is characteristic of modern industrial society. The crucial problem to which the syndicalists called attention was the sense of frustration and alienation from work that is felt by the individual worker when he is limited to the routine, repetitive performance of a single operation whose relation to the final product he neither sees nor feels, and when he is enmeshed in a bureaucratic organization in which there is progressively less scope for creative initiative and discretionary behavior as one moves from the apex towards the broad base.

The syndicalists also showed remarkable prescience when they warned of the evils that might result from seeking in the state a remedy for all the defects of modern society. They insisted that the modern state was no less bureaucratic and hierarchical in nature than modern industry. They argued that ever-increasing state control of the economic process, coupled with paternalistic measures designed to insure the individual's material well-being, would not only leave the central problems of an industrial society unsolved, but would run the risk of creating a new leviathan more fatal to individual freedom than the domination of private corporations. As socialists the syndicalists believed that the root of the evils of modern society

[30] *Ibid.*, p. 7.   [31] *Ibid.*, p. 11.

was the institution of private property in the instruments of production, but they insisted that state socialism would mean a fusion of the economic and political bureaucracies. Before this unique concentration of power the individual would be totally helpless; every trace of his individuality and his spontaneity might then be eliminated in a new and more efficient drive towards absolute uniformity and disciplined obedience.

In the middle of the twentieth century the increased size and complexity of industrial units in capitalist society serve to emphasize some of the problems posed by the syndicalists' analysis, while the example of the Soviet Union lends credence to their gloomy forebodings of the results of state socialism. It is interesting to observe that in England, where the Labor Party has been endeavoring to construct a democratic and non-authoritarian socialist society, there has been a considerable revival of guild-socialist theories. In books, journals, and pamphlets the extent and form of workers' and consumers' participation in the nationalized industries, ways of minimizing bureaucratic control, and methods of evoking a sense of personal responsibility and initiative in the individual worker have been extensively discussed. The major weakness in these discussions, as in the speculations of the non-Marxist socialists after the First World War, is their failure to formulate a new pattern of institutions to meet the needs of a modern industrial society. The positive proposals, in so far as they are not merely rhetorical pleas for a cooperative and federal industrial order, reduce themselves, on the one hand, to completely impractical suggestions for a return to a simpler society, or, on the other, to a series of relatively minor institutional changes—trade-union representation on the boards of nationalized industries, works councils and "co-determination" in the factory, consultative committees at various levels of government. The syndicalist prescription, that is, proves to be either a surgery so radical as to be fatal to the patient, or, as in the case of the Sankey Report discussed above, a palliative ointment.

Against this background, let us examine some of Laski's proposals for institutional changes, particularly in the political realm. His major premise is that it is "only by intensifying the active participation of men in the business of government that liberty can be made secure." [32] The present principle of tacit consent is, for him, "too theoretical in

[32] AMS, p. 387.

character. It results in the virtual annihilation of every individuality that is not either at the center of things, or finding its compensation for exclusion in some such activity as art." [33] Throughout, his tacit assumption is that man is predominantly a political animal or, at least, that he ought to be, if his personality is to be fully developed. Only on the basis of this assumption can he regard artistic activity as a compensation for the individual's exclusion from active participation in politics. While it may be natural for a student of politics to feel that other men would, if only they had adequate knowledge, leisure, and opportunities, share his passion for politics, the assumption is psychologically hardly more valid than a poet's belief that if men were given proper training and adequate opportunities they would naturally devote most of their time and energy to the composition of verse. As Laski admits when he complains of mass apathy and indifference, we have no reason to believe that most men do, in fact, have a deep and abiding interest in politics. Moreover, if, with Laski, we maintain that human personality is exceedingly complex and that men's interests, as expressed in the numberless groups and associations that they create, are highly diverse, we cannot insist that political activity is the high road to self-fulfillment or that it is necessarily a higher form of self-expression than other human pursuits.

At no point does Laski advocate a system of direct democracy; for him anything but a representative system of government is not only inadmissible but undesirable.[34] He does believe, however, that a much larger number of persons can be given an active role in the processes of government if his proposals for territorial and functional federalism are carried out and if all citizens are assured of adequate educational opportunities and sufficient leisure. He maintains that decisions on the problems that confront each industry or profession should be entrusted to those who understand the problems and are most affected by their solutions, that is, all those who participate in the industry or profession. For each "function" there must be a representative assembly, made up of representatives of management, labor, technicians, the consumer, and of allied functions, with power to make regulations and decisions binding on all who participate in the in-

[33] FS, p. 88.
[34] See his statement: "We cannot, even in our remotest dreams, give every man some actual share in the business of administration." *Ibid.*

dustry.[35] Laski makes no attempt to deal with the crucial problem —what proportion of the total seats in each such industrial assembly is to go to each of the groups to be represented, and, above all, what is to be the balance between management and labor. But, in view of his desire for the achievement of "economic democracy" and the abolition of the autocratic control over the industrial process that is characteristic of capitalism, it would seem that he anticipates that the workers of various grades will constitute a majority in each industrial assembly.[36]

As we have already observed, Laski never accepts the abolition of the state that is implied in the pure theories of syndicalism or guild socialism. He believes that the traditional organs of government based on geographical units must be retained in the new society in order to deal with those problems which are of primary concern to the consumer. In 1918 and 1919 he advocates a national federation of the various industrial councils, a producers' parliament, to deal with general problems of production and to settle differences between the industrial assemblies.[37] The present political parliament would continue to deal with problems of consumption. Thus there would be two coordinate legislatures in the society, and within each of the two main spheres, consumption and production, there would be extensive decentralization and devolution of power to subordinate geographical and functional units. Questions involving the relationship between production and consumption would constitute a matter for "joint adjustment" between the two bodies, while disputes between the two legislatures would probably have to be referred to a special tribunal for settlement.[38]

In 1920 Laski no longer advocates the idea of two equally powerful legislatures; he maintains that the political legislature should not only be responsible for creating the units of industrial government, but also retain general supervision over the activities of the industrial councils by drawing "the large outline of the social plan," leaving to

[35] See *The State in the New Social Order*, Fabian Tract No. 200 (London: The Fabian Society, 1922), pp. 12–13; and FS, pp. 70–71.

[36] See his comments in his Introduction to John Stuart Mill, *Autobiography*, The World's Classics No. 262 (London: Humphrey Milford, Oxford University Press, 1924), pp. xvii–xviii; see also FS, pp. 77–78.

[37] See FS, pp. 72–73; and AMS, p. 88.   [38] See AMS, pp. 88–89.

the workers in each industrial council the elaboration of "creative detail." [39] His statement in 1922 that final control must lie in the whole citizen body, and not in any vocation or area or rank, if the lives of the many are not to lie at the disposal of the few, indicates the extent of his movement away from the guild-socialist idea.[40] He explicitly abandons the proposal for a federation of the industrial councils into a national producers' parliament; the solution of general industrial questions is really the solution of problems of citizenship which come within the scope of Parliament. This view that traditional political institutions represent all men as citizens is contrary to his earlier insistence that the state represents men only as consumers and that a new central body is therefore needed to deal with the problems of production. More significantly, once Laski accepts the position that the state represents all men as citizens, he has, in effect, abandoned the basis of his rejection of the traditional state organization and the theory of state sovereignty. As a result he is forced to modify his early position that the main field of labor action should be industrial rather than political and that the diversion of labor's energies into political struggles is a tactical error. As early as December, 1918, we have a preview of the new Laski position; he argues that, particularly in the United States, where "a political democracy confronts the most powerful economic autocracy the world has even seen," [41] it is "impossible for labor even to dream of victory, unless it attempts to capture the actual machinery of the state; and that implies not less political than industrial action." [42]

Finally, however, we must consider whether Laski's proposals for a series of industrial councils, dominated by workers' representatives and given power by the state to regulate the conditions of production and to carry out the details of economic planning, constitute a practical program for implementing his ideals of "industrial democracy" and "economic federalism." A major difficulty is that any plan for vesting control over the processes of production in workers' representatives runs counter to the hierarchical structure that is required by

[39] "Democracy at the Crossroads," *Yale Review,* n.s., IX (July, 1920), 795.
[40] See *The State in the New Social Order,* p. 15.   [41] AMS, p. 116.
[42] "British Labor Reconstruction Proposals and the American Labor Attitude," *Proceedings of the Academy of Political Science,* VIII (Feb., 1919), 62.

the gradations in skills, techniques, and expert knowledge characteristic of modern industry. The decision to alter a given method of production, to install a new machine, to expand the plant, or to hire additional expert employees must be made largely in terms of such factors as technical efficiency, financial cost, and judgment as to future demand. Inasmuch as competence in assessing these factors is necessarily confined to a small group of experts and administrators, it is difficult to see how the responsibility for such decisions can be widely dispersed among the working force. A workers' council in a privately managed or state-operated factory may well be useful and practicable in dealing with the reactions of the workers to technical changes as well as in working out policies in regard to hiring, promotion, wages and hours, working conditions, and discipline. In respect to major decisions, however, the functions of the workers' councils must, it seems, be advisory and consultative—criticizing the proposals of management, conveying to the upper levels of the bureaucracy an understanding of the attitudes and wishes of the workers, and forcing the administrators to pay attention to the human implications of their decisions. If we admit that only a small minority possess either expert technical competence or knowledge of the larger economic situation in which a given plant or industry is involved, we must conclude that "economic democracy" as a method of making the major decisions in industry is not a feasible goal and that the term "democracy" should be used only in reference to the political system.

Presuming that the question of the proper sphere of activities of industrial councils were resolved, we would still face the problem of the proper way to organize such bodies. As we have seen, Laski does not deal with the primary question—what is to be the balance between the number of representatives of the workers and of management. Moreover, the choice of representatives of the workers is not without complications. If officials of the trade unions are chosen to represent the workers on the council,[43] the result may be to strengthen existing bureaucratic tendencies in union organization by increasing the power of professional "workers' representatives," whose interests may not be identical with those of the ordinary worker. There is no reason to believe that the average employee will be more actively concerned

[43] Laski suggests this; see *The State in the New Social Order*, p. 13.

in the work of the industrial council than he now is in the activities or the government of his trade union.[44] The fact that a union is represented as such on the council may serve to limit union independence and freedom of action; it would be difficult, for example, for a union whose representative on the council had approved a new retirement scheme to decide later to advise its members to reject the plan. Exclusion of union officials from the industrial council, on the other hand, would create a sense of hostility among the union leaders, who might well fear the council as a device of the employers to weaken the independent power of the union. Even if the council were to retain a real independence, the existence in each plant of two separate and possibly conflicting vehicles of workers' action would create serious problems. In any event, it is not likely that, particularly at the outset, a large number of workers would feel any great enthusiasm for, or interest in, the work of the industrial council. Finally, a system of workers' councils will probably never be regarded by labor as anything more than a supplement to working-class political parties designed to influence political action at the national level with respect to such economic problems as minimum wages, maximum hours, welfare schemes, governmental controls, or nationalization of certain industries.

In closing this survey of Laski's views of the relationships between politics and economics, we should look for a moment at his comments on the rights of property. The present system of private property and inheritance not only allows individuals to amass wealth because of their skill in such antisocial or socially useless activities as gambling and real-estate speculation, but also confers large amounts of property on certain persons through the accident of birth. The ownership of property confers rights that are purely prescriptive in

[44] At moments Laski seems aware of the danger of projecting "a wanton idealism" (AMS, p. 92) into our view of the trade unions. He recognizes that his plans for a large measure of industrial self-government "predicate a trade unionism far more virile and intelligent than in the past." (FS, p. 81). He warns that if the unions do not rise above their traditional concentration on greater job security and increased material benefits for their members and fail to arouse their creative impulses for self-government, the next years may well see the emergence of a new kind of industrial feudalism in which the workers will exchange liberty for comfort and in which the proposed industrial councils will serve no useful purpose or, worse, will be only "a means towards lulling the creative tenets of trade unionism into somnolence." *Ibid.*

nature and bear no relation to the performance of any service. In contrast, Laski asserts that the "society towards which we are moving will be organised upon the basis of functions, and the rights it will confer will be dependent upon the functions we perform." [45] The amount of property that any individual is permitted to hold will be limited to a proper return for the service he renders in satisfying social needs; only in terms of this principle can the individual interest be harmonized with the common good. He holds, however, that this revamping of the property system must be carried out gradually on the basis of changing men's convictions by persuasion; if, he warns, "the problem of social change is to be restricted to a struggle between property and poverty, we shall end either by the establishment of an iron industrial feudalism or an anarchy in which our intellectual heritage will perish." [46]

Laski's concept of property as the payment for a service rendered to society clearly implies that high rewards for speculative or monopolistic activities are indefensible and that inheritance rights should be sharply curtailed. But his principle gives us no clear standard for dealing with most of the actual problems of income and property distribution. How are we to measure the social need that is satisfied by the function performed by a given individual? If we rely on the forces of supply and demand to gauge the value of each contribution, the skillful entrepreneur or administrator, or the popular entertainer, will continue to be able to command a very high return for his services. If, however, we allow the government or some other central authority to set the proper reward for each function, we have an authoritarian solution that involves a nonrational estimate of the social value of a given vocation or service by those who make the decision.

2 . MARXISM AND LENINISM

We have already noted that Laski's early socialism was sharply critical of the statist and bureaucratic implications of both Marxism

---

[45] *The State in the New Social Order*, p. 8.
[46] "Lenin and Mussolini," *Foreign Affairs*, II (Sept., 1923), 54.

and Fabianism and that his own position was much closer to that of Proudhon or the pre-Marxist English socialists such as Bray and Thompson, whose doctrine he calls "the most fruitful hypothesis of modern politics." [47] We must now examine in greater detail his attitude towards the theories of Marx and Engels and their practical implementation by Lenin, paying particular attention to the problems of the role of violence in the transition to socialism and the need for a dictatorship after the revolution.

For Laski, Marx's major accomplishment was his detailed and final exposition of the central thesis of all earlier socialists—the complete moral inadequacy of capitalist civilization. He thus places the stress on the element—the ethical criticism of capitalism—which Marx, in his "scientific" and "non-Utopian" socialism, maintained was not the focus of his analysis.[48] Laski's fundamental sympathy for Marx arises from his belief that a relentless passion for justice was the driving force in Marx's life as it was in his own. Marx's purpose, he says, was

the desire to take from the shoulders of the people the burden by which it was oppressed. . . . He transformed the fears of the workers into hopes, he translated their effort from interest in political mechanisms to interest in social foundations. . . . He was often wrong, he was rarely generous, he was always bitter; yet when the roll of those to whom the emancipation of the people is due comes to be called, few will have a more honourable, and none a more eminent place.[49]

He admits the great historical significance of *The Communist Manifesto,* but he also points out how much it owed to the *Manifeste de la Démocratie* published four years earlier by Considérant; he notes that almost every detail of the Manifesto's program of action

[47] PTE, p. 315.

[48] He argues that Marx's vital perception was "that a society dominated by business men and organized for the prosperity of business men had become intolerable. Hardly less splendid was his insistence that no social order is adequate in which the collective energies of men are not devoted to their common life." *Karl Marx: An Essay* (London: The Fabian Society and George Allen and Unwin, Ltd., 1922), hereinafter cited as KM, p. 45. In his letters to Holmes during this period, Laski frequently belittles the originality of Marx's contributions and notes that he admires him less and less as the years pass. He writes: "What is good is all taken from Hodgskin and Thompson, the two early English socialists. . . . Anyhow, I propose to attack him in this Fabian tract and argue that reformism is by all odds the safest road to tread." *Holmes-Laski Letters,* I, 358 (Aug. 7, 1921).

[49] KM, p. 46.

was lifted from the proposals of the very pre-Marxist socialists whose views Marx subjected to a critical condemnation that was often inaccurate and always unfair. According to Laski a democratic system was totally alien to Marx's temperament; Marx was essentially a prophet who had to dominate every movement he entered, and who had no patience with difference; "contemptuous . . . of all who did not think exactly in his fashion, he never learned the essential art of colleagueship." [50] Marx dismissed liberty as a purely bourgeois ideal and was openly scornful of democracy as a bourgeois invention designed to deceive the people; for him, history was the story of clashes between determined minorities contending for power. Laski stresses the fact that, as early as 1848–1849, in the *Neue Rheinische Zeitung* articles, Marx had insisted that it would be necessary to institute a revolutionary terror "to abridge and concentrate the hideous death agonies of society." [51]

In general the views upon which Marx based his conclusions were "partial and incomplete" and, "vast and patient as were the researches he undertook, he was not always exact in his measurement of evidence." [52] His penetration into the motives and desires of men, what Laski calls "the inner substance" of their lives, in no way matched his profound insight into the workings of the material environment. His view of human nature is abstract, materialistic, and in direct contradiction with the totality of the facts. Nor is his economic interpretation of history any more adequate than his psychology; "the insistence upon an economic background as the whole explanation is radically false." [53] Laski also rejects the central elements in Marx's economic theory; he regards the labor theory of value as far from self-consistent and maintains that the iron law of wages is clearly invalidated by the fact that the wages of the workers do rise above the bare costs of necessities, thanks to such factors as trade-union organization.[54] Laski admits that Marx's law of the concentration of capital, by whose opera-

[50] *Ibid.*, p. 25.   [51] *Ibid.*, p. 17.   [52] *Ibid.*, p. 25.   [53] *Ibid.*, p. 33.

[54] Laski argues that the worker found Marx's value theory appealing "not by virtue of any logical estimation of its theoretic adequacy, but because it summarized the most poignant experience he knew," (*ibid.*, p. 30) that he was poor though he produced more than he could consume, and that the surplus he created was divided among a relatively small class of rich, and often idle, men. The Marxian law of wages will, he maintains, "win new adherents at every period of commercial depression"; for at these times "the impact of capitalism upon the wage-earner will closely resemble what Marx insisted is its normal relation." *Ibid.*

tion capitalism inevitably produces its own antithesis, socialism, is somewhat more plausible. Capitalism, as it matures, does tend to produce large monopolistic units, and the community does come to feel that some form of state administration of these monopolies is essential. He argues, however, that this movement does not inevitably bring about a transition to socialism and, in particular, that it need not lead to the revolutionary transition anticipated by Marx. The people may decide that legislative control, administrative regulation, or selective nationalization is an adequate safeguard against the danger that industries essential to the community's welfare may be exploited by private interests.

The main weight of Laski's attack on Marxism is directed against its insistence on the inevitability of a violent revolution in the transition to socialism and the corollary, the belief in the necessity of an iron dictatorship during the period of consolidation. While conceding that Marx expressed some doubts as to the necessity of revolution in England, he affirms that, on the whole, Marx no less than Lenin believed that a peaceful transition to a democratic socialist society was impossible. Laski's first objection to the revolutionary method is the essentially practical one that, given the overwhelming power of modern governments and of their instruments of control, the accomplishment of a revolution is now a qualitatively different problem than it was in 1848 or even in 1870; no revolution is possible in the face of a hostile army and navy, and that hostility is certain unless the revolutionary group has already attained control of the government by winning a majority. Also, differences in national background and religion cut across the solidarity of the working class, particularly in a nation such as the United States, and appeals to these loyalties may prove stronger than the economic motive on which Marx relied.

Laski's main ground for rejecting the Marxist doctrine, however, is his belief that security and freedom will vanish from the earth if profound belief in any cause is held to be justification for a resort to revolutionary violence. Violence is particularly inappropriate as the means of transition to a socialist or communist society in which the maximum development of men's cooperative and harmonious impulses will be essential; he notes that "the condition of communism is the restraint of exactly those appetites which violence releases." [55] The example of the Russian Revolution makes it clear that the resort to violent overthrow of existing institutions "entails the suppression of tolerance and kindliness, sows cruelty and hatred, anger and suspicion, into the soil of human relations, has impaired at every point the intellectual heritage of the Russian people, and has been impatient of reason and fanatically hostile to critical enquiry." [56] For Laski the good society is one that provides for the fullest possible release of the creative energies of its members and in which intellectual and spiritual goods are valued more highly than material possessions. It is impossible to reach the goal of this society by the path that Marx recommends, since he not only overaccents the economic motive, but, by advocating the resort to violence, he urges us to fly to exactly those evils from which we are seeking release.[57]

His objection to the theory of the dictatorship of the proletariat is equally strong; he observes that neither Marx nor Lenin gives us any idea of how long the dictatorship is to continue; nor do they demonstrate why we should have any confidence that, at the height of their power, the dictators will be willing to surrender their authority. In a phrase that is prophetic of the course of events in the Soviet Union, he warns that the dictators "may begin by asserting that they have seized power for a great end; they are bound to continue by holding power for its own sake." [58] For Laski the evils of dictatorship are equally apparent in the practice of Communism and Fascism.

Lenin and Mussolini alike have established a government not of laws but of men. They have degraded public morality by refusing to admit the terms upon which civilized intercourse alone becomes possible. By treating their opponents as criminals, they have made thought itself a disastrous adventure. . . . They have penalized sincerity in politics. They have given rein to passions which are incompatible with the security

[55] *Ibid.*, p. 42.

[56] "Lenin and Mussolini," *Foreign Affairs*, II (Sept., 1923), 48.

[57] He argues: "That wrong can be wiped out with wrong, that we are to regard ourselves as the victims of blind and impersonal forces against which it is useless to strive, that the possessive impulses of men cannot be transcended by creative effort— these and things like these are a gospel of impossible despair. In that aspect, surely, the older socialists were right who made the basis of their creed a doctrine of right and fraternity and justice. For right and fraternity and justice imply love as their foundation; they do not spring, even at the last vain striving, from a doctrine founded upon hate." KM, p. 44.

[58] "Lenin and Mussolini," *Foreign Affairs*, II (Sept., 1923), 54.

of life. They have insisted on the indispensability of themselves and their dogmas even though we cannot afford to pay the price incurred in the enforcement of that notion.[59]

The Marxist-Leninist view is that the great goal of the movement, the liberation of mankind from privation and fear, legitimizes any action that is a means toward this end. The corollary of this view is a contempt for freedom of inquiry and for the methods of argument and persuasion that involves a denial of what, to Laski, is the plain lesson of scientific knowledge and of human experience, that "the only permanent basis of power is action built upon the wills and desires of the mass of men." [60] In our complex and fragile civilization, the product of centuries of arduous labor and painful struggle, social changes must be made peacefully; reform of the social constitution must be a continuous process rather than a violent overturn of established institutions.

It may well be that the time has come for a revolution in the temper of human affairs; certainly no modern state can at once widely distribute political power and seek to maintain great disparities of fortune. But the only revolution that can hope for permanence is that which wins by slow persuasion the organized conviction of men. To endanger that process by exalting violence . . . will, in the end, disrupt the foundations of the social fabric. Great events . . . depend, in the last analysis, upon the spirit which surrounds the circumstances of government. If that spirit is habituated to methods of violence, we cannot maintain the traditions of civilization.[61]

As we have seen, Laski brackets Lenin and Mussolini in his condemnation of dictatorship; save in intensity, he finds no difference in their methods, and he believes that Fascism's "ultimate spirit is in no wise dissimilar" [62] from that of Soviet Communism. In view of the important role that the discussion of the genesis of Nazism and

[59] *Ibid.*   [60] *Ibid.*, p. 53.

[61] *Ibid.*, p. 54. For a somewhat different emphasis, see his statement in 1920: "For what is really in question today is, as Mr. MacDonald emphasizes, the existence of capitalism. I think, with him, that its destruction by concession is infinitely better than its destruction by revolution. But it may well be that a capitalism such as that of Sir Eric Geddes in England or of Judge Gary in America is incapable of necessary concessions; and in that event the direct action of the trade unions is destined to be the necessary path of attainment." "Parliament and Revolution," *The New Republic*, XXII (May 19, 1920), 384.

[62] "Lenin and Mussolini," *Foreign Affairs*, II (Sept., 1923), 48.

Fascism plays in his writings during the 1930's, it is interesting to note his early analysis of the causes of Fascism. In 1923 he attributes the rise of Fascism to Italian disillusionment after the Treaty of Versailles and to "the ill-considered effort of the left-wing Italian socialists not merely to link themselves to the Third International but also to seize control of industry in some of the great towns." [63] He notes that while "Lenin's system has won for itself international ostracism and armed intervention, that of Mussolini has been the subject of widespread enthusiasm" [64] among leaders in government and business in other countries. In view of the essential similarity in the ultimate spirit and methods of the two systems, he finds it "difficult to avoid the conclusion that the different reception of their effort is the outcome of their antithetic attitudes to property." [65]

[63] *Ibid.*, pp. 48–49.   [64] *Ibid.*, p. 52.
[65] *Ibid.*, p. 53.

Part Two

1925-1931

4

The Nature of the State and Political Power

UNTIL 1930 at least, Laski's approach to the analysis of political problems continues to be historical and undogmatic. From his historical studies he draws the conclusion that no particular form of state or government and no single theory of the state can be regarded as permanent or absolutely valid.[1] Each theory of the state and the man who formulated it must, therefore, be studied in the light of the environmental situation. He notes that one of the major values of this historical approach to the study of political ideas is that we learn to be tolerant of the beliefs of others even if we regard them as completely erroneous; the clear lesson to be learned from the record of the past is that "any error of wide circulation may possibly contain some great element of truth, and will certainly contain an important index to the aspirations of men."[2] Once that lesson has been mastered, we can no longer regard our own political beliefs as absolutely certain and eternally true; "to understand why men have held particular political opinions is to compel the scrutiny of one's own faith with an inescapable knowledge that its value is limited."[3]

Examination of Laski's writings during the period from 1925 to 1931 reveals that the major theme of his earlier works, the 'attack on the sovereign state, is given less attention. He may have believed that his early critical writings had laid the groundwork for the new positive theory of the state which he attempts to set forth in the comprehensive volume, *A Grammar of Politics,* published in 1925. There he comments that "it would be of lasting benefit to political science if the whole concept of sovereignty were surrendered. That, in fact, with which we are dealing is power; and what is important in the

[1] See "On the Study of Politics" (1926), reprinted in *The Danger of Being a Gentleman and Other Essays* (New York: The Viking Press, 1940), hereinafter cited as DBG, esp. pp. 36–42; and "Law and the State" (Nov., 1929), reprinted in *Studies in Law and Politics* (New Haven: Yale University Press, 1932), hereinafter cited as SLP, esp. p. 237.

[2] "On the Study of Politics," DBG, p. 41.   [3] *Ibid.,* p. 40.

nature of power is the end it seeks to serve and the way in which it serves that end." [4] Laski now seems to recognize more clearly than he had in earlier writings that the legal theory of sovereignty is unassailable on its own ground, although, as a static and purely formal system, it may be inadequate as a general theory of the state. "The ideal State of formal jurisprudence," he notes, "need not consider public opinion, the wills of other States, the impact upon itself of internal and competing powers, ethical right, or political wisdom." [5] Any political philosophy that is to be useful and meaningful must "seek a bridge between the purely logical world of ideal concepts, in which alone the juristic theory of the State dwells, and the actual world about us, in which the States that we know have to perform their function." [6]

He still maintains that until we know the content of a specific decision made by any government we cannot say that the decision promotes the interest of the whole community. Nor can the state's command be defended as an expression of the general will of the community, since no such will exists. "The will of the State," he insists, "is the will of certain persons exercising certain powers. . . . The will of the State may be made to approach 'generality' the better it is organized for that end. But organization as such can never assure it of generality until we know the purpose to which it proposes to devote its powers." [7]

As late as 1929 Laski still asserts that his is a pluralistic theory of the state, "rooted in a denial that any association of men in the community is inherently entitled to primacy over any other association." [8] He rejects the orthodox theory of state sovereignty because it "makes

[4] *A Grammar of Politics* (4th ed., 10th impression; London: George Allen and Unwin, Ltd., 1950), pp. 44–45; the first edition was published in 1925 by Allen and Unwin in England and by the Yale University Press in the United States; hereinafter cited as GP.

[5] "Law and the State," SLP, p. 239.

[6] *Ibid.*, p. 240; see also: "A theory of the state which emphasizes formality at the expense of substance is not likely to possess final value. It abstracts the legal system from the context in which alone its meaning can be found." *Ibid.*, p. 270.

[7] *Ibid.*, pp. 256–57.

[8] *Ibid.*, p. 259; it should be noted that the whole tone of this essay, which appeared in *Economica* in Nov., 1929, is much more pluralistic and resembles his early writings more than do many of the other pieces written between 1925 and 1929. It is possible that he wrote it some time before it first appeared in print.

unity upon the ground that unity in some given realm of conduct is held by those who operate the machinery of the State to be desirable. It does not tell us why it is so held; it does not tell us whether its recipients will so regard it; and it does not, finally, tell us whether it ought so to be regarded." [9] As a substitute for this orthodox theory, he now proposes a purely pragmatic standard for determining the nature and extent of the powers of the state. The state must possess such powers as are necessary for the accomplishment of the purpose it seeks to serve, and those powers should be organized in such fashion as to guarantee, as far as possible, that it will actually translate that goal into actions. We must remember that the state is in fact the small group of men who actually operate the government; instead of concentrating our attention on "the abstract metaphysics of politics," we must deal with the real problems of political life—to what range of subjects should the orders of those who govern refer, and how can these men be prevented from abusing the power entrusted to them. Laski argues that "the sovereignty of the State is a power only to fulfil certain purposes and obligations," [10] and that each individual must judge the government's use of its power by examining, in terms of the purpose ascribed to the state, the effects of governmental actions upon his own life.

Obviously Laski's pragmatic standard for determining the proper extent of the state's powers makes possible a very powerful or a very weak government; the definition of the purpose of the state will be crucial in determining the range of its powers. It is, therefore, significant that the greatest changes in his position occur in his discussions of the state's function and of its relations to other social groups. The state, which previously he described as coordinate with other associations, is now defined as "the keystone of the social arch," [11] "the coordinating factor in the community," [12] and "the fundamental instrument of society." [13]

The modern State is a territorial society divided into government and subjects claiming, within its allotted physical area, a supremacy over all other institutions. It is, in fact, the final legal depository of the social will. It sets the perspective of all other organisations. It brings within its power all forms of human activity the control of which it deems de-

[9] *Ibid.*, p. 273.   [10] GP, p. 662.   [11] *Ibid.*, p. 21.   [12] *Ibid.*, p. 98.
[13] *Ibid.*, p. 39.

sirable. . . . It moulds the form and substance of the myriad human lives with whose destinies it is charged.[14]

This description of the state, closely resembling that given by orthodox theorists, is a far cry from the "discredited state" of Laski's early writings. When he discusses the purpose of the state, he is equally generous and expansive. Borrowing William James's definition of good as the response to demand on the largest possible scale, he uses it to define the state as "an organisation for enabling the mass of men to realise social good on the largest possible scale."[15] In more concrete terms, he asserts that the state is "entrusted with power in order that it may satisfy, or organize the satisfaction of, the wants of men on the largest possible scale. It acts through a body of agents, the Government, to that end and no other end."[16] This formulation of the state's purpose, though it is obviously based on the Benthamite principle that the state should act to promote the greatest happiness of the greatest number, gives to the state a far more positive role than does the utilitarian theory.

Although he still insists that the will of the state cannot be equated with the will of society as a whole, he now admits that the state's will is an urgent aspect of the whole, "in the same sense that the skeleton is a vital aspect of the body," and that it "may be the largest will we normally encounter";[17] it is "the will which is adopted out of the conflict of myriad wills which contend with each other for the mastery of social forces."[18] He specifically recognizes what he had previously denied—that the state differs in kind and not merely in degree from other human associations:

I cannot, in any fundamental way, withdraw from its jurisdiction. I cannot . . . appeal from the tribunals it has created. It is the ultimate source of decision within the normal environment about which my life is lived. Clearly, that attaches to its will an importance for me greater than that which belongs elsewhere.[19]

How are we to reconcile the diverse and sometimes incompatible demands of the different groups and individuals that make up a community? Laski now flatly rejects the anarchist or syndicalist solution of this problem by his statement that the will of any given association

[14] *Ibid.*, p. 21.
[16] "Law and the State," SLP, p. 245.
[18] *Ibid.*, p. 35.
[15] *Ibid.*, p. 25.
[17] GP, p. 28.
[19] *Ibid.*, p. 38.

cannot be made a final will; he also admits that the "problem of so weighting associations that each receives not merely an equal, but, more, its due place in an institution which congeals them into unity is an insoluble one." [20] His new position is that the state represents men as consumers, as "centres of universal decision," in contrast to the specific interest groups, which represent men as producers. In order to protect men as "undifferentiated persons" whose needs are identical, the state must be given the power to coordinate the various functions in society and to enforce and interpret the common rules by which the rights of groups are defined. The state is defined as

the body which seeks so to organise the interests of consumers that they obtain the commodities of which they have need. Within the State, they meet as persons. Their claims are equal claims. . . . Clearly, *a function of this kind,* however it is organised, *involves a preeminence over other functions.* The State . . . is, in administrative terms, a government whose activities are shaped by the common needs of its members. To satisfy these common needs, it must control other associations to the degree that secures from them the service such needs require. The more closely a given function—education, for example, or the provision of coal—lies to the heart of the society, the more closely it will require to be controlled. [21]

Although this view of the state as the final coordinating agency in society represents a major shift away from Laski's earlier pluralism, he is still anxious to preserve a measure of independence for other social groups. In controlling associations the state should concentrate its attention on their general activities which interest every member of the society; on the other hand, group activities that are "primarily specific in their incidence" are of concern to the state only to the degree that their results bear upon the rest of the community. This formulation, however, is virtually meaningless since there are few, if any, group activities that do not affect the rest of the community. And if the state as the supreme coordinator is given the power to demarcate the respective spheres of "general" and "specific" group activi-

[20] *Ibid.,* p. 69.

[21] *Ibid.,* pp. 69–70; italics mine. See also the following statement of the state's task: "It sets the conditions within which other associations move only because its mission is to enable the citizen, through those associations, to be that best self of which he is capable. . . . It is protecting the plane upon which the interests of men, and therefore their rights, are, broadly speaking, identical. It co-ordinates the activities of other groups with a view to that end." *Ibid.,* p. 131.

ties, there is, in theory, no limit to the extent of the control which it may exercise over associations.

Laski's discussions of the proper extent of action by the state show the influence exerted upon him after his return to England in 1920 by the Fabians, especially Beatrice and Sidney Webb, and by his membership in the Labor Party, which had become one of the two major parties.[22] He argues that the state can fulfill its function of protecting the interests of men as consumers only if there is approximate economic equality in the community. This equality, in turn, can be assured only if the government so controls "the production and distribution of wealth that the general interest of the community is not regarded as the happy result of a mere sum of private interests, but is a recognised minimum in which each citizen has an equal share." [23] The state's interest in the production of essential goods and services is therefore "immediate, direct, and comprehensive. It must ensure such a supply of them as will serve the total need of the community. It must see to it that their quality is adequate. . . . The failure to secure these services being fatal, it is obvious that the State cannot risk their production by private enterprise." [24] This line of argument demonstrates the extent to which Laski's increasing stress on the need for governmental action to mitigate the inequalities that result from the "normal" workings of economic institutions is leading him away from his original antistatist position. The state must be given sufficient power to enable it to control other associations, particularly economic groups, so that each citizen will be assured that minimum of well-being which is essential to his life and to the performance of his civic duties. It is charged with the task of adjusting and shaping men's diverse wants and demands into a general pattern that will provide the maximum amount of satisfaction for the greatest number of citizens.

Laski's new formulation of the state's function shares with the Fabian view of the state a common ancestor, the basic utilitarian formula of the greatest happiness of the greatest number. Although

---

[22] In his letters to Holmes, Laski frequently mentions conversations with the Webbs and his great admiration for them. See, e.g., *Holmes-Laski Letters, 1916–1935,* ed. by Mark DeWolfe Howe (2 vols., Cambridge: Harvard University Press, 1953), I, 464 (Dec. 5, 1922) and II, 902 (Dec. 4, 1926).

[23] GP, p. 87.   [24] *Ibid.,* p. 435.

Laski admits this, he maintains that his position differs from utilitarianism in that he rejects the egoistic nature of impulse as well as Bentham's elaborate calculus of pleasures and pains. He argues, in fact, that good "is either social; or it is not good at all. If man is to live in community with his fellows it is a necessary condition of his life that what he attains should, at least in the long run, involve benefit also to others. Social good, therefore seems to consist in the unity our nature attains when the working of our impulses results in a satisfied activity." [25] Alternatively, he defines this social good as "such an ordering of our personality that we are driven to search for things it is worth while to obtain that, thereby, we may enrich the great fellowship we serve." [26] This attempt to "socialize" Benthamism is as unsuccessful as it is obscure. The initial equation between "good" and the maximum satisfaction of human wants, with no discrimination among them, ignores the obvious difficulty that the satisfaction of certain wants may be undesirable; and the assertion that the good of one person necessarily involves the good of other men is untenable, even when limited by the proviso, "in the long run," unless one postulates an automatic mechanism to preside over and adjust the conflicting wants and aspirations of men. Further, the definition of social good, which includes the phrase "things it is worth while to obtain," indicates that Laski has undertaken no serious analysis of this concept; this is a major weakness since the idea of social good, as the basis of his analysis of the state's purpose, is the cornerstone of his political philosophy. Finally, it must be noted that if social good is defined in terms of individual psychology as that personality structure which drives me to search for the good, there can be, by definition, no conflict between my good and the good of others; this equation of individual and social good, however, comes perilously close to the idealist's notions of a "real will" and a "real self" which Laski clearly rejects when he asserts that "the starting-point of every political philosophy is the inexpugnable variety of human wills." [27]

Even if we pass over the problem of the precise meanings to be attached to such terms as "social good," "social demands," and "human wants," we must ask whether it is, or should be, "the business of those who exercise authority in the State to satisfy the wants of those over

[25] *Ibid.*, p. 24.   [26] *Ibid.*, p. 25.   [27] *Ibid.*, p. 31.

whom they rule" [28] or to satisfy "the wants of men upon the largest possible scale." Most of us would agree that in general a government should frame its actions so that certain wants of the citizens are satisfied. But in particular situations a government may be obliged to act to protect what it believes to be the interests of the people even though that action fails to reflect, or even contradicts, the expressed desires of the citizens at that moment. Laski's formulation ignores the crucial problem of leadership in a democratic society as well as the extent to which leaders may and should shape popular demands and desires. Even more serious, however, and more surprising, in view of his interest in defending the autonomy of social groups, is his statement that it is the state's task to satisfy the wants of men. Every group and association in society exists in order to promote given interests and to satisfy certain wants. Unless we assume that the state is to swallow up these groups by assuming the functions that they now perform, we must specify the particular human wants and needs whose satisfaction is the state's peculiar function. The orthodox liberal theory of the state held that the maintenance of peace and order was its special task. Most of us would now reject this formula as too limited and would add that the state should also maintain certain minimum standards of material well-being for all citizens and provide certain opportunities for individual development. Although Laski has no desire to endow the state with absolute powers over the community and over the myriad groups that live within it, his penchant for sweeping generalizations and rhetorical phrases at the expense of careful analysis leads him to formulate the state's purpose in dangerously vague terms, such as "the maximum possible satisfaction of human wants."

By 1931, when he published *Politics,* Laski's position seems to have swung even further away from his early pluralism and back towards the orthodox theory of the state. He now finds the essence of the state to be its power to enforce its norms upon all who live within its boundaries and its supremacy over all other forms of social grouping; the state's will is a sovereign will, legally, though not morally, pre-eminent over all other wills.[29] He still argues that the state should

---

[28] *Liberty in the Modern State* (New York: Harper and Bros., 1930), hereinafter cited as LMS, p. 83.

[29] See *Politics,* The Hour Library (Philadelphia: J. B. Lippincott Co., 1931), here-

exercise its power in order "to make the response to social demand maximal in character," [30] and that the citizen judges the state by its ability to secure for him the conditions that are necessary to his attainment of happiness. Increasingly, however, he stresses the fact that this account of the state's purpose is purely theoretical and does not constitute a description of the activities of actual states. In fact the authority of a state is "a function of its ability to satisfy the *effective* demands that are made upon it"; [31] since only the possessors of economic power are able to make their wants effective at the centers of political decision, the state in its actual operations will seek to promote the interests of the dominant economic class. Only in a society in which economic power is equal or approximately equal will the effective demands of all citizens be equal; only under these conditions will the state's actions promote its theoretical purpose of securing the maximal response to social demand. Laski therefore maintains that the state "is compelled, if it seeks to realise its end, so to organise its activities as deliberately as [*sic*] mitigate the consequences of this material inequality. It has, by the use of the taxing-power, to hold the rich to ransom, in the effort to satisfy the demands of the poor." [32]

We have already suggested that an important reason for Laski's early attacks on the theory of the sovereign state was his belief that the state was hostile to the aspirations and claims of the workers and their unions.[33] During the period up to 1921 he insisted that the traditional state organization, being outmoded and unjust, was being and ought to be replaced by a new set of political institutions based upon the trade unions. By the mid-twenties, however, his interest in any form of guild socialism had completely evaporated. With the postwar decline of the Liberal Party, the Labor Party emerged as the alternative government; in 1924 Labor came to power for the first time, albeit as a minority government. After his return to England in 1920, Laski became more and more involved in Labor Party activities and came to regard himself as its intellectual spokesman.[34] As

---

inafter cited as P, pp. 13–16; the English edition, published in London by George Allen and Unwin, Ltd., has the title *An Introduction to Politics.*

[30] *Ibid.,* p. 38. [31] *Ibid.,* p. 19; italics mine.

[32] *Ibid.,* p. 54. [33] See above, chap. 1.

[34] During the 1926 general strike Laski carried on negotiations with the government on behalf of the unions. See *Holmes-Laski Letters,* II, 838–40 (May 2 and 23, 1926). Particularly during the period of the Labor Government in 1929–1931, he

he was forced to abandon his earlier hostility to political action on
the part of labor, his conception of the role of the state and of its
relations to other groups shifted towards the more conventional theory
of the state supported by the Webbs.

As a result, his analyses in the 1920's of the nature of the state and
of its powers are less clear-cut and more difficult to follow than his
earlier statements. Viewing the possibility that the Labor Party may
soon become the governing group in England, he now cannot afford
to minimize the powers of the state or its role as the instrument for
creating the new and more equitable social order that he desires. If,
on the other hand, he argues in favor of a strong state, with a large
measure of power over recalcitrant groups and individuals, his statements may be used in support of the actions of a Conservative Government, such as the rejection of the miners' demands, the breaking of
the general strike of 1926, or the passage of the "infamous" Trade
Union Disputes (Amendment) Act of 1927. Laski is unable, during
the 1920's, to resolve this dilemma of the political theorist who must
adjust his views to make them fit the shifting fortunes and tactics
of a particular political party. Although he places increasing stress on
the superiority of the state to other groups, he tends to qualify this
position by insisting that the state can actually fulfill its high purpose
and be justified in exercising its great powers only if, and to the extent that, the inequalities inherent in the present social and economic
order are removed. He carries along from the earlier period a large
measure of suspicion of political power; he still argues, as we shall
see,[35] that authority should be federalized and mass participation in
political activity increased. These principles, which reflect his continued adherence to the ideals of individual and group freedom, also
constitute, as limitations upon the exercise of power, weapons for
defending labor and its organizations against hostile action on the
part of a state that mirrors the interests of the capitalist economic
system. There is, therefore, a fundamental ambivalence in his attitude
towards the state's final coercive power; the state must be given the

---

frequently prepared memoranda and had discussions on current problems with Mac-
Donald, Sankey, Henderson, and other Labor Ministers. *Ibid.*, II, 1156 (June 11,
1929), 1160–61 (June 25, 1929), 1169–70 (Aug. 2, 1929), 1264 (June 28, 1930),
1289 (Oct. 11, 1930), 1296 (Nov. 22, 1930), and 1302–3 (Jan. 10, 1931).

[35] See below, chap. 6, section 1.

authority to control men and their groups in order that it may satisfy their common needs, but that authority must be regarded with suspicion as long as it can be used to promote the interests of the few and to hamper the activities of the underprivileged and their associations.[36]

Although Laski's view of the state, particularly in the 1930 and 1931 writings, is veering towards the Marxist conception of the state as the instrument of the dominant capitalist class, he has not yet arrived at a completely Marxist position. He states that the concept of justice in the modern legal system "thinks of the individual essentially as the owner of property; and it is for his protection that it is above all concerned"; [37] in consequence, "the citizen who is without property cannot, in any real way, enjoy the rights which are theoretically at his disposal." [38] At the same time he argues that since universal suffrage means that the masses are winning the power to control the instruments of government, they are bound to use that power to make political institutions responsive to their needs. The citizen who does not possess property "is forcing the state to extend its conception of justice so as to include his interests not less than those of the owners of property." [39] The amenities whose enjoyment was previously dependent upon the ownership of property are "now increasingly organised for the multitude by the state at the cost of those who are able to enjoy them without state-action." [40] This growth of the political power of the masses poses sharp problems for any defender of the Marxist interpretation of politics; a state that is compelled by the political power of the vast majority of propertyless citizens to frame its policies in terms of their needs and to levy ransom on the wealthy in order to pay for benefits for the masses cannot easily be described as an instrument for promoting the interests of the owners of property. The paradox that political institutions that are supposed to reflect and to support a given set of class relationships may be used to change those relationships and to limit the rights of property is one that has embarrassed all Marxist analysts. The

[36] He admits this ambivalence when he says, in discussing the principle that underlies his proposals for changes in political institutions, that it "agrees that a coercive authority is necessary, but it is distrustful of a coercive authority." GP, p. 272. See also his discussions of trade-union freedom from state interference and the right to strike, esp. LMS, pp. 135–50 and 155–63.

[37] P, p. 74.   [38] *Ibid.*, p. 75.   [39] *Ibid.*   [40] *Ibid.*, p. 78.

Leninist solution is the argument that the improvements won by the workers in democratic societies are concessions that they are able to wrest from capitalist democracies because capitalism in these areas draws in extra profits from its imperialist control over backward areas; for a time, it can use these gains to "bribe" its own workers into acquiescence.

In the 1920's and the early 1930's, Laski is not prepared to accept this Leninist solution of the problem. He endeavors to ignore the difficulty. At one moment he states categorically that "those who dominate the State at any given time naturally equate the public welfare with their conception of good; and this conception, quite inevitably, is inextricably bound up with the preservation of their power"; [41] at the same time he maintains that the propertyless are using, and will increasingly use, their political power to shape the contours of the state and its laws to fit their needs. He does not see that anyone who advocates, as he does, the use of the instruments of political democracy to effect a gradual transformation of a capitalist economic system into a socialist or, at least, a more equal society cannot, at the same time, assert that those political instruments are the exclusive property of the economically dominant group. A belief in "gradualism" is logically incompatible with an analysis of the state and the political process solely in terms of economic classes; after 1932, as Laski's economic determinism becomes more rigid and fatalistic, he increasingly comes to doubt the possibility of a gradual and democratic transition to socialism. During the period with which we are dealing both strains are present; he uses the thesis that the state is an instrument of capitalist domination as a tool of analysis and as a weapon against the traditional political parties, while he emphasizes the use of political power in the advance towards a new social and economic system in order to spur on the Labor Party and its supporters to more vigorous action.

As we have already noted, one strand in Laski's thought continues to be marked by a strong suspicion of authority and a constant desire to set limits to the powers of government. In his anxiety to discredit

---

[41] "Justice and the Law," SLP, p. 280. See also: "The substance of law, broadly speaking, will be determined by the wants and needs of those who dominate the economic system at any given time. . . . What the courts do day by day is to apply rules the object of which is to protect the interests of the existing order." *Ibid.*, p. 278.

the idealists' analysis of the state, he carries his realism to the point of defining the will of the state as "the decision arrived at by a small number of men to whom is confided the legal power of making decisions." [42] A few pages earlier he gives a quite different definition of the state's will when he calls it "the will of government as the orders of that will are accepted by the citizen-body." [43] Frequently he warns that the agents through whom the state's purpose is expressed may misinterpret that purpose or pervert it to their own ends. The final answer to all the schemes which, from Plato's *Republic* on, have advocated rule by a wise and expert elite is the fact that men have learned that "if, over any considerable period, they are governed by a section of themselves, it is in the interest of that section that they will be governed"; [44] no one can presume to speak for the masses of ordinary men about the effects of governmental policies on their lives. It is the clear lesson of history that "no class of men can retain over a period sufficient moral integrity to direct the lives of others. Sooner or later they pervert those lives to their own ends." [45] Laski maintains that the holders of power, even if they are not dictators, "will always deny freedom if, thereby, they can conceal wrong," [46] for it is the law of power's being "to hate the process of rational examination. It will not, unless it must, brook criticism of its pronouncements." [47] Realizing that "every ground which exists for entrusting power to a body of men is a ground also for erecting safeguards against their abuse of the authority confided to them," [48] men have endeavored in every age to create an institutional pattern through which power must be exercised and by which it can be controlled. As a result of these limitations on the exercise of authority, power has now become "by its very nature, an exercise in the conditional mood. Those who exert it can only have their way by making its objects

[42] GP, p. 35.   [43] *Ibid.*, p. 29.

[44] *The Dangers of Obedience and Other Essays* (New York: Harper and Bros., 1930), hereinafter cited as DO, p. 208. See also the statement: "The danger of leaving to the State a sovereign position among other associations lies in the fact that it must always act through agents and that those agents are drawn from a body of experience which is not necessarily coincident with the general interest of the community. They will even tend, as a rule, to identify their own experience of good with the common needs of mankind." GP, p. 71.

[45] GP, p. 290.   [46] LMS, p. 212.

[47] "The Dangers of Obedience," DO, p. 10.

[48] "Procedure for Constructive Contempt," SLP, p. 222.

commend themselves, as, also, its methods of pursuing those objects, to those over whom it is exerted." [49]

Since any system of direct democracy is impossible in a modern national state, the government must be made and kept responsible to its citizens if we are to minimize the dangers of divergence between the interests of rulers and those of the ruled and abuse by the rulers of their power. The only way to guarantee that the government in any state will actually carry out the purpose of the state is "to take steps to see that the decisions made by the State take full account of the interests that will be affected by those decisions. . . . *The sovereign power* must be compelled, *a priori,* to make a comprehensive effort to embody the wills of those over whom it rules in its will before it is entitled to act upon them." [50] The system of government must be democratic, for in a democracy, where there are regular opportunities for the people to change their rulers, the interests of those who wield power are more securely linked with the interests of the people than under any other form of government. Rousseau's remark that the English are free only on election day is a constant reminder, however, that free elections at regular intervals are a necessary but not a sufficient guarantee of responsible rule. Laski holds that the traditional separation-of-powers and the checks-and-balances doctrines of the eighteenth-century theorists, designed to prevent the irresponsible use of power, lead in practice to a confusion of powers and to a government far more irresponsible than the British Cabinet system. As opposed to a distribution of power among the three coordinate branches of a government, he advocates that the centers of authority be greatly multiplied by conferring power on territorial and functional bodies and that the voluntary associations of men be brought into direct contact with the state and its agents. Only by these means will the government constantly be forced to recognize the real needs and desires of its citizens and to make its decisions embody their wills to the greatest possible extent. Only thus can we insure that the governors will in fact seek to promote the well-being of all the people.

Before examining Laski's concrete proposals for implementing this goal of federalizing authority by associating social groups with the exercise of political power, we should look for a moment at his dis-

[49] LMS, p. 270.   [50] "Law and the State," SLP, p. 255; italics mine.

cussion of the nature of groups and of their relation to the state. We note first that, by 1925, he has abandoned his earlier adherence to the doctrine of the real personality of groups; he now denies the existence of any group will over and above the organized wills of the members of the group. He maintains that when we speak of the will of the Conservative Party or the will of England, we are actually referring to "wills so united as to give a predominant appearance, not of some will over and above the separate wills of which it is compounded. . . . Corporate personality, and the will that it embodies, is real in the sense that it makes those upon whom it acts different from what they were before. But it remains different from the uniqueness which makes me separate from the rest of the universe." [51] The group, that is, is real, not as "a complete finite entity to be immediately and recognisably differentiated from other complete and finite entities," but "as a relation or a process. It is a binding together of its individual parts to certain modes of behaviour deemed by them likely to promote the interests with which they are concerned. . . . It lives, not as a thing apart from its members, but in and through what they do." [52] This more nominalistic analysis of the nature of groups is far more compatible with Laski's emphasis on the importance of the individual than was his earlier position that the group is a person in every way as real as the individual.

He now recognizes that there is a crucial difference between the nature of the state and that of the voluntary association; the latter lacks the instruments of ultimate coercion possessed by the former. He still maintains that the other associations of men are as natural as the state and denies that they "owe their existence to the state, or that the latter is entitled, by means of its agents, to prescribe the terms upon which they can live." [53] There is no necessary or a priori unity in society; groups have different and sometimes conflicting interests, while each individual is a center of diverse interests whose individuality cannot be reduced to the sum of his group affiliations. "Our groups do not grow together," he says, "into a vast monistic whole. We build them together as and how we can. We find the means of

[51] GP, p. 32.

[52] *Ibid.*, p. 256; note also his insistence that society is not something other than its members, "but exactly and precisely . . . men and women whose totality is conveniently summarized in a collective and abstract noun." LMS, p. 13.

[53] LMS, p. 174.

connection by the discovery of kindred purpose, of sameness in difference, of like origin. The oneness we achieve is a contribution we ourselves make. But we make it only in a partial way." [54] Although admitting that the state has men's "interests in trust to a degree with which no other body can . . . compete," [55] he holds that its coordination of the functions of other groups must, if it is to be legitimate and adequate to its purpose, be a creative coordination which not only takes account of the interests of individuals and groups, but weaves them into a pattern of satisfaction that represents a genuine increase in the well-being of all parties concerned. Recognizing that voluntary associations are "the spontaneous expression of felt needs in the experience of men," [56] to which political institutions have not made an adequate response, the state must make use of these groups and of their knowledge if it hopes to understand and satisfy the wants of the countless citizens "whose wills can hardly hope, in any other articulate and coherent form, to reach the central focus of power." [57] If, on the other hand, the state ignores the claims that these associations make in the name of their members, it will discover that men will refuse to admit its title to obedience and will follow instead the commands of their church or trade union.

In dealing with the crucial problem of the degree of control that the state may properly exercise over group activities, Laski, while admitting that associations cannot be conceded a liberty to overthrow the state, insists that a government may interfere with an association only when it has "moved to action which cannot logically be interpreted as other than a determination to overthrow the social order." [58] As long as groups confine themselves to the expression of grievances or the advocacy of opinions or actions, no matter how subversive or seditious, they should be free from any control by the government. At another point in the same volume, however, he argues that voluntary associations should be immune from state control unless "their *ideas and conduct* are intended directly to alter the law, or to arrest the continuity of general social habits." [59] In discussing the question of government control of trade unions and strikes, he says: "No limitation upon freedom to associate is, I urge, permissible unless it can be

---

[54] GP, p 261.   [55] *Ibid.*, p. 75.   [56] P, p. 67.
[57] "The Recovery of Citizenship," DO, p. 67.   [58] LMS, p. 168.
[59] *Ibid.*, pp. 134–35; italics mine.

demonstrated that clear and decisive advantage to the community, including, be it remembered, trade unionists themselves, is likely to result." [60] It is apparent that there are major inconsistencies among his various formulas; the phrases "intended directly to alter the law" and "intended to arrest the continuity of general social habits" are so vague that they would give a government far greater control over group action and opinion than would the first formula, which limits government interference to situations in which a group has clearly acted with revolutionary intent. Nor is the "clear and decisive advantage to the community" formula of any great use; if interpreted literally, it means that a government would not be permitted to act to prevent or delay a major strike or lockout unless it first persuaded the members of the community, including, it would appear, the workers and the managers concerned, that such action would be to their advantage. Laski's position seems to be that as long as essential industries remain under private ownership, with no restriction by the state on the employer's liberty to make what profits he can, there is no justification for attempts by the government to prevent interruptions of production in such industries by denying the workers' right to strike.[61]

It is important to note that Laski's conception of authority as federal in nature, with its stress on the devolution of power to functional associations and on the participation of voluntary groups in the processes of administration, has shifted, as compared with his earlier writings, from a descriptive category to a normative principle. That is, his original attack on the theory of the centralized and sovereign state rested on the charge that the theory no longer adequately represented actual political facts; industrial and professional groups were, to an increasing degree, making the rules that regulated their fields of activity, with the result that the state as the general coordinator of social life was fast disappearing. Now the main residue of his earlier pluralism seems to be the argument that the state can adequately accomplish its essential task of maximizing the satisfaction of human wants only if it is compelled to incorporate in its processes of decision-making the wills and demands of the groups that stand between the state and the individual. Representatives of voluntary associations ought constantly to meet with and

[60] *Ibid.*, pp. 137–38.   [61] See *ibid.*, pp. 158–59.

advise government officials at all levels, and the power to make detailed regulations, particularly of economic life, should be handed over by the state to representative bodies in industry. Authority, that is, can no longer be described as federal in nature; Laski's thesis is that it must be federalized if the state's purpose and the goals of its citizens are to be realized.

To this end, the state should give to the interests and groups affected by a decision their due place in the inquiries and negotiations that precede that decision. To each government department and agency should be attached permanent, specialized advisory bodies made up of representatives nominated by the groups concerned with the agency's work; each such committee should be consulted by government officials before a decision is made on any subject falling within the sphere of its special knowledge. Each advisory committee would have power to comment on proposals for new legislation, to suggest new laws or administrative changes, and to examine orders issued by a government department under powers delegated to it by the legislature.[62] Advisory councils of this sort, on the national, regional, and local levels, will, according to Laski,

interpret law, and therefore they will make the law. For they will bring into the light of day the true consequences of law, as those are felt by the men who suffer them. They will determine, therefore, the way in which it is applied. They will indicate, accordingly, necessary change and necessary amendment. They will give each interest in the community organic connection, as an interest, with the State. They will infuse its purpose with their own purposes.[63]

Laski also proposes the establishment of committees of members of the legislature to advise the various executive departments. Each committee would be in constant touch with the Minister and would carry on inquiries; it would thus be able to bring before the legislature accurate information and competent opinion about the work of the administration, although, in contrast to the committees of the American and French legislatures, it would neither make formal reports to the assembly nor have power to initiate or amend legislative proposals.

He continues to advocate that Parliament devolve limited rule-making powers upon territorial and functional assemblies in order

[62] See GP, pp. 377–87.   [63] *Ibid.,* p. 386.

to relieve the central government of some of the tasks that now overwhelm it and in order to draw a larger number of people into an active relationship with the work of government. The areas of local government need to be revised to make them correspond to the functions to be performed; also, each local body should be given general control over all administrative functions within its area, and the confused complex of separate bodies dealing with education, health, housing, transport, etc., in a given locality should be eliminated. He insists that the central government must retain the power to set and enforce minimum standards in such fields as education, housing, and health, as well as a general reserve power to alter, as social needs change, the areas of local government and the sources from which control is exercised. In addition, the central government will have control over local taxing powers as well as a general right to inspect and report on all activities of local authorities.

Territorial decentralization, however, is not sufficient by itself; he maintains that "any geographical system of political structure is inadequate to embody the lives it seeks to express." [64] Since, in modern society, men's vocational interests are more central than their common interests and problems as neighbors, Laski advocates that a representative body be established to govern each industry left in private hands. Each such industrial council will represent equally the owners, the vocations, the direct consumers of the industry's product, and the government; to it will be delegated the power to make rules, binding on the whole industry, relating to wages, hours, working conditions, stabilization of production, etc., subject to the approval of the central Ministry of Production and the ultimate control of the legislature. Under each industrial council district councils will be created to carry out similar functions in the industry within geographical areas.

Laski believes that the institutional structure that he proposes—a network of advisory committees at every level of government, together with a series of industrial councils as the organs of representative government in the economic realm—will greatly increase the freedom of the average citizen by effecting a wide distribution of power within the state. The system, he says, "provides for the admission that law affects only a small part of social life; and it there-

[64] "The Recovery of Citizenship," DO, p. 69.

fore surrounds each organ of legal competence with bodies entitled
to advise and so made that their advice is fully weighed." [65] Under
this arrangement, he concludes,

ordinary men and women are given the opportunity to make fully
known that upon which they believe their happiness to depend. It will
be open to the State to deny their will, but it will be the nature of this
system to make that denial a much more difficult, sometimes even a
more perilous, adventure than it is to-day. As a system, also, it strives
at every angle of its compass to make its working a mechanism of education to those who encounter it. [66]

Although he continues, at least until 1929, to call his theory of the
state "pluralism," it is obvious that his proposed scheme of advisory
councils and subordinate rule-making bodies has little, if any, connection with his earlier pluralism. The suggested advisory committees
are purely consultative; the power to make decisions is left with
the Minister and the Cabinet, subject to whatever control Parliament and the electorate can exert. In the event of an unfavorable
decision by the Minister, the advisory council has no recourse save
an appeal to the groups that its members represent. The devolution
of authority to make regulations to local authorities and to industrial
councils is kept within narrow limits by the extensive powers of
supervision and taxation left to the central government. These bodies
will be confined to making decisions on matters of detail within a
general framework laid down by the central government, and their
principal duties will be of an administrative rather than a political
character.

Leaving aside the question whether Laski's state should be called
pluralist, federal, or unitary, we must ask whether the pattern of
political institutions that he describes is practicable and whether,
compared to the traditional state organization, it is more likely to
achieve the goals of keeping government responsible to popular needs
and checking abuses of political power. Laski recognizes that his
system, with its stress on greatly increased popular participation
in all phases of governmental activity, demands of the citizens a
higher level of education and a more active and continuous interest
in the processes of politics than does the traditional state. He admits
that his thesis depends "upon the assumption that the average man

[65] GP, p. 429.   [66] *Ibid.*, p. 430.

is, in fact, a political animal. It involves the argument that he can be made to show interest in affairs of State and that such interest may be made to coincide with understanding adequate to the democratic conduct of affairs." [67] However, he immediately concedes that many persons in modern society show no interest in political matters, and "ask only that their private affairs remain unfettered by public interruption." [68] In fact, he states that "it is a grave error to assume that men in general are, at least actively and continuously, political creatures. The context of their lives which is, for the majority, the most important is a private context. . . . The characteristic of social life is the unthinking obedience of the many to the will of the few." [69]

It is not sufficient to show that his thesis depends upon an assumption that he himself terms "a grave error." We can agree with his statement that, under the present system, the level of popular interest in, and understanding of, the processes of politics and administration is low. The crucial question is—Is this widespread indifference to politics a "natural" human trait, or is it a result of the institutional structure of the modern state? If it is largely the consequence of insufficient knowledge and inadequate opportunities for participation in politics, Laski may argue that it will disappear, gradually, at least, under the system that he proposes. The available evidence on this central problem does not appear to be conclusive. Attempts during the last few years in England, a country where the degree of popular interest in politics is generally considered to be higher than in other democracies, to provide increased opportunities for greater citizen participation in the work of government, particularly in the operation of the nationalized industries, have not been conspicuously successful. The national and regional consumers' councils appointed by the ministers for the nationalized industries have complained in the reports issued during the brief period of their operation that few consumers use them to make complaints or suggestions.[70] On the other hand, the results of the experience of Germany under the Weimar

[67] *Ibid.*, p. 42.   [68] *Ibid.*

[69] *Ibid.*, pp. 18–19. See also the flat statement: "Man is not by nature a political animal. He gives his attention rather to the results than to the methods of institutions." *Communism,* Home University Library of Modern Knowledge, No. 123 (New York: Henry Holt and Co., 1927), hereinafter cited as C, p. 179.

[70] See A. M. de Neuman, *Consumers' Representation in the Public Sector of Industry* (London, 1950).

Republic, in which the administration of much of the social insurance
and labor relations programs was left to such bodies as the labor
courts and the works' councils, seem, in general, to have been en-
couraging.[71] We may conclude that even if consultative bodies do
not have the great significance that Laski gives to them, they can be
a useful weapon against bureaucratic tendencies in administration
by focusing informed outside opinion upon governmental action and
by giving reliable information and advice to the larger public.

Laski's proposals for devolving limited powers on local and industrial assemblies raise other problems. General policies, particularly
in economic matters, must be decided at the national level, and the
work of local bodies must be largely confined, as he admits, to carrying out the administrative details involved in implementing the
over-all plan. A large measure of local participation in such fields as
regional planning, housing, health, and education is, however, clearly
desirable as a technique for insuring that local needs will be satisfied in an appropriate way and as a method of giving more people a
share in the business of government. Reform of the areas of local
government to make them meaningful in terms of modern problems
is as necessary in England and the United States today as it was
when Laski advocated it in 1925.

Decentralization of power becomes a much more perilous venture
when it is extended to industrial assemblies.[72] The industrial councils which Laski proposes imply something very close to a cartel
organization for each industry; a single price would be fixed for
the product by the central government; there would be complete
publicity in respect to methods, costs, and research developments
throughout the industry, and regulations by the council, binding on
all firms, of the details of hours, wages, and labor relations. Under
this system the rigidities already apparent in modern industry would
be intensified and the element of competition virtually eliminated

[71] See Franz L. Neumann, *European Trade Unionism and Politics* (New York:
League for Industrial Democracy, 1936); Nathan Reich, *Labour Relations in Republican Germany* (New York: Oxford University Press, 1938); and Frieda Wunderlich, *German Labor Courts* (Chapel Hill: University of North Carolina Press, 1946).

[72] For a general discussion of the movement to set up economic councils in various
European countries after the First World War, and of the theory of functional repre-
sentation, see Lewis L. Lorwin, *Advisory Economic Councils,* Brookings Institution
Pamphlet Series No. 9 (Washington: The Brookings Institution, 1931).

from private economic activity. Also the composition of each industrial council presents serious problems. Laski's plan provides for equal representation for the owners, the workers, direct consumers, and the government; this arrangement makes possible the domination of the council by either business or labor, unacceptable to the other, or, more probably, a complete stalemate. What will be the position of the government representatives who are supposed to guard the public interest? Will they seek to arbitrate between the other groups or, by playing one group off against the others, will they attempt to run the industry? Will the attitudes of the government representatives shift with changes in the party in political power? Merely to pose these questions suggests the insoluble problems involved in determining the relative weights to be given to the various groups represented in an industrial council or assembly. It would seem far wiser to leave general economic regulation and control to the political legislature and to the agencies of the political executive, while allowing the details of wages, hours, and working conditions to be settled, as far as possible, by management and labor through trade unions and nongovernmental machinery.

5

Obedience, Liberty, and Equality

1. THE PROBLEM OF OBEDIENCE

IN *A Grammar of Politics* Laski begins his analysis of the problem of obedience by considering man's nature as a social being. If men are to live together in peace, there must be rules to regulate their social relationships and a government to enforce the observance of these rules; thus, the obligation to obey the commands of government arises out of the fact that man is by nature a community-building animal.[1] Particularly in regard to matters that the society deems essential to its existence, "spontaneity ceases to be practical, and the enforced acceptance of a common way of action becomes the necessary condition of a corporate civilisation." [2] Since men are not purely rational beings, theories that attempt to explain the obedience of the many to the few solely in terms of rational factors, such as consent, fear of the consequences, or utility, are inadequate. He concludes: "The State as it was and is finds the roots of allegiance in all the complex facts of human nature; and a theory of obedience would have to weight them differently for each epoch in the history of the State if it were to approximate to the truth." [3]

When, however, Laski proceeds from this general survey of the basis of allegiance to the state to a consideration of the moral problem of the obligation to obedience, he reverts to the strongly individualistic thesis of his early writings. The state, he says, is to be judged by what it does in practice to enable men to realize the best that is in themselves. "Our obligation to obey the State is, law apart, an obligation dependent upon the degree to which the State achieves its purpose. We are the judges of that achievement." [4] Force, which he defines as "the compulsory subjection of the individual to an experience he would not voluntarily share," should be used "in those directions

---

[1] See GP, pp. 17–18. [2] *Ibid.*, p. 18. [3] *Ibid.*, p. 22.
[4] *Ibid.*, pp. 26–27.

only where the common sense of society is on the side of the type of conduct it seeks to compel." [5] Even where the law has spoken it has no moral right to claim my obedience unless I discover in my own experience that it operates to make possible the enrichment of my personality. "If," Laski states, "I hold that its [the state's] power is being in fact exercised, not for the ends implied in its nature, but for the ends incompatible therewith, the civic outcome of such perception is the duty of resistance." [6] As a result, however, of his new sense of the state's role as the promoter of men's common interests, he places greater qualifications on this right and duty of resistance; I ought not to resist, he concedes, if I believe that the state is honestly trying to fulfill its purpose, and, for most men, this conviction will be the result of such inquiries as they make.

Laski also formulates his views on the problem of obedience in terms of a theory of rights. As a member of society, I have an inherent right to whatever is necessary to my self-realization as a moral being; therefore, "I judge *the State, as the fundamental instrument of society,* by the manner in which it seeks to secure for me the substance of those rights." [7] "Every government is thus built upon a contingent moral obligation. Its actions are right to the degree that they maintain rights. When it is either indifferent about them, or wedded to their limitation, it forfeits its claim to the allegiance of its members." [8] The individual must scrutinize every command of government to determine its compatibility with this system of rights; he has the right to disobey if his rights are infringed upon. Again Laski qualifies this individualistic theory by adding that the right of disobedience "is, of course, reasonably to be exercised only at the margins of political conduct. No community could hope to fulfil its purpose if rebellion became a settled habit of the population." [9]

The confusions in Laski's treatment of the question of obedience to the state are even more marked than in his early writings. First, we note that on occasion he reverses his usual argument—that most citizens normally obey the orders of their rulers with little hesitation or critical searching of their consciences—and states that, in fact, the citizen does not give his allegiance to the state simply because it is acting in his interest, but "examines what is done in its name

---

[5] *Ibid.*, p. 33.   [6] *Ibid.*, p. 39.   [7] *Ibid.;* italics mine.
[8] *Ibid.*, p. 57.   [9] *Ibid.*, p. 62.

and makes a judgment upon the moral quality of the order he is asked to obey." [10] More significant are the conflicting statements that he makes when he discusses the reasons why men ought to obey. At moments he relies upon his early ultra-individualistic theory that "the only ground upon which the citizen can give or be asked to give his support for the state is upon the conviction that what it is aiming at is, *in each particular action,* good. . . . We should not even support a given state because its intentions are sincere." [11] In this mood he denies that violation of the law is wrong in itself or in its effects upon the individual; "every Government," he notes, "claims that it is wrong to break the law. To the pluralist that judgment can only be made when it is known what law is broken and under what circumstances." [12] To the argument that *jus est quod jussum est,* he responds with a flat denial that "submission is ever a moral obligation unless, as an act, it carries with it the individual conviction of rightness which makes it moral." [13] At other times he seems to accept, at least in part, the views of the critics of his individualistic theory of obedience, who argued that his position would lead to anarchy by making disobedience and rebellion normal features of political life. He warns that individuals should not disobey authority unless the beliefs that are offended by the commands of the state are really vital and unless the government demonstrates that it has no intention of respecting the rights or promoting the wellbeing of the citizens. In this view, disobedience and, a fortiori, rebellion are the ultimate reserve weapons against perversion of the state power, to be used only in the marginal situation where the dictates of authority seem to deny all that men hold most certain and most valuable in their experience.[14]

When Laski is emphasizing his belief that the actual incidence of state power is largely a function of the property system that obtains in a society, he tends to support the view that the claim of authority upon the individual is "legitimate proportionately to the moral ur-

10 "Law and the State," SLP, p. 249.
11 "The Dangers of Obedience," DO, p. 16; italics mine.
12 "Law and the State," SLP, p. 260.
13 GP, p. 288. Note also: "The real constraining force upon ourselves is not the legal obligation to obey the government, but the moral obligation to follow what we regard as justice." *Ibid.,* p. 63.
14 See LMS, pp. 73–74.

gency of its appeal." [15] In an unequal society the authority of the state, which is predominantly lodged with those who possess economic power, is normally exerted in their interests; the large majority of citizens who do not possess property have, therefore, no moral obligation to obey. Authority's title to allegiance would be sound only if the commands of the state recognized men's rights and embodied their needs and their experiences. He repeatedly refers to Ulster's refusal in 1914 to accept the Home Rule Act, the denial by churchmen of the validity of the decisions of the Judicial Committee of the Privy Council, and the resistance of the South Wales miners to the Munitions Act of 1915 as examples of "the thesis that the exercise of authority is surrounded by a penumbra of anarchy." [16] With these incidents in mind, he argues that "no state can act in the face of considerable opposition from its citizens, if the latter are deeply and conscientiously moved by the issue in dispute," [17] and that "every generation contains examples of men who, in the context of ultimate experience, deliberately decide that an anarchy in which they seek to maintain some principle is preferable to an order in which that principle must be surrendered." [18]

The marked qualifications and limitations that Laski sometimes imposes on this thesis that the individual conscience is the only true source of obedience to law can best be understood as reflections of developments in the English political scene and of his involvement in those changes. When we remember that the Labor Party became the governing group in England in 1924 and again in 1929, we can see some of the difficulties of his position. Let us imagine a situation in which a Labor Government with a real majority has come to power and is beginning to make fundamental moves in the direction of the equal society. The minority who wield great economic power may resent the loss of their privileges and the use of the power of the state for purposes that are antithetical to their basic code of political, economic, and moral wisdom and justice. In this situation Laski's

[15] GP, p. 249. [16] *Ibid.*, p. 250.

[17] "The Dangers of Obedience," DO, p. 15.

[18] LMS, pp. 71–72. See also the comment that while the spirit of contingent attack which he advocates may lead to disorder, this danger is outweighed by the fact that that spirit "makes government itself vigilant to the opinion about it; and men who prefer, in the internal life of a State, the path of perpetual peace to that of organised protest will, sooner or later, lose the habit of freedom." GP, p. 85.

theory that obedience to the law is a matter for the judgment of the
individual conscience and his references to Ulster and South Wales
would provide a convenient legitimation of their interest in resisting
the government's attempts to build a new and more equitable social
order. If such thoughts crossed Laski's mind during the period from
1925 to 1930—and it seems incredible that they should not have
occurred to him—there would be good reason for him to qualify and
to tone down his earlier defense of disobedience. The passages in
which he maintains the original individualistic theory of allegiance
in its pristine purity may then be regarded as evidence not merely of
the persistence of older ideas side by side with the new, but also of
the continued need for a defense of the interests of "ordinary men
and women" against the hostile state, as long as it is dominated by
the interests of the owners of property.

By 1931 Laski shifts the ground of obedience away from the moral
adequacy of the state's commands as judged by the individual and
makes the obligation to obey a function of the degree to which the
state secures to the individual at least a minimum of material well-
being. More accurately, he establishes as the criterion of the moral
quality of state actions the extent to which they secure to the citizen
the material benefits that constitute the general conditions of his
happiness. He maintains that the state's "claim to allegiance must
obviously be built upon its power to make the response to social demand maximal in character. . . . We can only argue that legal imperatives may be imposed if, in their operation, we satisfy at the
least sacrifice as much as we can of human want."[19] There are, he
concludes, "certain general conditions of happiness, affecting all citizens alike, which are the minimum bases of a satisfactory social life.
These, at the least, the state must secure to its members, if it is to
count upon their continuous obedience to its rules."[20] This thesis
is obviously a development of Laski's view that the state is entitled
to allegiance only if it secures to its citizens those rights that are the
conditions of self-realization; the rights now stressed as essential
to the development of the individual are economic and material demands. The theory is useful, too, in that it justifies the title to obedience of a government which undertakes measures leading to greater
economic equality at the same time that it leaves room for disobedi-

[19] P, pp. 38–39.   [20] *Ibid.*, p. 44.

ence in the present society, which, in his opinion, is becoming ever more sharply divided into the two nations of rich and poor. In the present situation, "the right to resist the law is the reserve-power in society by which men whose demands are denied may legitimately seek to alter the balance of forces in the state." [21]

A similar evolution can be observed if we examine Laski's discussions of the nature of the individual and of his relationships to other men. He sometimes speaks of "that uniqueness of individuality, that sense that each of us is ultimately different from our fellows, . . . that is the ultimate fact of human experience." [22] The individual must find the source of his decisions in the experience "which is the one unique thing that separates him from the rest of society. . . . His true self is the self that is isolated from his fellows and contributes the fruit of isolated meditation to the common good, which, collectively, they seek to bring into being." [23] He concludes: "Each of us desires the good as he sees it; and each of us sees a good derived from an individual and separate experience into which no other person can fully enter. Our connection with others is, at the best, partial and interstitial. . . . The ultimate isolation of the individual personality is the basis from which any adequate theory of politics must start." [24]

Together with this belief that man's true self is his isolated and nonsocial self, Laski also holds the view that social groups and institutions play a major role in determining the individual's fate. In this mood he argues that "an individual abstracted from society and regarded as entitled to freedom outside its environment is devoid of meaning," [25] and that "the organised effort of a determined group of men may, with patience, change the character of those institutions; but the individual who stands apart from his fellows is unlikely to be their master." [26] His analysis of rights is social and functional rather than individualistic; "I have . . . no right to do as I like. My rights are built always upon the relation my function has to the well-being of society." [27] We do not possess rights "as avenues of

---

[21] *Ibid.*, p. 59.   [22] LMS, p. 17.   [23] *Ibid.*, p. 18.

[24] *Ibid.*, p. 21. See also: "I am not a part of some great symphony in which I realize myself only as an accident in the *motif* of the whole. I am unique, I am separate, I am myself; out of these qualities I must build my own principles of action." *Ibid.*, pp. 74-75.

[25] *Ibid.*, p. 12.   [26] GP, p. 18.   [27] *Ibid.*, p. 95.

personal enjoyment. . . . By a functional theory of rights is meant that we are given powers that we may so act as to add to the richness of our social heritage. We have rights, not that we may receive, but that we may do." [28] Finally, side by side with the emphasis on the ultimate isolation and uniqueness of the individual, Laski argues that "our immersion in political affairs extends, whether we recognise it or no, to the ultimate substance of our lives. The only privacy man can hope to enjoy is that of judgment; and even judgment entails consequences of social import." [29]

In a sense there is no inconsistency in his stress on both the individual and social aspects of human personality. But, captivated by his own rhetoric, he often tends to give each aspect an undue importance as he discusses it; we are given too many divergent "unique," "final," and "ultimate" characteristics of men, and when we stop to add up the account we discover that man is both "ultimately isolated" and "fundamentally social," that his "true self" is both his private self and the self that meets in fellowship with others and works for the common good. As the years pass Laski lays ever greater emphasis upon the social aspect of men's lives. He insists that organized groups are the only vehicles through which the individual can realize his potentialities or make his desires and opinions effective. More and more frequently he argues that individual liberty and uniqueness are meaningful only to a handful of men in our society and that only in the context of equality of knowledge and of economic power will ordinary men have the opportunity to exercise initiative and to discover or express their individual uniqueness. The freedom and uniqueness of the individual are therefore regarded as values that can be enjoyed only in the future; the immediate accent is on group action to remake the social order and on the temporary subordination of individuals, especially if they block the march to the good society, to the demands of justice and equality. No theories are entitled to be regarded as socialist, Laski states, unless they "admit the right, and duty, of the State to subordinate individual claim to social need, not as an occasional incident of its operation but as a permanent characteristic of its nature." [30] Here we arrive at the conflict between liberty and authority, which is related to our next theme, the rela-

---

[28] *Ibid.*, pp. 40–41.   [29] *Ibid.*, p. 43.
[30] "The Socialist Tradition in the French Revolution," SLP, p. 68.

tionship between liberty and equality. Once one becomes convinced that the entire structure of social institutions must be remade, perhaps for the sake of an eventual increase in men's freedom, one is seemingly driven to exalt—at the expense of liberty—the authority which is regarded as the instrument for creating the new order.

2. LIBERTY, EQUALITY, AND NATURAL RIGHTS

Laski's argument in *A Grammar of Politics* that freedom consists in opportunities for self-realization is basically inadequate because he never tells his reader what he believes to be the nature of the self that is to be realized. He discards the idealist's notion of the real self as the common object of the strivings of all men but offers no substitute for it. He tells us, for example, that "if social institutions permit me so to express myself that my life acquires a satisfactory balance of impulses, I am, in a creative sense, free." [31] The fatal weakness appears in the crucial phrase, "a satisfactory balance of impulses"; the phrase is meaningless, since he does not specify a set of general norms of conduct applicable to all individuals. At the same time he condemns Bentham's egocentric individualism, which is the logical consequence of allowing each individual to determine for himself what constitutes a satisfactory balance of his impulses. As a result Laski is forced to remain on the level of vague generalities and to assume without demonstration that certain norms are universally accepted and understood. Although he states that the permanent essence of freedom is "that the personality of each individual should be so unhampered in its development, whether by authority or by custom, that it can make for itself a satisfactory harmonisation of its impulses," [32] he is obviously not willing to allow individuals to pursue certain courses of action that he regards as "anti-social," or to permit a man to proceed unhampered if the balance of impulses that he finds satisfactory involves, for example, a marked stress on the acquisitive impulse or on the drive to dominate other men. Similar difficulties inhere in his assertion that the "purpose of society . . . is to enable each man to be himself at his best. Freedom is the system

[31] GP, p. 66.   [32] *Ibid.*, p. 102.

of conditions which makes that purpose effectively possible." [33] These conditions—such as adequate education, reasonable wages and hours of labor, and the absence of special privilege—are the same as the rights that Laski postulates; rights and freedoms are defined in identical terms, and in both definitions, everything turns on the unanalyzed concept, "the opportunity to be one's best self."

In 1925 Laski still maintains that since liberty is something positive it cannot be defined as the absence of restraint. "Historic experience has evolved for us," he asserts, "rules of convenience which promote right living. To compel obedience to them is not to make a man unfree." [34] Again, he makes no attempt to define or concretize the notion of "right living." He notes that his creative impulses suffer no frustration when the law ordains that he must educate his children. What, however, is to be done with the eccentric who does feel that his personality is invaded by the state's command that he educate his children? And, more significant, how does Laski's generalization help us to deal with the problem of liberty that arises when the state ordains that the education of children must be of a certain kind— completely secular, for example, rather than religious? His thesis that restraint only becomes an invasion of liberty "where the given prohibition acts so as to destroy that harmony of impulses which comes when a man knows that he is doing something it is worth while to do" [35] is meaningless unless we are told what things are worth while doing, or unless it is agreed that each man has the right to do whatever he believes is good. Laski also defines freedoms in historical terms as "opportunities which history has shown to be essential to the development of personality." [36] While this formulation is somewhat more intelligible than his psychological and ethical definitions, it gives no support to the newer economic freedoms in which he is particularly interested. It also assumes that we have adequate knowledge of what is essential for personality development and that there is general acceptance of that knowledge.

Laski argues that men cannot achieve freedom when a few citizens enjoy special privilege, or when the rights of some depend upon the pleasure of others, or when the incidence of the power of the state

[33] *Socialism and Freedom*, Fabian Tract No. 216 (London: The Fabian Society, 1925), p. 8.
[34] GP, p. 142.   [35] *Ibid.*, p. 143.   [36] *Ibid.*, p. 144.

is biased in favor of one group. All three of these obstacles to the enjoyment of liberty flourish in our society; "to speak, therefore, of the present order as one built upon freedom is to regard the interest of the few who can achieve it as coincident with the general well-being of society." [37] The individual's power to secure the satisfaction of his demands "depends upon the possession of property; and since *freedom means the power to satisfy demands,* freedom is a function of property." [38] Merely noting this new definition of freedom, we observe that for Laski the essential conditions of liberty—the absence of privilege, adequate opportunities for all, and the principle that "differences in the social or economic position of men can only be admitted after a minimum basis of civilisation is attained by the community as a whole" [39]—also constitute, when taken together, the essence of equality. Liberty and equality are, therefore, in his view, complementary and inseparable.

In the late twenties an important change takes place in Laski's view of freedom. In the Preface to the second edition of *A Grammar of Politics,* written in October, 1929, he says: "In 1925 I thought that liberty could most usefully be regarded as more than a negative thing. I am now convinced that this was a mistake, and that the old view of it as an absence of restraint can alone safeguard the personality of the citizen." [40] Both in this and later editions of the *Grammar,* however, he leaves unchanged the 1925 discussions of liberty in the body of the text; but in 1930 he outlines his new view of liberty in *Liberty in the Modern State.* The first words of this volume are: "I mean by liberty the absence of restraint upon the existence of those social conditions which, in modern civilization, are the necessary guarantees of individual happiness." [41] This definition obviously does not embody the traditional view of liberty as the absence of restraint upon the actions of the individual; in essence it is the same as Laski's earlier view that freedom is the system of conditions enabling the individual to attain self-realization by satisfying his demands. In succeeding paragraphs, however, and in general throughout the work, he uses the term "liberty" in the traditional sense; he states, for example, that every rule and every compulsion is "a limitation

[37] *Socialism and Freedom,* p. 8. [38] *Ibid.;* italics mine.
[39] GP, p. 157. [40] GP, Preface to the second edition.
[41] LMS, p. 1.

upon freedom. Some of them are essential to happiness, but that
does not make them for a moment less emphatically limitations." [42]
He now insists that there is an antithesis between liberty and authority, that "a man's freedom is born of a limitation upon what his
rulers may exact from him." [43] He also concedes that, while liberty
may be unreal if a man has no security in employment or insufficient
education to enable him to express his needs and opinions, economic
security is not liberty, and "deprivation of knowledge is not a denial
of liberty. It is a denial of the power to use liberty for great ends." [44]

He admits that "equality is not the same thing as liberty. . . .
Men might be broadly equal under a despotism, and yet unfree."
He now argues that "in the absence of certain equalities no freedom
can ever hope for realization." [45] Only if the economic power of all
citizens is approximately equal will each be able to make use of his
freedom in order to seek his own happiness in his own way. He
regards liberty as "essentially an expression of an impalpable atmosphere among men. It is a sense that in the things we deem significant
there is the opportunity of continuous initiative, the knowledge that
we can, so to speak, experiment with ourselves, think differently or
act differently, from our neighbours without danger to our happiness
being involved therein." [46] While he is convinced that liberty can
exist only in a democracy, he believes that even under democratic
government there must be "ways and means of protecting the minority against a majority which seeks to invade its freedom." [47] In
the last analysis, liberty means being faithful to oneself and to one's
own values; therefore, it "cannot help being a courage to resist the
demands of power at some point that is deemed decisive; and, because of this, liberty, also, is an inescapable doctrine of contingent
anarchy." [48]

[42] *Ibid.*, p. 3.   [43] *Ibid.*, p. 14.   [44] *Ibid.*, p. 5.

[45] *Ibid.*, p. 7; see also the statement: "The citizen who asks for freedom is entitled to the conditions which, collectively, are the guarantees that he will be able
to go on the road to his happiness, as he conceives it, unhindered." *Ibid.*, p. 27.

[46] *Ibid.*, p. 29.   [47] *Ibid.*, p. 30.

[48] *Ibid.*, pp. 281–82. In 1929, while he was writing *Liberty in the Modern State*,
he wrote to Holmes: "I find myself defending the good old-fashioned thesis that I
really may not know what is best for me, but that if I am not allowed the chance
to find out, there will be no 'I' left at all to make decisions. And so I am thoroughly
enjoying myself by attacking all bureaucrats and moral reformers on the ground . . .
that the supreme blasphemy is the endeavour of the creedmonger with a principle to

Although Laski stresses the importance of liberty, he believes that in our age men are interested in freedom not so much for its own sake as for the sake of the satisfactions it is able to bring them. The freedom desired by the poor is "the freedom to enjoy the things their rulers enjoy. The penumbra of freedom, its purpose and its life, is the movement for equality." [49] He argues that by equality he does not mean identical treatment for individuals who differ in capacity and need, although he does advocate "identity of response to primary needs" [50] as well as the guarantee of a minimum standard of living for all. Rather, equality is "an insistence that there is no difference inherent in nature between the claims of men to happiness. It is therefore an argument that society shall not construct barriers against those claims which weigh more heavily upon some than upon others." [51] Approximate equality of wealth is essential if political equality and justice are to be attained. Differences in wealth or status over and above the minimum standard guaranteed to every citizen must be open to achievement by all, and they must be capable of being shown to be necessary to the enhancement of the common welfare. Each man has the right to "such a share of the national dividend as permits him at least to satisfy those primary material wants, hunger, thirst, the demand for shelter, which, when unsatisfied, prevent the realisation of personality"; [52] in return for this minimum payment, the individual has a duty to perform such functions as will produce the amount required for his maintenance. No one has a right to income or to property except as a return for functions performed on behalf of society. Laski rejects the communist plea for equality of income for all; he does not even believe that his "common civic minimum" should be the same for all members of the community; "the minimum we settle for each occupation will clearly involve differences built upon the costs that occupation involves." [53] Above this minimum we must "also pay wages in such a fashion that we attract into each social [*sic*] necessary occupation a sufficiency of talent to run them [*sic*] adequately." [54] For manual labor, differences

enforce to make man in his own image." *Holmes-Laski Letters, 1916–1935*, ed. by Mark DeWolfe Howe (2 vols., Cambridge: Harvard University Press, 1953), II, 1174 (Aug. 20, 1929).

[49] LMS, pp. 218–19.   [50] GP, p. 160.   [51] LMS, p. 9.
[52] GP, pp. 183–84.   [53] *Ibid.*, p. 197.   [54] *Ibid.*, pp. 197–98.

in reward above the minimum will be based on individual output; for work that is not quantitatively measurable, rewards are to be set at the levels that will give the society an adequate number of doctors, lawyers, teachers, and other professional workers.

As is so often the case, Laski's concrete proposals for attaining "economic equality" are a good deal less dramatic and revolutionary than his abstract discussions of the subject. The concept of a basic minimum income, adequate to satisfy the primary needs of the individual, which has been a familiar ideal in the Western democracies since 1900, has, with the development of programs of unemployment and old-age benefits, extensive free social services, and full-employment and minimum-wage legislation, to a large extent now been translated into practice, even in the United States, the last stronghold of *laissez-faire*. A corollary of this rise of the "welfare" or "transfer-payment" state has been the extensive use of graduated income and inheritance taxes that have brought about a marked change in the patterns of distribution of both income and wealth. Progressive taxation has curtailed the rights of property to an extent that does not fall far short of Laski's suggestions; in Great Britain and, to a lesser degree, in the United States, it is now difficult to live on inherited property without performing any useful social function.

Laski invites confusion by his constant use of the term "economic equality" when he means equality of opportunity and a minimum income to provide for each citizen's basic needs. His rejection of the theory of equal incomes for all demonstrates that he is not, in fact, advocating equality. His principle that, above the basic minimum, each worker should be paid in proportion to his output is obviously not egalitarian, as the results of the piece-work and Stakhanovite systems make clear. His proposals with respect to nonmanual labor would make it necessary for some central authority, presumably an agency of the state, to determine what occupations and services are socially necessary, the degree to which a given function is more useful than another, and the scale of payments that will guarantee to the society an "adequate" supply of accountants or doctors or engineers. He makes no attempt to indicate how such decisions are to be made. Nor is it clear that the determination of wages by a central authority will result in an income distribution more equal than that attained by reliance on a relatively free labor market. The experience of the

Soviet Union shows that under this system the incomes of managerial, professional, and technical personnel may be at least as far above those of ordinary workers as they are in a market economy.

Laski's main thesis is that inequality is an inherent characteristic of capitalist society, while a socialist society will necessarily be the "equal society" that he advocates. This position creates difficulties for him; on the one hand, he frequently states that universal suffrage means that the citizen is using his political power to effect a reduction of economic and social inequalities, but, on the other hand, he argues that since inequality and injustice are inherent in capitalist society, equality can be attained only when capitalism is transformed into socialism. By carrying on the analysis in terms of simple dichotomous concepts such as "capitalism" and "socialism," he ignores the fact that the capitalism of 1930 may be qualitatively different from that of 1830 or 1880. He is therefore led to make sweeping statements such as the following: "Any society, in fact, the fruits of whose economic operations are unequally distributed will be compelled to deny freedom as the law of its being." [55] "Discussion of inessentials can be ample and luxurious; discussion of essentials will always, where it touches the heart of existing social arrangements, meet at least with difficulty and probably with attack." [56] In fact, of course, critics of capitalism, including socialists and Communists, enjoyed virtually unlimited freedom in both England and the United States in 1930, and in both countries discussion of economic and social "essentials" by Laski and many other writers was "ample and luxurious," while in the Soviet Union, where capitalism had been eliminated, freedom to criticize was conspicuously absent in 1930.

At one moment Laski argues that freedom is meaningful only to the small minority in capitalist society who own and control property, but in the next breath he maintains that men now enjoy greater political and religious freedom than ever before. Particularly after the onset of the depression in 1929, he seriously overestimates the control that the economically powerful exert over the political process as well as the degree to which ordinary men in capitalist society are the prisoners of poverty, ignorance, and "dumb inertia." The masses have been so brutalized by the system of inequality that their only response to their situation is "a sense of angry despair or sodden

[55] LMS, pp. 220–21.   [56] *Ibid.*, p. 224.

disillusion." [57] The poor "do not know the power that they possess. They hardly realise what can be effected by organising their interests. They lack direct access to those who govern them." [58] This under-rating of the political awareness and effectiveness of ordinary men, which occasionally comes perilously close to despair and contempt, leads Laski to be unduly pessimistic about the ability of democracy to deal with its long-range problems and with the crisis of the depression.

The crux of Laski's analysis of the relationship between liberty and equality is his categorical assertion that

in an unequal society it is necessary to repress the expression of in-dividuality. Every attempt at such expression is an attempt at the equaliza-tion of social conditions; it is an attempt to make myself count, an insistence on my claim, an assertion of my right to be treated as equal in that claim with other persons. To admit that I ought to have that freedom is to deny that the inequality upon which society rests is valid. And, accordingly, every sort of devious method, conscious and uncon-scious, is adopted to prevent my assertiveness.[59]

The argument assumes what, in the light of history, appears to be highly dubious—that the expression of individuality has been at a minimum in societies in which significant social and economic in-equalities exist. The assertion that every attempt to express one's in-dividuality is an attempt to equalize social conditions seems ground-less. There are forms of self-expression that have little if any con-nection with social or economic equality; in fact, it may be argued that when the individual creates truly personal outlets for self-expression, he is, to that degree, differentiating himself from other men rather than asserting his claim to be treated equally with them. As long as economic inequalities are not too great and social stratifica-tion remains relatively open and fluid, there would appear to be a positive correlation between social and economic differentiation and the range and vigor of individual self-expression. The expression of individuality flourished in fifth-century Athens but was virtually absent from Sparta, which embodied, to a far greater degree than Athens, Laski's ideal of a society in which social and economic condi-tions were roughly equal for all citizens. Every rigidly egalitarian society of which we have record has been compelled to curtail indi-

[57] "A Plea for Equality," DO, p. 221.   [58] P, p. 26.
[59] LMS, pp. 245–46.

viduality and spontaneity lest they destroy the inelastic pattern of group life on which the community depends.

During the last two centuries the opportunities for individual freedom and self-expression have been greatest in the countries where there has been a large measure of political freedom—France, England and the older Dominions, the United States, Scandinavia, and Switzerland. In all these societies there exist inequalities of income and status; this suggests the inadequacy of Laski's thesis that individual self-expression depends upon an equal society. We note, however, that in each society the hierarchy of wealth and status has been a gradual slope rather than a pyramid in which an apex of great wealth and power rises sharply from a base of mass poverty and ignorance. In these countries a large middle class has played a vital political and cultural role, and there has been a good deal of social and economic mobility. Finally, judged by world standards, these societies have been the most advanced in industrial technique and in per capita wealth. These examples indicate that liberty, in the sense of a wide range of choice for each individual in determining his manner of life and thought, is incompatible with a rigidly egalitarian society and, also, with a society in which a small group, by their monopoly of wealth and power, dominate a large mass of persons who are impoverished and ignorant. Liberty seems to reach its maximum development for the individual and for most individuals in a society when the range of inequality is not too great, when income and status groups are relatively open and fluid, and when each person has sufficient access to opportunities for education and training to permit him to develop as far as his abilities permit. In order that the benefits of freedom may be widely realized in a society, it is essential that almost every citizen receive an income that covers at least the necessities of life; obviously this condition is most easily met when the resources and productivity of the nation are great.

From the premise that every attempt by an individual to exercise his right to liberty will be challenged by the powerful because every effort at self-expression is an effort to equalize some privilege now held by the few, Laski draws the conclusion that the more consciously we can seek that equalization as a desirable object of social effort, the more likely we are to make attacks upon liberty more rare, the evil results of such attack less frequent. No man's love of justice is strong enough to survive the right to inflict punishment in the name of the creed he professes; and the simplest way to retain his sense of justice is to take away the interest which persuades him of the duty to punish. Scepticism, it may be, is a dissolvent of enthusiasm, but *enthusiasm has always been the enemy of freedom* . . . . we cannot argue with men who are in a passion. Nothing is so likely to engender passion as the perception that they are called to sacrifice a privilege. The way, therefore, of freedom is to arrange the pattern of social institutions so that there are no privileges to sacrifice.[60]

In flatly asserting that enthusiasm has always been the enemy of freedom, Laski ignores the enthusiasm and zeal that were characteristic of the Puritan Revolution, the American and French Revolutions, and other great historical movements for freedom, and he overlooks his own impassioned denunciations of injustice and inequality. Even more curious is his argument that since the surest way to arouse the passions of the privileged and to destroy freedom is to call upon them to surrender a privilege, we should, in order to safeguard freedom, carry through a total renovation of social institutions, involving the abolition of all privileges. Surely, the more drastic attack on privileges, arousing more intense passions in more people, will constitute a far graver threat to freedom. There seems little reason to believe that men of wealth and power will accept a greater evil with better grace than a lesser one.

"If we have a society of unequals," Laski asks, "how can we agree either about ends or means? And if this agreement is absent how can we, at least over a considerable period, hope to move on our way in peace? An unequal society always lives in fear, and with a sense of impending disaster in its heart." [61] If, as Laski argues, agreement about means and ends is a necessary condition of social peace, the prospect for modern society can only be the hopeless one of perpetual conflict. In fact, however, the reverse of this position seems to be more nearly true. Men will always disagree about the means that will best attain a given end, and in a democratic society there is not— and indeed there should not be—universal agreement on all ends. Nor is there any guarantee that greater social and economic equality will mean greater homogeneity of thinking about values or techniques. There is even less reason why a thinker such as Laski, who argues in

[60] LMS, pp. 285–86; italics mine.   [61] *Ibid.*, pp. 251–52.

favor of the values of individual self-expression and spontaneity, should regard such homogeneity as desirable. Even if one accepted his contention that social violence is the necessary consequence of disagreement about ends and means, it would not follow that a program of radical social and economic changes is the way to lessen the differences between the opinions of social groups and thus minimize the possibility of violent conflict.

In conclusion, we should look briefly at Laski's theory of natural rights. We have seen that he defines the rights that inhere in each man as a member of society as "those things without which I cannot, in Green's phrase, realise myself as a moral being," [62] or as "those conditions of social life without which no man can seek, in general, to be himself at his best." [63] Since the purpose of the state is to make it possible for each man to achieve this self-realization, it must secure the substance of these rights to every citizen; rights, therefore, "are prior to the State in the sense that, recognised or no, they are that from which its validity derives." [64] Rights are correlative with functions, and, though their content varies with changes in time and place, the general test of rights is their utility to all the members of the state. As we have observed, Laski also holds that rights, "regardless of the exact function to which they relate, are at a minimum basis, identical. The State, at that level, must secure them for each of its citizens." [65]

The citizen has the right to work and, if he is unemployed, the right to the means to live. He has the right to a living wage, reasonable hours of labor, and adequate leisure. He has the right to such education as will enable him to perform his duties as a citizen, as well as the right to participate in the government of industry. Politically, he has the right to vote and to be chosen for public office. He has the right to the freedoms of speech, opinion, religion, association, and assembly, and to full judicial safeguards before the courts of law. Finally, each man has the right to own property to that extent which "enables the decent satisfaction of impulse"; "if what I own is, broadly speaking, important for the service I perform" and "can be shown to be related to the common welfare as a condition of its maintenance." [66]

[62] GP, p. 39. [63] *Ibid.*, p. 91. [64] *Ibid.* [65] *Ibid.*, p. 95.
[66] *Ibid.*, p. 130.

We have already discussed the difficulties that are involved in any effort to formulate a theory of natural rights.[67] Even Laski is forced to concede that a state may exist for a considerable period without recognizing the rights that he has postulated, although he insists that it has no moral claim to allegiance unless it maintains these rights. The basic weakness in his formulation of a theory of rights is the same one we noted in discussing his analysis of the state's purpose and his original conception of liberty. He defines rights as the conditions without which the individual cannot be his best self or realize himself as a moral being, although he rejects the ethical theory of an idealist such as T. H. Green that is basic to this concept of rights; and he fails to give an alternative statement of the nature of this "best self" or of the conditions required for its realization. In the early 1930's he abandons this formulation and defines a right as "a condition without which, in the light of historic experience, the individual lacks assurance that he can attain happiness." [68] He offers no analysis of "happiness"; presumably he regards it as a condition that is approximately the same for all individuals in the society. If, however, men differ sharply in their conceptions of happiness, there may be great variations in their ideas of their rights, since the latter are held to be the conditions that they regard as essential to their well-being. Laski has no warrant for asserting, for example, that all men have a natural right to participate in the government of industry, unless he is prepared to defend the position that all men do, in fact, regard such participation as necessary to their attainment of happiness. Finally, there are conditions of individual well-being that no state can hope to secure for its citizens. The state cannot confer upon all citizens as rights such essentials to well-being as physical health and a personality that makes possible satisfactory relationships with other people, though it may attempt to remove or to prevent restrictions that keep the individual from achieving them.

[67] See above, chap. 2, section 2.   [68] P, p. 45.

6

Economic and Political Change

1 . POLITICS AND ECONOMICS

As EARLY as 1925 Laski dismisses the guild-socialist movement with the remark: "In 1920, guild socialism was the fashionable doctrine of the time; its influence is now almost negligible. Its importance has come to lie in its emphasis upon industrial decentralization, and it is generally agreed that it is not a theory of the state." [1] He explicitly rejects the syndicalist idea, saying that "no function can, in any final way, be entrusted with ultimate powers. At some point, co-ordination in the interests of those who live by the results, as against the interests of those who live by making the results, of the function is essential. We cannot . . . leave . . . the government of coal-mines solely to the miners." [2] His opposition to workers' control over industry is as complete and as confident as his previous rejection of state ownership and control; he states: "There is no reason to suppose that the ownership of the American mines by the United Mine Workers of America would be more careful of the public interest in coal than has been the case under their ownership by corporations like the present interests." [3]

To the state, as the guardian of men's common interests and common needs, is entrusted the vital task of coordinating and organizing the activities of the various functional groups in the society; "it will so direct the functions which produce the required services as to secure effective conditions of response." [4] Laski also finds that this essential coordination cannot be accomplished by creating, in place of the state, a system of associations or an economic parliament to harmonize conflicting group interests. The problem of weighting each function properly in order to determine the composition of such

[1] "Political Science in Great Britain," *American Political Science Review*, XIX (Feb., 1925), 99.
[2] GP, p. 64.   [3] *Ibid.*, p. 439.   [4] *Ibid.*, p. 69.

a body is insoluble, and "vocational bodies . . . are not, by their very nature, built to deal with the general issues which must be faced by society as a whole." [5] Any system of functional representation would also destroy the quality of direct intelligibility that must be preserved if democratic government is to be maintained; thus "for the immediate future it seems clear that we must surround the administrative self-determination of functional units with the territorial control of the State." [6] He explicitly rejects the Webbs's proposal that two co-ordinate national assemblies be established, one to deal with political affairs and the other to handle social and economic problems. The Webbs's Social Parliament, possessing all the financial and taxing powers of the present House of Commons, would soon come to dominate the Political Parliament, while any attempt to compart-mentalize authority in the two legislatures would prove completely unworkable, since the "making of policy . . . seems to involve a single assembly charged with the oversight of the whole field of administration." [7]

To a far greater extent than in his early writings, Laski now concedes that the decisions that must be made in the daily operation of complex political and industrial organizations require expert knowl-edge and skill, which the ordinary citizen or worker cannot be ex-pected to possess. He does not, of course, advocate rule by the experts; "however much we rely upon the expert in formulating the materials for decision," he says, "what ultimately matters is the judgment passed upon the results of policy by those who are to live by them." [8] Co-ordination of the activities of the various experts so that the broad policies approved by the public are carried out is the function of the politician, who, by indicating the limits of the possible, forms a bridge between the experts and the people. The complexity of modern po-litical problems means that the judgment of the citizens "can be asked for only on the larger issues, and, very certainly, that those issues, to be decided, must be consistently reduced to the simplest terms. A democracy, in other words, must, if it is to work, be an aristocracy by delegation. But the fact of delegation is vital." [9] Laski recognizes the

[5] *Ibid.*, p. 73.   [6] *Ibid.*, p. 140.   [7] *Ibid.*, p. 339.

[8] *The Limitations of the Expert*, Fabian Tract No. 235 (London: The Fabian Society, 1931), p. 12.

[9] GP, p. 43.

dangers to representative and democratic government involved in the rise of the positive state and the growing importance in political life of extremely complex, quasi-technical economic problems; the legislature is overburdened, while increasingly the executive and the administration are becoming the central pivot of the state. Parliamentary government faces the new and perilous task of reconsidering the nature and privileges of property at a time when the inadequacy of the mechanisms that link the citizen to his representative, the executive, and the constantly expanding civil service means that those who rule have little real understanding of popular needs and desires.[10]

In 1930 Laski first emphasizes a thesis that he is later to repeat and develop in detail; he argues that the success of nineteenth-century representative government

> was built upon an agreement between parties in the state upon fundamental principles. There was, that is, a kindred outlook upon large issues; and since fighting was confined to matters of comparative detail, men were prepared to let reason have its sway in the realm of conflict. For it is significant that in the one realm where depth of feeling was passionate—Irish home rule—events moved rapidly to the test of the sword; and the settlement made was effected by violence and not by reason.[11]

He believes that, since the First World War, this general agreement among parties and groups within the state has virtually disappeared. The eclipse of English liberalism is a result of its fundamentally individualistic attitude that cannot cope with the demands of the workers or with their unions; the Liberal social legislation of the 1906–1914 period is characterized as an effort "to mitigate social inequality by recognition of individual claims, and to build machinery for their satisfaction which continued to neglect the fact of trade unionism." [12] The decline of Liberalism has meant the growth of the Labor Party and its increasing hold upon the workers; to maintain that hold, the party must move toward the redefinition of the property system desired by the workers while pressing for higher taxes on the wealthy to pay for the new benefits demanded by the poor.

[10] See "The Present Evolution of the Parliamentary System," in Laski, Ch. Borgeaud, *et al.*, *The Development of the Representative System in Our Times* (Lausanne: Payot et Cie., 1928), pp. 7–17.

[11] LMS, p. 238.   [12] *Ibid.*, pp. 236–37.

The gap between the principles of the Labor Party and the Conservative Party is, therefore, far wider than the prewar differences between Liberals and Conservatives. "Persons of wealth thus find themselves threatened from both sides. On the one hand, taxation abstracts an ever-increasing portion of their income; on the other, public ownership deliberately narrows the realm within which a large fortune can be made." [13] At the same time the underprivileged are increasingly skeptical of the ability of traditional political institutions to achieve the equality which they demand. The result is that "the grounds of social antagonism to-day make the prospect of agreement between classes far more difficult than in the past simply because the cost of concession is so much greater." [14] Laski concludes that in England, for the first time since the seventeenth century, "what is coming rapidly into the foreground of discussion is the very thesis of parliamentary government itself." [15] British democracy can survive only if major reforms are made in political and economic institutions. We have already discussed his suggestions that a series of advisory councils be attached to each governmental agency and that the power to deal with many of the details of economic regulation be delegated to industrial councils; now we must look at the economic changes that he proposes.

He no longer believes that the hierarchical structure of modern industry can be replaced by a cooperative organization of the various functional groups. Authority to make decisions must be confined to the minority at the top of the hierarchy; workers' councils can only endeavor to make the authority exercised a responsible authority that takes into consideration the wills of those affected by its decisions. They will advise and consult with the men responsible for industrial government in much the same manner that the citizens' councils will advise those who make political and administrative decisions. The first step in destroying what Laski calls the present "irresponsible autocracy" in economic life is to make industry, like medicine, the law, or teaching, a profession in which "monetary gain is subordinate to rules conceived in terms of function, and the purpose of function

[13] "The Prospects of Constitutional Government," *Political Quarterly,* I (July–Sept., 1930), 312.
[14] *Ibid.,* p. 316.
[15] "The Mother of Parliaments," *Foreign Affairs,* IX (July, 1931), 569.

is social service." [16] To this end the functionless owner of capital must be removed from control of business enterprises and transformed from "the residuary legatee of industry" into a person who receives a fixed dividend for the use of his wealth. The rules by which industry is governed can then be made by those who actually work in it; although a hierarchy of authority will still exist, it will, arising naturally out of function, reflect the gradations of skill and ability among the working force rather than differences in wealth or social status. In each industry, whether nationalized or under private management, there should be a constitution that provides for standard hours and wages, proofs of qualification for positions in the industry, and mechanisms for consultation with the workers about hiring and dismissal, promotion, and changes in technology. Laski believes that this abolition of a parasitic class of functionless owners is "more likely than any single source of invention to secure that full-hearted cooperation on the part of the rank and file which is the real road to an increase in productivity." [17]

"Any industrial system," he says, "must satisfy the principles of justice; it must give to the worker a secure and adequate livelihood, reasonable conditions of work, and a full opportunity to share in the making of the conditions upon which his happiness in work will depend." [18] What sort of economic organization will meet these conditions? First, we note that Laski is not at all certain about the extent to which some form of socialized ownership must replace private ownership. At one point he argues that wherever "functionless property is the controlling factor in industrial production, the abolition of its rights is the necessary path to justice." [19] The rights of the owners are to be bought out by legislative enactment; "they would then have the right to a dividend; but they would surrender alike profits and control." [20] Since the ownership of almost all industrial property is for Laski "functionless," this proposal would mean the transfer of almost every industrial enterprise from its present owners to the government. In a later, more detailed discussion of the problem in the same volume, however, he states that private ownership and private profit are to be eliminated only from those industries "urgently affected by a public character which are monopolistic in their nature." [21] The

[16] GP, p. 202. [20] *Ibid.* [18] *Ibid.*, p. 433.
[19] *Ibid.*, p. 208. [17] *Ibid.*, p. 212. [21] *Ibid.*, p. 436.

production of "urgent commodities" that are not naturally monopolistic is "the natural and proper sphere of the consumer's co-operative movement"; [22] the production of "definitely desirable, but not necessarily urgent" commodities may be left to private initiative, under suitable government regulation, while in the realm of commodities not invested with a public character the state will have no direct concern with the amount of profit or the form of industrial government. Each of the private companies that fall into the last two categories is to be controlled by a Board of Directors, in which half of the seats are reserved for the elected representatives of management and labor, in equal proportion, and the other half of the seats are held by the representatives of invested capital. The investors are also entitled to one third of the surplus earned by the company after the payment of operating costs, including the dividend to stockholders. Thus the owners of capital retain at least a share in the profits and in the control of the business, and the rights of functionless property are not abolished.

At another point in the *Grammar,* he argues that the production of "those elements in the common welfare which are integral to the well-being of the community" [23] must be socialized. In *Socialism and Freedom* he argues for socialized ownership of all essential industries, adding that the decision as to the range over which socialization should extend is not a matter for dogmatic statement, but should be the result of inquiry and experiment.[24] In 1928 he says that Marx was right in holding that "no State . . . can rightly order its life so long as *the fundamental instruments of production* are the plaything of private gain." [25] Although he insists that socialization does not necessarily mean nationalization, he specifically states that essential services must be nationalized and their ownership vested in the state. Far more important, however, than Laski's conflicting statements about the proper sphere of socialized ownership or his distinctions between socialization and nationalization is the fact that, in complete contrast to his earlier views, he advocates a large measure of state ownership and control of industry, as well as state regulation and intervention

[22] *Ibid.*   [23] *Ibid.,* p. 204.

[24] See *Socialism and Freedom,* Fabian Tract No. 216 (London: The Fabian Society, 1925), pp. 10–11.

[25] "The Value and Defects of the Marxist Philosophy," *Current History,* XXIX (Oct., 1928), 28; italics mine.

in the nonsocialized sector of the economy. All of the diatribes against state control, nationalization, bureaucracy, paternalism, and Fabianism are forgotten; he is now convinced that only the state has the power to regulate private economic power and to foster social and economic equality. The attitude of the Conservative Government towards the general strike of 1926 and its 1927 legislation to curb the power of the unions were merely the last in a series of events that persuaded Laski that labor was bound to meet with hostility and repression if, by confining its energies to the industrial sphere, it failed to obtain control of the state. His conclusion is that "either the State must control industrial power in the interest of its citizens, or industrial power will control the State in the interests of its possessors." [26]

When he states, "I understand by Socialism the deliberate intervention of the State in the process of production and distribution in order to secure an access to their benefits upon a consistently wider scale," [27] we can see how completely his socialism has lost its early Proudhonian and syndicalist flavor. Ignoring all his former warnings of the dangers to initiative and freedom involved in bureaucracy and state control, he states that most of "the accusations of bureaucracy brought against public ownership are the crude type of propaganda which seeks to postpone its inevitable victory." [28] Previously he inveighed against the deadening effects of the hierarchical structure and the habits of routine of the civil service; now he says that there is "not . . . any danger in this country of a civil service wedded to routine and averse from experiment. The evidence rather suggests that ministers are less ready for change at the pace forced upon them than that they have to goad their subordinates into new ways." [29] While recognizing that his proposals for constant and extensive regulation of industry by government will be criticized as "the apotheosis of officialism," he insists that there is no alternative to state control except pure *laissez-faire.*

The problem, in fact, is not whether government intervention is desirable. The truth is that government intervention is essential, and the problem

[26] GP, p. 109.

[27] "The Socialist Tradition in the French Revolution," SLP, p. 68.

[28] *Socialism and Freedom*, p. 11.

[29] Introductory essay to Sir Henry Taylor, *The Statesman* (Cambridge: W. Heffer & Sons, Ltd., 1927), p. xxv.

is simply of methods whereby it can bear its maximum fruit. For to leave to the unfettered play of economic forces the supply of those needs by the satisfaction of which we live is to maintain a society empty of all moral principles; and such a society more surely moves to disaster than at any period in history.[30]

All that now remains of his previous antistate viewpoint is the argument that the producers in a nationalized industry have the right to participate in determining the conditions under which they work, in settling, that is, questions of wages, hours, and factory conditions, and that the workers have "the right to be consulted in the making of policy for the industry."[31] Policy making itself is "a matter which must rest with those who speak in the name of the community";[32] the workers have only "a right to be heard, to explain their point of view, to emphasise doubts, and, at the margin, to resist decision."[33] Each nationalized industry will be managed by a governing board and several regional boards, made up of members elected by the managers and technicians and by the vocations, and of other members nominated by the appropriate Minister to represent the public; in each factory there will be a works' committee to discuss with the management such subjects as work regulations, distribution of hours, payment of wages, the settlement of grievances, safety and welfare provisions, factory discipline, training, and education.[34] These works' committees, Laski believes, "are the root of freedom in the factory. The individual worker is himself helpless before the size of modern organisation. He can only make himself felt by the evolution of institutions through which his will has a full opportunity of expression. In committees such as these there is, I think, a reasonable guarantee that this will be the case."[35] Over and above the basic minimum wage guaranteed to every worker as a citizen, wage rates will be settled by the trade union of each vocation in the industry in discussions with the governing body.

In each private industry a national council and several district councils will be established, representing equally the owners, the vocations, the direct users of its products, and the government, with power to issue orders dealing with wages, hours, and working conditions, the stabilization of production and employment, the creation of ma-

[30] GP, p. 489.   [31] *Ibid.*, p. 441.   [32] *Ibid.*
[33] *Ibid.*   [34] See *ibid.*, pp. 445–53.   [35] *Ibid.*, p. 453.

chinery to settle disputes, and the collection and publication of information about costs, output, methods of manufacture, and research. After approval by the Ministry of Production and subject to the control of the legislature, the orders of these councils will be binding upon all firms in the industry. At the factory level there will be works' committees like those in the nationalized industries. All companies left under private management will be required to submit to the government full information about their costs, assets and liabilities, and profits. In addition the government must have the power to fix prices and to control the entry of new firms and must act to prevent the sharp fluctuations of the business cycle by endeavoring to estimate supply and demand and by stabilizing the currency; it must control the issue of capital, attempt the centralized control and distribution of raw materials, and reduce the costs of food and essential raw materials by an efficient system of zonal distribution.[36]

Laski admits that the economic system he proposes is "frankly collectivist" in that it "attempts a wholesale planning of the methods whereby the purpose of industry is achieved."[37] This collectivism is necessary because the "working-classes of the world have no longer any faith in capitalism. They give to it no service they can avoid. It involves industrial dislocation as the law of its being. It implies a distribution of property at no point referable to moral principle. It means waste and corruption and inefficiency."[38] Under the system of private property and the market economy we have "both the wrong commodities produced, and those produced distributed without regard to social urgency."[39] Since the amassing of wealth is the primary activity in capitalist society, its attainment becomes the standard by which all else is judged and valued; this profit-making motive, which mistakes means for ends, is totally inadequate as the foundation of a well-ordered society. In a society in which the power of demand is so unequal that the different classes seem to be different nations, the state "is compelled to use its instruments to protect the property of the rich from invasion by the poor. It comes to think of order as the final virtue. It neglects its larger aims. It perverts the equal aid it owes to all in the effort to afford the special advantage required by some."[40] Social conflict can be avoided and the foundations of the

[36] See *ibid.*, pp. 489–91.   [37] *Ibid.*, p. 504.   [38] *Ibid.*, p. 507.
[39] *Ibid.*, p. 175.   [40] *Ibid.*, p. 176.

social order made secure only by compelling the state to organize the satisfaction of "the passion for equality," which is "a permanent feature" of human nature. To this end, far-reaching use must be made of the power of the state; essential industries must be nationalized and the right to inherit property sharply curtailed; there must be comprehensive regulation of private business, each citizen must be guaranteed an adequate minimum wage, and the government must provide suitable educational opportunities and welfare services for all. We must create a new society based upon the conception that property is the return for service to the group, a society in which wealth no longer dominates our lives and perverts all our relationships and institutions.

Laski believes that these major reforms are the minimum concessions acceptable to the masses, who now reject the assumptions of capitalism and refuse it their allegiance. He warns that

if we are to avoid revolution, the concessions must be large enough to assure a world-order in which the average man is assured of the opportunity to realise his best self. That means . . . equality; and equality means, undoubtedly, great sacrifice on the part of those who now enjoy the gain of living while bearing very partially the cost of that gain. . . . the classes in the possession of power . . . have to prove their goodwill to the disinherited. Only as that proof is rapid and substantial shall we be able to maintain the best prospects of the human race.[41]

The question immediately arises, can such great social and economic changes be accomplished peacefully through the normal channels of representative government? It is sometimes asserted that Laski's doubts that the workers would be able to win their goals by democratic methods first arose during the depression of the 1930's, particularly as a reaction to the failure of the MacDonald Labor Government in 1931. While these events obviously influenced him deeply, as we shall see,[42] it is important to realize that as early as 1925 he was not completely confident that the changes he proposed as the minimum alternative to revolution could be achieved democratically. He comments:

We are running a race with time in this country. Our system requires radical revision; and the stage is set for changes as vast in the economic régime as those of the nineteenth century were in the political. It is not

---

[41] *Ibid.,* p. 540.   [42] See below, chap. 7.

easy to be confident that parliamentary institutions are as fitted to the former as, unquestionably, they were to the latter. Governments which attack the citadel of property take their lives in their hands; for great social changes have to be paid for, and their cost does not produce reasonableness in the payers. . . . One remembers that a fairly small change like Home Rule produced the Ulster Volunteers. Will big changes produce the necessary restraint in those adversely affected by them? [43]

Repeatedly, during the late 1920's, Laski returns to this theme; the choice we face is concessions by the ruling class on a far greater scale than history has ever witnessed or acceptance by the workers of the Communist position that violent revolution is inevitable.[44] And repeatedly he asks: "Will a class, which has hitherto enjoyed a virtual monopoly of effective authority in the state, acquiesce peacefully in its own extinction?" [45] Although he does not give a direct answer to the question, he clearly indicates that he is not optimistic about the willingness of the ruling class to abdicate from power peacefully; he warns that "there are, in every community, groups of powerful men who make it a matter of principle to deny the validity of all concession. They display an ignorant hostility to change every whit as dangerous and provocative as the challenge they confront." [46] Marx was surely right "when he argued that no class, at least so far in the historic record, has been willing peacefully to abdicate from its power." [47] After the accession to office of the second minority Labor Government in 1929, Laski asks: "What demands will Mr. Mac-Donald have to satisfy when, perhaps after the next election, he has a definite majority in the House of Commons? Will he be permitted peacefully to satisfy demands which imply an immediate alteration of the existing social system?" [48] When we recall developments in Spain, Italy, Yugoslavia, and Ulster in 1914, we are forced to ask

[43] "English Politics Today," *The New Republic*, XLIII (July 8, 1925), 173–74. See also the warning: "Faith in the power of reason is not the strongest of human impulses; and we shall know more of its tenacity when Socialism begins to move nearer the realisation of its central aim." *Socialism and Freedom*, p. 6.

[44] See C, pp. 32, 90, 181–82, 240, 243, *etc.*

[45] "The Prospects of Constitutional Government," *Political Quarterly*, I (July–Sept., 1930), 312.

[46] C, pp. 240–41.

[47] "The Value and Defects of the Marxist Philosophy," *Current History*, XXIX (Oct., 1928), 29.

[48] "The New Test for British Labor," *Foreign Affairs*, VIII (Oct., 1929), 82.

ourselves, "Can a social conception of property-rights replace an individualist conception without conflict and violence?" [49] He insists that labor in Britain will be entitled to maintain its belief in the possibility of a peaceful transition from capitalism only if MacDonald can successfully carry through fundamental reforms and can secure, within a short time, an independent majority in Parliament.

During the entire period of the MacDonald Government, Laski warns the leaders of the Labor Party and the Opposition that the masses, who now realize that the inequalities of the present order are indefensible on any ground save that of traditional rights, are demanding, with increasing determination, the abolition of the system of private property, which prevents them from escaping from their poverty. The wealthy, on the other hand, feeling that their privileges are threatened, answer the threat by a renewed resolve to defend their position at any cost. In this atmosphere of ever greater tension, we have "no final assurance that there is, on either side of the social equation, a sufficient volume of goodwill to make us optimistic about peace over any long period." [50] Laski urges the powerful to "reform, if you would preserve"; like the prophets, he couples his exhortations with dire prophecies of the disasters that will ensue if his warnings go unheeded. His pessimistic conclusion is that "human nature being what it is, men do not easily surrender what they have the power to retain; and they will pay the price of conflict if they think they can win. They do not remember that the price of conflict is the destruction of freedom and that with its loss there go the qualities which make for the humanity of men." [51] His last comment on this problem before the crisis of 1931 and the defection of MacDonald is made in July, 1931. After noting that the allegiance of the workers to the Labor Party depends upon their conviction that the new society which they demand can be achieved by democratic and parliamentary means, he sums up his dissatisfaction, and, presumably, that of the workers, with the results of the first year and a half of the MacDonald Government by the brief comment: "Ex-

[49] *Ibid.*

[50] "The Prospects of Constitutional Government," *Political Quarterly*, I (July–Sept., 1930), 315.

[51] LMS, p. 256. See also the comment: "We have no inherent reason to suppose that those who possess, and enjoy, power will surrender it for ideals they do not share." P, p. 150.

perience of the present administration has not deepened that conviction." [52]

2 . MARXISM AND LENINISM

We have seen that in his early writings Laski, though he generally accepted an economic interpretation of politics, rejected Marx's philosophy of history as "radically false." By 1927, however, he argues that "there is no department of human life in which the governing ideas and institutions will not be found, upon examination, to be largely a reflection of a given set of economic conditions." [53] Early in 1931 he remarks that "the thesis of the materialist interpretation of history seems to me, in its large outline though not in its particular details, a thesis that is unanswerable." [54] His analyses of the legal system and of such historical movements as the French Revolution indicate a general commitment to the basic Marxist tenet that "the primary mechanism of change in a society is the system of production which obtains." [55] Nevertheless, he holds that historical events are misread if they are seen entirely in economic terms; "religion, race, nationality, these have their ideologies which shape, even as they are shaped by, the economic environment." [56] Historical materialism, because of its excessive rationalism and its overemphasis on economic factors, ignores the fact that men's rational interest is often "overcome by distracting counter-currents of loyalty which afford them satisfaction superior to that which reason might afford." [57] Laski refuses to deal with the basic issue; if, as he maintains, many human actions are nonrational and if the Marxist interpretation ignores or underrates the nonrational factors in behavior, the Marxist view of

[52] "The Mother of Parliaments," *Foreign Affairs,* IX (July, 1931), 572.

[53] C, p. 78.

[54] "Communism as a World Force," *International Affairs,* X (Jan., 1931), 23.

[55] "The Value and Defects of the Marxist Philosophy," *Current History,* XXIX (Oct., 1928), 23; for his analysis of the legal system, see "Justice and the Law," SLP, esp. pp. 277–87; and for his discussion of the French Revolution, see "The Age of Reason," SLP, esp. pp. 45–47.

[56] "The Value and Defects of the Marxist Philosophy," *Current History,* XXIX (Oct., 1928), 27.

[57] C, p. 79.

history must be inadequate and erroneous not merely, as he admits, in its details, but in its very foundations. His eclecticism is so uncritical that he can accept and use Marx's central thesis as an analytic instrument at the same time that he rejects a thoroughgoing economic determinism as historically and psychologically false; often he dilutes Marxism to the point where it is no more than an insistence that the economic system is one of the important causal factors in social change; he states, for example, that "ideologies produce economic systems, just as economic systems produce ideologies." [58]

Laski modifies another fundamental Marxist tenet, the belief that there exist inevitable laws of historical development that enable us to predict at least the next stage of social evolution; he argues that the "laws" that govern a given system of production are "merely tendencies which are, at each instant of time, subject to a pressure which makes prophecy of their operation at best a hazardous adventure." [59] He notes that even if economic classes disappear, it does not necessarily follow that other forms of class rule, such as the rule of a doctrinal aristocracy, will not emerge. He also criticizes Marx for his assertion that the movement to socialism and communism is the inevitable result of the breakdown of capitalism; the sequel to that breakdown, he argues, may be anarchy and the emergence of a nonproletarian dictatorship. This criticism is obviously the result of a superficial reading of Marx, since Marx's frequent appeals to the workers to prepare and organize to carry out the revolution imply that the attainment of socialism is not simply a mechanical inevitability.[60] Laski also notes that the Marxist affirmation that a new system of production will emphasize better tendencies in human nature, and precisely the tendencies a communist society requires, is "no more than a prophecy which may be justified in the event." [61] He questions the certainty of the Communists that capitalism will be unable to check their propaganda or stem their relentless sweep to victory; he cites the examples of postwar Italy, Bulgaria, and Rumania

[58] *Ibid.*, p. 87.

[59] *Ibid.*, p. 84. Note his remark that "the error of communism lies in its refusal to face the fact that this is a complex world. Its panacea is unreal simply because the world is too intricate for panaceas to have universal significance." *Ibid.*, p. 243.

[60] See Karl Marx and Friedrich Engels, *The Communist Manifesto* (New York: International Publishers, 1932).

[61] C, p. 177.

to demonstrate that "the counter-offensive of capitalism has been proportionate to the vehemence of communist claims." [62] The reader is most amazed by his rejection of the major thesis of Marxism, the belief that capitalism will inevitably collapse and give way to a new economic system. For when he admits "the possibilities that better industrial organisation and the prospects of scientific discovery might easily make of capitalism a system able to satisfy the main wants of the workers," [63] he is denying not merely Marx's major premise but also his own repeated assertions that the demands of the workers can be satisfied only if capitalism is replaced by a new economic system.

In his discussions of the world Communist movement, Laski frequently stresses its similarities in organization and in temper with the Roman Catholic Church; in both institutional systems, "there is the same width and intensity of discussion before dogma is imposed; there is the same authoritarian imposition of dogma; and there is the same ruthless purging of dissident elements which show unwillingness to accept the decisions made." [64] Like the early Jesuits, the Bolshevists are unyielding dogmatists, characterized by fanatic loyalty, rigorous discipline, and complete confidence in the inevitable triumph of their cause. He maintains that the strength of Communism's psychological appeal, especially to the underprivileged, lies in the fact that "it has a faith as vigorous, as fanatic, and compelling as any in the history of religions"; [65] the movement has made its way "by its idealism and not its realism, by its spiritual promise, not its materialistic prospect." [66] He is critical of the rigorous controls and party discipline of Communism, and says that, in working towards its goal of world revolution, the Third International persistently underestimates the need for flexibility and diversity in its campaigns in different countries. To the present-day reader it is obvious that his assumption that the International was primarily concerned with promoting international revolution is erroneous; even in 1927, the Comintern had been transformed from an international revolutionary organization into an instrument of Soviet foreign policy, while the international position of the Soviet Union had become the dominant factor in Communist decisions to give or withhold support from non-Russian revolutionary movements.

[62] *Ibid.*, p. 198. [63] *Ibid.*, p. 87. [64] *Ibid.*, p. 192.
[65] *Ibid.*, p. 246. [66] *Ibid.*, p. 250.

Laski points out that the Communist tactic of persistent attacks on social-democratic leaders, and the strategy of "the united front from below," with its effort to substitute Communist for reformist leadership in working-class organizations, have not proved successful. Such tactics cannot hope for success; socialists will not cooperate with the Communists while the latter are pursuing a policy of Machiavellian maneuver, the essence of which is described by Longuet's citation of the line from Racine, "I embrace my rival, but it is the better to choke him." [67] The Communist strategy of constantly attempting to create situations of conflict and confusion among the masses, which they then utilize for their own purposes, may easily backfire and give rise to repression and to dictatorship from the Right; to Laski, Mussolini's ascent to power demonstrates that the lessons of the Russian Revolution can be learned and put into practice by the forces of reaction.[68] He notes too that the Communist emphasis on national self-determination, although a useful propaganda device for winning the support of colonial and subject peoples, is a double-edged sword that can be used to defend nationalist movements against domination by the Soviet Union and the Comintern.

By the end of 1930, as the threat of Fascism became greater, Laski seems to have become much more impressed by the success of these Communist tactics which, previously, he regarded as inept as well as immoral. He expresses admiration for the manner in which the national parties in the Comintern

are articulated to the whole; the way in which it is able to produce what appears to the outsider some new kind of miracle—unity of outlook; the way in which its knowledge of what has to be done extends over the whole of the civilised globe, with a certitude to which the ordinary observer is unable to pretend—that surely is an object for our admiration. The way in which it has crushed out disunity in each national movement and . . . has been able to penetrate the workshops of the country and to build up, cell by cell, nuclei of communist propaganda, particularly in times of national distress or crisis, so that in a great crisis they may have very real and widespread influence, is extraordinary. The way in which it is able to discredit among the working classes the normal operation of the social democratic party, by demanding on behalf of the

[67] *Ibid.*, p. 211.   [68] See *ibid.*, pp. 236–37.

proletariat always more than the social democratic parties are prepared to grant, is a strategy of which it is difficult to be too eulogistic.[69]

More than twenty years later it is not difficult to be wiser than Laski in assessing the wisdom of these Communist tactics. We know, for example, that in Germany dissident elements were indeed eliminated from the Communist ranks and the Party completely destroyed and rebuilt in the image of the Russian model;[70] the Communists, by their savage attacks on the Social Democratic leadership and their tactical alliances with the Nazis, were successful in weakening the socialist movement and in confusing and disillusioning many workers. We also know, however, that the beneficiaries of these tactics were not the Communists but the Nazis, who capitalized on the confusions and suspicions among the workers that the Communists did so much to foster.

Laski is aware of the extent to which the Leninist techniques for seizing and holding power were modeled on the strategy developed by Babeuf and his followers in their attempt to overthrow the Directory in France. The direction of the whole revolutionary conspiracy by a small, secret central committee headed by Babeuf, the special efforts to infiltrate the police and the army, the persistent efforts to spread rumors that would discredit the government and stir up the people, the advocacy of a period of absolute dictatorship by the central committee in the name of the proletariat, and the insistence on rigorous controls over the press and political activity—all these elements have "provided ever since the methodology of revolutionary socialism at least in its large outline."[71] Laski concludes:

The detailed resemblances between the programme of Babeuf and that of the Russian communist are remarkable enough; but even more remarkable is the similarity of ultimate temper which runs through the two movements. There is the same exhilaration of spirit, the same bitterly drawn distinction between friend and foe, the same urgency that all things be made new, the same power relentlessly to dissect the weak-

[69] "Communism as a World Force," *International Affairs,* X (Jan., 1931), 25-26.
[70] See Ruth Fischer, *Stalin and German Communism* (Cambridge: Harvard University Press, 1948).
[71] "The Socialist Tradition in the French Revolution," SLP, p. 87; see, in general, pp. 87-99.

nesses of contemporary society, the same capacity for self-confident optimism, the same genius for propaganda and invective. Lenin, so to say,
is the Babouvistes writ large.[72]

Laski's major quarrel with Marx and, even more, with Lenin and
the Communists, is with their belief that the transition from capitalism to socialism can be accomplished only by a violent revolution
against the established order, followed by a period of proletarian dictatorship to prepare for the advent of communism. The Communist
justifies the resort to violence on the grounds that the capitalist class,
like all ruling groups, will never surrender its power voluntarily and
that the machinery of the state, which is the instrument of that class,
must be destroyed and replaced by new instruments of working-class
rule. The bureaucracy and the armed forces must be completely
smashed, traditional parliamentary institutions liquidated, and violence systematically employed to destroy the power of reactionary
elements; the more complete and intense is this dictatorship of the
Communist party as the vanguard of the proletariat, the shorter will
be the period of transition to the new classless society in which all
coercion and violence will have disappeared. Laski notes that violence
is not justified by the Communist for its own sake, but is regarded
as a *saeva necessitas;* "since the workers are, historically, the rising,
and the capitalists the falling, class in society, revolutionary violence
is force used to further the natural evolution of society; violence used
against communism is violence used in the service of reaction." [73] In
his criticisms of the "True Socialists," Grün and Hess, Marx says that
only the utterly stupid, the cowardly, or the complete Utopians can
still believe that the capitalists will be moved by rational arguments
to surrender their power for the sake of social justice. Since it is sheer
folly to expect anything of the ruling class except the defense of its
own position by every available means, the proletariat must realistically prepare for its great historic mission, the violent overthrow of

---

[72] *Ibid.,* pp. 98–99. In 1927 he writes to Holmes: "Did I tell you that I had traced
the origins of the famous 'Dictatorship of the Proletariat' to Babeuf? As that is Marx's
chief claim to strategic creativeness, and as I dislike Marx intensely it gave me peculiar pleasure, as there is little doubt but that he had read Babeuf with great care."
Holmes-Laski Letters, 1916–1935, ed. by Mark DeWolfe Howe (2 vols., Cambridge:
Harvard University Press, 1953), II, 998 (Nov. 20, 1927).

[73] C, p. 142.

the decaying capitalist system and the systematic use of force to extirpate all remnants of the power of the ruling class.

To this Marxist-Leninist theory of revolution and dictatorship Laski is completely opposed, at least during the 1920's. In 1925 he states the core of his answer to the Communist thesis: "Revolutions do not achieve the direct end at which they aim; and the weapons of which they are driven to make use destroy by their character the prospects they have in view." [74] Revolution is "probably incompatible with the maintenance of civilised life; for, if it is attempted on any large scale, its destructiveness will reduce the standard of living for vast populations to the level of the Indian ryot." [75] Even if a Communist revolution were successful, the resulting destruction, together with the hatred and bitterness engendered, would make impossible the emergence of the society of justice and fraternity that is supposed to be its goal. He maintains that the special conditions that made the Bolshevik Revolution successful in Russia are not likely to occur again in any modern state; Lenins and Trotskys are rare, while "few governments are as outrageous as that of Tsarist Russia or as confused and incompetent as that of Kerensky." [76] It is impossible for a secretly armed minority to seize power as long as the armed forces remain loyal to the government, and the Communists have no reason to hope that in other countries the army and navy will be as totally disorganized and as susceptible to revolutionary propaganda as they were in Russia in 1917. He notes that an unsuccessful revolution would lead to a dictatorship of the Right and to increased misery for the masses. The argument that ideal right must demonstrate by its might that it is right indeed, while it may justify a Communist revolution, "justifies also a Fascist revolution, at least to those who are convinced Fascists." [77] Remarking that "it is permissible to doubt whether the method of violence is ever the midwife of justice," [78] he resists the idea that dictatorship, even of the proletariat, means liberty or equality

---

[74] GP, p. 506.   [75] *Ibid.*, p. 540.   [76] C, p. 236.

[77] *Ibid.*, p. 173. See also his statement that, to the student of history, "a frank surrender to a deliberate philosophy of violence in which the battle is to be to the stronger without regard to the end they seek to serve, must, inevitably, sound like a betrayal of civilization itself." "The Value and Defects of the Marxist Philosophy," *Current History*, XXIX (Oct., 1928), 28.

[78] C, p. 181.

or justice; the experience of Russia reminds us that it "is in simple fact the exchange of one tyranny for another," [79] and that a dictatorship is incapable of voluntarily abdicating from power.

In his argument against the Communist thesis, Laski also asserts a proposition that elsewhere he seems to deny, namely, that under modern democratic government the wants of the people obtain a response that is more adequate than at any previous time. In 1927 he states that, in his opinion, few governments are prepared to risk the tremendous costs inherent in revolution if, by concessions to the masses, they can purchase its avoidance. He denies one of Marx's central theses—the law of the increasing misery of the proletariat—when he asserts that the condition of the working class has shown a marked improvement during the last century. In opposition to the Communists he argues that democracy has such notable successes to its credit that we are not entitled to act on the assumption that social justice is unattainable through the ordinary institutions of representative government "until we have made much further experiment than has so far been attempted"; [80] no one, therefore, "has a right to abandon the prospect of constitutional effort until he is forced by his opponents to change his ground." [81] He concludes: "The sceptical observer is unconvinced that any system has the future finally on its side; that it is entitled, from its certainties, to sacrifice all that has been acquired so painfully in the heritage of toleration and freedom, to the chance that its victory may one day compensate for a renunciation that, on its own admission, is bound to be grim and long." [82] In our age, when the weapons at the disposal of those who have recourse to violence are so catastrophic that social conflict is inevitably the

[79] "The Value and Defects of the Marxist Philosophy," *Current History,* XXIX (Oct., 1928), 28. See also his statement that "a regime which, like that of a proletarian dictatorship, is avowedly built on the use of hatred and fear and calculated relentlessness" cannot breed the habits of freedom which are essential if the communist society is ever to come into being. *Ibid.,* p. 27.

[80] C, p. 180.

[81] "Machiavelli and the Present Time," DO, p. 260. See also the comments that the "effort at constitutional transition . . . loses nothing by being attempted; and much may be lost by its willful and deliberate abandonment," "The Value and Defects of the Marxist Philosophy," *Current History,* XXIX (Oct., 1928), 28; and that in a period of universal suffrage it ought to be possible for socialists "to capture the seat of power at the polls, and throw upon the capitalist the onus of revolt." C, p. 172.

[82] C, p. 244.

parent of social disaster, "we must rather have faith in the power of reason to direct the human spirit to the prospects of concession and sacrifice. We must rather seek to persuade our masters that our equality is their freedom." [83]

As we have already seen, Laski's prophecy is that if the rulers of our society ignore the demands of the people for equality and fail to heed his warning that they must make great sacrifices if conflict is to be avoided, the masses will increasingly turn to the Communists for a violent solution of their problems. He argues that Communism's greatest strength lies in the fact that its indictment of capitalist society is so largely true. "To men whose environment is poisoned by insecurity, and for whom, in general, there is little hope of future benefit, the only wonder is that the promise has not proved more seductive." [84] The workers of every country see in Russia a state which, "with all its faults and weaknesses, seems to them to lie at the service of men like themselves. They recognise in the demands it makes, and the principles to which it gives allegiance, their own demands and principles." [85] To them the important facts about the Russian experiment are "that all must toil, that communal experiment is in the interest of the masses, that no one is preferred save in terms of principle." [86] The only way to counter the appeal of Communism is to prove by actions that its promises can be matched by the results obtainable by the methods of reason and cooperation.

By 1930 the paralyzing effects of the great depression were evident throughout the world. During the twenties Laski had noted that in periods of contraction the effects of capitalism upon the workers are very similar to what the Marxists maintain are the normal results of its operations—large-scale unemployment, wage cuts, and general misery, side by side with the existence of vast unused productive capacity and the elimination of many of the concessions made to the workers by employers and the government in more prosperous

[83] "A Plea for Equality," DO, p. 237.

[84] C, p. 240. See also his statement that Marxism is "the inevitable creed of men who suffer from economic oppression. It draws its nourishment from every refusal to act with justice and generosity. It is fed by the conflicts which, at every margin of civilization, haunt our lives with the instinct of coming disaster. National hatred, economic war, racial antagonism, religious conflict, to all who suffer the results of these, the message of Communism is real and it is telling." "The Value and Defects of the Marxist Philosophy," *Current History*, XXIX (Oct., 1928), 29.

[85] C, p. 242.   [86] *Ibid.*, p. 243.

periods. As the depression continued and deepened, Laski's hopes for a peaceful transition to the new social order faded; he saw anger and despair mounting among the workers, while the rich and powerful, bent on protecting their privileges at the expense of the poor, seemed less willing than ever to make the sacrifices that he regarded as essential if social peace were to be maintained. His earlier doubts about the possibility of achieving socialism by democratic and constitutional methods were sharpened, and, as we shall see,[87] he moved closer to the Communist position that violent revolution is inevitable. As early as December, 1930, he stated that the conditions that Lenin postulated as necessary for successful revolution might develop within a month in Germany and that, if a new war should break out in Europe, those conditions would be a real possibility, especially in the defeated countries.[88]

Although his pessimism became more pronounced in 1930 and 1931, his general commitment, up to 1932, is to the methods of rational discussion and peaceful change, and his basic outlook is that of an eighteenth-century rationalist. During the 1920's he repeatedly urges that the discovery of new knowledge and its wider diffusion through the processes of education are the only means to a satisfactory and peaceful solution of the complex problems that we face. "It is the conquest of knowledge that is the real source of our hopes, its conquest and its extension to the common man. *For the real root of conflict is ignorance. . . .* we can only make men citizens by training their minds to grasp the world about them. *When the masses can understand they will have the courage to act upon their understanding.*"[89] The difficulties of the modern state, which are mainly moral in character, have to be met "by the elevation of the popular standard of intelligence, and the reform of the economic system."[90] Repeatedly he urges that the discovery of knowledge, which is the only road to man's earthly salvation, is possible only if students are thoroughly trained in "the habit of skepticism." Like Mill, he believes that toleration of new ideas and of unorthodox behavior is "not merely desirable in itself, but also politically wise, because no other atmosphere of activity offers the assurance of peaceful adjustment";[91] and, like Mill, he is

[87] See below, chap. 9, section 2.
[88] See "Communism as a World Force," *International Affairs*, X (Jan., 1931), 29.
[89] GP, p. 240; italics mine.   [90] *Ibid.*, p. 317.   [91] LMS, p. 280.

convinced that persecution will never be able to achieve a final suppression of significant truth. His fundamental belief is that "truth can be established by reason alone; that departure from the way of reason as a method of securing conviction is an indication always of a desire to protect injustice." [92]

Laski's emphasis on the role of knowledge and reason in social affairs, his faith in the efficacy of methods of persuasion to accomplish necessary changes, his hostility to irrational dogmas of all sorts, his cosmopolitanism, and his critical attitude towards traditional institutions make him the heir of the *philosophes* of eighteenth-century France, who, as men and as thinkers, exerted so strong an attraction upon him.[93] He remarks that in the eighteenth century the great man of letters is "the spiritual leader of the nation"; [94] it is difficult to avoid the feeling that this is also his conception of his own role in modern society. Just as the *philosophes* had used the power of thought and persuasion to destroy the foundations of a social order that linked social and political rights to the accident of aristocratic birth, so Laski attempts to employ the weapons of learning and literary skill to discredit an institutional system which, it seems to him, makes political and social power a function of an irrational and unjust distribution of private property. Like the French thinkers, he is aware that he is separated from the masses by his superior capacities, but, like them, he believes that it is possible to raise the average citizen towards his own level of intelligence and political awareness; his own faith is that which he ascribes to the philosophers and the romantics, "a religion of service to one's fellowmen." [95] He maintains that the French intellectuals remained, down to 1789, definitely reformist in outlook; but the total failure of the monarchy and the aristocracy to heed their criticisms or to embark upon the reforms that they warned were essential led the people to turn from the *philosophes* to the men of action. Thus violence and terror destroyed the *ancien régime* which had refused to make concessions while they would have been acceptable. There is a striking parallel with Laski's analyses of the defects of capitalist society, his proposals for major reforms, and his warn-

[92] *Ibid.*, p. 288.
[93] See his essays on "The Age of Reason," "Diderot," and "The Socialist Tradition in the French Revolution," reprinted in SLP.
[94] "The Age of Reason," SLP, p. 19.
[95] "Diderot," SLP, p. 41.

ings of the inevitable outburst of violence if great concessions are not made.

He feels the closest kinship with Diderot, who for him summarizes the fundamental characteristics of the spirit of the eighteenth century —"its infinite curiosity, its passion for omniscience, something of its endless talent for the making of systems, its faith in the destiny of man, its desire to end the needless infliction of pain, its confidence in the power of science to conquer the realm of nature, its happy certitude in the ability of man to overcome the need for the supernatural." [96] This statement can be taken as—and perhaps was meant to be—a summary of the main elements in the personality of Laski as well as that of Diderot. He continues:

He tested the life about him to the full. He met everyone and examined everything. Save Rousseau, he never lost a friend. . . . He had the power to be interested in all that is a part of human experience . . . . when he died, in 1784, it could be truly said of him that he was at the centre of every effort in his age which sought the betterment of its quality; that, if he did not plan the battle, it could not have been so fruitfully won if he had been absent when the essential decisions were made.[97]

In the final paragraph of this extended portrait of Diderot, from which we can catch a glimpse of Laski's ideal image of himself, he tells us that Diderot

moved always amid the play of great ideas and he kept, without compulsion, the affection of his friends. Above all, he had the joy he accounted so high, of fighting consciously in what Heine called the "Liberation War of Humanity." What haunted him in life was the longing for that immortality which comes with the recognition by a later generation that one of the forerunners has served it well . . . . for Diderot that yearning has not been vain.[98]

[96] *Ibid.*, p. 48.   [97] *Ibid.*, p. 52.
[98] *Ibid.*, p. 65. I am indebted to Franz Neumann for calling my attention to the elements of self-portraiture in these comments by Laski about Diderot.

Part Three

1932-1939

7

The Nature of the State and Political Power

BEFORE DISCUSSING Laski's writings during this period, we must survey the events that marked the end of the Labor Government in 1931 and the conclusions that he drew from them. By 1931 the depression had become critical in England; the number of persons unemployed, which had been large even before 1929, increased steadily, and unemployment-insurance payments constituted a heavy drain on declining government revenues. The Prime Minister, MacDonald, and Snowden, the Chancellor of the Exchequer, decided that these payments must be reduced if the credits needed to maintain the pound and to keep Britain on the gold standard were to be forthcoming; this proposal was opposed by most of the members of the Labor Party in Parliament and in the country. The disagreement was the culmination of a process of estrangement between the Prime Minister and a few of his colleagues, on the one hand, and the majority of the members of his Ministry and his party, on the other.

The crisis came in August, 1931. After consultations with MacDonald, Baldwin, and Sir Herbert Samuel, King George V first accepted MacDonald's resignation and then called on him to form a new Government. MacDonald's new Ministry was made up of four of his Labor colleagues and representatives of the two Opposition groups. At once all but fourteen of the Labor members of the House of Commons went into opposition and chose Arthur Henderson as their new leader. According to Laski, MacDonald consulted neither his colleagues nor his party during all these maneuvers.[1] Almost immediately after the formation of the new Government, the King granted its request that Parliament be dissolved, and in October, 1931,

[1] But cf. the accounts given by Viscount Samuels in his *Memoirs*, by Viscount Snowden in *An Autobiography*, and by Sidney Webb in "What Happened in 1931: A Record," as cited in W. Ivor Jennings, *Cabinet Government* (2d ed., Cambridge: Cambridge University Press, 1951), pp. 40–42.

a general election was held. During the campaign the National Government called on the people to give it a mandate to save the nation and the pound. The Labor Party, deprived of its three most noted leaders, MacDonald, Snowden, and Thomas, and bewildered and embittered by the events of the preceding months, suffered an overwhelming defeat; it polled about six and a half million votes to fourteen and a half million for the various "National" parties. Every ex-Minister in the Labor Party except George Lansbury lost his seat; there were only fifty-six Labor members in the new House, opposing four hundred and seventy-one Conservatives and almost one hundred Liberals and MacDonald Laborites.[2]

Laski asserts that during the election campaign MacDonald, Snowden, and their new Conservative and Liberal colleagues warned the voters that a Labor victory would cause foreign investors to lose confidence in British financial stability and would therefore mean a "flight from the pound." In his view this argument was, in effect, a threat that the forces of capitalism would not permit Labor to carry out its program, even if it received a majority of the votes. It is, he says, "an announcement that finance-capital will not permit the ordinary assumptions of the constitution to work if these operate to its disadvantage. Socialistic measures, in a word, are not obtainable by constitutional means."[3] Before the election the new Government assumed powers to effect by order-in-council the economies it believed necessary, and within a month of its formation it abandoned the gold standard, the maintenance of which was presumably the reason for its creation. After the election the President of the Board of Trade was given the power to impose duties on all imports, up to one hundred per cent of their value, if their volume seemed to him to be abnormal. To Laski these measures mean that control over revenue and expenditure have passed from Parliament to the executive; they "are the formulae of an executive dictatorship which open up vistas it is indeed difficult to contemplate with equanimity. The conventions of

[2] See Keith Hutchison, *The Decline and Fall of British Capitalism* (New York: Charles Scribner's Sons, 1950), p. 210.

[3] "Some Implications of the Crisis," *Political Quarterly,* II (Oct.–Dec., 1931), 467; he adds that the implication of this position is "tantamount to an insistence that if socialists wish to secure a state built upon the principles of their faith, they can only do so by revolutionary means." *Ibid.,* p. 468.

the British Constitution have not, I think, been more violently outraged in our time." [4]

For Laski the events of 1931 raise serious questions about the conventions that underlie the operation of English government. He
argues that MacDonald's actions have seriously undermined the
principle of the collective responsibility of the Cabinet; during the
last months of the Labor Government, and particularly during the
August crisis, most of the members of the Cabinet had no real sense
of the Prime Minister's plans or intentions. He maintains that the
purpose of a resignation or a dissolution is to allow a Cabinet to seek
a new mandate from the voters, not to permit a Prime Minister to
appeal from his colleagues to his opponents. He asks if MacDonald
is entitled, in case he disagrees with his new colleagues, to force their
resignations and, having somehow formed another government, to
ask for another election. He is disturbed because Parliament was at
no point consulted about the change in government and is deeply
concerned about the role of the King in the formation of the National Government. MacDonald should have advised the King to send
for Baldwin or Arthur Henderson, instead of taking over as the
head of the new Government. "He was chosen by the King to carry on
the Government, borrowing the majority necessary for that purpose
from a Coalition of his opponents. . . . The new Cabinet, in fact,
was born of a Palace Revolution." [5] The appointment of MacDonald
as Prime Minister served to conceal from the voters the fact that the
new Government was in essence a Tory Government. He is now the
Tories' prisoner; inasmuch as he has virtually no party support of
his own, he holds office merely "as the King's favourite, a person,
and not a representative leader. And . . . once Mr. MacDonald
differs upon an important point from the Tories, we shall either have
an ordinary Tory Cabinet, or a manoeuvring for position in which
the real balance of power will turn upon the will of the King." [6]

In Laski's view the conventions of parliamentary government were
even further outraged by the announcement on January 22, 1932, that,

[4] *Ibid.*, pp. 468–69.

[5] *The Crisis and the Constitution: 1931 and After*, Day to Day Pamphlet, No. 9
(London: L. and V. Woolf and The Fabian Society, 1932), hereinafter cited as CAC,
p. 34.

[6] *Ibid.*, p. 36.

because of the inability of the members of the Cabinet to agree on fiscal policy, Lord Snowden, Sir Herbert Samuel, Sir Donald Mac-Lean, and Sir Archibald Sinclair were to be allowed to speak and vote in the House in opposition to Cabinet dec'sions. He notes that this decision implies a free vote in the House on every question of financial policy, since "the agreement to differ" in the Cabinet must be extended to members of the groups in Parliament. Such practices mean the death of collective responsibility and of the system of party government founded thereon. He concludes that "the National Government is, effectively, a Tory Government in which certain non-Tory statesmen are permitted to remain on the understanding that, despite their dissent, Tory measures will go into effective operation. A position more likely to destroy the meaning of principle in politics it would be difficult to find." [7]

Laski insists that the drastic realignment of parties in Britain brought about by the 1931 crisis is even more significant than these constitutional changes. In contrast to the postwar situation of three parties and occasional minority governments, there are now two completely antithetic groups, the Coalition and the Labor Opposition. Since 1918 there has been a gradual consolidation of the forces of capitalism in response to increased taxation of the wealthy to pay for the program of social welfare, as well as to growing demands for socialization of basic industries. This consolidation is "the real meaning of the post-war decline of the Liberal Party. Its historic mission ended when the margins of concession which capitalism could hope to make began to be reached." [8] When the prospect of a majority Labor Government became a real threat, the Liberals and Conservatives joined together to prevent any attack on the system of private property. On the other hand, the postwar years have witnessed a gradual movement to the left by the Labor Party. The experience of the two minority governments, especially that of 1929 to 1931, has convinced Laborites "not of the necessity of making terms with capitalism, but of the impossibility of patching it up." [9] "The crisis of 1931 has at last awakened the Labour Party to realise that the purpose of Socialists is Socialism . . . and that disaster is the inevitable consequence of a policy of quarter-measures." [10] In essence, therefore,

[7] *Ibid.*, p. 64.   [8] *Ibid.*, p. 40.   [9] *Ibid.*, p. 42.
[10] *The Labour Party and the Constitution*, Socialist Programme Series, No. 2 (Lon-

there are now only two parties in England, and between the Conservative-Liberal defense of capitalism and the Labor Party's commitment to socialism there can be no compromise. "The difference between the National Government and the Labour Opposition to-day is an irreconcilable difference of fundamental political philosophy." [11]

Laski defines parties as "predominantly organizations which seek to determine the economic constitution of the state." [12] The party, that is, is "a mechanism to control public opinion about property in the particular way its members deem desirable." [13] The obvious objection to this analysis of the nature of democratic parties is based on the fact that Conservatives and Liberals, or Republicans and Democrats in the United States, have not held opposing views of the basis of the economic system. Laski admits the facts, but draws from them the singular conclusion that "since 1689, we have had, for all effective purposes, a single party in control of the state." [14] Only since the rise of the Labor Party have there existed two parties in the sense of organizations that differ about the economic foundations of society. His definition of the nature and function of political parties is, therefore, valid only for the contemporary situation, if, indeed, it is applicable at all, and cannot be used to explain the "normal" operations of the party system. He ignores the sharp differences between Liberals and Conservatives before the First World War, which, in the conflict over the 1909 Budget and the powers of the House of Lords, led to a constitutional crisis far more serious than any question that was to arise during the period of Labor rule from 1945 to 1951. He also asserts that the same forces that led Liberals and Conservatives to join together in the defense of capitalism are "compelling the consolidation of Republican and Democrat in the United States as a party of property seeking to resist the invasion of its hitherto uncontrolled empire." [15] He does not identify the group or party that is carrying on the invasion. Actually, the restrictions imposed on cap-

---

don: The Socialist League, 1933), hereinafter cited as LPC, p. 1. See also the statement that "the doctrines in battle together are mutual and exclusive opposites between which there is no prospect of final adjustment." *Democracy in Crisis* (Chapel Hill: University of North Carolina Press, 1933), hereinafter cited as DC, p. 164.

[11] CAC, p. 50.

[12] *Parliamentary Government in England* (New York: The Viking Press, 1938), hereinafter cited as PGE, p. 61; all references are to the second printing of 1947.

[13] *Ibid.*, p. 77.　　　　[14] *Ibid.*, p. 72.　　　　[15] *Ibid.*, p. 75.

italist freedom during the 1930's were carried through by the Democratic Party. In 1954, the realignment of American parties predicted by some writers, which would involve a union of conservative Southern Democrats with Republicans, has not yet occurred. Far less likely is the outcome predicted by Laski—the consolidation of the two major parties to meet the threat of a mass socialist movement.

Laski frequently bases his argument upon the assumption that the Labor Party is a true socialist party; he ignores the fact that its political leaders, Attlee and Morrison, and the influential trade-union leaders are not doctrinaire socialists. He says, for example, that the evolution to socialism cannot be "so gradual as slowly to accustom the owners of economic power to the transformation. *The announced programme of the Labour Party itself excludes that possibility. It is committed by its terms to a direct parliamentary attack upon the central citadel of capitalism.*" [16] But the 1937 program of the Party, which advocates such reforms as increases in old-age pensions and unemployment insurance, the abolition of the means test, and the nationalization of such essential services as transport, public utilities, and coal mining, can hardly be described as a direct attack on capitalism's central citadel. At other moments, however, Laski, reversing his position, berates the Labor Party and its leaders because they still believe that the state is a neutral factor in society, available to the party that wins a majority in Commons, rather than the instrument of the owning class. He says: "The whole mind of the party was so concentrated on the parliamentary process as to produce the impression that it really believed that political democracy operated in a vacuum independently of the economic framework within which it was contained." [17] Mr. Attlee is attacked because he is convinced that Labor's opponents will permit it to govern if it wins a majority,[18] while the Party leaders are criticized for rejecting unity with the Communists, penalizing militant trade unionists, and using "all the influence at the disposal of the party machine to damp down discussion of the strategy of power." [19] At times, then, Laski is well aware that the Labor Party is a left-wing democratic party, pledged to extend social reforms and to undertake the socialization of certain basic industries, and that its program is not so alien to British traditions nor so com-

---

[16] *Ibid.,* p. 69; italics mine.   [17] *Ibid.,* p. 152.
[18] See *ibid.,* p. 154.   [19] *Ibid.,* p. 158.

pletely opposite to the principles of the Conservatives that a Labor victory will mean the death of the system of parliamentary government. More frequently, however, viewing the Labor Party as Laski writ large, he tends to identify his own Marxist beliefs with the views of the Party and of the working class. On the basis of this identification, he assumes that the struggle between Conservative and Labor parties is a clash between two diametrically opposite forces, "capitalism" and "socialism," that will inevitably lead to violence.

He maintains that the abyss which now separates the basic principles of the two parties calls into serious question the viability of the whole system of British democratic government; the successful operation of that system has depended, as Balfour noted, on agreement about fundamental issues between the parties that have alternately governed the country. He warns:

But the day has passed when political parties were united about the national way of life; they differ today not over the incidentals, but the foundations, of political principle. Our constitution is to be tested by stresses and strains more profound than any to which it has been subjected since the seventeenth century. It is necessary to adapt it to purposes alien from the ends it has hitherto served. The task is not an easy one, since it seeks to alter the historic contours of the State.[20]

The normal alternation of Government and Opposition in the seats of power, possible because both parties were confident that neither would make any major change in national habits or institutions, is no longer practicable. The Conservatives and their allies have shown that they will resort to any means, no matter how outrageous to the accepted conventions of the constitution, to prevent Labor from attaining power or from carrying out its program if it does win a majority; one section of the community "has set definite limits to the area in which the will of the other (which may at any moment become a parliamentary majority) may operate."[21]

Crucial to this argument is Laski's conviction that the defenders of capitalism not only sabotaged the Labor Government of 1931 but will repeat this sabotage in the event of a future Labor victory at the

[20] LPC, p. 28. Also, "For the first time in British history since the Puritan Rebellion parties confronted one another with respective ways of life which looked to wholly antithetic ends." DC, pp. 39–40.

[21] "Some Implications of the Crisis," *Political Quarterly,* II (Oct.–Dec., 1931), 469.

polls. The grounds for this belief are difficult to discover. Laski is certain that in 1931 the Labor Government suffered "a stab in the back,"
but he seems unsure of the assassin's identity. Sometimes MacDonald
and Snowden are the villains; at other times he argues that "the flight
from the pound" was engineered by "the capitalist interests of Great
Britain." Unable to persuade the Labor Government to embark upon
the reduction of unemployment pay, they "deliberately painted a
black picture of Great Britain's approaching bankruptcy in order
to injure the nation's credit abroad." [22]

In support of his "sabotage" theory, Laski relies heavily on statements supposedly made by the Conservatives and MacDonald and
Snowden during the 1931 campaign, warning that a financial crisis
would be inevitable if a Labor Government were returned to power.
Partisan speeches made during a campaign are hardly reliable evidence of changes in fundamental political attitudes. Americans are
accustomed to hear before every election solemn warnings by spokes-
men of each party that a victory by their opponents will be followed
by every catastrophe that can be imagined and by some horrors that
cannot even be named. Certainly no respectable Republican orator
since 1932 has failed to assure his listeners that another Democratic
victory would mean financial collapse, the end of republican institutions, dictatorship, and grave peril to the American way of life. No
serious commentator on American politics has relied on these prophecies to prove the existence of an impassable gulf between the two
parties or to assert that the Republicans would resort to sabotage if
the Democrats were re-elected. The disinterested observer finds in
the campaign oratory of British politicians no real basis for the certainty with which Laski concludes that if the voters were to give
Labor a mandate to create a Socialist regime, "the financial interests,
and their political representatives the Tory Party, would take action
against it which, *mutatis mutandis,* would be equivalent to the action
taken by Lord Carson and his friends against the Home Rule Bill in
1914." [23] Incidentally, one cannot but be struck by the complete reversal, in a period of ten years, in Laski's attitude towards the problem
of resistance to the state's will. In the early 1920's he repeatedly defended the Ulster rebellion and similar efforts to resist the sovereign

[22] CAC, p. 47.   [23] *Ibid.,* p. 49.

state, which supported his thesis that no government can force its will on a minority determined to defend its own view of right. Now the same examples are cited with complete disapproval to prove that the Tories will forcibly resist Labor's efforts to govern.

The experiences of the New Deal in the United States and of the Labor Government in England from 1945 to 1951 indicate that complaints by some businessmen about "insane" fiscal and economic policies do not necessarily mean that they will, by sabotaging governmental regulations, endeavor to bring about the downfall of the regime by extraconstitutional means. Any democratic government that enjoys a large measure of popular support can, it seems, employ its wide powers over currency, taxation, and spending to control industry and finance with little fear of a revolution from the Right, particularly in a period of economic depression when the popular attitude towards business leaders tends to be severely critical and when a large majority of the citizens look to the government for effective action to promote recovery. However, the movement of political events throughout the world after 1932, as Laski interpreted it, served merely to strengthen his belief that we had entered a period in which the capitalist class would destroy democracy in their effort to maintain their power and privileges. The triumph of Nazism in Germany, President Roosevelt's difficulties with the Supreme Court, the failure of the Blum Popular Front regime in France, the Spanish civil war, these and other developments of the 1930's were simply additional examples of his thesis that the logic of capitalism was now in contradiction to the logic of democracy. Differences were ignored and qualifications omitted, and each day the picture became simpler and clearer to Laski. Political democracy leads to demands for major economic reforms and, finally, to the movement towards socialism; capitalism, unwilling to surrender its privileges, moves to smash the instruments of democracy. The only political possibilities are, therefore, the opposite alternatives of Fascism and revolutionary socialism.

After this brief historical survey, we must examine some of Laski's general statements about the nature of the state during the 1930's. First, we note that he explicitly rejects the doctrine of pluralism; he now argues that the sovereignty of the state, the target of his early attacks, is essential if the state is to fulfill its function, the maintenance of a given system of class relations. Pluralism's fundamental weakness was that it

did not sufficiently realise the nature of the state as an expression of class-relations. It did not sufficiently emphasise the fact that it was bound to claim an indivisible and irresponsible sovereignty because there was no other way in which it could define and control the legal postulates of society. It was through their definition and control that the purposes of any given system of class-relations was [*sic*] realised. If the state ceased to be sovereign, it ceased to be in a position to give effect to those purposes.[24]

He acknowledges that for him "the pluralist attitude to the state and law was a stage on the road to an acceptance of the Marxian attitude to them." [25] The state is "simply the executive instrument of the class in society which owns the means of production"; [26] if, therefore, we seek, as the pluralist does, to limit the power of the state, we must first destroy the class structure of society. Only with the attainment of the classless society will the need for the state's sovereignty and coercive power disappear. Only when conflicts based upon property have been eliminated can we conceive of "a social organisation in which the truly federal nature of society receives institutional expression. And in such a social organisation, authority can be pluralistic both in form and expression." [27] In good Marxist fashion, Laski does not completely abandon his earlier goals; he insists, however, that their achievement must be postponed until a prior objective, the classless society, has been attained. He says that the reason for his shift from pluralism to Marxism is that only by means of the latter theory can he "explain phenomena like the state as it appears in Fascist countries. That state seeks the total absorption of the individual within the framework of its coercive apparatus precisely because it is there, nakedly and without shame, what the state, covertly and apologetically is, in capitalist democracies like Great Britain or the United States." [28]

[24] "The Crisis in the Theory of the State," in Vol. II of *Law: A Century of Progress, 1835–1935.* Published by the New York University School of Law (New York: New York University Press, 1937), hereinafter cited as CTS; reprinted as introductory chapter to the 4th edition of *A Grammar of Politics*, 1938, pp. xi–xii.

[25] *Ibid.*, p. xii.   [26] *Ibid.*, p. xiii.   [27] *Ibid.*, p. xii.
[28] *Ibid.*, pp. xii–xiii.

His Marxist analysis of the state is formulated as early as 1933: "each economic regime gives birth to a political order which represents the interests of those who dominate the regime, who possess in it the essential instruments of economic power." [29] He now refers to democracy as "capitalist democracy," since it is the political system that has been created and maintained to meet the needs of those who own the means of production in capitalist society. He totally reverses his original pluralist position by defining the state as a national society "which is integrated by possessing a coercive authority legally supreme over any individual or group which is part of the society." [30] This supreme coercive power is called sovereignty: "it is by the possession of sovereignty that the state is distinguished from all other forms of human association." [31] The essence of any state, which appears clearly at every moment of crisis, is "the fact that its authority depends upon the power to coerce the opponents of the government, to break their wills, to compel them to submission. . . . Normally, that is to say, the basis of state-sovereignty is the contingent power to use the armed forces of the state to compel obedience to its will." [32]

Laski now also denies the validity of the traditional views of the nature and purpose of the state, which he adopted during the 1920's as he abandoned his original antistatism; he rejects, that is, the theory that the state stands above groups and classes and attempts to promote the general interest; he denies that it seeks to realize the rights that are the necessary conditions of the development of its citizens; and he denies that the purpose for which it maintains law and order is the maximum satisfaction of demand.[33] All these propositions describe the ideal state of the philosophers; they refer only to the state in theory, while Laski is concerned only with what the state is in practice. All past and present theories of the state are merely ideologies, whose function is to justify the use of power by masking the real nature of the state. In opposition to them he demands a realistic analysis of the activities of actual governments. On the other hand, his own theory of the state is not an ideology; based on the facts and

---

[29] DC, p. 50.

[30] *The State in Theory and Practice* (New York: The Viking Press, 1935), hereinafter cited as STP, p. 8.

[31] *Ibid.*, p. 9. He adds that "neither unwisdom nor injustice makes any difference to the formal legal right of the state to exact and enforce obedience to its orders." *Ibid.*, p. 10.

[32] *Ibid.*, p. 14.   [33] See *ibid.*, p. 179.

on the only true philosophy of history, the theory of historical materialism, it enables us to predict and explain actual political events and movements.

He insists that every society "must seek to sustain some stable relations of production in order to continue as a society. It has to put behind those relations the force of law. It needs, that is, a coercive instrument to secure the continuance of those relations simply because, otherwise, it will not continue to earn its living." [34] The state's "primary function is to ensure the peaceful process of production in society. To do so it protects the system of productive relations which that process necessitates." [35] The men who constitute the government have the right to exercise the state's sovereignty and, thereby, to determine how the fruits of the productive process are to be distributed. Since every society contains groups whose relation to the process of production is fundamentally different, conflicts are inevitable both between the groups and "between the ideas each group puts forward as the expression of its idea of good, which is born of the experience it infers from its position." [36] The members of the dominant group, which controls the machinery of the state, may believe that they are attempting to promote the good of the whole society, the greatest possible satisfaction of wants, but their conception of social good reflects the values they have acquired from their experience, and that experience is a function of their relation to the productive process. Indeed, for all of us, it holds true that our conception of social good is "born, in predominant part, of our place in the scheme of social relationships." [37]

At certain periods, rapid and continued changes in the methods of production make it impossible for the society to exploit fully the new productive potentialities as long as the old system of property relations obtains. Some group in the society then seeks to liberate the potentialities it sees in the productive process by changing those relations; if, however, it wishes to establish new property relations, it "must seek to capture the state in order to use the coercive power of the community to re-define them." [38] Consequently, the basic struggles in any society are "always struggles between economic classes to secure control of the sovereign power." [39] In these class struggles the

[34] *Ibid.*, pp. 92–93.   [35] *Ibid.*, p. 93.   [36] *Ibid.*, pp. 94–95.
[37] *Ibid.*, p. 97.   [38] *Ibid.*, p. 98.   [39] *Ibid.*, p. 99.

state is not a neutral agency, standing "over and above the conflicting groups, judging impartially between them. By its very nature, it is simply coercive power used to protect the system of rights and duties of one process of economic relationships from invasion by another class which seeks to change them in the interests of another process." [40] Particularly when the system of property relations is threatened, the state must move "to protect the vested interests involved in the class-relations of the particular society. . . . Its government must act as the executive committee of the class which dominates, economically, the system of production by which the society lives." [41] The proof of this thesis is that whenever, in any state, the continuity of essential services is threatened, as it was, for example, by the general strike in San Francisco in July, 1934, "the government will intervene, with all the coercive power at its disposal, to assure the maintenance of that continuity." [42] The claim that the state intervenes in such situations in order to protect the community and its overriding needs is only a pretext to conceal the state's real goal, which is to act as the agent of the capitalist class.

Laski maintains that the main features of the legal system in a capitalist democracy are determined by the needs and wants of the ruling class; law is a response to effective demand and only the economically powerful can make their demands effective. In a capitalist society the law's primary function is to put the state's final coercive power behind the fundamental premises of the regime of private property, while in a socialist state such as the Soviet Union the main purpose of the law is "the protection of those social relationships which develop in a community where the instruments of production are publicly owned." [43] On the basis of his analysis of the English law of sedition and the attitude of the courts in cases involving trade unions and of the role of the United States Supreme Court as the guardian of the principles of *laissez-faire* in the half-century after 1880, Laski rejects both the formalist and the realist views of the function of the judiciary.[44] The courts, as a part of the coercive machinery of the

---

[40] *Ibid.*, p. 100.   [41] *Ibid.*, p. 115.   [42] *Ibid.*, p. 117.

[43] "Law and Justice in Soviet Russia," 1935, reprinted in DBG, p. 61. The entire essay is a remarkable demonstration of Laski's enthusiasm for Soviet institutions at this time and of his completely uncritical acceptance of the virtues of the Russian legal and penal systems.

[44] He argues: "The formalist has forgotten the degree to which the postulates of

state, must protect as fully as possible the interests of those who own the means of production. He argues that in a capitalist society "the main ethos of the laws . . . will be the protection of such relations as ensure the successful making of profit by the class which owns." [45] He does not explain how we can fit into this pattern of explanation such crucial examples of modern legislation as minimum-wage laws or progressive personal and corporate income-tax laws. His discussion of the judiciary, particularly in the United States, as the defender of *laissez-faire* was beginning to be outmoded when it was written, and it became increasingly less accurate as time passed. It was in 1936 and 1937, during the period of what Laski calls the final collapse of capitalism, that American judges, especially those on the Supreme Court, reversed their earlier tendencies to shape the law in the interests of the business community.

For Laski, the differences between the judicial systems of capitalist democracies and those of Fascist dictatorships are distinctions of degree rather than of kind, of methods rather than fundamental objectives; in both cases, the courts must protect the basic postulates of capitalism.

The difference between a democratic State and a dictatorial is the difference between the ability in the one to use, in a large degree, the forms of free consent to the State-purpose, and the need, in the other, to discipline the citizen-body to this end. . . . But the Anglo-American system uses the methods of free consent, so far as the judicial function is concerned, because it knows that, *a priori,* there is small likelihood of any refusal to accept the State-purpose. . . . The German method achieves by brute force a coincidence of view that in Great Britain and America is accomplished by deep-rooted traditions that the judiciary has rarely sought fundamentally to challenge.[46]

He notes that in the United States the legislative and executive branches have used various methods to force the Supreme Court to

---

judicial logic are provided for the judge by the State; they [*sic*] have over-emphasized the independence of the Courts and made its [*sic*] law a body of principles judicially determined which live apart from the sources which give its character to the living law. The realists have . . . in their turn, failed sufficiently to notice that, as an instrument of the State-power, the range within which he [the judge] is in fact free to undertake this selection [of a *ratio decidendi*] is more narrow than their view makes it desirable for them to admit." "The Judicial Function," DBG, p. 107.

[45] *Ibid.,* p. 109.   [46] *Ibid.,* p. 129.

change its views: judges have been impeached; [47] Congress has altered the Court's jurisdiction and the number of the judges; amendments have overriden Court decisions; and when vacancies have been filled, the political departments of the government have been careful to appoint men of "sound" views. These facts prove that "the judicial will must subordinate itself to the purpose the State declares, so long as the latter, through its legislative branch, persists in this purpose." [48] On the whole, this conclusion seems to be borne out by the American experience; in the long run the Court has bowed to the will of Congress and the President, although it has often been able to delay for a number of years action desired by a majority. The facts cited by Laski demonstrate, however, the inadequacy of his major thesis. If the courts are regarded merely as a part of the state's apparatus of coercion, which exists for the sole purpose of defending the interests of the ruling class, how are we to explain the bitter and protracted struggles between the judiciary and the President and Congress that have occurred from the days of Jefferson and Marshall to the period of the New Deal?

And what is the reason for the conflicts, to which he repeatedly refers, between English judges, whose training in the common law has given them a profound bias in favor of *laissez-faire,* and the men responsible for the legislation and administration of the modern state? [49] When he is attacking the judges and warning them that the "ignorance of, and hostility to, modern social reform of the contemporary Bench may easily make it necessary to build a system of administrative tribunals to prevent it from being wrecked by judges who deny the existence of the defects it seeks to remedy and minimize the power of the efforts made to deal with them," [50] he is compelled to admit that modern legislation and administration are not shaped, as is the common law, by the demands of a business civilization. He thereby denies the central principle of the simple and monolithic Marxist analysis of the state which he has adopted.

Laski maintains that the emergence of Fascism conclusively demonstrates the validity of the Marxist theory of the nature of the state

[47] In fact, however, since the unsuccessful attempt to impeach Justice Samuel Chase in 1804–5, impeachment proceedings have not been brought against any member of the Supreme Court of the United States.

[48] "The Judicial Function," DBG, p. 130.

[49] See PGE, pp. 297–302 and 305–12.   [50] *Ibid.,* p. 312.

and its legal system. He insists that the marriage of capitalism and democracy is a phenomenon peculiar to the period of capitalist expansion. When capitalism enters its phase of contraction, as it now has, "the price of the concessions expected by democracy then appears too high. The assumptions of capitalism then contradict the implications of democracy." [51] Since the continuance of democracy means the transformation of capitalism into socialism, Fascism appears on the scene to rescue capitalism. He states: "By the abrogation of democracy, in one form or another, it has entrusted unlimited political power to those who own and control the means of production." [52] Fascism has crushed opposition parties, trade unions, freedom of opinion, and free elections; it has brought churches, press, radio, cinema, and publications under its control; and it has converted the bureaucracy and the judiciary into its instruments. It has thus demonstrated that it is essentially "the destruction of liberal ideas and institutions in the interest of those who own the instruments of economic power." [53]

As long as its armed forces remain reliable, the Fascist regime can crush all internal discontent. It therefore "offers the capitalist a position in which the satisfaction of the profit-making motive is the first consideration of state-policy. The problems of capitalist democracy are solved by the simple process of eliminating the democratic element in that union." [54] Fascism leaves undisturbed the private ownership of the means of production, which is the foundation of capitalism. "There is a change in the form of the state, a substitution of naked dictatorship for parliamentary democracy, but that is all." [55] It destroys "the institutions of working-class democracy"—the trade unions, socialist parties, and the cooperative movement—which threaten the basis of capitalist power. By the resort to Fascism capi-

---

[51] STP, p. 111.   [52] *Ibid.,* p. 112.

[53] *The Rise of European Liberalism* (London: George Allen and Unwin, Ltd., 1936), hereinafter cited as REL, p. 247; all references are to the second impression of 1947. The American edition (New York: Harper and Bros., 1936) has the title *The Rise of Liberalism.*

[54] STP, p. 113.

[55] *Ibid.,* p. 172. See also the statement: "The truth is that the essence of any state is necessarily supreme coercive power which lies at the service of those who own the instruments of production in a given society. At bottom, the fact that this society is politically democratic does not make any differences to the consequences of this principle." "What Is Vital in Democracy?," *Survey Graphic,* XXIV (April, 1935), 180.

talism "was able to maintain the title of the capitalist to profit without the need to satisfy the demands of an electorate for a continually advancing standard of life. When, that is to say, the contradiction between the economic oligarchy of capitalism and its democratic political foundation was revealed, where the adventure was possible, the contradiction was resolved by suppressing the democratic foundation." [56] Laski dismisses the objection that there has been Fascist interference with "freedom of enterprise" with the flat statement that "the character of that interference, both in Italy and Germany has been interference of capitalists in the interests of capitalist recovery." [57]

Laski makes no changes in his theory of Fascism as he watches Nazism operating in Germany during the late 1930's. Fascism is simply the naked form of capitalist domination of the state, while democracy is a more veiled form of class rule. "Fascist dictatorship," he says, "enables the uneasy marriage between capitalism and democracy to be dissolved by the simple expedient of forcing the masses, by terror, to renounce their claim to increased material welfare. It is vital to the understanding of this process to recognise that, under it, the class-relations typical of capitalism remain unchanged." [58] In 1938 he writes: "The Fascism of Western Europe is the necessary protective armament of an economic system that can produce only upon a restricted scale and which is unable to solve the problems of distribution." [59] Since Fascism maintains the capitalist contradiction between the forces of production and the relations of production, it is unable to transform its rule of terror into rule by consent by offering the masses improvement of their material circumstances. In fact, in its attempt to maintain the profits of the capitalist class, it must resort to an aggressive foreign policy and to imperialist ventures so that popular attention will be diverted from domestic difficulties. The emergence of Fascism "offers no more to the owners of economic power than a temporary and hazardous breathing-space before they encounter a new challenge. . . . It is, by its nature, an attempt only to arrest in the interest of privilege the decay of that

[56] STP, p. 177.   [57] *Ibid.*, p. 132.   [58] CTS, p. xv.
[59] "The Prospects of Peace in Europe," in Benjamin S. Rowntree, *et al.*, *Wharton Assembly: Addresses, 1938* (Philadelphia: University of Pennsylvania Press, 1938), p. 49.

capitalist enterprise which has now passed into its phase of final contraction." [60] At every point we see that Fascism is for Laski the
crucial phenomenon that reveals the true nature of the state; it
demonstrates clearly that the state's "coercive power must be used
to protect the stability of a given system of class-relations; it cannot be
used to alter that given system." [61] The obvious corollary of this
conclusion is, as we shall see, the belief in "the inevitability of revolution as the midwife of social change." [62]

It is difficult to conceive of an explanation of Fascism that would
be more inadequate or more disastrous in its implications than Laski's
view that it is "the institutional technique of capitalism in its phase
of contraction." [63] His analysis is erroneous because he does not see
that Fascism is an essentially new phenomenon of the twentieth
century and not merely the last stage of "bourgeois" rule; it is a
basically irrational mass movement, in which the humanistic values
of Western civilization are rejected. The Leader and the Party destroy
the independence of all the institutions and organizations of the free
society—churches as well as trade unions, chambers of commerce and
business associations as well as socialist and labor groups, the freedom
of the businessman as well as the right of the worker to organize and
to strike.

As a means of analyzing the factors in the rise of Fascism, the mid-
nineteenth-century apparatus of a rationalistic economic determinism,
which Laski borrows from Marxism, is altogether inappropriate.
Although we still have no really adequate account of the genesis and
nature of Fascism, it is obvious that it is a complex phenomenon
having its roots in certain general characteristics of modern society:
the bureaucratic and hierarchical structure of the large units of social,
economic, and political life; the frustrations imposed upon the worker
by the monotonous routine and the incredibly detailed division of
labor of the industrial process; the growth of a large new middle
class of salaried workers who are uprooted from traditional sur-
roundings and highly anxious about their precarious social and economic position; the decline of the old middle class of independent

[60] CTS, p. xxv.   [61] STP, p. 115.
[62] *Ibid.*, p. 119; also, see below, chap. 9, section 2.
[63] REL, p. 248.

merchants and craftsmen; the great influence of standardized mass media of communication and propaganda; and the serious psychological and social strains incident to modern total war and to its consequences—inflation, depression, family disorganization, and social and moral disintegration. If we take Germany as the *locus classicus* of Fascism, we must add to these general characteristics of modern society various historical factors peculiar to that nation which played a part in the growth of the Nazi movement—the late achievement of national unity, the failure of the 1848 liberal revolution, the persistence of the political power of the large landowners and the military class, the relatively late and extremely rapid process of industrialization, the basic Lutheran tradition of "inner morality" and political quietism, the superficial socialism of the workers which concealed their basic conservatism, and the split in the labor movement between socialist and Communist groups.

The consequences that followed from the acceptance of Laski's analysis of Fascism were nothing short of disastrous; those who were influenced by him during the 1930's were led to adopt attitudes and to pursue courses of action that constituted one of the factors in the failure to check Nazism before 1939. The mistaken conception that Fascism was simply the final stage of a declining capitalism, together with the belief that capitalist democracy and Fascism were basically similar since both were forms of capitalist exploitation of the masses, not only weakened the will to resist Fascism among large sections of the working classes in the Western democracies, but drove a wedge between conservatives and radicals in each country at precisely the moment when they should have joined together to defend the free society against the all-out attack of Nazism. The Laski-Marxist onslaught against "capitalist democracy" was a pure gift to the Nazi propagandists who were endeavoring to exploit group differences within the democracies and, in particular, to convince the workers that their real enemies were the "plutocrats" who dominated English and French society. It is understandable that many workers, when faced with the choice between Fascism as the overt rule of the privileged class and "capitalist democracy" as a more subtle form of capitalist domination, lapsed into the mood of cynical apathy or "revolutionary defeatism," so evident in France in 1939. The attacks

on the "bourgeois" governments of England and France and the
insistence that the interests of the rulers and those of the masses
were completely contradictory constituted serious obstacles to the
effective rearmament that was imperative if the threat of Fascist aggression was to be met. Although Laski, like many other Left-wing
leaders, was clearly anti-Fascist, he continued, until 1937 at least, to
oppose any serious effort to rearm.[64] Finally, by reducing the alternatives of political action to two polar opposites, Fascism and revolutionary socialism, Laski and his followers frightened off conservative and liberal groups and so lessened the chances for a strong anti-
Fascist coalition within each of the democracies.

Laski's failure to understand the real nature of Fascism is only
one of the consequences of his acceptance of a simple Marxist analysis of the state. We cannot here undertake a thorough critical survey of Marxist-Leninist political theory;[65] we can only point out
a few of its major weaknesses. First, the theory rests on a view of the
class structure of capitalist society which, however relevant it may
have been in 1850, is descriptively inaccurate and analytically useless
when applied in studies of the political sociology of a contemporary
democratic society. The theory divides society into two totally antagonistic social and economic classes, the bourgeoisie and the proletariat; in so far as remnants of other classes exist, they have no real
importance in the class struggle that underlies conflicts for political
power, and, by the inexorable laws of capitalist development, intermediate classes are bound to sink down into the proletariat. The
theory, which divides capitalists and workers on the basis of the
criterion of ownership of the means of production, predicts that, because of the concentration of capital, the number of capitalists will
constantly decrease. This picture of a bipolarized society has little
relevance to the class structure of contemporary Britain, France, or
the United States; ownership of the means of production is not confined to a small capitalist class, and ownership and effective eco-

[64] See his support of Cripps's opposition to rearmament by the National Government in "Stafford Cripps, Socialist Leader," *The Nation,* CXLIV (Jan. 23, 1937),
92–93.

[65] There is no single work which concentrates its critical attention on the Marxist
theory of the state that is comparable to the classic criticisms of Marxist economic
theory. But see the recent volume by John Plamenatz, *German Marxism and
Russian Communism* (London: Longmans, Green and Co., 1954).

nomic control are to a large extent divorced.[66] The proliferation of
bureaucratic structures in private and public enterprise, together
with the great increase in the number of necessary technical personnel have meant the growth of a large stratum of white-collar
and technical workers, referred to as the "new middle class." This
group, which numerically more than compensates for the decline
of the old middle class, has nowhere demonstrated an identity of
interest and of political outlook with the "proletariat." Finally, the
role of the farm bloc in American politics, the political strength of
the French peasant proprietors, and the solicitude displayed by both
parties in England for the rural vote demonstrate that independent
farmers are still a politically powerful group, whose interests are not
the same as those of the factory worker or the salaried employee.

The Marxist prediction of the increasing misery of an ever larger
proletariat has failed even more dismally. Because of the great increases in industrial productivity since 1850, the power of trade
unions, and the protective and welfare legislation of the modern
state, the material status of the industrial worker has, as even Laski
admits, shown significant improvement during the past century. This
ameliorative trend has been accompanied by a general decline of
revolutionary sentiment; the average worker, particularly in the
United States, feels that he has an important stake in the continuance
of the present economic and political system. Economically as well as
politically, the working class is by no means a homogeneous group;
the division between organized and unorganized workers, members
of craft and of industrial unions, workers in production and workers
in distribution, and workers in domestic and in export industries, as
well as splits along sectional, racial, religious, and national lines, make
it impossible to speak of the "working-class" attitude towards many
important political issues.

The moment this dichotomous analysis of the class structure is
discarded, the entire Marxist theory of the state as the instrument
by which the ruling class represses and exploits the proletariat collapses. In the complex, multi-group democratic state a government
can rely on the general support of only a small group of party regu-

[66] A Brookings Institution study entitled "Share Ownership in the United States,"
reported in the New York *Times,* July 1, 1952, p. 1, indicates that about 6,500,000
individuals in the United States own publicly held stocks.

lars; since other groups of voters outside this circle are less firmly attached to the party in power, changes in their attitudes must be carefully noted; finally, on the outer fringes are the voters least committed to support of the government's program and most likely to swing over to the opposition party at the next election, giving it the majority it needs to govern. To this last group, called the "floating vote" in England, the politician in office devotes his anxious attention since his re-election largely depends upon their votes; in England, the group is principally lower middle class and its geographical locations can be indicated with some accuracy.[67] In the United States, because of its greater size, much larger population, more complicated social and political structure, and weaker party organization, the concept of the "floating vote" is less useful; however, in a specific election, it can be demonstrated that the victory was due to shifts in the votes of a fairly definite group, such as the Midwestern farmers in 1948. Any given government will, of course, tend to favor certain groups in the society over others. The Harding and Coolidge administrations were peculiarly sensitive to the needs and desires of the business community, while the New Deal, particularly during Roosevelt's first term, consciously sought to increase the power of organized labor. But no democratic government can ignore the demands of a large group, especially if that group is neither one of its completely loyal supporters nor one of its irreconcilable opponents.

When we survey political developments in the Western democracies since 1900, we are forced to reject Laski's thesis that the state "is always the servant of that class which owns, or dominates the ownership of, the instruments of production." [68] He admits that the modern state performs a large number of functions for the benefit of the workers, especially in the fields of education, welfare, social insurance, health, and housing, and that these services, which are of greatest benefit to the lowest paid workers, are largely financed by taxes that increase progressively as incomes rise. Yet he insists that it has always been the central purpose of the state "to remove from the path of the capitalist the obstacles that stood in the way of making profit." [69] Many capitalists would doubtless argue that some of the

[67] See W. Ivor Jennings, *The British Constitution* (2d ed., Cambridge: Cambridge University Press, 1947), pp. 43–47.

[68] STP, p. 295.   [69] PGE, p. 152.

democratic governments of the twentieth century have been very unsatisfactory executive committees of their class and that as coercive instruments they have proved, to an unfortunate extent, to be boomerangs.

Laski attempts to meet this central difficulty in several ways, none of which can be said to be satisfactory. First, having drawn a distinction between the expanding and contracting phases of capitalism, he maintains that it was possible for the state to offer benefits to the workers while capitalism was successful, but that they must be curtailed or abandoned in the present period of decline. The implication of this argument is that in the heyday of capitalism the state did not function as the instrument of capitalist exploitation, at least not to the extent that it does in the era of contraction. But, actually, the modern state is far more susceptible to pressure from labor than the state of 1850. And if it is the law of capitalism's being to maximize profit and to reduce labor costs to the minimum, why should capitalists have been willing, even during the period of expansion, to have their profits reduced by the amount that these benefits cost? On the basis of a Marxist analysis the only possible source of the government revenues which, in the days of prosperity, were used to finance these concessions was the profits of the capitalist class. Yet Laski tells us that when contraction began, the concessions were withdrawn since they then became a threat to profits.

At other times he maintains that these benefits must be regarded as the results of preliminary phases of the class struggle; they are gains that "have had to be fought for grimly by those upon whom they conferred benefit." [70] Although he admits that such concessions have been extensive, he insists that the "owners of the instruments of production are compelled . . . to give way at certain points, even, on occasion, at critical points; but they surrender the outworks, they do not yield the central citadel." [71] The admission that the capitalist class can be forced at critical points to grant concessions to the exploited class reduces the Marxist analysis to absurdity, an absurdity which cannot be concealed by resorting to the use of such metaphors as "outworks" and "the central citadel." A Marxist should be aware that continued quantitative changes can mean a change in quality and that it is Utopian to expect that at a given moment the walls of

[70] STP, pp. 148–49.   [71] *Ibid.*, pp. 149–50.

the capitalist citadel will collapse and be replaced immediately by a
new socialist structure. Laski's statements about the nature of capitalist democracy are completely contradictory. He states that it confines the effective enjoyment of the rights it confers to the owners
of property, but, a few pages later, he urges that "where the members of a state enjoy fundamental political rights in a degree real
enough to make effectively possible the transformation of dissent
into orthodoxy, I believe that it is the duty of the citizen to exhaust
the means placed at his disposal by the constitution of the state before resorting to revolution." [72]

Laski maintains: "Political forms have always been a mask behind which an owning class has sought to protect from invasion the
authority which ownership confers; and, when the political forms
have endangered the rights of ownership, the class in possession has
always sought to adjust them to its needs." [73] It follows that in a
capitalist society "the democratic form of the state, where this exists,
merely masks the power of a plutocracy and its dependents who are
no longer finding it suitable to the interests they seek to safeguard." [74]
His view makes political power entirely derivative from, and sub-
servient to, economic power; political forces have little freedom of
movement since the postulates of the legal and political systems are
determined by the system of productive relations.

The belief that political power is virtually impotent to deal with
economic power may have been warranted by the situation that Marx
confronted in the mid-nineteenth century; but in our day political
power can, in almost every country, dominate economic forces and
bend them to its will. Fascism and Communism are the extreme
cases of the mastery of political over economic power; but even in
Britain nationalization and comprehensive controls over production
and distribution have meant extensive political influence on the economic realm, while in the United States the government interferes
in economic life to an extent that would have been inconceivable
to most Americans twenty-five years ago. The present level of defense
expenditures, to say nothing of regulatory and welfare activities,

[72] *Ibid.*, p. 188.   [73] *Ibid.*, p. 293.

[74] *Ibid.*, p. 295. See also the statement: "I expect, therefore, to see the slow erosion
of political democracy in all capitalist states in the next two generations." "What Is
Vital in Democracy?," *Survey Graphic*, XXIV (April, 1935), 204.

means that in the years ahead the government will, by its taxing and spending policies, exert a powerful influence on the operation of the economy, no matter what the theories of the administration may be. For good or evil, the twentieth century is as much the age of political power as the nineteenth century was the era of economic hegemony. A theory of the state that mirrors the conditions of a vanished past is, therefore, bound to appear outmoded and irrelevant to our situation. Laski, who argues that "the adequacy of any political theory lies in its power to explain the events which occur," [75] defends the Marxist-Leninist theory of the state on the ground that it "has so defined its nature and functioning as to enable us to predict with assurance the course its operations will follow." [76] By this test the Marxist theory has conclusively demonstrated its inadequacy during the last twenty years.

Since Laski believes that private property is the main source of power and that the effort to break the hold of those who possess economic power must be the main goal of social action, he forgets all his previous warnings about the dangers of unchecked political power and abandons his proposals for limiting the exercise of authority by the government. The ambivalent attitude towards the state and its power which we noted in his writings during the late 1920's disappears. Since the capitalist state is essentially coercive authority in the service of the holders of economic power, it is futile to attempt to circumscribe its power by legal or political mechanisms.[77] On the other hand, the new socialist state must be given all the powers it needs in order to reshape legal and political institutions to bring them into harmony with the underlying economic forces, and its efforts to create the new society must not be hampered by the existence of limitations on governmental power. He argues that capitalist democracy can no longer win obedience to its principles since men no longer accept its ends as just; consequently, "no mere changes in political machinery are adequate to the proportions of the problem. . . . political forms, of themselves, can accomplish nothing." [78]

[75] "Political Theory and the Social Sciences," in *The Social Sciences,* Report of a Conference under the Auspices of the Institute of Sociology and the International Student Service, British Committee (London: Le Play House Press, 1936), p. 123.
[76] CTS, p. v.
[77] See his criticisms of the theory of the *Rechtsstaat,* STP, pp. 154–55.
[78] DC, p. 149.

He now believes that the schemes that he had advocated for devolving some of the powers of the central government to subsidiary
bodies are of no great value. The subjects that take up most of Parliament's time—regulation of trade and industry, tariffs, currency, defense, foreign affairs, and the judiciary—are precisely the matters
that cannot be handled by local or functional assemblies; "where the
residence of the sovereign power is, there, inescapably, will the solution be sought." [79] It is interesting to compare his early defense of
American federalism, and the variety of experiments and solutions
that it permits,[80] with his statement that "American federalism was
an admirable expedient in the days of fairly self-contained agricultural communities within the state; to-day, with large-scale industry
of national ramifications, it is, as the problem of dealing with child-
labour makes evident, a grave hindrance to that uniformity of legislation which, over an increasing area, the great society requires." [81]
No longer is he concerned about the dangers associated with the increasing resort to rule-making by administrative agencies; he dismisses this problem with the remark that "the protest against the
growth of delegated legislation collapses as soon as it is submitted
to serious scrutiny." [82]

The fundamental change in his view of the political process is indicated by his assertion that "every political conflict is the battle of two
active minorities for the possession of the inert multitude." [83] Once
one of these active minorities has obtained the electoral support of
enough members of the inert mass to give it a majority, it is entitled
to use that majority "to govern in terms of its will" [84] and to employ
all the power of the state to carry out its program. He flatly rejects
his earlier thesis that no government can or should ignore the opposition of a minority that is determined to follow its own view of
right or justice. Indeed, he insists that if any party, that is, the Conservatives, or any influential group of citizens, that is, the capitalist

[79] PGE, p. 173.   [80] See above, chap. 1.

[81] DC, p. 153. See also his comment that federalism is "a scheme of government
which suits the habits of a state which is still in its youth; it is not suited to the habits
of one that has definitely attained maturity." "The Public Papers and Addresses of
Franklin D. Roosevelt," *University of Chicago Law Review,* VI (Dec., 1938), 29.
See also "The Obsolescence of Federalism," *The New Republic,* XCVIII (May 3,
1939), 367–69.

[82] PGE, p. 294.   [83] DC, p. 111.   [84] CAC, p. 45.

class, refuses to accept the dictates of a government that possesses a majority in Parliament, there is no possibility of a peaceful settlement of political issues. "We cannot seriously argue that no government is entitled to take any decision which may outrage the conscience of a significant minority." [85] It is "impossible to conduct the process of ordered government upon the terms that a majority must not use its power when a minority threatens resistance. . . . Normally, a government that is challenged is obliged, so long as it feels confident that it has public opinion behind it, to meet the challenge." [86] Under Laski's treatment, the decrepit sovereign state appears to have made a complete recovery.

[85] STP, p. 73.

[86] *Ibid.,* pp. 73–74. See also the statement that once a socialist party "commands the will of the electorate its title to defend its programme with all the resources of the state behind it seems to me beyond question." DC, p. 250.

8

Obedience, Liberty, and Equality

1. THE PROBLEM OF OBEDIENCE

IN A LECTURE delivered early in 1932 we hear the last echoes of Laski's theory that the individual citizen is obliged to obey the command of the state only if he is convinced that its decision embodies justice and the right. The title of any organization to our loyalty "depends upon the ethical adequacy which pervades its exercise of its power. And of that exercise individuals must in the last resort be judges." [1] In 1932 and 1933, as he adopts the Marxist position, this individualistic theory of obedience disappears from his writings, and the focus of his attention shifts from the individual to the class. He is interested, not in the minority that refuses in the name of conscience to obey, but in the conditions under which the great majority, the proletariat, will withdraw their allegiance from the state that exists to protect the interests of their exploiters. While capitalism is expanding, the decisions of authority are generally accepted because of "the sense among those to whom they apply that, for one reason or another, the difference they will make is not worth fighting about." [2] Now, however, men deny the validity of capitalist democracy because the maintenance of inequalities, which is the basis of capitalism, can no longer be squared with the fundamental principle of democracy, "the assertion that men and women have an equal claim upon the common good." [3] More concretely, Laski maintains that, for the masses, capitalist democracy "is not attacked because it is regarded as inherently wrong, though that is the main motive of its outstanding critics; it is attacked because it is unsuccessful." [4]

In this discussion he seems to accept the Marxist argument that capitalism inevitably means increasing privation for an ever-

[1] "Nationalism and the Future of Civilization," DBG, p. 241.
[2] DC, p. 155.   [3] Ibid., p. 184.   [4] Ibid., p. 185.

expanding proletariat and that misery forces the workers to revolt against the system. The rest of his analysis is, however, a denial of this basic Marxist tenet. He argues that capitalism, during its period of expansion, was able to make great concessions to the demands of the workers and to offer them a constantly rising standard of living; the masses therefore became accustomed to continuous improvement. The tendency of modern legislation since the Industrial Revolution, he concedes, "has been to soften by governmental action the harsh contrast which would otherwise obtain between the lives of the rich and the poor. And, on any long view, the ability of the state to win the loyalty of its citizens depends upon its power continuously to soften the contrast." [5] In discussing the years after the First World War, he admits that "in no period since 1832 have so many concessions been made to the workers by their masters; in no period, either, has the response to those concessions seemed so unsatisfying." [6] He notes that the process of capitalist development has resulted in the *embourgeoisement* of large sections of the working class and that the average English, American, or French worker has no well-developed proletarian consciousness. "How should he have it," he asks, "who so often possessed a house, or a savings-bank account, a motor-car, or a modest insurance policy? How should he who so largely has shared in a standard of living rising generally until quite recently?" [7]

The onset of what Laski calls the present period of capitalist contraction, in which capitalism can no longer continue to offer concessions to the masses, cannot, therefore, be dated earlier than the 1920's. It is not clear whether he means that there has been an absolute decline in the worker's standard of living, or merely that the system is no longer able to maintain the previous rate of improvement. Often he implies that the sense of allegiance to capitalist democracy has disappeared because the economic system can no longer offer to the masses the constantly higher standard of living that previous benefits have led them to expect. In order to regain the loyalty of its citizens in the face of the challenge of socialism, capitalist democracy must do one of two things: "Either the possessing class by which it is controlled must be willing to tax itself on a *constantly augmenting scale* for the benefit of the masses, or its volume of pro-

[5] STP, p. 59.   [6] PGE, p. 18.   [7] STP, p. 267.

duction must so constantly expand as to make possible *an ever-greater standard of life* for the ordinary wage-earner." [8] The governing class can maintain its authority only "by proving that its power is continuously coincident with an increase of material well-being for the working classes, or that, where sacrifices have to be imposed, their incidence is genuinely equal. The former . . . is a function of an economic recovery which is dubious; the latter is prohibited by the psychology which our inegalitarian system has created." [9]

Laski's picture of the evolution of capitalism during the period before 1929 contradicts every essential element in the Marxist theory that he claims to accept. He states that the standard of living of the average worker rose constantly, while Marx held that the condition of the proletariat was growing steadily worse. Laski concedes that the state has increasingly organized for its citizens the material conditions of an adequate life by providing for the poor a wide range of services that the rich can buy for themselves,[10] while the Marxist theory insists that the state is the coercive instrument by which the capitalist class protects its privileges and its profits. Laski admits that the development of capitalism has given a large number of workers a real stake in the present system and he laments the *embourgeoisement* that has resulted from their material prosperity, while Marx built his system on the postulate that the deterioration of the position of the proletariat and the middle class would inevitably lead to the growth of revolutionary consciousness among the members of an ever-expanding proletariat. Laski says that as long as "the system of private ownership in the means of production produces a continuous improvement in working-class conditions which satisfies the workers' established expectations, the latter will accept, even if doubtfully, the state as it is. But immediately that improvement fails over any considerable period, the workers will develop a revolutionary consciousness." [11] His argument is thus that the threat of revolution arises when capitalism can no longer satisfy the workers' expectations of constant improvements, while Marx maintained that

---

[8] PGE, p. 22; italics mine.   [9] DC, p. 224.   [10] See STP, p. 59.

[11] *Ibid.*, p. 109. See also the statement that we can expect a revolution in any state only when the class excluded from the benefits of ownership finds that "the material well-being it expects is, over a period, denied at the level it deems possible of realization, and when it connects that denial with the system of class-relations which the state maintains." *Ibid.*, pp. 145-46.

revolution would occur because a shrinking capitalist class would confront an increasing number of workers whose standard of living was barely sufficient to keep them alive.

Laski's position seems to be that, until 1929, capitalism behaved in a manner that contradicted the Marxist analysis at every important point; suddenly, when the depression began, capitalism reversed its previous tendencies and began to demonstrate the contradictions that Marx had seen in the middle of the nineteenth century and that, in his opinion, made revolution imminent in 1848 and in 1870. At the crucial point, the explanation of the breakdown of capitalist society, Laski rejects, even in the crisis situation of the 1930's, the economic determinism of the Marxist theory. Marx had argued that the internal contradictions of the system and, particularly, the fall in the rate of profit, would lead to an increase in the misery of the workers, which would deepen their awareness of their proletarian status and their determination to move to a revolutionary overthrow of the hollow shell of the old order. Laski, on the other hand, is compelled to assert that the primary factor in the movement for revolutionary change is the set of psychological expectations (that is, the assumptions that inequalities will be progressively lessened and that material benefits will be increased) created in the minds of the workers by the operations of successful capitalism. When the decline of capitalism makes further concessions impossible, the revolutionary consciousness of the workers is aroused and they move to capture the state so that the amelioration of their position can once more be resumed.

In effect Laski is arguing that the basic reason for the overthrow of capitalism is its long record of successful accomplishments rather than its progressive deterioration. He states: "The more real their [the masses'] access to the good life, the more they resent the barriers which remain in their path; and if these are stoutly defended, the pressure against them only becomes proportionately the more keen." [12] The present "egalitarian temper" of the average worker, engendered by the state's efforts to lesson the distinctions among its citizens based on wealth or birth, "feels the burden of remaining inequalities much more fiercely than was the case when they seemed, by their extent, a part of the fixed order of nature." [13] The more

[12] DC, p. 187.   [13] *Ibid.*, p. 218.

closely one studies Laski's discussions of the evolution of capitalist society, the more one is forced to conclude either that he did not understand Marx's analysis, or that he saw its inapplicability to modern conditions, but was unwilling to abandon it because he wanted to retain the revolutionary appeal and the "scientific" authority associated with the Marxist formulae.[14]

Viewed in its own terms, Laski's theory that the masses will no longer give their allegiance to capitalist democracy, since it cannot fulfill their expectations, is based on several highly dubious assumptions. The central assumption is that, faced with a severe depression like that of 1930, a democratic government must adopt a sharply deflationary policy, which involves reduction of expenditures and, consequently, the curtailment of benefits and the elimination of social services. The effect of this policy is to accelerate the rate of unemployment and the decline in wages. Capitalist democracy, that is, "had to lower the standard of life just when democratic expectation looked to its dramatic expansion proportionately to the increase in productive power." [15] Social reform is expensive, and in a period of depression it is a grave danger to the interests of the ruling class. It interferes with profit making, the central postulate of the capitalist system; it threatens capital accumulation and encourages investors to withdraw their capital to other countries; and it necessitates levels of taxation that the rich are unwilling to accept. As a result, the "reformers are pushed aside, and the stern reactionaries take their place." [16] If the voters, after an experience of reactionary rule, elect a leftist government, it will be sabotaged by the vested interests.

Laski formulated this view that drastic deflation is the response of capitalism to depression on the basis of the actions of the National Government in England in 1931 and 1932; but he continued to adhere to this position as late as 1938 and 1939, when the American

[14] There may, of course, be some truth in his argument that the steady rise in per capita production and consumption during the last century has created a general expectation of continuous improvement and the possibility of widespread dissatisfaction if the rate of progress is not maintained. But it is obvious that this thesis, which, in characteristically paradoxical fashion, Schumpeter advanced when he argued that capitalism's success is the basic reason for its decline, is incompatible with the Marxist analysis to which Laski declares that he adheres. See Joseph A. Schumpeter, *Capitalism, Socialism and Democracy* (2d ed., New York: Harper and Bros., 1947), esp. pp. 61–62 and 143–45.

[15] DC, p. 54.   [16] *Ibid.*, p. 25.

New Deal had clearly demonstrated that a "capitalist democracy" could meet the problems of depression by the opposite technique of inflationary measures. The government simply disappointed business-men—and Laski—by refusing to make a balanced budget its prime consideration. It sharply increased payments to the unemployed and the underprivileged, and in the midst of the depression it inaugurated a series of long delayed social reforms. These payments, financed largely by government borrowing, not only restored morale and prevented the drift towards a revolutionary temper, but also revived effective demand and thereby stimulated the private sector of the economy. In 1935 Laski flatly rejects the argument of Keynes and Salter that it is possible to construct "a *via media* between capitalism and socialism directed by the state in the interests of the whole com-munity, but without any change in the essential structure of class-relations." [17] Their view assumes, in contradiction to the facts, "that, amidst the economic struggle of classes, the state can be an impartial arbiter concerned only for total well-being," [18] and that law has the power to override the capitalist drive for profits.

Laski's second major assumption is that the depression of the 1930's is the final collapse of capitalism; without a change in capitalist rela-tions of production, industrial recovery is impossible. This thesis, confidently advanced during the depth of the depression, is still main-tained in 1937 and 1938 in the face of the general recovery of both the American and British economies. Ignoring the actual increases in production, he continues to assert that the contradiction between the relations and the forces of production makes it impossible for production and consumption to increase.[19] Finally, Laski assumes that in order to avoid widespread resistance and disobedience, capi-talist democracy must offer the workers a constantly rising standard of living; anyone who denies the validity of the Marxist-Leninist view of the state must show that the actual states that we know "are inherently capable, granted the class-relations they maintain, of ful-filling demand on the largest possible scale, and that, therefore, they

---

[17] STP, p. 163.   [18] *Ibid.*, p. 162.

[19] The National Bureau of Economic Research index of physical output for all manu-facturing industries in the United States, which stood at 266 in 1924 and rose to its peak of 364 in 1929, had recovered to 301 in 1935 and 376 in 1937; see U.S. Bureau of the Census, *Historical Statistics of the United States, 1789–1945* (Washington, D.C.: Government Printing Office, 1949), p. 179.

have a moral claim to the obedience of their members on this ground." [20] The case "for the maintenance by the state of the present system of private property in the instruments of production must be that this results in a greater total satisfaction to all who are affected by its maintenance than would be the case under such an alternative system as socialism." [21] It is obvious that no previous social or economic system has been asked to satisfy such demands for a never-ending improvement in material conditions. But it must be noted that the United States, operating under a capitalist system, combined with some state intervention, seems to be the only country whose citizens now enjoy the prospect of a large, and continuously increasing, volume of available goods and services. Since the standard of living of the average American is higher than that of the Soviet worker or the semisocialized British citizen, the American worker is not convinced by the socialist argument that his well-being will be improved by a shift from private to public ownership.

By Laski's criterion, therefore, American capitalist democracy today has a better title to the allegiance of the ordinary citizen than any other political and economic system, unless one insists that capitalism must be compared with a purely ideal socialism rather than with actual examples of socialism. His adoption of a purely materialistic standard of judgment is a fatal error. Since he bases the state's title to allegiance on the level of material satisfactions that it provides for its citizens, he surrenders the right to criticize capitalism for its ethical and social shortcomings and for its tendency to build its system of values on the foundation of the "cash-nexus." He assumed in 1932 that the final collapse of capitalism had begun and that, therefore, it could be attacked as a failure; the assumption was unwarranted, and so American capitalism, at least, emerges untouched by his critical assault. He tells us that our obedience to the state "is, and can only be, a function of our judgment upon its performance. That judgment, moreover, is never one which each citizen can make upon the same postulates, intellectual or emotional. What he decides will be the product of the place he occupies in the state, and the relation of that place to his view of what he ought to attain." [22] If American capitalism continues to offer greater economic benefits to the average worker, Laski can hardly complain if the American

[20] CTS, p. v.   [21] STP, pp. 22–23.   [22] *Ibid.*, p. 64.

remains a victim of *"embourgeoisement,"* unable to see the advantages that socialism will bring to him.

2. LIBERTY, EQUALITY, AND NATURAL RIGHTS

The concept of liberty is not one of Laski's principal preoccupations during the 1930's. His continued criticism of the idealists' view of freedom implies that he still adheres to the definition of freedom as the absence of restraint, which he adopted in 1930. However, he frequently argues that only in a socialist society can liberty in a positive sense be achieved; this commitment to the Marxist version of the concept of freedom is difficult to reconcile with his Hobbesian definition. His chief concern is to show that freedom, in any sense of the term, has no meaning except in the context of equality. Without equality freedom is, in Hobhouse's phrase, a name "of noble sound and squalid result." [23] In a capitalist society the liberties that are supposed to exist under democracy are purely formal and lacking in substance except for the owners of property; the "bourgeois" liberty of "capitalist democracy" means that government must not interfere with the rights of property in any way that is objectionable to capitalists. "The liberty of capitalist democracy is essentially an aristocratic conception. It is an attempt to deny the right of government to invade certain spheres of behaviour in which the dominant members of the society wish to be left alone." [24]

Yet he concedes that the liberal state "represented a definite gain in social freedom upon any previous social order," [25] and the contrast that he draws between the political equality characteristic of democratic government and the inequality and autocratic rule implied in a capitalist economy is meaningful only on the assumption that the political liberties of the average citizen are far more substantial than he admits. He recognizes their reality when he states that capitalist democracy "offered a share in political authority to all citizens upon the unstated assumption that the equality involved in the democratic ideal did not seek extension to the economic sphere." [26]

[23] Quoted in DC, p. 207.
[25] *Ibid.*, p. 62.
[24] *Ibid.*, p. 202.
[26] *Ibid.*, p. 53.

But in discussing the emergence of Fascism as capitalism's response to crisis, he notes that from 1870 to 1930 the social-service state made extensive and expensive concessions to the demands of the masses for greater social and economic equality; Fascism, which represents capitalism's abandonment of democracy, is explained as the consequence of the use by the people of their political power in order to curtail inequalities. Hence, capitalist democracy means, in turn, merely formal and unsubstantial political liberties, political rights without social and economic rights, and great political power for the masses together with extensive social and economic concessions. The confusions and contradictions that mark Laski's analysis arise from his use of the terms "capitalist democracy" and "liberalism" to cover three distinct periods and their different political and social philosophies—the period of *laissez-faire* liberalism and the negative state, the new liberalism and the positive state that developed in England after the 1870's, and, finally, the period of what Laski calls "the decline of capitalism" and the movement towards Fascism after 1929. Because he makes no distinction between these three phases of "capitalist democracy," Laski alternates between the position that real liberties are confined to the few who own property and the thesis that the present capitalist crisis inevitably means the destruction of the significant political liberties as well as the economic and social gains of the positive state.

He devotes an entire volume, *The Rise of European Liberalism,* to an effort to trace the development of liberal and democratic ideas and their association with the rise of capitalism. His analysis of liberalism, which makes it simply the ideology of capitalism, seriously underestimates the role of philosophical, religious, and scientific factors in its formulation and diffusion. The greatest danger, however, in a genetic analysis is the tendency to judge the later phases of a historical process, such as the growth of liberal and democratic ideas, in the light of the intentions and purposes of those who shaped the early stages. While it is undoubtedly true that the desire of businessmen for freedom from the restraints of feudalism and mercantilism played a large part in the development and spread of liberal doctrines, the need to obtain support from the lower ranks of society drove them to formulate in universal terms the rights and liberties they wanted for themselves. With the achievement of universal suffrage in the nineteenth century, other groups in the society have been able to use the ideas and the techniques of political democracy to further their own ends.

Even in his discussion of the origins of liberal democracy Laski overworks the association between the achievement of democracy and the ascent to power of the capitalist class. The Puritan Revolution is explained as the revolt of businessmen against the Stuart despotism that was hostile to their interests. The result of the Revolution was "to make an English state apt to the purposes of men of property," [27] while the demands of the farmers and laborers who had fought the battle were totally ignored. After 1688, Laski states, the property of the businessman "is safe alike from the assault of state and church for the simple reason that, equally with the country gentleman, he now has at last his hands on the levers of political power." [28] At another point, however, he argues that it was the Industrial Revolution that brought the middle classes to power.[29] It is clear that if all important political, social, and cultural developments since the Renaissance are "explained" by a simple reference to the portmanteau concept, "capitalism," none of them is given an adequate explanation.

Laski holds that the ethos of capitalist societies is "an effort to maximise material well-being for the owners of capital; their liberty means that restraints will not, so far as possible, be laid upon the conditions of that maximisation." [30] The ethos of capitalism is "its effort to free the owner of the instruments of production from the need to obey rules which inhibit his full exploitation of them. The rise of liberalism is the rise of a doctrine which seeks to justify the operation of that ethos." [31] The motive of profit making is the essential motive on which the liberal state was constructed and which it still maintains as its central principle. Liberalism cannot "transcend the environment by which it was begotten"; it is "the prisoner of the end it had been destined to serve. For the men who served it did not believe in its claims apart from that end. . . . the liberty they cherished was, in sober fact, a freedom denied to the overwhelming majority of their fellow-citizens." [32] These assertions ignore the im-

---

[27] REL, p. 112.   [28] *Ibid.*, p. 102.   [29] See DC, p. 53.

[30] *Ibid.*, p. 204.   [31] REL, p. 25.   [32] *Ibid.*, pp. 262–63.

portant limitations imposed upon private economic power and upon profit making in democratic societies during the past half century. And the events of the last decade, particularly in England, have demonstrated that capitalists may remain loyal to the democratic process and to the liberal principles of constitutional change even when their own interests are adversely affected. Liberal democracy has been able to transcend its origins, and the prediction that the holders of power "will prefer rather to overthrow democratic government than to suffer the abrogation of the privileges associated with property" [33] has not been fulfilled.

Laski compares the situation of England after the First World War with that in the period from 1815 to 1832. Economic dislocation has induced popular dissatisfaction with fundamental institutions; the ruling class, panic-stricken by the threats to their power and security, attempt to repress those whom they can no longer persuade. The rulers of English society, facing, "for the first time since the Chartist movement, a decisive challenge to the ultimate sources of their power," [34] have launched a series of attacks on civil liberty: the Trade Union Amendment Act of 1927, the Incitement to Disaffection Act of 1934, and the Uniforms Act of 1936. Teachers and writers find that they can hold any views they like so long as they do not effectively criticize the present social order, while freedom of thought is limited, for all save a small minority, to the owners of property. After this long catalogue of infringements upon civil liberty in England by the capitalist government and its police, and in spite of his frequent assertions that the freedoms of capitalist democracy have no real meaning for the vast majority, Laski concludes his survey of civil liberties by saying: "I admit gladly that, so far, there has been no attack in this country on the central citadel of our freedom. But I do say with emphasis that the conditions are present here out of which such an attack could easily develop." [35] He also argues that, in the present capitalist crisis, "the passion of conflict makes reason its slave. Those dominate the political scene who are prepared to use

[33] *The Prospects of Democratic Government, Bulletin of The College of William and Mary in Virginia,* XXXIII (April, 1939), 6.

[34] "The Outlook for Civil Liberties," in Bertrand Russell, Vernon Bartlett, G. D. H. Cole, *et al., Dare We Look Ahead?* (London: George Allen and Unwin, Ltd., 1938), p. 167.

[35] *Ibid.,* p. 189.

the means which will accomplish the end. In such a period there is rarely the prospect of either tolerance or rationalism. . . . *Clearly, in this atmosphere, the liberal theory of constitutional government can have no meaning."* [36]

He insists that there has been no real change in the English political system since the triumph of the commercial class in 1688; "the English state of the past two hundred and fifty years is the institutional expression of that liberalism which received its first classical expression in Locke. It was the affirmation of the right of the property-owner to be protected against arbitrary interference in the enjoyment of his property." [37] Yet he argues that the recognition of unions and the extensive program of labor and social-insurance legislation were "the price paid by capitalists to the working class for their co-operation in the overthrow of a social control exercised by a landed aristocracy." [38] Again we note the tenacity of the aristocracy's hold on power; broken in the Puritan Revolution, in 1688, and in 1832, it is overthrown once more in the late nineteenth century. Laski's "concession theory," by explaining the continued expansion of capitalism until 1929 in terms of new scientific discoveries and technological advances, ignores Marx's argument that the capitalism of the mid-nineteenth century was no longer capable of exploiting the potentialities of the productive forces and had become a fetter upon the process of production.

In discussing the period from 1870 to 1930, Laski employs the revisionist thesis that political and industrial organization by the workers can counteract the immutable laws of capitalist development; but in his analysis of the period of contraction he suddenly shifts to the orthodox Marxist argument. If the crisis is weathered and production and living standards rise, he can once more abandon the Marxist framework in order to explain the stabilization in terms of noneconomic factors, such as scientific discoveries or rearmament. The Marxist thesis that capitalist collapse is inevitable can be put aside until the next period of depression. The predictions of imminent collapse and revolution are made after the onset of depression; if they are not fulfilled, the events can be explained after the fact by supplementing the fundamental hypotheses of Marxism with addi-

[36] REL, p. 247; italics mine.   [37] PGE, p. 10.
[38] LMS, Introduction to the Pelican edition, 1937, p. 19.

tional explanatory principles. The process is an intellectual activity that is comparable in its ingenuity and futility to the efforts to save the Ptolemaic hypothesis by constant additions of new epicycles to explain the movements of the heavenly bodies.

Another of Laski's favorite rhetorical devices is to dismiss as insignificant the controls over property and economic power in the modern democratic state, because they leave untouched "the essential implications of capitalism." These "essential implications" are never clearly defined. If high progressive taxes sharply limit profit making and the accumulation of wealth, if important business activities are subject to government regulation, if the laws guarantee minimum wages and maximum hours, insure the right to bargain collectively, and provide for a comprehensive social-insurance program, or, indeed, if major industries, such as coal mining, transport, banking, and communications, have been transferred to public ownership, the Marxist oracle can always reply that the central citadel of capitalism or its essential implications remain inviolate and that the reforms that have been made are merely concessions on minor details. The analysis is rooted in the fallacious assumption that there exists a fixed entity, called "the existing order," which has remained essentially unchanged since the replacement of feudalism by capitalism and that it can be altered only by a dramatic revolutionary upheaval, a Wagnerian finale in which the old order crashes in smoke and flames and a new society rises from the ashes.

Laski frequently reminds us that we are living in such a period of apocalyptic change; one society is passing through its death agonies and another is struggling to be born. In its death struggle capitalism will destroy its own offspring, the system of political democracy, in order to frustrate the creation of the new socialist society. He argues: "A fundamental change in class-relations requires now, as it required at the end of the fifteenth century, a revolution in the idea of property, of therefore, the state that is its guardian, if it is to be effective in altering the character of the forces of production." [39] Every society is sharply divided into the small but powerful group of men who

[39] REL, p. 243. Presumably Laski meant that there must be a revolution to alter the character of the *relations* of production. In the Marxist scheme, the forces of production do not require redefinition nor can they be changed by the state; the change in these forces has already taken place, and it is this which leads to the present contradiction between them and the capitalist relations of production.

are struggling to preserve the outworn past and the masses who are on the side of the future; each group has its faith and its battle cries, and each is driven by the logic of the situation and by its opponent's pressure to assume an ever more intransigent position. Revolution or counterrevolution, complete socialism or Fascism, these are the stark alternatives that confront us; the spirit of compromise and toleration upon which freedom depends is vanishing amidst the clash of opposing doctrines and warring groups. His prophecy of despair is that we must expect "the coming of an iron age in which the moral restraints placed by security upon the exercise of power can no longer hope to exert that influence we had come to believe was part of the settled habit of mankind." [40] Like every ruling group, our masters will fight for their privileges and power when they are challenged; "they prefer conflict to the alternative of abdication. . . . they cannot make the sacrifice involved in the choice of equality and the flight from greed." [41]

At the core of Laski's pessimism is his conviction that men are tolerant only when the matters upon which they differ are relatively unimportant; "men only agree to disagree when nothing that they regard as vital is the price of disagreement." [42] They "are not prepared to concede freedom where the things about which they care most profoundly are at stake." [43] Religious toleration, for example, came only when most people were no longer profoundly concerned about religion and when they realized that intolerance was economically unwise. Since capitalist democracy is now in a state of war, wherein men differ about the very foundations of society, freedom can no longer be maintained. Ours is an age of revolution and "the logic of a revolution excludes the possibility of compromise, if it is to be a successful revolution." [44] Violence and the collapse of normal democratic government seem inevitable no matter what course is followed. If a capitalist government refuses to grant the workers' demands and decides on a Fascist suppression of unions and working-class parties, there will be a revolution from below; "the working class is no more likely to watch unmoved the frustration of hopes upon which it is determined than it has been in other historic experience." [45] Even if a socialist government were allowed to come to

[40] STP, p. 291.   [41] LMS, Introduction to the Pelican edition, 1937, p. 28.
[42] DC, p. 192.   [43] *Ibid.*, p. 206.   [44] STP, p. 263.   [45] DC, p. 230.

power by constitutional means, which is unlikely, freedom would have to be sharply curtailed. The government would need, at least, wide powers to rule by decree to enable it to meet the crisis situation, and "it would have to suspend the classic formulae of normal opposition. *If its policy met with peaceful acceptance, the continuance of parliamentary government would depend upon its possession of guarantees from the Conservative Party that its work of transformation would not be disrupted by repeal in the event of its defeat at the polls."* [46] And if its program is opposed by businessmen, the government will be forced to meet the challenge to its authority by "the suspension of constitutional government." [47]

Conflict seems, therefore, to be inevitable, and, once men turn from persuasion to conflict, "the victors are bound to embark upon an attack on freedom in order to consolidate their power." [48] Laski still believes that revolution may well mean disaster for the entire fabric of civilized society, but he no longer argues that for this reason the socialist movement must do everything it can to avoid outraging the emotions of its opponents and to preserve democracy and the right to oppose the government in power. He now maintains that, "granted the real danger of conflict, the true burden of the argument is the obligation of the minority to accept the consequences of defeat." [49] He has discovered the key to the process of history; he knows not merely what has been and what is, but what must be. While he regrets the passing of freedom, he realizes that "the iron age" is the necessary transition to the new society. We must not delude ourselves by hoping for a continuation of the nineteenth-century tradition of liberty and toleration. Our only consolation is the knowledge that after the dark night of conflict we will find ourselves in the Promised Land of the classless society, where justice, equality, and true freedom will rule. Our rulers, by their refusal to surrender their privileges, have blindly chosen war in preference to peace. Thus we "enter upon a long period of winter. We can comfort ourselves only with the hope that a later generation will detect in its rigours the grim prelude to a brighter spring." [50]

The goal for which, at least temporarily, liberty must be sacrificed is the achievement of socialism; only in the classless society can the

---

[46] *Ibid.*, p. 87; italics mine.   [47] *Ibid.*, p. 219; see also STP, pp. 254 and 288.
[48] DC, p. 208.   [49] *Ibid.*, p. 248.   [50] REL, p. 264.

ideal of equality be realized, and only when equality is attained can liberty be given positive meaning for the masses and a true democracy established.[51] Laski assumes that there is a "constant drive of human impulse towards the establishment of greater equality in society. . . . Men take the view that differences in the state require justification; their exclusion from some privilege always leads to a demand for either its abolition or its extension to themselves." [52] By equality he means primarily economic equality, equality of income and property, and he insists that inequalities of status, power, and influence are almost always the results of material inequality. His ideal of equality is that each man should receive an identical return for his labor, an equal share in the social product; exceptions to this rule in the form of differences in reward can be allowed only if it is rationally demonstrated that such differences result in an increase in the total product and that those who are discriminated against benefit equally with those who are given a larger reward.

His discussion of equality involves several assumptions, all unproven and some, at least, highly dubious. He offers no evidence to demonstrate the existence of the universal impulse towards equality, and he concedes that no state has ever offered to its citizens the equality he demands. In fact most men in any contemporary democratic society do not appear to desire the abolition of differences in rewards and in the privileges associated with status. The average citizen hopes for improvement in his own position and in that of his family, and when his income is reduced he tends to resent the fact that a few people receive extremely large incomes that bear little relationship to their services to society. He hopes to rise in the social and economic hierarchy and he believes that his children can achieve a status superior to his. Since he is confident that some degree of upward mobility is possible, he is resentful of any complete egalitarianism that would blur the distinctions between him and those who are below him and that would lessen the opportunities for further advances by him or his children. There seems to be no evidence for Laski's assertions that each man "presses for the sacrifice of uniqueness for identity," [53]

---

[51] See "The Position and Prospects of Communism," *Foreign Affairs*, XI (Oct., 1932), 98; DC, pp. 207–8; and *The Prospects of Democratic Government, Bulletin of the College of William and Mary in Virginia*, XXXIII (April, 1939), 4–5.

[52] STP, p. 58.   [53] DC, p. 201.

and that those who are denied access to privilege inevitably seek to destroy privilege. Even in the ranks of labor in England or the United States, each group of workers is anxious to preserve the differences which mark them off from the less skilled or the less well paid. Laski is entitled to wish that his passion for equality were shared by the majority, and he may complain that the present unequal society has imposed on the workers the cruel illusion that they can improve their lot. But, he cannot, at the same time, assume that the workers are relentlessly pressing for a social and economic equality denied to them by the ruling class, or that a "political democracy is bound by its very nature to resent, and ultimately, therefore, to seek to overthrow, distinctions among its citizens which are built upon wealth or birth." [54]

His second assumption is that economic inequality is the root of all other inequalities; in the classless society there will be no significant differences in opportunities for advancement or in the returns men receive for their labor. While we have not yet observed a classless society in operation, we see in societies that have eliminated the system of private property no sign of the disappearance of marked differences in power, status, and opportunities for education. As early as 1920, Bertrand Russell, noting the fallacy involved in the assumption that material differences are the major factor in men's unequal advantages, argued that inequalities in power, which he regarded as characteristic of Communist society, were much more significant and vastly more dangerous than differences in wealth.[55] It may be true, as some maintain, that the effort to attain and to preserve strict economic equality necessarily leads to a concentration of political and social power in the hands of a few individuals; in any case, vast differences in political influence and social status still exist in the "socialist society" of the Soviet Union. Inasmuch as greater educational and occupational advantages are available to children whose parents occupy positions at the top of the bureaucracy than to workers' children, a new class structure, with different life-chances for the various groups, is emerging even though it is im-

[54] *Ibid.,* p. 218.
[55] See Bertrand Russell, *The Practice and Theory of Bolshevism* (2d ed., London: George Allen and Unwin, Ltd., 1949), pp. 111–13.

possible to accumulate private property. And the attempt to achieve economic equality by revolution and dictatorship, advocated by the Bolsheviks and accepted as virtually inevitable by Laski, is certain to intensify differences in the political power of individuals and groups within the society.

Laski also assumes that an equal society is compatible with the operation of a modern industrial system. But the experience of such different societies as the Soviet Union and the United States indicates that the gradations of payment necessary to maintain output and to obtain the proper number of skilled workers at each level of the complex industrial hierarchy render impracticable any rigidly egalitarian system of reward. In order to achieve satisfactory levels of production, the Soviet leaders have been forced to institute differentials in wages and salaries at least as great as those found in the United States; having rejected as Utopian earlier Bolshevik theories that the rewards for all types of labor should be approximately equal, they have introduced and intensified the Stakhanovite system, which offers material benefits and status differentials to workers who achieve or surpass given standards of output. Soviet experience thus fails to support Laski's assertion that a state founded on equality can not only succeed in operating a modern system of production, but also achieve a development of its productive capacity that far surpasses that of a competitive and unequal society.

It may be urged that Laski permits differences in wages if it can be shown that they lead to a greater social product and benefit all citizens equally. However, the main stress in his argument falls on the need for "economic democracy," equality in the gain of living as well as in its toil, and he insists that such equality requires the sacrifice of uniqueness for identity, at least in the material realm. His principle of differences in reward, which is entirely subsidiary, is nowhere adequately explained or defended. It is possible that in order to maximize total production in a complex industrial system involving a high degree of specialization, division of labor, and gradation in technical skill, a socialist management will be compelled to offer differences in reward as great as those that obtain in American capitalist society. In the absence of such wage differentials, production can probably be maintained only by compulsory regulation of labor to guarantee that the required number of workers for a given job will be available and to prevent employees from shifting to more attractive or less arduous occupations.

The second half of Laski's principle is utterly baffling. In theory it is possible to convince the entire working force that their welfare is linked to an increase in the total product and that a higher wage for coal miners, for example, is socially necessary in order to increase coal production. This demonstration will not be an easy task, since each group of workers tends to feel that its job is as socially vital and as arduous as any other occupation. But Laski also requires that we prove to the other workers that they will benefit equally with the coal miner if the latter is given a higher wage. How is this to be demonstrated? If a five per cent increase in the wages of miners leads to a five per cent increase in total social production and if we assume that prices and all other wages remain constant, it is clear that the increase in the real wages of the miner will be approximately twice the increase in the real wages of any other group of workers. And if increased wage payments to the miners lead to higher prices along with greater production, the real income of non-miners will remain fixed or will decrease while that of the miners rises or, at the worst, remains constant.

The last of Laski's important assumptions, and in a sense the most crucial, is that the elimination of private ownership is essential if economic inequalities are to be removed and that the workers are now aware that it is capitalism that prevents them from attaining the equal share in the social product to which they are entitled. It is, he asserts, the natural outcome of the worker's position that he accepts "as legitimate the public ownership of that to which difference in benefit is obviously traceable." [56] But many workers in capitalist society do not accept the conclusion that socialism is the proper remedy for such inequalities as they resent. During the last seventy years they have used the power of their unions and their ability to influence governmental action in order to increase their share in the national income, while accepting the basic framework of the capitalist system. The success of these methods in eliminating the harsh contrast between great wealth and abject poverty that characterized the nineteenth-century capitalist society that Marx condemned is particularly obvious in

[56] DC, p. 197.

Britain and the United States. As we have seen, Laski attributes these gains to a policy of concessions, which he describes as a substitute for equality. The average citizen may wonder why the elimination of the inequalities that cause him the greatest hardship should be regarded as a substitute for a movement towards greater equality.

Laski's insistence that there must be a total and abrupt shift from capitalism to socialism leads him to disregard or to belittle efforts to deal with specific problems and to eliminate specific injustices. His apocalyptic attitude, which resembles the temper of the early Christians in its scorn of immediate gains and in its expectation of a sudden and dramatic transition to a new and perfect world, is the root of his failure as an intellectual leader and a guide to political action during the 1930's. In his writings during the depression there is no mention of any proposals for government action to deal with unemployment or industrial collapse. His sole contribution is to underscore all the difficulties and problems and to insist that they are insoluble so long as his general prescription of socialism is not applied. Men such as Keynes and Salter, who were attempting to formulate rational and practicable solutions to the problems of the time, he regards with a mixture of scorn and amused pity, the usual reaction of the messianic prophet to the reformer. He insists that their efforts are futile since they ignore the basic problems, the incompatibility between the productive capacities of industry and the legal and economic relations of capitalism, and the impossibility of using the state, which is the coercive instrument of the capitalist class, to promote the general welfare. Their attitude is "an aristocratic approach, a cool and skeptical impatience of dogma, a passion for the rational solution of questions in their nature essentially rational, of which the appeal is by its nature a limited one." [57] As we shall see, his own reaction to the economic and political crisis is completely different from that of Keynes; he deserts his intellectual responsibility and follows the mass movement towards irrationality instead of endeavoring to guide men back to an intelligent analysis and solution of their problems.

[57] "The Position and Prospects of Communism," *Foreign Affairs*, XI (Oct., 1932), 106.

9

Economic and Political Change

1. POLITICS AND ECONOMICS

LASKI'S VIEWS on the relationship between politics and economics can
be summed up in the statement that political power and changes in
its distribution depend almost entirely upon economic power. The
state is the instrument of the dominant economic class; democracy is
confined within the limits set down by the requirements of capitalist
profit making; parties are the expression of opposite views of the
proper economic basis of society—at every point in his analysis, politics as an independent variable has virtually disappeared. In spite
of this insistence on the primacy of economic factors, he presents no
serious exposition of the principles of Marxist economics, and he
seems to have made no effort to master the modern techniques of
economic analysis, which recent writers such as Lange have employed as the basis of a new demonstration of socialist principles.[1]
Laski's economic theory consists of a few Marxist phrases, such as
"the relations of production are out of harmony with the forces of
production," and these phrases he applies only to the period of capitalist contraction. His usual argument is that this period dates from
1929, but the concept is sufficiently vague to permit him to date the
beginning of capitalism's final crisis in 1914 or even as early as the
beginning of the twentieth century.[2] At any rate, he is convinced
that 1929 marks the collapse of capitalism, but he fails to give an adequate explanation of the reasons for the breakdown.[3] His opinion

[1] See Oskar Lange and Fred M. Taylor, *On the Economic Theory of Socialism* (Minneapolis: University of Minnesota Press, 1938).

[2] See CTS, p. xiv.

[3] The thesis that the collapse of the capitalist system is inevitable is a crucial element
in the Marxist theory. Marx attempted to demonstrate that the rate of profit would
necessarily fall as capitalism developed, and that the system would, therefore, move
to its destruction. His explanation was not successful, and later Marxists, including
Hilferding, Luxemburg, Lenin, and Paul Sweezy, have endeavored to rehabilitate

seems to be that the capitalist collapse is the result of underconsumption, caused by the failure of the purchasing power of the workers to keep pace with increases in production. But it is impossible to be certain whether he believes that the income of the workers is decreasing or merely that their share of the national income is falling; indeed, he may mean that the real income of the workers has not fallen at all, but that it is increasing at a slower rate than the total production or the "productive power" of the society.

At one point he states flatly that "despite our immensely increased powers of production, the share of labour, the part, that is, of wages and salaries, has fallen consistently in the post-war epoch." [4] This statement is clearly inaccurate; the percentage of the national income of Great Britain that went to wages was relatively constant from 1911 to 1938, and, if salaries are included, "the share of labour" rose from forty-nine per cent in 1911 to sixty-two per cent in 1938.[5] In addition, the statement contradicts his assertion that there has been a marked and constant improvement in the position of the workers during the last hundred years. He also attributes the crisis in capitalism to a contraction of profits in the postwar period, which became especially severe during the depression. It is difficult to see how it was possible for both profits and wage and salary payments to decline after 1918, since national income increased until 1930. He maintains that after 1918 profits declined so sharply that the costs of social reforms jeopardized the essential relations of the capitalist system and endangered the title to profit that was "the assumption upon which capitalist democracy was founded." [6] His only explanation of this assumed fall in profits is that capitalist democracy became unable to

---

the argument; see Sweezy, *The Theory of Capitalist Development* (New York: Oxford University Press, 1942).

[4] STP, p. 167.

[5] The percentage of the national income represented by wages was 38.5 in 1911, 39.5 in 1924, 37 in 1929, 40.5 in 1931, and 37.5 in 1938; wages and salaries together represented the following percentages: 1911—49; 1924—60; 1929—58; 1931—64; 1938—61.5; see G. D. H. Cole and Raymond Postgate, *The British People, 1746–1946* (New York: Alfred A. Knopf, 1947), pp. 545–46. In the United States wages and salaries accounted for 58.1 per cent of the national income in 1929, 70.2 in 1934, 62.1 in 1942, and 67.2 in 1945; see U.S. Bureau of the Census, *Historical Statistics of the United States, 1789–1945* (Washington, D.C.: Government Printing Office, 1949), p. 12.

[6] STP, p. 177.

sell its goods in a profitable market. In fact, however, the level of production, sales, and profits in the United States rose steadily until 1930. In any case Laski does not tell us the reasons for the decline of profits and sales that he assumes. If he attributes the contraction to a decline in mass purchasing power, he is forced back to an underconsumption theory, and he must demonstrate that the ability of the workers to buy what they produced declined after 1918. But we have seen that their share of the national income at least remained constant and may have increased; real wages remained fairly constant in England from 1919 to 1924 and rose four or five per cent between 1924 and 1929.[7]

Extended analysis of Laski's economic discussions is unrewarding. His assertions are often so vague as to be incapable of precise interpretation; when his statements are clear they are often inaccurate or unsupported by evidence. Above all, his arguments are so inconsistent and are based on such contradictory assumptions that it is virtually impossible to say what his position is. We can merely summarize the general conclusions that he draws from his economic analysis. Since 1918 and especially since 1930, capitalism has entered a period of decline, marked by a fall in profits and wages; this is not merely a "normal" depression, which will be followed by another period of prosperity, but the final and irremediable collapse of the system. Only if the regime of private profits and private ownership of the means of production is replaced by socialism can we utilize the full productive powers of society and resume the upward trend of production and the standard of living. The necessary change in class relations cannot be achieved by the tactics of Fabian gradualism; "it is not a change that we can effect piecemeal, by reason of the closely knit texture of our industrial society." [8] Attempts by the state to regulate economic life in order to subordinate the profit motive to social needs or efforts at a gradual approach to socialism are impossible, since they assume that the state can act impartially in the face of class antagonisms. Such measures also disturb or destroy the confidence of capitalists that is a necessary condition of the successful operation of capitalist democracy. Laski says:

Conservatives and Liberals can secure this confidence because they are willing to abide by the rules upon which it depends. Socialists cannot,

[7] Cole and Postgate, *The British People,* p. 539.   [8] STP, p. 168.

without surrendering their claim to be Socialists. . . . I believe, therefore, that an attempt on the part of a Labour government to operate a
policy that will win the confidence of its opponents is doomed to failure;
the level of that policy would satisfy neither them nor its own friends.
And it would still leave wholly unsolved the central question of power.[9]
[The fundamental fallacy of Fabianism is that it] assumes the co-operation in the task of attack of the very men to whom the system stands not
merely as the protective armament of their own interests, but, not less
important, also as the guarantee of national well-being.[10]

What are the political implications of the present stage of capitalist collapse? The ruling class, in order to safeguard profits, the
lifeblood of the system, insists that previous concessions to the
workers be withdrawn and new benefits refused. More significantly,
capitalism in distress uses the state's power to suppress its opponents.
"To secure the conditions under which it may restore profit-making,
it embarks upon those experiments, wage-reductions, the destruction
of trade unions, the prohibition of strikes, and so on, which it believes
will assist that restoration. But when it does these things it enfolds
the society within the arms of a Fascist state." [11] The workers, however, to whom political democracy has come to mean state action to
secure increased wages, better working conditions, and a constant
expansion of the social services, attempt to use the institutions of
democracy to elect a progressive government pledged to protect their
gains. They then discover that for the owners of property the *raison
d'être* of democracy is the protection of capitalist rights and privileges.
Capitalism gives its allegiance to democracy on the condition that its
operations will not threaten the economic foundations of society;
when those foundations are endangered, it moves to suppress democracy.[12] Laski concludes: "Where capitalist democracy passes into its
phase of contraction, then either the democracy must transform the
capitalism or the capitalism will suppress the democracy." [13] Obviously, therefore, the belief of the Labor Party that "the opponents

---

[9] PGE, pp. 163–64.   [10] STP, pp. 250–51.

[11] *Ibid.*, p. 136; see also pp. 111–12.

[12] He maintains that "capitalism is willing to suppress democracy rather than
forego the privileges which accrue to ownership under the system of class-relations
that it involves." CTS, p. xvi; see also p. xxiv.

[13] "The Prospects of Peace in Europe," in Benjamin S. Rowntree *et al., Wharton
Assembly: Addresses, 1938* (Philadelphia: University of Pennsylvania Press), p. 49.
See also STP, p. 111.

of Labour have, equally with itself, the same interest in the maintenance of democracy" [14] is not only untrue but dangerously naive.

Since the workers refuse to surrender either their material benefits
or their democratic rights, they are driven to accept a "thorough-
going socialism" and to destroy the capitalist system that now aims to
eliminate both their economic and political gains. If they cannot
achieve the mitigation of social and economic inequality "by the
normal means of a given constitutional organization, they will be
driven to extra-constitutional means to attain it." [15] Thus we confront the classic revolutionary situation, a bipolarization of society
into two totally opposite groups.

Those who dominate the life of the regime deny its power to grant the
claims that are made. They regard the reformers as revolutionaries; they
insist that the revolutionaries are the enemies of society. They mobilize
the coercive power of the state to annihilate dissent. . . . The privileged
then begin to rally about those who promise by drastic action to restore
the traditional power of the state. Extreme produces extreme; and in
the clash of mighty opposites the prospect of rational compromise is lost.[16]

There are only three ways of avoiding this revolutionary situation:
first, the ruling class may sacrifice its privileges and cooperate in
the replacement of capitalism by socialism—Laski considers this possibility extremely unlikely; second, capitalism may achieve a new
economic prosperity that will permit the satisfaction of the workers'
demands at a new high level and the resumption of the policy of
concessions—this possibility is ruled out by his assumption that the
present economic decline is final and irreversible; finally, the capitalism of crisis might stabilize itself at a new and lower equilibrium "by
inventing a new ideology which persuaded men to be satisfied with
the material standards of its epoch of decay." [17] But this is impossible since "new ideologies are not invented out of whole cloth. They
rise and fall . . . with the rise and fall of new systems of class-
relations." [18]

Let us examine his attempts to apply this analysis of the political
manifestations of the capitalist crisis to the situation in the United

[14] PGE, p. 158.
[15] *The Prospects of Democratic Government, Bulletin of The College of William
and Mary in Virginia*, XXXIII (April, 1939), 8.
[16] STP, pp. 279–80.   [17] *Ibid.*, p. 169.   [18] *Ibid.*, pp. 169–70.

States and to the efforts of the New Deal to secure economic recovery while enacting a series of social reforms and regulations of business. He notes that in the United States and, to a lesser degree in England, "the slow erosion of capitalism" has not yet made the masses ready to accept a revolutionary strategy. In America the multitude is still dominated by "the illusion of an infinitely mobile society . . . the legend of infinite wealth to be exploited. . . . How profoundly rooted in American soil is the historic psychology of the *petite bourgeoisie* has been revealed remarkably by the great depression." [19] The persistence of this psychology renders it likely that in the United States, and even in England, the present crisis will lead to the rise of Fascism rather than to the emergence of a militant socialism.[20] As Laski surveys Roosevelt's New Deal policies, he is torn by two conflicting emotions, his belief that it is hopeless to try to use the power of the state to reform the capitalist system and his admiration for Roosevelt's energy and courage and for the "exhilarating spectacle" of a government acting vigorously to improve the condition of the people.[21] He refers to Roosevelt as "the first statesman in a great capitalist society who has sought deliberately and systematically to use the power of the State to subordinate the primary assumptions of that society to certain vital social purposes." [22] Roosevelt is attempting a revolution by consent; he "has, in effect, challenged American capitalism to coöperate with him in transforming itself into a social experiment." [23]

The dilemma that Laski faces is obvious; if he concedes that the New Deal government is attempting to subordinate the interests of the capitalist class to the welfare of the people, he is abandoning his Marxist theory of the nature and function of the state. Since he is unwilling to surrender his thesis, he revises his estimate of the signifi-

[19] *Ibid.*, p. 267.   [20] See *ibid.*, pp. 258 and 268.

[21] In 1934, writing to Holmes, he speaks of Felix Frankfurter: "He appears to retain deep faith in the New Deal—more, I imagine, than I can permit myself. But he can't outdo me in admiration for Roosevelt as a person even though I don't believe he can succeed. America excites us all as never in my lifetime. Even at this distance one has a sense of something big being tried; and the superiority of effort to our policy of do-nothingism is immeasurable." *Holmes-Laski Letters, 1916–1935,* ed. by Mark DeWolfe Howe (2 vols., Cambridge: Harvard University Press, 1953), II, 1470 (Dec. 16, 1934).

[22] "The Roosevelt Experiment," *The Atlantic Monthly,* CLIII (Feb., 1934), 143.
[23] *Ibid.*

cance of the Roosevelt innovations; "even if they wholly succeed, no radical would be tempted to regard them as anything more than a necessary historic phase in the slow evolution of American capitalism." [24] He argues that Roosevelt's program does not go beyond the aims of the 1906 Liberal Government of England, which "foundered upon the antagonism of the possessing class." [25] The argument that the Liberal program was a threat to the ruling class and that its accomplishment was prevented by capitalist antagonism contradicts his repeated assertion that, since 1688, there has been no threat to the owning group in England and that Conservatives and Liberals have been only two wings of a single party devoted to the defense of capitalism. He is certain that the leaders of American business will not permit the New Deal program to be carried out; the hostility of the courts indicates that business is determined that democracy shall not be used to interfere with the normal workings of the capitalist system.[26] He says: "The old industrial feudalism does not believe that its day is dead. . . . it calculates, not without reason, that the new religion, to secure objective establishment, must prove itself by the miracles it can perform. It realizes that it has the key to miracles in its own hands; and it sees no reason why it should surrender the key." [27]

He concludes then that the Roosevelt experiment seems doomed to failure, and he warns that that failure "means the end of political democracy in America, for the simple reason that it will prove itself thereby incapable of adapting to its purposes the institutions of its economic life." [28] Late in 1934 he notes that President Roosevelt, in his efforts to reform capitalism, "finds himself thwarted by the refusal of the vested interests to co-operate in the principles of his adventure. They have no confidence in the methods he proposes;

[24] *Ibid.*, p. 148.   [25] *Ibid.*, p. 151.

[26] See STP, pp. 158–60; and CTS, pp. xv–xvi.

[27] "The Roosevelt Experiment," *The Atlantic Monthly*, CLIII (Feb., 1934), 150–51.

[28] *Ibid.*, p. 152. In 1935 he asserts that the only result of cooperation in the efforts of a Roosevelt or a Lloyd George to achieve class collaboration is "to lull the masses into acquiescence by arousing in them false hopes certain to be belied in a short period. The process of class-collaboration was possible in the epoch of capitalism in expansion. Today, in the phase of contraction, it definitely puts its exponents on the other side of the barricade." "What Is Vital in Democracy?," *Survey Graphic*, XXIV (April, 1935), 205.

and since the recovery of the capital market is a function of their confidence, one essential condition of his success is wanting." [29] By 1938, however, he refers to the Roosevelt experiment as an indication of the vitality of "the principle of responsible and democratic self-government." The American people have had "leadership in a fuller sense than any of the older democracies of Europe; so far, they have responded to it in ample measure. If they continue that ardor of response, it may well be that it will become the splendid destiny of America to save Europe by her example as she will have saved herself by her energy and her determination." [30] Through this rhetorical fog, Laski appears to be suggesting the heretical notion that America, under Roosevelt's leadership, may succeed in its effort to use the power of government to harness capitalism and the profit motive to the public welfare. In any case, the argument that the New Deal is doomed to failure because of the antagonism and sabotage of the vested interests has disappeared for the moment.

This survey of Laski's discussions of the New Deal makes clear the extent to which his conversion to the Marxist faith has rendered him incapable of dealing with actual political events. His use of facts becomes more and more tendentious, and he forces events into a pattern to support his thesis that the preservation of democracy makes necessary an immediate and total shift to socialism. If facts that contradict his thesis become too obvious to be ignored, they are explained away as merely temporary stabilizations of the capitalist system. His basic theme is that class struggles are the fundamental factor in political change. History, he says, is "the competition of ideals for survival, the character of which is determined by their power to exploit productive potentialities at any given time"; [31] but he does not explain how ideals can accomplish the task of exploiting the potentialities of production. He insists that in this class struggle the power of the state is inevitably on the side of the owning class, and, in spite of

[29] STP, p. 249. Speaking of Earl Browder, he comments: "Yet I miss my guess if the failure of the Roosevelt experiment does not leave him, or some successor, one of the outstanding figures in the American scene." "Communism Faces the Wrath to Come," *The New Republic*, LXXXIV (Oct. 30, 1935), 339.

[30] "The Public Papers and Addresses of Franklin D. Roosevelt," *University of Chicago Law Review*, VI (Dec., 1938), 35.

[31] STP, p. 101.

the historical evidence that civil wars have often been the result of religious or political differences, he maintains that the unity of the state can be disrupted only by the struggle of classes.[32]

Laski insists that it is pointless to argue that reason and compromise are preferable to conflict and violence; everyone admits this, but the "weakness of the plea made for reason by its advocates is the final weakness that the conditions under which reason can operate effectively are absent from the system under· which we live." [33] If they are to demonstrate wisdom and self-restraint, our rulers need international peace and economic recovery as the conditions necessary to successful compromise. But recovery is impossible, given the "inherent and inescapable logic" of capitalism, and the prospects of peace between nations grow dimmer with the passing of each day. Peace at home and abroad depends upon the creation of a new harmony between the forces and the relations of production. "That new harmony means, as in the past it has always meant, a wholesale invasion of the privileges built upon vested interests. They have to be persuaded or coerced into giving way. And, historically, on any large scale and within any brief period of time, they have never, so far, been persuaded. For that persuasion requires a volume of mental adjustment which wholly contradicts the basic *Weltanschauung* of those who have to be persuaded." [34] "The sober truth," he concludes, "is that those who have power do not propose to abdicate from its possession." [35]

Finally, we must note, as one of the most striking characteristics of his analysis of the relationship between politics and economics, the absence of any discussion of the structure of the new socialist society— the organization of industry and political institutions, the problem of keeping the state responsible to its citizens while it exercises its vast new powers, or the participation by the workers in the government of industry. From his discussion of the measures that a Labor Government will be forced to take when it assumes office, we can see that his socialism has become progressively more centralistic. But he is no longer interested in these problems; he is concerned only with the single, crucial choice, that between a "thorough-going socialism" and Fascism. He alternates between apocalyptic warnings

[32] See *ibid.*, p. 143.   [33] *Ibid.*, p. 238.   [34] PGE, pp. 46–47.
[35] *Ibid.*, p. 48.

of the suffering and brutality that will engulf the world if men do not proceed at once to create the new society and chiliastic promises of the perfect world that will be ours with the abolition of capitalism. Like Marx he refuses to discuss the institutions of the new society. One sometimes wonders whether this Marxist aversion to any effort to describe the socialist society does not spring as much from a desire to avoid the painful task of positive construction as from a revulsion against the "unscientific" and "petty-bourgeois" predictions of Utopian Socialism. By concentrating on a criticism of present institutions and on the promise of a future paradise that remains undefined, the Marxist creates a kind of Sorelian myth that is largely immune to intellectual analysis. The combination of prophecies of disaster and promises of a millenium is as powerful as an instrument of appeal to mass emotion as it is unsatisfactory to those who are seeking for rational diagnosis and solution of political and social problems. The disciples of Marxism realize that the least attractive and least inspiring descriptions of Paradise are those which attempt to portray too many concrete details.

2. MARXISM AND LENINISM

We have seen that in this period Laski accepts what he believes to be the Marxist analysis of capitalist society and that he attempts, not without certain confusions, to use the principles of Marxism to interpret the events of the 1930's. He claims that Marx provided socialism "with a program and a philosophy more rooted in the objective facts that it encounters than any alternative of which we have knowledge," [36] and that his prophecies are likely to be fulfilled within the next half century in Europe and America as they have already been fulfilled in Russia. Perhaps the clearest statement of Laski's commitment to the Marxist faith is contained in an article written in 1935:

No tool at the command of the social philosopher surpasses Marxism either in its power to explain the movement of ideas or its authority to predict their practical outcome. On the nature and function of the State,

[36] "Marxism After Fifty Years," *Current History*, XXXVII (March, 1933), 695.

on legal institutions, on capitalist habits, on historiography, on the development of philosophical systems, Marxism holds the field against any of its rivals. On the breakdown of capitalist democracy, the decline of bourgeois culture, the rise of Fascism, the role of non-revolutionary socialism, it has insights not possessed by any alternative method of analysis. [37]

To what extent does Laski now agree with the Communists that violent revolution is inevitable in the transition from capitalism to socialism? Does he, after 1932, abandon his earlier commitment to an evolutionary and democratic approach to socialism and accept the Leninist thesis that the destruction of capitalism is impossible without recourse to violence and dictatorship? It is not easy to give a straightforward answer to this question; his statements are not free of ambiguities, and his views change with the passage of time and with changes in the external situation or the nature of his audience. In a single volume we find passages in which he insists that socialists must proceed by constitutional and democratic means, as well as statements that a peaceful achievement of socialism is extremely improbable, if not impossible. The reader who finds the discussion that follows confusing and complicated is invited to examine the transcript of the 1946 trial of Laski's libel action against a newspaper, the Newark *Advertiser,* which, in reporting a speech made by him, said that he had advocated a violent revolution.[38] After five days of discussion of the speech as well as numerous citations and counter-citations from his earlier books, articles, and speeches, few people in the courtroom can have been certain that they knew what his position actually was. In view of this confusion, the jury's finding, which was that Laski had not been libeled by the newspaper report, is perhaps understandable.

As we have seen, he asserts in 1931 that the position taken by the supporters of the National Government during the election campaign against the Labor Party is "tantamount to an insistence that if social-

---

[37] "A Key to Communism," review of *Marxism and Modern Thought* by N. I. Bukharin *et al., The New Statesman and Nation,* X (July 20, 1935), 102.

[38] See *Laski v. Newark Advertiser Co., Ltd., and Parlby* (London: The Daily Express, 1947). See also the accounts of the trial by Laski himself, "My Day in Court," *The Atlantic Monthly,* CXC (Nov., 1952), 65–68, and "On Being A Plaintiff," in Kingsley Martin, *Harold Laski* (New York: The Viking Press, 1953), pp. 263–67, and by the counsel for his opponents, Sir Patrick Hastings, *Cases in Court* (London: William Heinemann, Ltd., 1949), pp. 55–71.

ists wish to secure a state built upon the principles of their faith, they can only do so by revolutionary means. . . . That is, of course, the thesis of Lenin and Marx." [39] The progressive decline in the twentieth century of Britain's economic advantage over the rest of the world, coupled with the world-wide collapse of the capitalist system in the 1930's, means that the demands of the English workers can now be met only at the expense of the British capitalist class itself. Since two antithetical groups and their philosophies now confront each other, the agreement on fundamentals that has been the secret of the smooth functioning of the subtle conventions of British parliamentary democracy has disappeared. And Laski has increasingly grave doubts of the possibility that the capitalist class will cooperate in the liquidation of the regime of private property and of their own privileges. History offers no support for the belief that a ruling class, when threatened, responds by a magnanimous and altruistic renunciation of its power and perquisites; "no new social order has so far come into being without a violent birth." [40] Since there is no reason to believe that our rulers are wiser or more moral than their predecessors, it is highly probable that the capitalists will only yield in the face of superior force. So Laski is compelled to assume that the achievement of socialism will be marked by violence and by serious restrictions upon individual liberty and to reject the gradualism that is the predominant philosophy of the Labor Party. He denies the validity of the assumptions and tactics of gradualism because he is unable to share the faith of the majority of the Party that the democratic system will not be shattered by the conflict between Labor and the Conservatives. Of the alternative to gradualism, the Communist belief in the inevitability of revolution and dictatorship, Laski says in 1932: "I do not see how it is reasonable to deny the possibility—to put it no higher—that the communists are right." [41]

He repeatedly warns members of the British Labor movement that the road to power will be far more difficult than they imagine and that what they regard as the end of the road, the conquest of a Par-

[39] "Some Implications of the Crisis," *Political Quarterly,* II (Oct.–Dec., 1931), 468.

[40] DC, p. 213. See his statement that "capitalism is presented with the choice of co-operating in the effort at socialist experiment, or of fighting it; and I have given reasons for believing that it may well prefer the alternative of fighting." *Ibid.,* p. 233.

[41] "The Position and Prospects of Communism," *Foreign Affairs,* XI (Oct., 1932), 100.

liamentary majority, will in fact be only the beginning of their most serious problems—the overwhelming hostility of the press and other organs of opinion, widespread attempts by the capitalist class to sabotage the new government and its program, and desperate efforts to exploit the prestige of the monarchy in order to prevent the catastrophe of socialism. In 1933 he predicts that a Labor victory will be the signal for a financial crisis; if the leader of the Party refuses to emulate MacDonald by forming a National Government to deal with the crisis, the Conservative Prime Minister will refuse to summon the new Parliament and will govern by decree until the new House of Commons can be dissolved. The second election will take place in an atmosphere of extreme tension, and all the traditional forces in society, including the Crown and the churches, will be mobilized to "save the nation" from the disaster of a socialist victory. Whether this second election produces another Labor majority or a Conservative victory, it will be necessary to suspend the Constitution and the democratic system. He expects that in the crisis the main weapon of the anti-Labor forces will be an attempt to rehabilitate the ill-defined prerogative powers of the Crown; the leaders of society, who alone have access to the King, will not find it difficult to persuade him that he will be serving the best interests of the nation if he uses his prerogative to frustrate a socialist victory at the polls.[42]

Thus the ruling class may meet the crisis of a Labor electoral triumph by instituting what will be, in effect, a capitalist dictatorship, which, sooner or later, will face a revolutionary challenge from the masses. Despite his prediction that the newly elected socialist government will not be permitted to take office, he now maintains that it is probable that it will take power and embark upon bold measures, which will be attacked by the vested interests through "nonparliamentary means."[43] Again, this resort to sabotage will create a revolutionary situation. He concedes:

The assumption that a change in the basic character of a social order seems unlikely of accomplishment without violence is a challenge to two convictions which lie at the very heart of the liberal temper. It seems to deny the primacy of reason as a method of resolving social differences, and it visualises an atmosphere in which liberty as the expression of a

[42] See DC, pp. 88–91 and 119–26.   [43] *Ibid.*, p. 240.

constitutional system is deliberately put aside in the period of consolidation.[44]

However, this assumption must be made, since it is obvious that if the state is "at all costs to preserve a capitalist society, it will have to suppress those who are resolved upon its transformation." [45]

At the same time that Laski predicts that the measures of a socialist government will be met by capitalist sabotage, which will require the suspension of constitutional government, he insists that a Labor Government must carry out its socialist program boldly and must make an immediate attack on the central citadel of capitalist power. If, as in 1924 and 1929, a Labor Government shrinks from this task and attempts to maintain the confidence of business by limiting itself to halfhearted social reforms, it will immediately confront financial difficulties. More important, it will lose its hold over its own supporters, and "it will give way to new forces of the Left once it seeks a refreshment of authority from the electorate." [46] Although he advises Labor to attack boldly, he also warns that "a socialist government, unless it desires deliberately to provoke revolution, cannot ride rough-shod over the vested interests it proposes to attack. . . . It has to discuss, negotiate, conciliate, that it may attain the maximum possible agreement to its plans." [47]

While he accepts the Communist position that violence and revolution are virtually inevitable, he shrinks from accepting the Leninist conclusion—that socialists must prepare for the revolution so that they will be able to establish the dictatorship of the proletariat and to defend socialism against the attacks of reactionary forces. He rejects the Communist strategy on practical grounds and ignores the moral objections that he stressed previously.[48] Successful revolution is possible only when the authority of the government is completely broken, as it was in Russia in 1917; but "under the conditions of modern administration, except in the event of unsuccessful war, it is only seldom that a political system breaks down with such completeness." [49] English and American workers demonstrate an almost total lack of militant class consciousness; their "profound immersion" in bourgeois liberalism makes them totally unreceptive to revolutionary

[44] *Ibid.*, pp. 189–90.   [45] *Ibid.*, p. 211.   [46] DC, p. 240.
[47] *Ibid.*, p. 105.   [48] See above, chap. 6, section 2.
[49] DC, p. 236.

appeals. Although Laski frequently dismisses as worthless the argument that the national traditions of democracy and compromise in England and the United States make revolution unlikely in either country, he makes use of the argument himself in his criticism of Communist strategy.[50] He also insists that in both countries the outcome of revolutionary conflict is more likely to be a period of Fascist dictatorship than a victory for the proletariat.

He says that socialists must continue their efforts to win the support of a majority of the electorate for their program and must adhere to the principles of democratic constitutionalism. He ignores his own demonstration that violence is inevitable once the socialist government begins to carry out its program. Indeed, in arguing against the tactics of the Communists, he reverses his previous stand and suggests that a socialist government, by its prudence and wisdom, can prevent the forces of privilege from resorting to violence. "A socialism which pays reasonable tribute to the established expectations of vested interest is far more likely to succeed than a socialism which insists upon their forthright destruction." [51] He concludes his discussion with the comment that "a socialist government which succeeded to office in the classic constitutional way might, so long as times remained normal, await with confidence any threat to its authority"; [52] but he has already argued that the very fact that a socialist government has come to power guarantees that the times will not, and cannot, remain "normal."

To summarize Laski's position in 1933 then, we can say that he is convinced that violence will, in all probability, mark the transition to socialism, but he insists that socialists must continue to operate by legal and constitutional means and must refuse to engage in violence until their opponents move to smash their party or the government that they control. His position is uneasy, since he is attempting to marry the irreconcilable opposites of revolutionary doctrine and

---

[50] See *ibid.*, p. 255.

[51] *Ibid.*, p. 251. See also the statement that what a socialist government does "must seem to be just to the bulk of the opinion in society; and what it does must be done in such a way that the transition is not marked by the kind of abruptness which moves those affected to justifiable despair and indignation" (*ibid.*, p. 252); and the comment that, as far as it possibly can, "the obligation of a socialist government in normal times is to throw upon its opponents the burden of resistance." *Ibid.*

[52] *Ibid.*, p. 254.

democratic socialism. While he still hopes that a socialist government will be able to govern by constitutional methods in spite of capitalist opposition, his repeated predictions of violence and revolution and his constant emphasis on the abyss that separates the forces of Labor from those of Conservatism tend to make the possibility of democratic socialism more remote. He denounces all who try to insert intermediate terms into the political equation; repeatedly he criticizes the gradualist attitude of the large majority of the members of the Labor Party.[53] His effort to intensify social divisions and discontents would be intelligible if he were a Communist, concerned to create a revolutionary situation that he might exploit. Since, however, he is a democratic socialist, his approach is evidence of a kind of political schizophrenia. He states that reason and freedom are now threatened by the hate and fear which social conflict entails. "That is the prospect, grim and bitter and evil, we confront at the eleventh hour of what we might have made a great civilization. What we might have made, and what we still might make if the holders of power had the courage and the determination to steel themselves to sacrifice." [54] But the whole tendency of his writings after 1932 is to strengthen the irrational forces of hate and fear; he constantly stresses "the powerlessness of reason to prevent the use of violence when interests conflict to which men attach ultimate importance." [55]

This view that violence is inevitable is reiterated in a more theoretical fashion in *The State in Theory and Practice,* written late in 1934. During the libel trial in 1946, Laski admits: "At that time my view was that the relationship between classes, the decline in the well-being of the worker, was such as to make it inevitable that if the conditions continued, the relationship between classes would be resolved by force." *Q.*—"Inevitable revolution by violence?" *A.*—"Yes." [56] On the basis of his analysis of Fascism, he concludes that the state's power must be used to protect the class relations of the social and economic system and that "it cannot be used to alter that given system." [57]

The view here taken [Laski admits] is one that naturally disturbs many generous minds. *It postulates the inevitability of revolution as the mid-*

[53] See *ibid.,* pp. 217–18; and PGE, pp. 151–55.
[54] DC, p. 266.   [55] *Ibid.,* p. 159.
[56] *Laski v. Newark Advertiser Co., Ltd., and Parlby,* p. 107.
[57] STP, p. 115.

wife of social change; and it admits that there are phases of human evolution in which men cease to settle their differences in terms of reason, and resort to force as the ultimate arbiter of destiny.[58] . . . At this stage of economic development, the difference between classes can only be settled by force.[59] . . . My case has been that, whenever the class-relations of a given society make it impossible to distribute the results of the productive process, men whose expectations of material benefit are continuously disappointed will seek to change those class-relations; and I have suggested that, unless the possessing class voluntarily abdicates—the rarest event in history—the resultant position involves a social revolution. I have not suggested that the revolution will necessarily be successful; I have suggested only that such an attempt is inescapable.[60]

Laski insists that the only adequate answer to his argument would be the actual attainment of socialism by peaceful means in England, France, or the United States; but, he says, that evidence does not exist and is not likely to be forthcoming.

In discussing the question of the proper tactics for the working class to adopt, he appears to be moving towards a more favorable attitude to the Communist position when he states: "Because changes in the class-structure of society have rarely been made without revolutionary means, those who draw the inference that our experience is not likely to be different from that of the past, that, therefore, the expectation of revolution is legitimate, and *preparation for it the part of prudence,* have a case that has not been answered by the proponents of peaceful change." [61] But he continues to stress the *embourgeoisement* of large sections of the working class, particularly the technical and white-collar workers; he predicts that any attempt to carry out a proletarian revolution will lead to a Fascist regime, supported by the *grande* and *petite bourgeoisie,* as well as some of the unemployed workers.[62] The Communists' attacks on social democracy as "social fascism" and their effort to smash all workers'

---

[58] *Ibid.,* p. 119; italics mine. See also his statement: "The transition from feudal to bourgeois society was only accomplished by heavy fighting. There is no reason to suppose, unless we assume that men are now more rational than at any time in the past, that we can transform the foundations of bourgeois society without heavy fighting also and the assumption of greater rationality is an illusion born of special historical circumstances and now fading before our eyes." *Ibid.,* p. 243.

[59] *Ibid.,* p. 123.

[60] *Ibid.,* pp. 164–65.

[61] STP, p. 189; italics mine.

[62] See *ibid.,* pp. 255–58.

organizations that they cannot control he regards as serious errors that make the defeat of the proletariat certain. Of England and the United States, he says:

The obvious technique of anyone who desires to change the existing class-structure of society in these countries lies in the fullest possible exploration of the constitutional opportunities they offer. . . . if a constitutional victory is bound to prove illusory, the simplest way to demonstrate the illusion is to make the electoral victory of the working-class as speedy as possible. The tactic of the revolutionist, in British conditions, ought, on these terms, to be a united front with the reformist as the surest way of proving the futility of reform.[63]

The strategy that Laski recommends is a real united front of all working-class parties. This coalition of the workers will not be permitted to assume control of the state by constitutional means; nor will it be able to prevent the capitalist class from suppressing the democratic system, except in a period of collapse after an unsuccessful war or after a long period of tyranny that violates fundamental expectations.[64] The primary purpose of the united front is not, therefore, to gain either a parliamentary or a revolutionary victory for the working class; violent revolution is highly probable, but it is not likely that the workers will triumph in the struggle, even if they are united.[65] The creation of a strong coalition between reformist and revolutionary socialists only guarantees that, when violence and a Fascist dictatorship appear, the forces of the Left will give a better account of themselves than they did, for example, in Germany. His conclusion is pessimistic in the extreme; since the socialist society will come to birth only after a painful period of revolution, war, and dictatorship, "we must anticipate an epoch in which the attitude to liberty characteristic of Western civilization in general, and of Great Britain in particular, during the nineteenth century, will be at a discount." [66]

---

[63] *Ibid.*, p. 269.   [64] See *ibid.*, pp. 284–85.

[65] See *ibid.*, p. 294. See also his remark to Holmes in 1933: "I see no reason why there should necessarily be a communist victory. The breakdown seems to me more likely to result in a dark age of dictatorships without principle than in the triumph of any coherent body of principles. But that this civilisation drifts chaotically to its destruction seems to me the inescapable implication of the facts. Its contradictions cannot be resolved without an overturn of its foundations." *Holmes-Laski Letters*, II, 1443 (June 13, 1933).

[66] STP, p. 290.

Laski's discussions in 1937 and 1938 of the problem of revolution reveal no change in his position since the depression years of 1933 and 1934. Occasionally he seems to be suggesting that it is possible to attain socialism peacefully; at one point he states flatly that he does not "share the views of those who believe that conflict is inevitable." [67] But the general temper of the article in which this statement appears makes it clear that he does regard violence as inevitable the moment a serious effort is made to use the instruments of political democracy to achieve socialism.[68] He often concludes a discussion of the role of violence in the transition to socialism by posing the question, "whether a new class seeking to become possessed of sovereignty can use the institutions of the class it proposes to dispossess to effect that change in residence." [69] The reader is left in little doubt that his answer to this question is negative. Again, after analyzing the socialist program of the Labor Party, he asks the rhetorical question: "Are the psychological strains and stresses of such a programme not greater than a system of representative democracy can bear?" [70] A Labor Government cannot carry out a program of social reform because it does not possess the confidence of the ruling class. If it attempts to act upon its socialist faith, "it suspends the confidence of capitalists in its purposes which is necessary to the maintenance of that continuity which the functioning of the Cabinet in a parliamentary democracy requires. I see no escape from this dilemma; certainly no escape that is available in terms of institutional machinery." [71] He ridicules the

[67] "The Outlook for Civil Liberties," in Bertrand Russell, Vernon Bartlett, G. D. H. Cole, *et al., Dare We Look Ahead?* (London: George Allen and Unwin, Ltd., 1938), p. 188.

[68] Note the following statements: "Social divisions as profound as those we now encounter inevitably mean a battle for the possession of the state-power." *Ibid.,* p. 162. "Our governors will tolerate democracy, and the civil liberties to which it obliges them, without any difficulty so long as they approve of the ends to which that democracy is devoted. But there is no reason in our history to suppose that they regard democracy as an absolute which must be maintained regardless of those ends." *Ibid.,* p. 186. "After nearly three centuries of fortunate compromise we have come once more to the parting of the ways. I do not pretend to know the direction in which we shall travel. I am content only to hope that those who care for the freedom which alone gives life its quality will give a good account of themselves when the hour of trial arrives." *Ibid.,* p. 190.

[69] PGE, pp. 168–69.   [70] *Ibid.,* p. 14; see also p. 165.

[71] *Ibid.,* pp. 257–58. See also his argument that a Labor victory will mean, at best, that the forces of Conservatism will "lose that confidence in the government which

belief that violence and revolution are unthinkable in Great Britain because of its political traditions or the "genius for compromise" of its national character. "What was possible over a relatively minor controversy like Ulster is certainly not impossible over a major controversy like the foundations of the economic system." [72]

He continues to criticize Mr. Attlee and the majority of the members of the Labor Party for their naive belief that the institutions of political democracy have an existence independent of the capitalist profit making that they have been created to foster and protect. They are inviting "capitalists to co-operate in their own abdication," [73] and are basing their trust in the Conservatives' respect for the right of the majority to rule on the vain hope that "business men who have no confidence in the new order will yet so restrain themselves as to act as though they have. . . . That kind of self-restraint has not been their habit in the past." [74] The non-Marxist character of the Labor Party is the source of Laski's greatest concern; he fears that a Labor Government will adopt a policy of social reform and gradual movement towards socialism, rather than a full-scale attack on the central citadel of capitalism. But at the same time he argues that the greater the vigor and determination of a socialist government, the more likely is a resort to violence by the forces of the Right. The strategy that he recommends to the Labor Party is, accordingly, the one that by his own analysis makes revolution and the suspension of democracy most likely. To this criticism his answer would be that the alternative of gradualism is not a real possibility inasmuch as the state is the instrument of capitalist domination; any attempt by Labor to govern by conciliating its opponents will lead to a disruption of the labor movement and an easier victory for the forces of reaction.

---

is always the condition of a successful transition from one economic system to another. At the worst, they may hold the right of the government to make such changes one that they cannot permit without challenge. The first mood leads directly to what is nothing less than sabotage of the government. . . . The second mood, not less obviously, leads directly to civil war." *Ibid.*, pp. 23–24.

[72] *Ibid.*, p. 24.

[73] *Ibid.*, p. 154. See the comment that the "side-tracking of Marxism" by the Fabians has had "the serious effect upon the British Labor movement of weakening its realization that the conquest of power by socialism is a gravely difficult adventure by persuading it that the strategy of an epoch of prosperity is suited to an epoch of crisis." "The Fabian Way," *Current History*, XLI (Oct., 1934), 37.

[74] PGE, p. 154.

Fundamentally his deeply pessimistic conclusion is unchanged; we must move forward to the new socialist society, but there is no real hope that we can reach it without bitter conflict and the suspension of democratic liberties.

His acceptance of the inevitability of violence and his rejection of the traditional outlook of the Labor Party are reflected in his new and much more favorable attitude towards the Russian Revolution of 1917 and the Soviet regime. Whatever its costs in suffering and loss of freedom, the Soviet dictatorship is ultimately justified on the all-sufficient ground of historical necessity. If Lenin had been unable to persuade the Bolsheviks to attempt the Revolution, "the triumph of the bourgeoisie in Russia would have been inevitable. Whether that would have been for the benefit of Russia is not here my concern; the purpose of this book is not to justify but to analyse." [75] By smashing the old state apparatus and molding every institution and every individual to their requirements, the Bolsheviks demonstrated that they "had learned Marx's essential lesson that one can never play with revolution." [76] He insists that in order to carry out their aim, the abolition of private ownership in the means of production, the Bolsheviks had, inevitably, to resort to dictatorship; had they conformed to the tenets of parliamentary democracy, the Soviet experiment could not even have been attempted. He regards as well-founded the Bolsheviks' claim that their form of state is a higher form than that of capitalist democracy, and he makes the astounding assertion that "there has been more realization of personality under the Soviet regime than in any comparable epoch in history." [77]

Constantly he poses a sharp contrast between the spirit of hope and optimism found in the Soviet Union and the general sense of insecurity and anxiety that characterizes capitalist societies in the period of decline. He describes the universal mood of despair that has settled over the capitalist world since 1929. Then, turning to the Soviet Union, he notes: "No doubt its government was, in a rigorous sense, a dictatorship. . . . No doubt, again, its subjects paid a heavy price for the ultimate achievement to which they looked forward.

[75] STP, p. 266. One wonders whether an interpretation of the Bolshevik Revolution that makes its success depend on Lenin's powers of persuasion is compatible with the Marxist philosophy of history.

[76] *Ibid.*, p. 260.

[77] "A Leningrad Letter: II," *The Nation*, CXXXIX (July 25, 1934), 101.

Yet, whatever its defects and errors, the mood of the Russian experiment was one of exhilaration." [78] Capitalism, having ceased to confer material benefits on the workers, can no longer "exercise its old magic" over men's minds; Communism maintains unchallenged authority over its own citizens, and, despite intensive propaganda efforts to discredit the Soviet idea, the workers in other countries feel "a proud interest in every success the Russian experiment can show." [79] Communism is winning the contest with capitalism for the allegiance of the masses "because, alone among the welter of competing gospels, it has known how to win sacrifice from its devotees in the name of a great ideal. It offers the prospect . . . of losing one's life in order to find it. There is poverty, there is intellectual error, there is grave moral wrong; but there is also unlimited hope." [80] Russia, he insists, is "the one effective center of creativeness in a world which, otherwise, does not seem to know how to turn its feet away from the abyss," [81] "the one country in the world today in the life of which a mood of exhilaration can be detected." [82]

Laski is, of course, not the only writer of the 1930's who notes the prevalence of pessimism and despair and who, in describing the malaise of representative democracy, observes that most citizens are "enfolded in a purely private life, and devoid of interest in, or knowledge of, the political process." [83] Nor is he alone in calling attention to the general loss of self-confidence among the rulers, the universal skepticism about traditional values, and the hollowness of a set of standards that refers all activities and achievements to the single

[78] "The Position and Prospects of Communism," *Foreign Affairs*, XI (Oct., 1932), 96.

[79] *Ibid.*, p. 101. See also his statement that a man "may regret, as I regret, the bureaucratism of Moscow, and yet feel convinced that the defense of the Soviet Union is one of the highest duties a Socialist can fulfill." "Communism Faces the Wrath to Come," *The New Republic*, LXXXIV (Oct. 30, 1935), 339.

[80] "The Position and Prospects of Communism," *Foreign Affairs*, XI (Oct., 1932), 105. Note also his enthusiasm in 1936 for the draft of the new Soviet Constitution and the "wide and notable" gains in individual freedom that it represents. "A London Diary," *The New Statesman and Nation*, XI (June 20, 1936), 958–59.

[81] "The Position and Prospects of Communism," *Foreign Affairs*, XI (Oct., 1932), 104.

[82] "Marxism After Fifty Years," *Current History*, XXXVII (March, 1933), 696. See also the comment that he finds in Russia "a buoyant and optimistic faith I have never before encountered." "A Leningrad Letter: I," *The Nation*, CXXXIX (July 18, 1934), 70.

[83] DC, p. 67.

measuring rod of pecuniary gain. Nor is his explanation of this wide-spread disillusion unique; it is the orthodox Marxist interpretation—the decay of the economic and social system of capitalism is the basic reason for the ideological confusion. The skepticism of the ruling class about the values of democracy reflects their dislike of the ends for which the masses are endeavoring to use democratic instruments. And since the system can no longer satisfy the workers' demands for greater equality, they, too, are cynical about the values of "capitalist democracy" and are aware that "the narrow and formal character" of that democracy means that it does not offer "a recognition of an equal claim to a share in the common good." [84] In a word, "the *malaise* of capitalist democracy is incurable while it remains capitalist, for the simple reason that it is against the conditions inherent in capitalism that men revolt. The system, that is, has lost the power to win assent to its hypotheses." [85] It should be noted that Laski maintains both that the workers are in revolt against the foundations of capitalist democracy and that the inertia of the many ranges them on the side of the *status quo*.

His general thesis is that in this period of capitalist decay, as in the last days of the *ancien régime* in France, both the self-confidence of the rulers and the sense of security among the masses have evaporated. Consequently, the essential conditions of liberalism and democracy—tolerance of differences of opinion and trust in rational argument—have disappeared; liberalism "favored reason and toleration only on the implicit condition that these, as they worked, did not threaten the economic foundations of the regime itself." [86] The moment the demands of the masses endanger the essentials of capitalism, liberalism abandons its belief in freedom and rational discussion, and the businessman moves to suppress by force those who seek to introduce a new economic and social system. We have already called attention to the stress that Laski places on the thesis that the successful operation of democracy demands agreement on all major issues and that democracy has been able to function only when groups and parties have differed only about relatively insignificant details.[87] The theory that ideological, and therefore, social and economic, homogeneity is the necessary condition of successful democratic gov-

[84] CTS, p. xxiv.   [85] DC, p. 169.   [86] CTS, p. xxiv.
[87] See above, chap. 5, section 2; see also STP, pp. 74–75, and PGE, *passim*.

ernment is not only inadequate but also dangerous to democracy. The foundation of political democracy must be a multi-group society that sustains a pluralism of ideas, values, and interests.[88]

Laski employs the theory when he argues that if an equal and homogeneous society is created there will be universal acceptance of a given system of values and, especially, of common ideas of political right and wrong. "The different views of political right taken by men are largely born of their different positions and unequal claims in society; the more fully we can find a plane of relationships in which those differences are eliminated, the more possible does it become for law to seem just to those to whom it presents itself as obligatory." [89] The view that the elimination of the material differences between men and classes will mean the disappearance of different ideas of social and political good is a corollary of the Marxist view of the relationship between ideas and values and the economic substructure, and of the concepts of proletarian literature, science, art, politics, economics, and music as opposed to their bourgeois counterparts. But the theory is completely opposed to the remnants of liberalism and individualism in Laski's thinking that lead him to defend the right of the individual thinker to investigate freely and to proclaim the truth he finds. Laski's argument implies that there was more general agreement about fundamental values in England during the successful era of parliamentary democracy from 1850 to 1900 than there is in the present period of decay. If this is true, it follows that social homogeneity and economic equality were greater in the nineteenth than in the twentieth century. The obvious falsehood of this conclusion suggests the inadequacy of the entire argument that greater social and economic inequality has meant a decline in agreement on fundamentals and a collapse of democracy.

The basis of Laski's thesis is his belief that men's thoughts and their conceptions of good and evil are a function of their relationship to the ownership of the means of production. Men's "ideas of right and wrong are largely born of their position in society; and when this, with its profound habituations, is challenged, now, as in the past, they go forth to do battle in behalf of their ideas of right and

[88] See Robert M. MacIver, *The Web of Government* (New York: Macmillan Co., 1947).
[89] STP, p. 78.

wrong." [90] Men think as they live; since the rich and the poor live so differently that they are, in fact, "two nations," "they draw their notions of good and evil, right and wrong, from the way they live; and there is no bond of effective common understanding between them." [91] He maintains that those who advocate state regulation of economic affairs in the public interest are, in effect, calling for the imposition of ethical limitations on capitalism's inherent drive for profit; the fatal weakness of this demand is that it views ethical limitations "as standing apart from the economic process instead of being born of its operation. *The ethically valid is always pretty co-extensive with the economically possible. . . .* the function each class performs in the economic system will, broadly, shape its ideas of good." [92]

This is the classic Marxist argument that men's ideas and values are determined by their class positions and that all intellectual formulations, except those of the Marxist who speaks for the historically ascendant proletariat, are mere ideologies, disguised rationalizations of class interests and privileges. The Marxist theory of ideologies is fundamentally an anti-intellectual weapon of argument. Those who use it can dismiss opposing views without detailed examination or criticism of them; at the same time they are assured that their theories alone are "scientific" and non-ideological. While it would be difficult to deny that there is a relation between a person's beliefs and his social and economic position and that social and economic conditions play a major role in popular acceptance of given ideas and values, the formulation of an idea by an individual can never be explained or understood in terms of his class position. Sociological and economic explanations will never tell us why it was Luther who was driven to make the break with Rome or why Marx was impelled to devote his life to critical analysis of capitalist society. More important, it is completely fallacious to assert that socio-economic or psychological explanations of the genesis of an idea, even if they are

[90] CTS, p. xxiv.

[91] *The Prospects of Democratic Government, Bulletin of the College of William and Mary in Virginia,* XXXIII (April, 1939), 5.

[92] STP, pp. 163–64; italics mine. See also the statement that "our ideas are largely the outcome of our interests." "The Challenge of Our Times," *The American Scholar,* VIII (Autumn, 1939), 393.

adequate, are a substitute for a judgment of the truth or falsity of the idea. Scholars ought to insist that the argument that ideas can be impugned and dismissed because they are "bourgeois," "reactionary," or "radical" involves a surrender to a completely antirational attitude.

Laski's own career refutes the thesis that a man's ideas of what constitutes social or political good are a reflection of his social or economic status. His socialism or that of Marx, Engels, or Lenin, or the Fabianism of the Webbs, Shaw, Wells, Cripps, and Attlee, cannot be explained on the basis of personal experience of proletarian poverty and exploitation. In fact the leaders and the theoreticians of the European socialist movement and the critics of nineteenth-century capitalism, such as Matthew Arnold, Carlyle, J. S. Mill, and William Morris, to whom Laski so often refers, have, for the most part, been members of the middle or upper class. Their analyses of their society and their criticisms of its failings were based not on their experiences as members of the working class but on their insights into the problems and feelings of others. These insights were the fruit of the keenness of their observation, the power of their imagination, and their ability to analyze and to express what they felt and thought. Conversely, as Laski admits when he speaks of the *embourgeoisement* of large sections of the working class,[93] it is by no means true that all those who are objectively "proletarian" are driven by their economic status to accept "proletarian" ideas and values. The power of imagination and thought to transcend the limitations of an individual's personal and group interests alone gives to intellectual and artistic activities their meaning and their title to respect. If, as Laski argues, my thoughts are predominantly the reflection of my class position and the interests of my group, I am, in effect, shut up in a sealed room with those whose ideas and beliefs are replicas of my own, and our voices cannot reach the minds of those who are locked within the adjacent chamber. Sympathy, good will, understanding, love, all these are irrelevant; our beliefs are shaped by our experiences as members of a class, and "the others," whose experiences are so different, can never understand the words we speak or the hopes we cherish. Since there can be no effective com-

[93] See STP, pp. 254-55.

munication across the barrier that separates us, we can look forward
only to a violent breach in the wall, a struggle of two dumb forces
that will end only in the death of the weaker.

Laski does not merely describe or attempt to explain the despair,
the pessimism, and the flight from reason that mark the depression
years. Trapped by his belief that thought is powerless to master its
social environment, he joins the retreat from intelligence by calling
for faith and fervor rather than reason and persuasion. He becomes
the prophet, if not the advocate, of revolution and dictatorship as the
inevitable road to the new socialist society. Socialism, he maintains,
"has reached that stage where it cannot be suppressed by persecution, and has become militant in temper because the conditions of
victory are within its grasp. It has . . . all the characteristics of a
great religion—its dogmas, its missionaries, its sects acutely divided
from one another, its priests, its fanatics, its martyrs." [94] Every mention of the Soviet Union contains an admiring reference to the zeal
and fervor of the Communists, their absolute faith and devotion to
the cause, and their spirit of confidence and exhilaration. Forgetting
his earlier argument that "enthusiasm has always been the enemy
of freedom," [95] he insists that the British Labor Party "will need
the kind of religious enthusiasm for its ends which Russian Communism displays; the ability to convince its opponents that nothing
can turn it from its goal." [96] The Party must abandon its characteristic indifference to doctrine and its isolation from the international
movement. We need, he concludes, "the inexorable faith of Lenin
in the coming of our opportunity, his unresting preparation to be fit
for the hour when it came. British Socialism has passed the stage
when it could indulge itself in the carefree dreams of youth. The
time has come when it should assume the intellectual responsibilities
of manhood." [97] After describing the zeal of members of the Communist Party in the Soviet Union, he adds: "I wish my own party
could command the same fervent and selfless devotion from its
members." [98]

[94] DC, pp. 162–63.   [95] See above, chap. 5, section 2.
[96] CAC, p. 55.   [97] *Ibid.*, pp. 57–58.
[98] "A Leningrad Letter: I," *The Nation*, CXXXIX (July 18, 1934), 71.

Part Four

1940-1945

10

The Nature of the State and Political Power

DURING the years of the Second World War, Laski's political activities reached a new peak. In addition to his regular teaching duties and his membership on the National Executive of the Labor Party, to which he was first elected in 1937, he acted as a confidential adviser to Mr. Attlee during the first year of the Coalition Government, delivered countless lectures to labor groups, soldiers, and other popular audiences in all parts of England, and wrote many pamphlets for such groups as the Labor Party, the Fabian Society, and the National Peace Council as well as five books, a host of periodical articles, and a series of articles for the Washington *Post*. As a result his wartime writings are largely propaganda tracts, which deal with immediate issues in an unsystematic fashion. The relentless demand that he produce within a few weeks a pamphlet or an article to answer the Communist attacks on the "phony war" of 1939, to justify the Coalition Government of 1940, or to persuade Americans to support the British war effort diverted his energies from constructive or analytic channels and led him to concentrate his attention on the specific decisions taken by the Labor Party during a highly eventful period. At times he spoke and wrote as the semi-official spokesman of the Labor Party; at other moments, speaking for the Marxist wing of the movement, he issued sharp criticisms and solemn warnings to the Party leaders. Since he constantly shifted between these two roles, the reader is often confused as to which represents the real Laski.

A few months after the outbreak of the war, he argues, in a pamphlet published by the Labor Party,[1] that the Party's decision to maintain its independence is correct; its duty is to act as an Opposition that can criticize the weaknesses of the War Government and replace it at any moment. A vigorous Opposition is essential to the proper functioning of Parliament and to the maintenance of public interest

[1] *The Labour Party, the War, and the Future* (London: The Labour Party, 1939).

in its activities and, therefore, to efficiency and justice in wartime administration. The power to change the government by normal constitutional methods is necessary if democracy is to be preserved. It is far better that a Labor Opposition should exist, able to express popular dissatisfactions and grievances, than that "the process of criticism should be destroyed by the formation of those peculiar and complicated loyalties that are inherent in any all-party coalition." [2] The real benefits that result from the role of Labor as a genuine Opposition should not be sacrificed, especially since "the philosophic abyss on important points of doctrine which separates the Government from the Opposition would not be bridged by a weak compromise in which each sacrificed its vital principles for a superficial unity." [3]

In May, 1940, when Mr. Churchill replaced Chamberlain as Prime Minister, the leaders of the Labor Party accepted important posts in the new Coalition Government. Laski at once wrote a spirited defense of the Coalition, in which he ignored his previous support for the principle of an organized wartime Parliamentary Opposition. He insists that the Churchill Government is far more concerned with the threat of Fascism to democracy and the interests of the workers than was the Chamberlain Government.[4] In 1942, although still defending the Coalition, he adds the plaintive comment that "sometimes, I should have liked a more confident sense in the Labour leaders that they are hardly less indispensable to Mr. Churchill" [5] than he is to them. But he defends Churchill as the opponent of appeasement and "a foremost advocate" of understanding with the Soviet Union. Under the Coalition Government, he insists, the status of trade unions is higher than ever before, social services have been strengthened, and civil liberties kept flourishing. In the opinion of British Labor there is no available instrument of victory more likely to attain it than Mr. Churchill.[6] He completely rejects the idea that Churchill will resort to unconstitutional methods in order to remain

[2] "Government in Wartime," in Laski et al., Where Stands Democracy? (London: Macmillan and Co., Ltd., 1940), p. 20.

[3] Ibid., p. 21.

[4] See Where Do We Go from Here? (New York: The Viking Press, 1940), hereinafter cited as WDWG, pp. 72-73.

[5] "Democracy in War Time," in G. D. H. Cole et al., Victory or Vested Interest? (London: George Routledge and Sons, Ltd., 1942), p. 48.

[6] See The Strategy of Freedom (New York: Harper and Bros., 1941), hereinafter cited as SOF, pp. 41-49.

in power. "Mr. Churchill is the leader of our people, by consent, and not by coercion; and when and if that consent is withdrawn he will cease to be its leader." [7] For the working class the defeat of Hitler is the major historical necessity; British Labor cannot, therefore, take any action that may interfere with the victory over Nazism, and the Labor Party must accept the risks of coalition and agree to unpleasant compromises on policy. The only alternative, the Communist policy of revolutionary defeatism, is "a plain invitation to gamble with the independent existence of Britain. We should never be forgiven if we accepted it." [8] He expresses the hope that American opinion will press Churchill to realize the economic implications of the war and to inaugurate a program of important social and economic changes. "What is needed to give Mr. Churchill the requisite stimulus to new perspectives of action is a fresh and stiff breeze from across the Atlantic. . . . What he requires is to be pricked into the urgency of thought upon matters which he has not yet learned to see in their due relevance to this war." [9]

By 1943, however, Laski has become seriously disturbed by the failure of the Coalition Government to agree on any purposes beyond the defeat of Hitler or to make "any effective change in the parallelogram of social and economic forces in Britain." [10] Mr. Churchill, he now urges, "fights the war like a great aristocrat whose honour is involved in victory because the aristocrat accepts the challenge. He does not fight the war like a great statesman who sees beyond victory to the opportunities it might make." [11] He laments the fact that soon after the Coalition was formed Churchill "built himself a moral ascendency over the Labour leaders so complete that they were not prepared to seek for changes which might have created difficulties for him with his Conservative followers." [12] Although the members of the Labor Party insist that the victory will be lost unless basic changes are made in the relations of production before the war ends, the Party's leaders have not moved to make any of these changes. "There is, therefore, a decisive contradiction between the acts of the Labour leaders and the principles of their party"; since they do not

---

[7] *Ibid.*, p. 139.   [8] *Ibid.*, pp. 88–89.   [9] *Ibid.*, pp. 133–34.
[10] *Reflections on the Revolution of Our Time* (New York: The Viking Press, 1943), hereinafter cited as RR, p. 159.
[11] *Ibid.*, p. 219.   [12] *Ibid.*, p. 343.

dare to take the risk of going out of the Coalition Government, "they are compelled to fight the war, for all effective purposes, on the terms which the ruling class approves." [13] Laski's views on the Coalition have come full circle; he now urges the breakup of the Churchill Cabinet unless the Conservatives accept, as the price of the support of the Labor leaders, the demand that the movement to socialism shall at least be started during the war. This advice, as the party leaders recognized,[14] was the height of political folly; Churchill could probably have continued to govern even if Labor had gone into opposition, and had he been forced to hold a general election during the war, he would certainly have won easily. Labor's willingness to place its socialist beliefs above the safety of the nation would have been a powerful argument for the Conservatives in any postwar election campaign and might well have prevented a Labor victory in 1945.

Laski asserts that after three years during which Labor leaders have been "full partners" in the Coalition Government, there have been "no controversial measures which might endanger the unity of the nation by revealing in action the gap between the premises upon which the Tory party is prepared to act, and those which the Labour Party approves in its annual conferences." [15] By their insistence on maintaining the electoral truce, the Labor leaders have made it certain that all legislation affecting the postwar period will be determined by the heavily Conservative Parliament elected in 1935 and that the war will be won on the traditional terms of Churchill and the Tories. Since no significant measure has been enacted that would not have been passed had Labor remained in opposition, the result of the Coalition is that every essential principle of the Labor Party is frustrated for reasons that amount to no more than the argument that "the *raison d'être* of its existence is to keep its ministers in the War Cabinet on Mr. Churchill's terms." [16] Laski ascribes the serious errors of the Party's leaders to their failure to guide their actions by the Marxist philosophy of the state and to their blindness to the central importance of the class struggle. Their "parliamentarism"

[13] *Ibid.,* p. 405.

[14] See Attlee's letter of May 1, 1944, rejecting Laski's proposals, as quoted in Kingsley Martin, *Harold Laski* (New York: The Viking Press, 1953), pp. 150–53.

[15] *Marx and Today,* Fabian Society Research Series No. 73 (London: Victor Gollancz, Ltd., and The Fabian Society, 1943), hereinafter cited as MT, p. 15.

[16] *Ibid.,* p. 21.

causes them to seek compromises that do not disturb the Conservatives, just as the "collaborationism" of the union leaders induces them to accept an economic pattern in which they are bound to be the "junior partners" in a regime of monopoly capitalism.[17] The heads of the Party encourage its members to hope that Churchill and his party will cheerfully cooperate in the postwar effort to achieve socialism. He concludes his bitter attack by stating that, clearly, "the Labour Party is being trained by its leaders for the fatal rôle of cover for the preservation, even the strengthening, of those vested interests against the power of which it should be its historic function to organise."[18]

Of course [he says] we recognise the need to pay a pious homage at the Annual Conference to the principles of socialism; but, in the intervals, our main desire is to prove to our opponents that we are not, as they have urged, Utopian visionaries, but hard-headed practical men, like themselves.[19] . . . Nothing, I submit, is more likely to destroy the Labour Party than its acquiescence in a Cabinet the work of which is so profound a contradiction both of the ends and of the means which its leaders, as well as its rank and file, declare to be the condition of national salvation. Nothing, either, is so likely to prepare the way for that bitterness and disillusion out of which Fascism is born.[20]

Again, late in 1944, he gives bitter expression to his opposition to the policies of Attlee, Bevin, and Morrison: "I doubt whether Keir Hardie or Arthur Henderson would have seen in the policy of the British Labour Party, as exemplified by its leaders in the War Cabinet, much else than *a tentative approach to that alliance between employers and employed which, outside Britain, is called the corporate state.*"[21]

Laski's attitude toward political democracy undergoes similar shifts and reversals in response to external events. At the beginning of the war, in the face of the Nazi threat to the existence of Britain, he is driven to defend the virtues of English democracy, which before 1939 he regarded as a mask for capitalist domination. He now asserts that the values to which the masses have pinned their faith are those which are summed up in the system of parliamentary democracy;

[17] See *ibid.*, p. 19.   [18] *Ibid.*, p. 23.   [19] *Ibid.*, p. 30.
[20] *Ibid.*, p. 32.
[21] *Will the Peace Last?*, Peace Aims Pamphlet No. 28 (London: National Peace Council, 1944), p. 6; italics mine.

he grows lyrical about "the dynamic of democracy" that can and must be evoked in this conflict between democratic rule by discussion and Fascist rule by coercion. The system of constitutional and democratic government evolved during the past century and a half has come close to achieving the difficult balance between individual freedom and social order and to securing the peaceful accomplishment of social changes. Abandoning his previous argument that in a capitalist democracy the effective use of political rights is limited to the owners of property, he maintains that as the government has been compelled to appeal to an increasingly large electorate, it has responded more and more fully to the wants and desires of the masses.[22] A century ago trade unions were illegal, a national system of education, workmen's compensation, and public health services did not exist, and factory legislation was extremely primitive. Most important of all, the standard of living was, at best, one fourth of what it is today. These gains are the result of the operation of the principles of political democracy, which have allowed the workers to build their unions, political parties, and cooperative movements; every movement toward the positive state has been "a response made by the political party in power to the demands of the working-class voter to share in the gain as well as in the toil of living." [23]

He argues that as a result of the experience of the last one hundred and fifty years, it is now generally admitted that the popular will is the only effective basis of political power. Since the Nazis totally reject this principle, they are seeking to destroy the entire democratic and liberal heritage of Western civilization. Laski, who in 1938 and 1939 insisted that the capitalist class had no interest in defending democracy unless it operated to protect their possessions, their profits, and their privileges, now tells us that the experiences of 1940 brought about a spiritual regeneration of the British people and drove the ruling class "to renew its homage to the democratic idea." [24] *All* political parties, he asserts, share the liberal and democratic tradition and accept the ends it has in view—"to make the common man the master of his own destiny; to recognise in democratic freedom the atmosphere in which that mastery can alone be attained; to insist

---

[22] See *The Rights of Man*, Macmillan War Pamphlets No. 8 (London: Macmillan and Co., Ltd., 1940), hereinafter cited as ROM, pp. 5–6.

[23] *Ibid.*, p. 8.   [24] RR, p. 157.

that the attainment of democratic freedom means the admission of rights in the citizen which the State denies at its peril." [25] In sharp contrast to his earlier insistence that an unbridgeable abyss separates the principles of the two major parties, he says that all parties in Britain know that a planned society is inescapable in the present phase of social development.[26]

Occasionally, when he forgets his enthusiasm for political democracy as opposed to Fascist dictatorship, he reverts to the position that in a capitalist democracy the benefits of liberty and democracy are confined to a small minority; [27] but in general, from 1939 to 1942, while a Nazi victory was possible if not probable, Laski seems to rediscover the values of democracy and the liberal society. He tells us that Munich reminded the rulers and the people of Britain "that if they had important differences, they had also not less vital identities. It compelled them to the recollection that if they had great problems to solve, they had also great traditions to preserve." [28] It is interesting to compare his evaluation of the prospects of British democracy with his prewar statements; he now argues that the "virtue of the system was that it still left elbow-room—though not too much elbow-room —for that give and take which enables men to settle their differences by discussion and not by machine-guns." [29] He concludes with a glowing tribute to Britain and its democratic way of life: "Nowhere have I found in greater degree either the qualities which make private life lovely or *in public relations the instinctive embodiment of the anxiety for fair play* . . . . when all is said against this people that can be said, British leadership seems to me to have been a beneficent thing in the history of civilization." [30] Laski usually ridicules the idea that the English have a peculiar genius for political compromise and criticizes the Labor Party for its naive belief that the ruling class is committed to democracy as well as for its habit of building its outlook, "not upon any coherent philosophy, but upon a pragmatic ap-

[25] ROM, p. 29. [26] See SOF, pp. 106–7.

[27] See WDWG, p. 124; it is interesting to note that when he is defending the Western liberal and democratic tradition he speaks of "democracy," and that when he resumes his attack on the present order he refers to it as "capitalist democracy."

[28] "Democracy in War Time," in Cole *et al., Victory or Vested Interest?*, p. 40; see also the statement that "the 'common people' in this country live under institutions which give them a hope of self-fulfilment at least as great as that enjoyed in any other country." *Ibid.*

[29] *Ibid.*, p. 41. [30] *Ibid.*, p. 42; italics mine.

proach which insists upon dealing with each issue as it arises." [31] It is, therefore, surprising to hear him say, in the very language of the English Whig, that one of the finest of British qualities is "an intuitive understanding that the well-being of a people is born of the compromises of experience and not of the ruthless logic of ideas." [32]

By 1943, when the worst danger to Britain seemed to have passed and when it again became possible to contemplate the future that would emerge with the defeat of Nazism, his tributes to British democracy ceased and he returned to his earlier criticisms of capitalist democracy, negative freedom, and bourgeois liberalism. Once again he insists that the political institutions of capitalist democracy

are, inherently, the institutions of a negative freedom. Their function has been, first, to protect the rights of a special class of property-owners, and their dependents, from invasion by the masses whose rights were not rooted in the ownership of property. . . . And the second function of these political institutions has been to gauge the limits beyond which a refusal of concessions to the masses might jeopardize the whole system in which private property is the fundamental source of social power.[33]

Even British and American democracy cannot hope to avoid the descent into Fascism if they remain capitalist; the plain lesson of the past decade is that when "democratic institutions threaten the capitalist foundations of society, capitalists, if they can, embrace counter-revolution in order to overthrow democratic institutions." [34] This argument that the owners of property are willing to destroy democracy the moment it interferes with capitalism is offered as a justification of the coercive rule of the Soviet dictatorship.

If the Communist Party of the Soviet Union left the central principle of its faith to the chance decision of *an electorate still in the phase where the denial of the socialist idea is the rule rather than the exception,* that would be as remarkable as a willingness on the part of Western democracies to see without repining the access of socialist parties to the state-

31 *Faith, Reason, and Civilization* (New York: The Viking Press, 1944), hereinafter cited as FRC, p. 164.
32 "Democracy in War Time," in Cole *et al., Victory or Vested Interest?*, p. 42.
33 RR, p. 402.
34 MT, p. 18. See also the statement: "Faith in the democratic idea is no longer historically compatible with faith in the capitalist idea." *London, Washington, Moscow, Partners in Peace?*, Peace Aims Pamphlet No. 22 (London: National Peace Council, 1943), p. 23.

power. . . . This is why the Soviet citizen is constrained to the acceptance of the fundamentals of his faith. We who are dismayed at this constraint ought, after all, to remember that the main reason why we are left the freedom to criticize the fundamentals of our own faith is that no one expects that freedom to criticize will become freedom to change; where this danger is even suspected upon the horizon, there emerge with startling rapidity the Mussolinis and the Hitlers and the Francos to put a term to that freedom.[35]

The assumption on which his analysis of capitalist society rests is, again, that "the overwhelming majority" of the citizens are excluded from the possession of liberty.[36] After a brief interlude in which he seemed to recognize the strength of the ties that bind together all groups and classes in British society, he retreats to his private world of dogma; from that retreat, he emphasizes "the degree to which modern capitalism has made the institutions of political democracy a hollow façade behind which effective power is increasingly in the hands of business men." [37]

Before the war began in 1939, Laski maintained that Fascism must be regarded as the last stage of monopoly capitalism, in which the privileged class abandons democracy in order to preserve the essentials of capitalism from the threats of the labor and socialist movements. Once England went to war with Hitler, this analysis of Fascism no longer served his purposes; it provided no basis for attack upon the Communist arguments during 1939 and 1940 that since the war was, like the First World War, merely a conflict between two sections of the bourgeoisie, the working class should take no part in the struggle, but should endeavor to transform it into a revolutionary civil war against capitalism within each country. Immediately after the outbreak of the war, he published several pamphlets attacking this Communist policy of revolutionary defeatism and the People's Convention Movement in England; he insisted that it was not possi-

[35] FRC, pp. 158–59; italics mine.

[36] See *Will Planning Restrict Freedom?* (Cheam, England: The Architectural Press, 1944), p. 21.

[37] "The Economic Foundations of Fascism," review of *Business as a System of Power* by Robert A. Brady, *The New Statesman and Nation*, XXV (Mar. 27, 1943), 212. See also the statement: "What is remarkable, when we penetrate behind the formal facade of political democracy in Britain, is the depth of the abyss which divides the few who rule from the many to whom their orders are given." *Will Planning Restrict Freedom?*, p. 29.

ble to achieve a revolution under wartime conditions and that any such attempt in England would only increase the risk of a Nazi victory. He makes a sharp distinction between British and Nazi imperialism; the former has already passed through its expansive and aggressive phase, while the latter is just entering it. The essence of British imperialism has been the export of capital, which results in industrialization and the movement towards national independence in the subject territories, while Nazi imperialism, being purely exploitative, aims to enslave the conquered peoples.[38] He argues that an expanding imperialism is an infinitely greater threat to socialism and the interests of the workers than a contracting imperialism. British Labor supports the war because it recognizes that Hitler is the main threat to its own safety and to its hopes for the future.

He also asserts that "ever since the rise of Fascism, it is the common man who has been anxious to challenge its claims, and the privileged who have sought to come to terms with it." [39] The rulers of the capitalist democracies were prepared to make any surrender to Fascist aggression as long as their own vested interests were not endangered. He does not explain what privileges were threatened by the Nazi attack on Poland, or why this act of aggression presented a more serious threat to the ruling class than, for example, the seizure of Czechoslovakia in 1938. He insists that Fascist aggression could have been halted had the democracies taken a firm stand on Manchuria or Abyssinia. Chamberlain and the Conservatives were unwilling to embark on the policy of collective security, because it meant an alliance with the Soviet Union that would have threatened the vested interests of Great Britain, the defense of which was their primary concern. The failure to create a common front with the Soviet Union against the Fascist powers is, therefore, "essentially" the fault of the British and French leaders who were unable to overcome their profound prejudice against Soviet Russia and who were less terrified by Fascism than by Communism, which they believed would emerge as Fascism's "residuary legatee" after the overthrow of Hitler and Mussolini.

Laski's argument is a tissue of half-truths, and he vastly oversimplifies a complex situation. First, it is by no means certain that Chamber-

[38] See *Is This an Imperialist War?* (London: The Labour Party, 1940), pp. 4–6.
[39] SOF, p. 70.

lain and Daladier rejected an agreement with the Soviet Union simply because of their ideological hostility to Communism. An important factor in their hesitancy was the belief that the Soviet army, torn apart by the purges of the 1930's, was not an effective fighting force and that an alliance with Russia might be a military embarrassment rather than a help. Even after the Nazis attacked the Soviet Union, astute military analysts such as General Marshall, who had every reason to hope for a German defeat in Russia, felt that the Soviet armies would be defeated within a few weeks. Second, the Nazi-Soviet pact of 1939 demonstrates that we cannot assume that the Russians were determined to pursue a straightforward policy of opposition to Fascist aggression through collective security and that this strategy was ruined simply by the "vested interests" of Britain and France. In fact Laski surrenders the basic point in his argument by admitting that when, after March, 1939, Britain and France became anxious to conclude an alliance with Russia, Stalin and his advisers were not eager to accept the offer. Stalin "had no sense of obligation to the principle of collective security; he was as much entitled to use it as a convenience as were Mr. Chamberlain and M. Daladier." [40] It would appear that neither the Soviet Union nor the Western democracies wanted a war with Germany in 1938–1939 and that each side was prepared to use the traditional techniques of power politics in order to buy from Hitler a period of peace at the expense of the other.

In any event, the failure to check Fascist aggression was due far more to the almost universal abhorrence of war among the citizens of the democracies than to the anti-Communist machinations of the privileged classes. Now that many of the old arguments against rearmament and collective security are being revived by the left wing of the British Labor movement, it should not be too difficult to recall or appreciate the widespread agitation on the Left during the 1930's against rearmament or any other action that might lead to war. Laski himself admits: "It was only in the late autumn of 1938 that the Labour Party began in any full way to grasp that the forces of counter-revolution were threatening every gain the masses had so painfully made in the last century; and . . . that the safety of the world, at least as a democratic world, depended on a full alliance with the Soviet Union." [41] When Chamberlain returned to England,

[40] RR, p. 65.   [41] MT, p. 10.

having sacrificed Czechoslovakia to obtain "peace in our time," there was a general sense of relief and approval, even though it may have been mingled with a feeling of shame; this anxiety to avoid war was by no means limited to the "appeasers" or to the members of the ruling class. In the light of Laski's frequent statements during the 1930's that collective security through the League of Nations was futile in a world of capitalist states and in view of his opposition, shared by many members of the Labor Party, to the demands of Churchill and Eden for a rearmament program sufficiently extensive to give collective action against Fascist aggression a chance of success, his readiness after 1939 to ascribe to the ruling class in England and France complete responsibility for the repeated surrenders to Fascism and the failure to build an alliance with the Soviet Union is not merely inaccurate and superficial but totally irresponsible. Laski is not one of the happy few in England and the United States who have the right to join Churchill in saying, "I told you so," when they reflect on their actions and utterances during the period before the war.

In his analysis of Fascism in 1940, Laski discovers that the capitalists, who called in the Fascist leaders to defend their privileges, have now become subject to their rule by terror just as the workers are. "A capitalist society invoked the aid of Hitler because it could not, within the framework of democracy, resolve its own contradictions. But it has become the victim of the monster it sought to make the instrument of its salvation." [42] In contrast to his prewar argument that Fascism is the technique of rule of capitalism in its period of crisis, he now maintains that the Fascist leaders are the totally irrational "outlaws" of civilization, the "gangsters" who, called in as "junior partners" by businessmen and the leaders of military and civil administration to curb the ambitions of the masses, have become the masters of the society. They rule by terror over their former allies as well as their enemies, and their only concern is to perpetuate their own power.[43] Recognizing that the Nazis have destroyed or taken over all traditional organizations and institutions in society and not merely those of the working class, he states that the explanation of the Marxian critics of Hitler "omits the vital fact . . . that

[42] *The Labour Party, the War, and the Future,* p. 1.
[43] See WDWG, pp. 76–77.

he controls big business hardly less than he controls the working class"; [44] he does not mention that he defended the Marxist position during the 1930's. Fascism is no longer described as simply the last stage of capitalist domination; it is the total revolt of pure irrationality against the central tradition of Western civilization, a tradition that is shared by all groups and parties in the democratic states. The makers of Fascism are the marginal men, the total failures of organized society; they had contempt for the masses, but "they hated also, the forces of privilege because it was these which had made the rules that condemned them to failure." [45] They cannot re-establish peace and order since they are unable to solve the fundamental problems that led to their emergence; and they do not propose to permit the present reign of terror to end, since social peace would mean their downfall.

Laski's analysis of the factors accounting for the rise of Fascism is also much more complex than his prewar explanation of its genesis. In 1940 he lists five principal reasons for Hitler's success—nationalism and the desire for revenge after 1918, the economic crisis, the association in the popular mind between the Weimar regime and defeat and economic difficulties, the divisions among those who supported constitutional government, and the misery of a population thoroughly weary of increasing political strife and of weak and ineffective governments.[46] He is compelled to recognize that the Fascist movement received a large measure of support from the masses, "from little men, frustrated, bewildered, insecure, unhappy, because of the failure of capitalist democracy to solve their problems." [47] But when we ask why the masses who rejected "capitalist democracy" turned to Fascism rather than to socialism for a solution of their problems, Laski offers us no adequate answer. He does not probe the weaknesses of the Marxist political, sociological, and psychological theories that made it impossible for socialism to hold the allegiance of the workers in the face of the irrational appeals of Fascist slogans. He contents himself with resounding phrases that do not deal with the crucial issues: "Fascism is the epitaph upon those forces of privilege which seek to imprison the future by defending with violence

[44] *Ibid.,* p. 87. [45] *Ibid.,* p. 96. [46] See ROM, pp. 11–12.
[47] WDWG, p. 122.

an obsolete past." [48] Its essence "is the use of the outlaw by privilege to defend itself against the demand of the masses for justice." [49]

His fullest discussion of the origins and nature of Fascism is found in the volume published in 1943, *Reflections on the Revolution of Our Time*. Here again he stresses the importance of frustrated national ambition and the appeal to the unemployed, the *petit bourgeois,* and the *déclassé* intellectual. Fascism has been forced to destroy all groups that might serve as centers of resistance to the regime and has not confined its attacks to working-class organizations. Again he criticizes the Marxist thesis that Fascism is simply the political expression of monopoly capitalism in decay. The Marxists have not given sufficient attention to two other elements. First, they ignore "the fact that both Mussolini and Hitler were able to build mass-movements. . . . this ability . . . was built upon a skilful exploitation of nationalist sentiment. It promised success and unity to peoples which had been rendered miserable by failure and disunity." [50] Fascism promised to the people all the things that the Left parties promised, and "in its propaganda, was far more skilful in its psychological exploitation of the national tradition." [51] The Left, on the other hand, "was preaching a revolutionary doctrine without ever studying seriously the dynamics of power." [52] Second, the Marxist analysts overlook the significant fact that Fascism "has been driven by its own inner logic to the destruction of capitalism in its historic liberal form." [53] In order to deal with the problem of unemployment and to sustain their appeal to nationalist sentiments, the Fascist leaders have been compelled to adopt a large-scale rearmament program and an aggressive foreign policy; these policies have made necessary strict state control of foreign trade, profits, wages, prices, and consumption. While Laski continues to repeat his earlier formula that Fascism is "the retort of the propertied interests to a democracy which

[48] *Ibid.*, p. 149.

[49] "The Need for a European Revolution," in *Programme for Victory* (London: The Fabian Society, Routledge, 1941), pp. 5–6.

[50] RR, p. 93.   [51] *Ibid.*, p. 94.

[52] *Ibid.*, p. 95; he cites the surrender of the Social Democratic government of Prussia to von Papen in 1932 as evidence that "they desired to rule who were afraid to govern. . . . They refused to be the state; and they encountered opponents who were determined to utilize to the limit the full implications of its supreme coercive power." *Ibid.*, p. 96.

[53] *Ibid.*, p. 96.

seeks to transcend the relations of production implied in a capitalist society," [54] he also states—and this is the important new element in his analysis—that "the leaders of the Fascist parties have in each instance used the power of the state to make themselves the masters alike of the working-classes and of the capitalist class in the interest of perpetuating their own authority." [55]

Again and again he returns to this theme; the businessmen called in the outlaws and gangsters to obtain relief from the pressure of democratic and socialist demands and to restore among the masses the discipline that had been destroyed by the growing inability of the system to satisfy the workers' expectations. But having "preferred the risk of alliance with the outlaws to the possibilities involved in an alliance with the people," [56] the owners of property now find that their fears have led them into a prison where they are at the mercy of the Fascist reign of permanent terror. "The decision to place Mussolini and Hitler in power . . . was, in fact, the execution of bourgeois society." [57] In essence Fascism is a counterrevolution, whose purpose is "to adapt capitalist society to the conditions of modern technology, of a world-market, of a division of labour which has made the collectivist organization of social relationships inevitable. Fascism is capitalism rejecting its liberal origins in order to adapt its relations of production to a situation in which the liberal idea, politically, economically, and socially, would be fatal to the capitalist idea." [58] Clearly there is confusion here; Laski tells us that the Fascist leaders have enslaved the capitalists and executed capitalist society, and yet he argues that Fascism is essentially capitalism adapting itself to the requirements of modern technology. When every important element in the society and the economy has come under the control of the Fascist leaders, the society can hardly be described as capitalist, if the word is to retain any meaning. Once again he extends the concept of "capitalism" to the point of unintelligibility, just as he did when he failed to distinguish between the *laissez-faire* society and the modern positive state.

He offers the following explanation of the success of Fascism:

Counter-revolution succeeds when a quite special set of historical circumstances have taken a deep hold of a people. Its established expecta-

[54] *Ibid.*, pp. 100–1.   [55] *Ibid.*, p. 99.   [56] *Ibid.*, p. 136.
[57] *Ibid.*, p. 127.   [58] *Ibid.*, pp. 285–86.

tions are disappointed; its sense of failure is profound; it has ceased to be at unity with itself, and has lost, thereby, the capacity to respect its traditional political institutions. When these three conditions co-exist, the prospect of a counter-revolution is profound; when the second is absent, a revolutionary situation is emerging.[59]

According to this analysis, the sense of national failure and frustration is the critical factor that determines whether popular discontent with the established order will find its outlet in a revolutionary or a counterrevolutionary channel. Moreover, Laski sometimes emphasizes the complexity and diversity of the forces that advanced the Fascist counterrevolution; it was, he says, "built upon a coalition of forces each of which not only had a special interest in its success, but a secret hope that in the final co-ordination achieved it might become the dominant authority."[60] This emphasis contradicts his earlier view, which he never completely abandons, that Fascism is simply the creature of a threatened capitalist ruling class. Although he asserts that Fascism is compelled to plan for war and aggression and that "it therefore assumes a quasi-collectivist character in which *the state-power determines the ends to which the instruments of production are devoted,*"[61] he also maintains that Fascism "remakes the foundations of order to retain the claims of privilege."[62] His wartime opposition to Nazism and his desire to mobilize every possible force in order to insure its defeat are in conflict with his long-standing antagonism to capitalism and with his tendency to regard the capitalist class as the source of all evil. The first aim leads him to view the Fascist leaders as the outlaws of Western civilization, as gangsters who have made themselves the masters of the economically powerful as well as the oppressed, while his antipathy to capitalism drives him to identify the new enemy, Fascism, with the ancient foe, capitalism.

In explaining the rise of Fascism, he also attributes a good deal of significance to "the peculiar characteristics of German historical-economic conditions,"[63] and particularly to the fact that the impact of the French Revolution made the growth of the middle class to

[59] *Ibid.,* p. 290.   [60] *Ibid.,* p. 292.   [61] *Ibid.,* p. 304; italics mine.

[62] *Ibid.,* p. 303; see also the statement that Fascism "adapts capitalism . . . to the conditions which safeguard the forces of privilege against revolt from within." *Ibid.,* p. 305.

[63] *Ibid.,* p. 261.

power the victim of the hostility to Napoleon. The result of this special historical experience was that in 1918 "the German bourgeoisie was already, as a governing class, an economic anachronism, and the German proletariat was not yet ready to take its place." [64] When the problems of military defeat and the economic crises of inflation and depression were superimposed upon this power vacuum, respect for tradition and for law vanished; in this state of civil war, the "doctrineless nihilism" of Fascism found its opportunity. The movement, he insists, has no philosophy and makes no effort to build a new society. Hitler "achieved power simply in order to maintain power. He could not keep himself in power without terror; he therefore used terror." [65] "If a constitutive principle in fascism exists at all, it is simply and solely the principle that power is the sole good and that values attach only to those expedients which sustain and enlarge it." [66] The attempt to identify Bolshevism and Fascism is a "monstrous error." Bolshevism is a truly revolutionary doctrine, and the difference between it and Fascism is "the vital one that there is nothing in the nature of the Bolshevik state which is alien from the democratic ideal." [67] Fascism, being "a contradiction of the objective movement of history," [68] can never achieve peace, stability, or material security.

Laski's wartime analysis of Fascism represents some improvement over his previous view that it is the instrument created by the capitalist class to defend its wealth and privileges and to crush the organizations of the workers. But he never seems to recognize that his rejection of the orthodox Marxist theory of Fascism has important implications for his general philosophy of the state and his view of the historical process. He bases his explanation of the successful appeal of the Fascist movement almost entirely on such noneconomic factors as frustrated nationalism and the psychological disturbances among the old and new middle classes, and in his analysis of the roots of Nazism in German experience he lays great stress on historical events that are not primarily economic in character, such as the Thirty Years' War and the association of the ideas and institutions

[64] *Ibid.*, p. 262.   [65] *Ibid.*, p. 108.   [66] *Ibid.*, p. 103.

[67] *Ibid.*, p. 301; he does not explain how the democratic ideal can be defined to make it compatible with the Bolshevik theory of the state and the Party or with the Stalinist state in action.

[68] *Ibid.*, p. 122.

of the French Revolution with the Napoleonic invasion. His argument that a profound sense of failure among a people is the crucial factor that leads to the resolution of the capitalist crisis by Fascism rather than by a socialist revolution is based on the fundamentally anti-Marxist assumption that socio-psychological factors can effect a major shift in "the objective movement of history." When he maintains that under Fascism economic power is decisively subordinated to the demands of the dominant political group and that the state determines the ends for which the instruments of production are to be used—and he adheres to this view at least half the time—he is, of course, denying the validity of Marx's theory of the state. He tells us that a group of men who possessed little or no economic power, who were, in fact, total failures in capitalist society, have succeeded, by skillful propaganda and by the use of terror, in making themselves the masters of the state and, thereby, of the economy and the entire society. In so far as the Fascist leaders acquired wealth and economic power after they captured the state, they reversed the Marxist thesis that the state is coercive power in the hands of the dominant economic group and made economic power the derivative of political power.

The phenomenon of Fascism is fatal to Laski's Marxism, just as it destroys the basis of other nineteenth-century creeds, such as the belief that reason had finally triumphed over the passions or the faith that social progress would be continuous and automatic. We have seen that his version of the Marxist doctrine renders Laski incapable of dealing with the realities of the twentieth-century positive state; confronted with the problem of explaining Fascism, his theory of the state, already weighted down and encumbered by numerous reinterpretations and modifications, finally collapses. Although the war against the Nazis forced him to modify his earlier interpretation of Fascism, he never followed through the implications of these changes with sufficient consistency to realize that he had undermined his basic premises. Since he had neither the time nor the will to undertake a fundamental reassessment of his political beliefs, he went on repeating the old formulas and hypnotizing himself and his audiences by the use of a series of resounding phrases. Reality receded farther and farther from his grasp, but the words he uttered were so familiar and persuasive to him that he was not aware that he had, to a large extent, substituted a world of fiction and shadows for the world of facts. Occasionally, when some great event in the real world, such as the outbreak of war in 1939, forced its way into his consciousness, he attempted to modify his ideas to make them conform more closely to the facts. But the web of illusion was stronger than these realistic intrusions; since his energy was being drained off into a hundred different channels, he would hurriedly make the few changes that were essential to close the gaps and then sink back into the repose of the older and simpler formulations.

During the last two years of the war, for example, as the menace of a Nazi victory faded, he tended to revert to his earlier analysis of Fascism and to fall back on the simple dichotomies of good and evil, socialism and capitalism, the progressive and peace-loving Soviet Union and the reactionary and imperialistic capitalist world led by the United States. Once more he insists that "if the legal relations of capitalism are threatened, the evidence is now, I suggest, too massive to be denied that those who feel that they may lose by a change in the system will turn to Fascism as the method whereby they may protect their privileges." [69] We must choose either the nihilistic barbarism of Fascism or the idea of the Russian Revolution, either monopoly capitalism, which leads inexorably to Fascism, or planned production for community consumption. He states that it is

difficult to see upon what basis the civilized tradition can be rebuilt save that upon which the idea of the Russian Revolution is founded. . . . For, on the one hand, it satisfies the masses by its power to offer to them a sense of individual fulfilment now wholly unattainable within the confines of any alternative social system. And, on the other, it offers to the *élite* a vocation of leadership which seems likely to replace with real adequacy that wealth so often unrelated to function which has done so much to discredit the claims of privilege in our time. [70]

He offers no evidence to support the claim that the Soviet system offers its citizens a sense of individual fulfillment that no other sys-

[69] *London, Washington, Moscow, Partners in Peace?*, p. 22; see also the comment that "all over the world, those who defend the acquisitive society, whatever the rationalisations by which they defend it, are, in the end, driven to make a counter revolution in its name." *Ibid.*, p. 23.

[70] FRC, p. 51.

tem can now provide; and, to call the Stalinist dictatorship "a vocation of leadership" is, as he would say, "the happiest euphemism in
the history of the language."

In his general comments about the nature of the state, he continues
to employ the Marxist phrases that he adopted in the early 1930's.
"The character of a government, the ends, therefore, for which, if
it can, it will exercise its supreme coercive power, are set by the
parallelogram of forces in the society which it controls. The determining factor in that parallelogram is the relations of production in
the society." [71] Yet he states that in the middle of the nineteenth
century "the upper and middle classes in alliance in the Old World,
and the men of property in the New" discovered "that they could use
the state-power, both internally and externally, to protect their privileges from invasion." [72] We are not told what the "capitalist state"
was doing during the centuries that elapsed between the capture of
political power by the bourgeoisie and this "discovery" in the 1850's;
nor is it clear why Laski selects as the high point of capitalist exploitation of the machinery of the state the period of the last century,
during which, as he admits, democratic governments have been increasingly sensitive to the demands of an ever wider circle of citizens.

His primary concern is to berate the British Labor Party and its
leaders for their unwillingness to accept the fundamentals of the
Marxist philosophy. The theme of his 1943 essay on Marx is that the
future of the labor movement in Britain depends "on our ability
to recognise the bankruptcy of the traditional horror of principles
by which it has been permeated," and "on our willingness to adapt
the essentials of the Marxist philosophy to the situation we occupy." [73]
At the root of the movement's failures and difficulties lies the assumption that since the state power is a neutral factor in society, there
need be no real class struggle in England.[74] He attributes the Party's
failure to advance from a pragmatic program of social reform to a

---

[71] RR, p. 239; see also the statement that the purpose of the state power has always
been "to put the force of law . . . at the disposal of those who . . . owned or controlled the instruments of production in a given society." *Ibid.*, p. 294.

[72] *Ibid.*, p. 363.   [73] MT, p. 3.

[74] Note his charge that the Party is "incapable of realising that the state-power is
not a neutral agency vowed to some abstract common good, but a concrete weapon
used by men in the service of that class whose power over property enables them to
define the productive relations of society." *Ibid.*, p. 16.

thoroughgoing socialism to the great influx into the Party during the 1920's of people who were more interested in its success than in its doctrines. These nonsocialist opportunists forced the Party to accept the principle of "the inevitability of gradualness," based on the conviction that "there was some miraculous dispensation by which we should achieve our socialist transformation without fighting for it." [75] If this explanation is correct, Laski is, in effect, conceding that many British workers do not accept the views of the nature of the state and the class struggle which he advocates and which he usually attributes to them. The logical course for him to follow would be to adopt the Leninist solution and to assume that he and his followers know the real needs and desires of the masses better than they do themselves. But he is unwilling to break with the Party whose philosophy he rejects; indeed, he continues to serve as a member of its Executive Committee. In many of his books and articles he denounces the rank and file of the movement for their lack of insight into the dynamics of power and the leaders for their "collaborationist" tendencies, while at Party meetings and conferences he is not infrequently found employing his dialectical skill to defend the official program and actions of the Party leadership.

"The real truth . . ." Laski asserts, "is that once the Labour Party rejects the Marxist approach, it is bound to become no more than a party of social reform, and that the area within which social reform is possible depends upon the degree of well-being which leaves the masters of our present social order confident about their future." [76] Like the German Social Democrats, the British Laborites fail completely to understand the dynamics of political power and so hold to the naive belief that, in some way, England can "contract out" of the world phenomenon of the Fascist counterrevolution. The essence of this political wisdom which Laborites do not possess is the principle that force is the basis of every state and that "no government will permit a challenge, open or secret, to the imperatives behind which it places the fundamental authority of the state-power." [77] No capitalist state, no matter how democratic, will permit a challenge to the fundamental bases of capitalist social and economic relations; if necessary, it will exert to the limit its supreme coercive power in order to prevent any change in class relationships. The implica-

[75] *Ibid.*, p. 7.   [76] *Ibid.*, p. 20.   [77] RR, p. 389.

tions for the strategy of the Labor Party are obvious. No socialist party can hope to succeed to power in a normal, constitutional manner or to use the ordinary machinery of the state to accomplish the transition to socialism. A socialist government that has won an election must be prepared to face a determined capitalist effort to destroy democratic institutions. Socialists must be aware of the full implications of the state's coercive power and willing to utilize it to the full in order to carry out their program; they must not allow key positions in the civil service, the armed forces, and the courts to remain in the hands of their enemies. At every point they must adopt a positive attitude toward political power and not fall victims to the hesitation, indecision, and unwillingness to rule that have been the downfall of so many Left governments.

Just as the chief function of the capitalist state is the protection of the essentials of capitalism, the state in the new "planned democracy" must regard as its central task the defense of the system of public ownership of the vital instruments of production. The ideas of a Conservative Party will be persecuted immediately they appear to threaten the foundations of the planned society.[78] Under capitalism political parties must accept the fundamentals of capitalism and can operate successfully only as long as they do not disturb the confidence of the owners of property. Similarly, in the planned society political parties must accept the fundamental principle of social ownership of the means of production, and the field of political action will be limited to the relatively minor conflicts which arise from the different views of the various parties of "the best way to develop the public estate." [79] If this picture of the new "planned democracy," with its emphasis on the necessity for maximum exploitation of the state's coercive power, seems to be verging perilously close to Bolshevik theory, Laski reminds us that the Communists alone among Left parties have succeeded in bringing a socialist society into being. The magic of that success dispels all doubts from his mind. While conceding that the Russian Revolution "has offered opportunities to evil men of which they have taken large advantage," he at once adds: "Any fundamental change which depends for its effect upon new human relations and institutions must run the risks inherent in the exercise of power." [80]

[78] See *ibid.*, p. 406.   [79] *Ibid.*, p. 407.   [80] FRC, p. 143.

The new "realistic" Laski is contemptuous of the fears of those who wonder whether a centralized socialism may not entail a great and dangerous increase in the power of the state over the individual.[81] All states, he argues, have been based upon force and coercion rather than consent, because they have been unable to satisfy the wants of the people at a reasonable level. Only when the socialist society is firmly established and the defenders of the old order have faded away or been eliminated will we have, for the first time in history, a society based on a steady improvement in the material condition of all citizens; only then will government be able to rest on consent rather than coercion. But in order to reach this blessed state, in which coercive power will have "withered away," we must pass through an era of transition in which the exercise of power will be greatly intensified. Only the naive and the sentimental can still believe that these "grim necessities" may be avoided. Those who comprehend the inevitable course of history and the scientific principles of political power know that

any belief passionately held will seek to obtain power; and, if it does obtain it, it will fight with all its strength not merely to maintain the power it has won, but, if it can, to extend the area of its authority. . . . and where the possession of a belief gives birth to controversy, it is only where its consequences are deemed unimportant that men are prepared to abide by the results of reason and peaceful discussion.[82]

Although Laski usually dismisses fears of bureaucracy as propaganda on behalf of the privileged class, he recognizes the need for safeguards against *"the danger that a planned society will lose its democratic habits and fall into the hands of bureaucrats greedy for power."* [83] He says: "Unless we recognise that decentralisation is the secret of freedom, government becomes 'they' instead of 'we'; and that sense of aloofness is fatal to the fulfilment of personality. Do let us ceaselessly remember that planned democracy is planning for

[81] He insists that "the major part of the attack upon the state as bureaucratic is a technique for preserving essential social power in private hands." *Will Planning Restrict Freedom?*, p. 4. See also the comment: "Planning always seems to involve bureaucracy to those persons who can buy for themselves the service that the planners propose to organise for the whole community." *Ibid.*, p. 20.

[82] FRC, pp. 160–61.

[83] *Will Planning Restrict Freedom?*, p. 10; italics mine. See also his warning that "a planned society may easily be built by the sacrifice of individual freedom to that collective state-power operated by the rulers of the society." RR, p. 180.

the individual citizen, and not against him." [84] He offers no detailed discussion of the institutions that must be created in order to utilize the ordinary citizen's experience in the process of planning, but he insists that these institutions "should not so operate as to slow down unconscionably the processes of social change." [85] He confines himself to vague generalizations about the importance of decentralization, direct and continuous participation in civic affairs by all citizens, and a high level of popular interest in social and political problems.

Laski defends the freedom of the individual against what he describes as the tendency within the Labor Party to discipline spontaneity in the name of conformity and unity. "Expulsion becomes almost a monthly experience in the administration of the party; and expulsion rapidly breeds the mind accustomed to regimentation." [86] Warning against the dangers of the idea that members of the Party must accept without question the decisions of their leaders, he insists that the left-wing tendency to "identify the ethically right with what its leaders deem politically expedient at some given moment of time" [87] has had disastrous results. He urges that the insights of one's conscience, when one is sure of them, should never be sacrificed to the demands of any strategy. Our deepest obligation is not to any party or church, but "to that inner self in each one of us which we can never yield to any one's keeping without ceasing to be true to our dignity as human beings." [88] How is this emphasis on the freedom of the individual conscience to be reconciled with Laski's view that socialists must be realists about political power, prepared, if necessary, to suppress the liberties of those who do not accept the socialist faith? First, he obviously did not find it difficult to hold contradictory positions at any given moment. He superimposed a layer of Marxism on top of his earlier neo-Benthamite liberalism and never seemed to realize that the two strata could not be fused into a consistent philosophy. Depending on the circumstances and on his audience, he

[84] "Choosing the Planners," in G. D. H. Cole *et al.*, *Plan for Britain* (London: George Routledge and Sons, Ltd., 1943), pp. 123–24.

[85] *Will Planning Restrict Freedom?*, pp. 10–11.

[86] MT, pp. 28–29.   [87] *Ibid.*, p. 28.

[88] FRC, p. 33. See also: "The preservation of individuality, its extension, indeed, its ability to affirm its own essence, that is, I believe, the central aim of any ethic that Marxism can endorse." MT, p. 28.

was capable of moving rapidly from a collectivistic to an individualistic position. He may well have been unconscious of the major inconsistencies in his position; he was so fluent in speech and in writing that he could move down any of several paths with equal ease, and there was never the time nor, perhaps, the will to discover the extent to which they diverged.

Despite his insistence that a man's first obligation is to act in accordance with the dictates of his own conscience rather than to follow the strategy of any organization or party, he remained a member of the Labor Party's Executive Committee for fourteen years, although he often violently opposed the programs and policies adopted by the Party. He was never willing to carry his opposition to the point of resigning from the Executive Committee or from the Party. Such behavior may be understandable on the part of a trade unionist to whom loyalty to the movement and the solidarity of labor are the primary virtues, but, as an intellectual and a defender of the primacy of the individual conscience, Laski had much less excuse for his willingness to conform. He seems to have been so enamored of prestige and the sense that he was close to the seats of power that he was never willing to break with the Party leadership. For example, throughout the 1930's he called for a united front of working-class parties to meet the threat of capitalist reaction and Fascism, and in 1938 he castigated the Party's leaders for their refusal to allow the affiliation of the Communist Party. In 1937 and 1938 a movement arose within the Party, headed by Sir Stafford Cripps, that advocated a united front of all Leftist groups and, later, a broad popular front which would include all the opponents of the Conservatives, including the Liberals. Although he was a member of the Executive Committee, Laski was one of the leaders of the united-front movement; the activities of the group were sharply condemned, however, by the Party, and after several preliminary maneuvers Cripps, Bevan, and George Strauss were expelled from the Party in 1939. No doubt Laski would have voted against these expulsions had he not been in the United States at the time. No doubt he believed that once again party unity had been purchased at the expense of individual freedom to discuss and criticize official policy. But in spite of his objections to the practice of expulsion and his agreement with the policies advocated by Cripps and the others, he made no move to protest by resigning from the Executive Committee or by following the Cripps group out of the ranks of the Labor Party.[89]

Finally, it is difficult to reconcile Laski's statements of his concern for the freedom and spontaneity of the individual or the fulfillment of human personality with his repeated references to the Soviet dictatorship as the *locus classicus* of these values. He asserts that the Russian Revolution has been built upon the acceptance of the principle of the inherent dignity of human personality.[90] His judgment of the Soviet regime is:

When the last word has been said against Russian bureaucracy, against the hindrances to the political self-expression we know in Britain and the United States, against the scale upon which its terror has been conducted, against the ugly Byzantinism of its party infallibility, the solemn truth remains that *in the Soviet Union, since the October Revolution, more men and women have had more opportunity of self-fulfilment than anywhere else in the world.*[91]

And, after stating that the new socialist society will be able to extend the idea of constitutional and representative government to areas such as the management of industry, from which it is now completely absent, he goes on to assert that we see "the effective beginnings" of such constitutional government in industry in the Soviet Union, where millions of citizens help to shape the conditions under which they live and work.[92]

[89] Cf. the account and the somewhat different interpretation of these events given in Kingsley Martin, *Harold Laski,* pp. 99–105.

[90] See RR, p. 202.   [91] FRC, p. 57; italics mine.

[92] See RR, p. 49. See also the statement that "it is a fact beyond dispute that the economic system of the Soviet Union has given to the ordinary worker the right to a say in the conditions under which he labours which he can only secure in a capitalist society either . . . by the possession of extraordinary talent, or . . . because he has behind him a strong trade union of whose policy the employer must take account." FRC, p. 145.

11
Obedience, Liberty, and Equality

1. THE PROBLEM OF OBEDIENCE

LASKI CONTINUES to focus his discussion of the problem of obedience to the state and its laws on the conditions under which the state can retain the allegiance of "the masses" rather than on the issue of the obedience of the individual citizen. Men respect the law, he argues, when they feel that they have the great ends of life in common. In the present era of capitalist contraction, this agreement on fundamentals has disappeared, since it is no longer possible to satisfy men's expectations of an ever higher standard of living. "A democratic society . . . depends . . . upon its capacity continuously to maintain respect for the laws it seeks through its government to enforce. . . . And the habit of respect for law is . . . born of the citizen's sense that the society as a going concern affords him and his like the capacity to satisfy the expectations he deems legitimate." [1] He insists that "every system of consent in modern history has required a faith as its basis that men can accept; and the roots of that faith are its ability, as a going economic concern, to satisfy the wants it encounters." [2] Now that capitalist democracy is unable to meet the people's demands for expanding welfare, the traditional discipline of the state is in decay, and men refuse to give their allegiance to the government or to its laws. The response of the ruling class to this spirit of disobedience is Fascism and the destruction of democracy.

While he maintains that every system of consent in modern history has been rooted in the ability of the economy to satisfy popular wants, he also argues that, up to the present time, no economic system has been able to satisfy the needs of men. [3] Since it is his general position that all previous states have been built on coercion rather than consent, he has no grounds for the assertion that in the period

[1] RR, p. 182.　　　[2] *Ibid.*, p. 123.　　　[3] See FRC, p. 170.

of its expansion capitalist democracy was able to create the faith that is the basis of allegiance. He ignores this problem and simply states that only by the transition from capitalism to socialism can a "common faith" be re-established as the basis for widespread popular consent to government. He assumes that socialism will inevitably mean constantly increasing production and real wages and that an economics of expansion is no longer possible under capitalism, even in the United States.[4] Only when the potentialities of the productive forces in society are liberated from the shackles that now bind them will the conditions of expanding welfare for the masses be recreated. The termination of the present age of anxiety and of decay in traditional values can only be effected "by restoring to the state the power to enforce its traditional discipline; and this power is a direct function of the economic success of the property-system which the state supports." [5]

Laski is still uncertain whether the withdrawal of popular allegiance from capitalist democracy is the result of the inability of capitalism to continue the previous advances in material well-being or of a real decline in the standard of living of the masses. He states that in recent years "the improvement in the condition of the masses was at no point equal to their expectations of improvement"; [6] this statement suggests that no deterioration has occurred, but that the workers' hopes for further improvements have not been fully met. A few pages later, however, he asserts that capitalism "involves a progressively increasing number of employed [sic; presumably, this should be "unemployed"], and a lower relative wage for those whom it does employ. Capitalism . . . progressively raises prices without a corresponding increase in wages. . . . Capitalism, finally, ceases to be capable of that continuous expansion which enables it to make continuous concessions of welfare to the many." [7] The statement that the real wages of the worker must decline in the present stage of capitalism is, as we have noted, not demonstrated. He also asserts that the insistence that society offer its members ever greater material well-being as a condition of their loyalty to the state is a new and revolutionary demand that has arisen only in the twentieth century. "A revolution has already shaped itself in men's minds," he says,

[4] See RR, p. 151.   [5] Ibid., p. 169.   [6] Ibid., p. 143.
[7] Ibid., pp. 191-92.

"which makes them judge the states under whose authority they live by their power to offer the masses economic security upon the basis of expanding welfare. That, in our time, has become the meaning of freedom to the masses all over the world." [8]

He associates this psychological revolution with the erosion of the authority and influence of organized religions, which, in earlier centuries, helped to support the state's claims to the obedience of its citizens.[9] This admission plays havoc with his thesis that obedience to the state has always been a simple function of the level of material satisfaction. He goes on to assert that in our day the socialist faith has generally replaced religious creeds. "As scientific progress subdues nature to the purposes of man, the idea of the heavenly city of early Christianity gives way to the dream in which the reward of man's effort is not salvation in the life to come but happiness upon this earth itself. And so long as the expansion of well-being continues, the scheme of values upon which the security of civilization depends maintains its hold upon mankind." [10] Today, the churches have little or no influence on the behavior of men, and religious influences follow, rather than lead, secular patterns. "Whatever religious faith may do for individual happiness, it is difficult not to conclude that it has no relevance to the collective problem of happiness by which our civilization is confronted." [11]

How are we to explain this revolution in the minds of men which has led them to insist on material well-being in this world and to reject promises of future happiness in the heavenly realm? In particular, how can we explain the general demand in the present century for a state and a social order that will guarantee to the individual a progressively rising standard of living? Obviously, the question is crucial since, according to Laski, it is this new attitude of the masses that has made them reject capitalism and democracy, its political manifestation. He says that this decisive change in men's expectations and the decline of religious beliefs in favor of a secular and materialistic outlook are the results of the discoveries of science which, especially in the last century, have made possible for the first time in history adequate control over the forces of nature. The attitudes which he describes are widely held in the advanced industrial

[8] *Ibid.*, p. 297.   [9] See *ibid.*, p. 198.   [10] FRC, p. 60.
[11] *Ibid.*, p. 137.

societies of Western Europe and the United States, though it might
be difficult to demonstrate that such expectations of continuous material improvement characterize the peoples of non-Western nations
such as China and India, or even the Soviet Union. To the extent
that Laski's thesis holds true for the Western world, it involves a
drastic reversal of the Marxist analysis and of the predictions based
upon it. He argues that the scientific revolution has made possible
the spectacular success of capitalism and a marked rise in the general
standard of living since 1850 and that these achievements have given
rise to new expectations and demands among the masses. Marx predicted that the collapse of capitalism would mean increasing misery
for a constantly expanding proletariat and, consequently, the rise
of revolutionary attitudes among the workers. Laski explains the
popular dissatisfaction with the present political and economic systems and the demand for the creation of a socialist society as the consequences of the masses' expectations of constantly expanding welfare.

He finds it difficult to decide whether he approves or condemns
this new materialistic attitude of the masses. He frequently criticizes
the desire for more and more material possessions as a manifestation
of the sickness of an acquisitive society. Repeatedly he condemns a
society in which every man is valued in terms of the volume of his
possessions; and he speaks of the remarkable spiritual transformation that took place in England during the war, when the drive for
material prosperity and individual acquisition was overshadowed by
a sense of mutual aid and participation in a great cause, which
transcended the interests of the individual. And he contrasts the materialism and self-seeking that are characteristic of capitalist society
with the emphasis on nonmaterial values that one finds in the Soviet
Union. Speaking of the Russian revolutionary idea, he says, "year in
and year out of its history, men and women, both young and old,
found in it the inspiration which made them feel that they were a
part, however small, of the great world-purpose which has the future
on its side." [12] The principles of the Bolshevik Revolution have "the
mysterious power of renovating values, of renewing the faith of man
in himself, at a time when the dark shadows seem, otherwise, likely
to close about him." [13] The clear implication of these statements is
that the value of the Soviet experiment lies in the sense of common

[12] *Ibid.*, p. 54.   [13] *Ibid.*, p. 64.

purpose that it inspires, and not in the higher standard of material well-being that it offers. Indeed, Laski now argues that the principles of Bolshevism have been successful in renovating values and renewing men's faith, whereas his usual position is that only economic expansion and a resumption of material improvements for the masses can lead to the emergence of a new set of generally accepted values. The same confusion is evident in his statements that "the purpose of any scheme of values in a society is to promote the habits among its citizens which permit of expanding welfare," [14] and that the revolutionary necessity which we now confront is the need "to find new values in the imposition of which the conditions of expanding welfare can be rediscovered." [15]

At other moments Laski not only approves the materialistic desire of the masses for a constantly rising standard of living, but argues that the Soviet Union is superior to any capitalist society because it can offer its people progressively increasing material benefits.[16] The Russian economic system, he states, is differentiated from all others by "the fact that its central principle is that of expansion for all, and that it is undominated, even uninfluenced, by any interest which can seek wealth or welfare through the technique of restriction." [17] "In the narrow economic sphere, there is a more genuine basis for economic freedom for the masses in the Soviet Union than they have elsewhere previously enjoyed." [18] The central significance of the Russian Revolution, according to this argument, is not that it has transcended the materialistic values of capitalist society, but rather its "assertion that a man may not be excluded from the essential goods that civilization has achieved simply because he is not an owner of the instruments of production." [19] The Soviet experiment, he says, makes it clear that socialism means the resumption of the improvement in the material condition of the masses and, as a result, a restoration of men's common faith and their allegiance to law. Laski specifically accepts the view that material improvement means, *ipso facto,* spiritual and intellectual progress and that a good society is one in which men's demands are satisfied at a constantly increasing rate. "I am concerned only to affirm that, as a working assumption for the people who live, not upon the heights, but in this workaday

[14] RR, p. 416.   [15] *Ibid.,* p. 417.   [16] See FRC, pp. 57–58.
[17] *Ibid.,* p. 58.   [18] RR, p. 48.   [19] *Ibid.,* p. 80.

world, adequate external circumstances are likely to mean adequate internal fulfilment." [20] He continues: "Good, on this view, is the satisfaction of demand on the largest possible scale; and a good society is one built upon an institutional basis which enables it perpetually to reach out to an ever increasing satisfaction of demand." [21]

Laski is here advocating a quantitative and materialistic conception of the good life and of the good society that he condemns in his attacks on an acquisitive capitalist society. We have seen that on the basis of this materialistic criterion the "capitalist" system of the United States must be judged to be superior to the "socialist" system of the Soviet Union. His analysis of the conditions under which men will now obey the state is correct in so far as it describes the popular materialism of Western society and the conviction that the state should guarantee to each citizen at least a minimum of well-being. He errs, however, in assuming that this attitude will necessarily lead the worker to demand the replacement of capitalism by socialism. By a program designed to prevent depressions or to cushion their effects and by the measures of the welfare state, a government may well be able to satisfy the popular demand for economic security without abandoning the capitalist system. The great danger, about which he seems totally unconcerned, is that the citizen, by equating material satisfactions with freedom and self-fulfillment, as Laski encourages him to do, may be willing to accept an authoritarian system of government, provided that it promises to defend his economic security and grant him greater material benefits. No critic aware of the profoundly materialistic temper of modern Western man should encourage men to define the good society as the one that provides its members with the largest volume of possessions or to identify freedom with economic security or material satisfaction.

2. LIBERTY, EQUALITY, AND NATURAL RIGHTS

Laski uses the occasion of the Hobhouse Memorial Lecture in 1940 to proclaim the death of the doctrines of liberalism. "We must," he says, "if we are to be honest, admit that the liberalism for which Hob-

[20] FRC, p. 138.   [21] *Ibid.*

house battled so bravely has suffered an eclipse as startling and as complete as that which attended the doctrine of the divine right of kings after the Revolution of 1688." [22] He begins by distinguishing between the negative liberalism of Locke, Smith, and the Benthamites, which stressed the freedom of the individual from the interferences of arbitrary and inefficient governments, and the positive liberalism of Green and Hobhouse, who argued that governments should act to remove hindrances to the good life. He then proceeds to ignore this distinction and to engage in extended polemic against the doctrines of *laissez-faire,* which he identifies with liberalism. Liberalism, he asserts, has now become the instrument of those whose vested privileges will be adversely affected by an extension of democracy from the political to the economic realm; in its doctrines we see reason performing its "traditional function of clothing with respectability the title of men to power who actually held power." [23] A brief examination of what he describes as the principles of liberalism—the assumption that commercial activity is the index of advancing civilization, that legislation interfering with the success of the businessman is a hindrance to progress, that a low level of material well-being for the masses is natural and inevitable [24]—demonstrates the extent to which he equates liberalism with *laissez-faire* doctrines. Liberalism, he argues, has declined because it refuses to recognize that, particularly in the economic realm, "massive social controls," requiring social planning, are essential if freedom is to have any meaning in the lives of the vast majority. The example that he offers in defense of his thesis is peculiarly revealing; he argues that in the United States the "outworn doctrines of liberalism" have been the bulwark of the opposition to the Roosevelt reforms. The radical thus finds himself in agreement with the extreme conservatives who insist that the title of "liberalism" belongs to the nineteenth-century political and economic views of the Liberty League rather than to the efforts to use the power of government to control certain aspects of economic life and to promote the general welfare.

In his discussions of liberty, Laski abandons the view that freedom means the absence of restraint, although he never explicitly rejects

---

[22] *The Decline of Liberalism,* L. T. Hobhouse Memorial Trust Lectures No. 10 (London: Oxford University Press, Humphrey Milford, 1940), p. 3.

[23] RR, p. 415.   [24] See *ibid.,* pp. 414–15.

this definition that he adopted in 1930. In its place he uses a confused mixture of Marxist and idealist definitions of freedom. The only element in his analysis which seems to be quite clear is the assertion that freedom is not essentially what most men think it is—self-determination as opposed to the determination of one's actions by some external force, such as the state. Whenever we are assured that "real" freedom is the recognition of necessity, obedience to law, or the realization of one's best self, most of us tend to suspect that behind the dialectical subtleties an attack on freedom is perhaps being prepared. Clearly freedom in the ordinary sense is not the sole good; it may not even be the highest good; we may decide to limit certain freedoms in order to achieve other values, such as security, peace, and the protection of the weak. But if we begin by extending the connotation of freedom to make it embrace virtually every human value, we are no longer able to relate liberty to other human goals and to indicate what the effect on freedom will be if we endeavor to achieve other aims by given means.

Laski, we know, has a very low opinion of the freedom that exists in "capitalist democracy." The liberty achieved in the century after 1815 has operated on a narrowly political plane and its benefits have been confined to a small number of citizens. Essentially, freedom has meant security for the individual citizen from government interference, and the free society has been "overwhelmingly, a society in which the ultimate purpose was to protect the unfettered initiative of the business man." [25] Since he admits that since 1870, and particularly since 1918, collectivist tendencies have been predominant in the actions of democratic states, we might expect that he would also admit that in this period the people have enjoyed an increasing measure of the "positive freedom" that he advocates, together with the essential elements of the traditional "negative freedom." On rare occasions he concedes that national education, insurance against unemployment, illness, and the insecurity of old age, and state regulation of hours and wages have meant striking additions to the freedom of the average citizen, but normally he ignores these gains and insists that there has been a marked decline in freedom since 1918, when the capitalist system began to contract. He derives this con-

[25] "Choosing the Planners," in G. D. H. Cole *et al., Plan for Britain* (London: George Routledge and Sons, Ltd., 1943), p. 112.

clusion from the postulate that freedom is a function of "the security men feel about the foundations of the social order; and that security in its turn, is a function of the capacity for economic expansion of that social order." [26]

He argues that "there is no effective freedom in a society if there are wide differences between citizens in their access to the good things of life"; [27] liberty must be set in the context of equality by eliminating the claims on the stock of common welfare of the owning group, who perform no useful social function. Equality he now defines, in a manner that defies comprehension, as "the admission of a plane of general satisfactions in social organization where the minimum satisfaction of equal needs is at a level which permits the increasing fulfilment of personality." [28] To make liberty real for the masses, we must move to an equal society like that of the Soviet Union where the goods of civilization are open to all, not merely to those who own the instruments of production. We must, during the next generation, build this equal society or abandon democracy, for democracy cannot survive the impact of that "class war which is the normal condition between citizens who have the security that property gives and citizens who have nothing but their labour-power to sell." [29] One wonders what has become of the large number of English and American workers whose possession of homes, cars, and savings accounts has led to their total *embourgeoisement*.

We must, Laski insists, move ahead from the negative concept of freedom to a new, positive conception, and he offers a variety of explanations of the meaning of positive freedom. First, as we have seen, he states that men now "judge the states under whose authority they live by their power to offer the masses economic security upon the basis of expanding welfare. That, in our time, has become the meaning of freedom to the masses all over the world." [30] At another point he adopts the view that freedom is the recognition of necessity; "every society is built upon a system of postulates the continuing life of which its members must agree to respect; and their freedom is only available within the limits of that respect." [31] It follows that

---

[26] WDWG, p. 162.

[27] "Democracy in War Time," in G. D. H. Cole *et al., Victory or Vested Interest?* (London: George Routledge and Sons, Ltd., 1942), p. 38.

[28] RR, p. 208.   [29] FRC, p. 89.   [30] RR, p. 297.
[31] *Ibid.*, p. 382.

if the introduction of planning into a capitalist democracy is to be compatible with the maintenance of freedom it must have behind it the general consent of citizens. . . . When a society accepts the decision to plan it is, thereby, providing itself with an overriding purpose to the general principles of which the mass of citizens must conform. Their freedom becomes a function of its necessities; the limits of their permissible initiative are set by the logic it implies.[32]

Most of us will agree that the recognition of inevitabilities is necessary, provided, of course, that the necessities that we recognize are real and are not merely our private wishes raised to the level of historical or metaphysical inevitabilities. In political action, as in all human activities, the exercise of freedom of choice proceeds always within a framework of necessity, those elements in the situation which are "given" and unalterable, the "brute facts." But if all the elements in the situation are determined by forces outside the actor's control, he is left with no freedom of choice. Freedom exists only where the situation is, at least in part, "open-ended" before the actor wills and acts. Only as he recognizes the factors that are already determined and distinguishes them from those that are susceptible to influence by his actions can he make a rational and proper use of his freedom. In this sense we can say that the exercise of freedom depends on the recognition of necessity. To say this, however, is not to assert that freedom *is* the recognition of necessity; this definition retains an honorific term although its meaning has been eliminated by the adoption of a totally deterministic theory of human action.

Laski's view of freedom as the recognition of the necessary principles of the social order also rests on his thesis that the life of every society is based on a series of generally accepted postulates that no citizen can be permitted to reject. Once we admit that a capitalist or a planned society is based on certain general principles to which all citizens must conform and that they are free only within the limits set by the "overriding purposes" of the society, we are forced to accept Laski's conclusion that freedom of action and opinion is confined to relatively insignificant matters of detail. Once we start down this path, it is fatally easy to join Laski in excusing the manifold limitations on individual freedoms that are found in a society such as the Soviet Union, since each restriction can be defended as

32 *Ibid.*, p. 383.

one of the necessities entailed in the society's "overriding purposes." When the abandonment of almost all liberties has been rationalized away in this fashion, one can always argue that since the society recognizes necessity it is, after all, really free in spite of the massive prohibitions imposed on every aspect of its citizens' lives. Given this view of freedom, it is not surprising that Laski concludes that the ideas of any group such as the Conservative Party will inevitably be persecuted once they are held to threaten the foundations of the new socialist society.[33] Nor is it strange that he argues that in the planned society, as in the Soviet Union, the primary function of the trade union will not be to defend the interests and well-being of its members, but rather to increase output and to further the achievement of the goals set by the community. The union will not have to concentrate its efforts on protecting the interests of the workers, since it will be "assisting in the development of an estate no longer subject to the claims of vested interest." [34]

Laski also insists that "citizens who participate in a great end about which they are agreed find a freedom in its service which makes right and duty reciprocal terms." [35] He cites the examples of Britain during the war and of Russia since the Revolution to prove that men find freedom in the service of a great purpose that transcends their personal interests. The difficulties inherent in this view are obvious. Although a man may be free when he decides to sacrifice his individual liberty, in whole or in part, to the service of some cause, he is in no sense free if he is compelled to submerge himself and his interests in a social purpose. Even if his sacrifice is voluntary, he can hardly be said to find freedom in surrendering himself to a higher goal; to the extent that he relinquishes control over his own actions and decisions, he loses his freedom. He may accept this loss because he holds that the defeat of Nazism or the propagation of the teachings of his faith is more important than the exercise of his individual freedom; and he may feel a profound sense of satisfaction and emotional fulfillment in the service of the cause. No amount of dialectical refinement, however, can alter the fact that the individual gives up a part of his freedom when he surrenders the direction of his conduct to some authority. No member of the armed forces during the last war was under the illusion that he was free under military discipline.

[33] See RR, p. 406.   [34] *Ibid.*, pp. 397–98.   [35] *Ibid.*, p. 386.

Satisfaction, comradeship, the sense of sharing in a great purpose, exhilaration, all these he may have found if he was fortunate, but he well knew that he had sacrificed much of his freedom for the duration of the war.

Laski's argument that men find freedom by surrendering their individuality to a great social purpose is closely linked to another definition of freedom that he often gives. "The essence of freedom, given the framework of necessity within which each must discover it," he says, "is, I think, to be found in what I have called the sense of continuous initiative, the conviction that each of us, even if involved in a social purpose which transcends our private purpose, can yet contribute to its definition some emphasis which is our own." [36] The "sense of a capacity for growth, which enables its possessor to affirm his or her personality, is the very secret of freedom." [37] He insists that in 1939, even in the democratic nations, only a "tiny minority" found in their daily lives this self-fulfillment that gives one the conviction that one is free. The idea of freedom, he says, "involves the organisation of those opportunities for continuous initiative through which alone the common man can find significance. That is why, despite its immense price and its colossal blunders, the Soviet Union reaches out towards something that is genuinely new in civilisation." [38] At another time he speaks of freedom as the creation of "the positive conditions in which a people can affirm its own essence." [39]

In a sense these definitions of freedom as the power of the individual to affirm himself or his own essence and as the possession of opportunities to exercise continuous initiative are compatible with the view that we have defended, namely, that freedom is the power of the individual to be determined in his actions by his own will rather than by any external force. The difficulty is that terms like "self-affirmation," "self-fulfillment," "self-realization," and "the realization of one's own essence" are so vague that if we use them as definitions of freedom we run the risk of becoming so confused that we are able to find freedom in situations where it is, in fact, completely absent. Laski, for example, sees unparalleled opportunities for continuous

[36] *Ibid.*, p. 390.   [37] *Ibid.*, p. 391.

[38] *London, Washington, Moscow, Partners in Peace?*, Peace Aims Pamphlet No. 22 (London: National Peace Council, 1943), p. 21.

[39] "Democracy in War Time," in Cole *et al.*, *Victory or Vested Interest?*, p. 54.

initiative for ordinary men and women in the Soviet Union; he asserts that in spite of the fact that the Communist dictatorship plans the growth of its citizens' individuality, it has achieved for millions of men the "positive freedom" that arises out of the sense of a capacity for growth. As we have observed, he solemnly maintains that in the Soviet Union since 1917 "more men and women have had more opportunity of self-fulfilment than anywhere else in the world." [40] The parallel between Laski's views of "positive freedom" and those of the Bolsheviks is not simply a deduction from his assertions that self-fulfillment and the sense of continuous initiative flourish under the Russian regime as they do in no other society; he himself explicitly makes the identification. He states:

Broadly speaking, their opponents looked upon liberty as the absence of interference with their disposition of power; *the Bolshevists regarded freedom as the positive organization of opportunities for ordinary people to exercise a creative initiative.* To achieve this end, they were driven to the idea of planned production for community consumption; and they required possession of the state-power if they were to accomplish this purpose.[41]

In order to reach these goals in the situation which confronted them, they had to accept the necessity of a system of dictatorial rule and the impossibility of democracy in the Western sense.

The strange results to which acceptance of a "positive" view of freedom has led writers such as Laski make one hesitate before abandoning the more clearcut "bourgeois" idea of freedom. The powerful argument of Dostoyevsky's Grand Inquisitor—that since freedom is an impossible burden for the ordinary man, the rulers must assume the task of making the decisions that will give men what they really desire, peace and satisfaction—although unacceptable, is more logical than the effort to retain the name of freedom while demanding its surrender in the name of the exigencies of great historical movements or theological doctrines. Why, it may be asked, have political philosophers so often ignored the essence of liberty by defining freedom as obedience to law or to a higher purpose, as the realization of the individual's highest self, or as the recognition of necessity? It is understandable that men of action, anxious to wield political power, may be tempted to define away the concept of free-

[40] FRC, p. 57. [41] *Ibid.,* pp. 156–57; italics mine.

dom that stands between them and unbridled authority. But why are scholars such as Laski, who have no hope of wielding power, led to this conclusion? One important reason seems to be that thinkers whose sensitivity makes them recoil from the evils and inadequacies of their society tend to become impatient of individual freedom and the complex process of persuasion as the means to the realization of their vision of the good life and the good society. As Laski noted in his early writings, the Utopian resents the failure of other men to share his vision of the good and their unwillingness to move to the immediate realization of his ideals. His readiness to sacrifice freedom to his blueprint of the perfect society, which can be built if only the objections and hesitations of shortsighted and stupid men are swept aside, is intensified when he also believes that he has discovered the key to the process of historical change. His proposals then are not only eminently desirable, but embody historical and metaphysical necessity; in the face of his sense of intoxication and his drive to overcome all obstacles, the protests and the doubts of individuals pale into insignificance.

Another reason for the attempts to redefine freedom is that many men seem unwilling to accept the fact that both freedom and authority, or freedom and necessity, exist and that they sometimes come into conflict. Since Rousseau, thinkers have persisted in the effort to prove that there is no opposition between freedom and authority provided that we understand the true nature of freedom. The reconciliation is not difficult if, with the idealists, we define freedom as obedience to one's real or best self, and if we assume that the state is the embodiment of that self. But clashes between the demands of authority and the freedoms of men occur from time to time in spite of such intellectual resolutions of the dilemma. Freedom has meaning only in the presence of restraint; if there were no hindrances to our freedom of action we would be unable to comprehend the meaning of liberty. And restraints by authority are often necessary to preserve the freedoms of some men from interference by others. Sometimes we may do freely that which authority compels us to do. Freedom and authority are not simply contradictories, nor are they inevitably complementary.

12

Economic and Political Change

1. POLITICS AND ECONOMICS

THROUGHOUT the war period Laski monotonously repeats the slogan that capitalist relations of production are out of harmony with the forces of production and that this disharmony compels an economics of scarcity at a time when modern technology has made possible continually expanding welfare for all. Even in the United States, capitalism can no longer expand; in fact production is restricted so that profits will not be endangered by an oversupply of goods, the share of the wage earners in the national income is progressively reduced, and the size of the reserve army of the unemployed increases. His explanation of the crisis in capitalism now seems to be a simple underconsumption theory. Capitalism distributes an excessive and constantly increasing proportion of the national income to the rich, whose claims to profit, rent, and interest are the first charge on the social product. As a result, the masses are increasingly impoverished and their capacity to consume can never overtake the social capacity to produce.[1] As usual, his statements about economics are extremely confused; he argues that total production is curtailed because of the restrictionist policies of capitalism, and yet, in discussing the United States, he says that "it is, above all, notable that *despite the increase in the national income between 1933 and 1941,* the proportion which went to the working-class was smaller than in 1929."[2] Despite the evidence that the tremendous increases in American production during the war were accompanied by a marked improvement in the general standard of living, although a large proportion of the national product was being channeled into war production, he continues to

[1] See RR, pp. 191–92; and MT, pp. 25–26.
[2] *London, Washington, Moscow, Partners in Peace?*, Peace Aims Pamphlet No. 22 (London: National Peace Council, 1943), p. 13; italics mine.

insist that capitalism now means a progressive decline in real wages and an ever larger number of unemployed workers.

He argues that if Britain and America remain capitalist societies they will not be able to avoid the destruction of democracy and the resort to Fascism. Increasingly the workers, who are denied the benefits to which they believe they are entitled, look with favor on the Soviet Union where the economic system is capable of expansion. "This central idea of the Russian Revolution that we must, as a society, plan production for community consumption has taken a hold upon mass-opinion with something of the vigour of a new faith." [3] The Soviet Union, having resolved the contradictions of capitalism, can offer its people a rising standard of living, and it has no interest, as capitalist states inevitably do, in war or aggression. The United States, on the other hand, will probably have fifteen million people unemployed after the war. [4] Discussing the relations that will obtain between the great powers after victory, he says, "the relations of production in a society which neglects justice and denies self-government to its citizens will make it difficult for that society to maintain friendship with another society in which justice and self-government are highly valued"; [5] the latter society is, presumably, the Soviet Union. He maintains that the only way to counter the appeal of Communism to the workers is to have a labor government that will carry through a forthright socialist program. Since "sinister interests" and "prescriptive titles to well-being" alone prevent the expansion of production and the use of the community's resources for the well-being of the many, we will, as soon as the present "dark age of privilege" is abolished, automatically move into "an era of vast and creative economic expansion." [6]

Only by eliminating social and economic privileges through social ownership of property and by planning social and economic life in the interest of the whole community can we fully mobilize the workers in support of the war and make the Four Freedoms meaningful in their lives after victory. A number of fundamental principles must be recognized immediately, even if they cannot be completely ap-

[3] FRC, p. 150.

[4] "The American Myth and the Peace," *The Nation*, CLVIII (Feb. 12, 1944), 181.

[5] *London, Washington, Moscow, Partners in Peace?*, p. 19.

[6] "Choosing the Planners," in G. D. H. Cole *et al.*, *Plan for Britain* (London: George Routledge and Sons, Ltd., 1943), p. 115.

plied until after the victory over Nazism: certain sectors of the economy, such as land, fuel, transport, electric power, and the credit system, must be placed under public ownership; the educational and public health systems must be radically reformed and extended; a great housing program must be started; there must be provision for economic planning to prevent the recurrence of mass unemployment and depression; and the state must control imports and exports.[7] These proposals, he says, "do not assume the establishment of a socialist state at the end of the war. . . . Their purpose is the different, though related, one, of safeguarding our political democracy against those forces of counter-revolution which are present among ourselves." [8] The program outlined would constitute a beginning of the necessary movement to the socialist society. It would reassure the workers of the possibility of achieving their socialist aims by peaceful and democratic means and would provide "the time for that psychological readjustment to great innovation which offers the surest basis for the avoidance of conflict." [9] This program is the minimum response that can satisfy the demands of the masses. "It is the central thesis of the Labour Party's doctrine that, in the absence of such changes before the end of the war, the fruits of victory will have been thrown away." [10] Inasmuch as the actions of the Party's leaders in the Coalition Government are a complete denial of this thesis, they are compelled to fight the war on the terms of the ruling class, the restoration of "traditional Britain," rather than the strengthening and extension of democracy and freedom.

Laski advances a series of arguments to demonstrate the necessity of using the war period to inaugurate these fundamental changes in the social and economic system of England. The psychological conditions created by the war have prepared men for great and rapid changes and made them more willing than ever before to accept great sacrifices for the sake of social goals. He states: "I have never known the mind of this country more open to great experiment, nor have I ever known the common people of Britain more determined upon

[7] See RR, pp. 349–51; and "The Need for a European Revolution," in *Programme for Victory* (London: The Fabian Society and George Routledge and Sons, Ltd., 1941), pp. 26–31.

[8] RR, p. 352.

[9] "The Need for a European Revolution," in *Programme for Victory*, p. 31.

[10] RR, p. 405.

its inception. . . . There is a greater chance to-day of what may be termed a revolution by consent in Britain than at any time in history." [11] He thus advances the curiously un-Marxist thesis that the war offers a great opportunity, which will never be repeated, of securing general consent for a peaceful transition from capitalism to socialism and a complete redefinition of the state purpose.[12] He insists that this sense of national unity and this willingness to embark on great changes will evaporate with the end of hostilities. After victory the ruling class, no longer needing the support of the masses, will be far less willing to accept sacrifices of their power and privileges; they will then "look for their directives rather to the privileges of the past than to the hopes of the future." [13] Among the masses fatigue and inertia, which are always the main support of the opposition to change, will inevitably follow the tremendous physical and mental strains of the war years. When the war is over, "men will want, more than anything, a routine of thought and habit which does not compel the painful adaptation of their minds to disturbing excitement. . . . In the grim crucible of war, a nation can build that pattern of reform which makes possible recovery after the war." [14]

If the government proceeds at once to demonstrate, by deeds rather than words, to the British people and to the whole world that "to win a democratic victory, capitalist power has actually begun to strip itself of its privileges," [15] we can ensure the foundations of our democratic society. But if, ignoring the implications of the revolution of our time, we miss the present chance to embark on major reforms, "the opportunity we now have will not recur in any time of which we need to take account. We shall then enter upon an epoch of which little will be remembered save the suffering it unnecessarily caused. That is the choice before us." [16] If the necessary changes are not made before hostilities cease, England will rapidly move to a situation of intense class conflict and, inevitably, to violent revolution. Laski also

[11] "British Democracy and Mr. Kennedy," *Harper's Magazine*, CLXXXII (April, 1941), 469. See also the statement that not "since the seventeenth century has there been in Britain a deeper anxiety to probe into the roots of its problems, a greater willingness to experiment on a scale proportionate to their intensity." RR, p. 332.

[12] See RR, pp. 417–18.

[13] "Choosing the Planners," in Cole *et al.*, *Plan for Britain*, p. 125.

[14] RR, p. 228.   [15] WDWG, p. 154.

[16] H. J. Laski, Wilfred Wellock, P. W. Martin, *The Economic Revolution*, Peace Aims Pamphlet No. 5 (London: National Peace Council, 1941), p. 24.

argues that the movement towards socialism in Britain is an essential element in the strategy of fighting Nazism by provoking revolutions among Hitler's victims, both inside Germany and in the conquered nations. Precepts and propaganda will never evoke resistance among those who suffer under Fascist rule; the old order of capitalism does not win the allegiance of our own people, and it inspires among the conquered people no willingness to risk everything for the defeat of Nazism. He insists that "if we are to appeal to the German workers, the best form that appeal can take is the proof, in our own society, of our capacity to do justice to the interests of our own workers." [17] We must offer the peoples of Europe the model of a new society that Hitler and Mussolini cannot hope to match. "We can fight the counter-revolution successfully if we fight it with a revolutionary idea; but nothing less than this idea will suffice if our victory is to be a creative one." [18]

In any case, the European Revolution is unavoidable; if Britain fails to give it leadership by her example, it will seek direction and support from the Soviet Union.[19] "The only questions to be raised are whether its birth-pangs can be abridged and its purpose made beneficent. If the victory of this country were to be set in the perspective I have described, I think that abridgement and that beneficence can be secured; without it, I believe we shall enter upon an era as dark as any in the human record." [20] The reconstruction of Europe will be impossible unless England takes a leading role in the task of rebuilding. She will be unable to assume that leadership if she cannot offer Europe the example of a just and truly democratic society, and if her own failure to reach agreement on the basic principles of reform leaves her torn by internal dissension and class conflict in the postwar period. "Internecine conflict here will be so grave a pre-occupation that we shall lack the power and the energy to preside over that European reconstruction in which our leadership will be so obviously essential." [21]

He also asserts that from 1917 to 1941 "there was no capitalist society which was not anxious for the downfall of the Soviet Union, unwilling to build normal relations, either social or political with its peo-

---

[17] RR, p. 319. [18] *Ibid.*, p. 320. [19] See SOF, pp. 57–60.
[20] "The Need for a European Revolution," in *Programme for Victory*, p. 33.
[21] *Ibid.*, p. 16.

ple." [22] A further argument in favor of beginning the transition to socialism during the war is that we will thereby demonstrate to the Russians that the forces of privilege in the West will no longer be able to threaten their security. "Peace in any durable way depends upon our ability to arrive at a *modus vivendi* with the Soviet Union. We shall achieve that only as we get at the root of Soviet suspicion of our motives; and the way to remove that suspicion is to make it plain that there is nothing in the operation of our social institutions which makes us desire, or even connive at, the breakdown of the Soviet experiment." [23] Finally, he is convinced that the inauguration of a revolution by consent in Britain will also have important consequences in the United States. Sometimes he argues that the English revolution is essential because only a socialist Britain can evoke the necessary response from a progressive America. "The Britain of the old order, with its slums, its mass unemployment, its profound privileges, has nothing to say to the new America which, under President Roosevelt's leadership, is struggling to be born." [24] At other times he urges Britain to begin the task of fundamental social transformation in order to help create in the United States a widespread demand for similar experiment, which will arrest "the danger—omnipresent in the United States in existing conditions—that big business will use the war-emergency to stifle the struggle of the New Deal to continue." [25]

To the objection that the tremendous responsibilities and burdens of Britain's wartime leaders make it impossible for them to give their attention to plans for fundamental changes after the war, Laski replies that the program of change that he urges is an essential part of the strategy of total war. The morale of the common people, which is the key to successful war production and to victory, depends on the demonstration that the postwar world will be one in which their needs and desires will be satisfied. He insists that "the separation of victory in the field from the building of the conditions which enable the victory to be used is an artificial and static conception of totalitarian war which mistakes altogether its inherent nature." [26] Churchill is prepared to be responsible for any change, no matter how great, if only he can be made to see its direct relevance to the attainment

22 FRC, pp. 145–46.   23 *The Economic Revolution*, p. 23.
24 *Ibid.*, p. 24.   25 RR, p. 216.   26 *Ibid.*, p. 284.

of victory. It is the essential task of the Labor members of his Government to persuade him that the full support of the workers at home and the willingness of the peoples of Europe to revolt against Fascism depend upon an immediate beginning of a fundamental redistribution of economic power in Britain. Indeed, the leaders of the Labor Party should insist that Churchill's acceptance of this policy is the price he must pay for their support.[27] The Party leaders fail to press these demands upon the Conservatives; as usual they cling to habit without philosophy, and, faced with the tremendous problems of the postwar period, they refuse to recognize that "only upon a Marxist basis can we diagnose them correctly, and hope, thereby, successfully to solve them." [28] By the middle of 1943 Laski has become convinced that the unwillingness of Attlee, Bevin, and Morrison to insist that the Coalition Government accept his program for a wartime revolution by consent means that we have failed "to utilize the revolutionary impetus of this war to lay the foundations of those conditions, both economic and social, which would ensure to us the prospect of full employment after the war. That failure only means," he concludes pessimistically, "that the struggle for those conditions will come later rather than now, that it will, in all probability, be established by coercion instead of founded on consent." [29]

His argument that Labor should insist that at least the first steps to socialism must be taken before the end of the war, even at the risk of disrupting the Coalition Government, is based on his analysis of British political and economic life. In his view a small group of "vested interests," "the privileged class," who are violently opposed to any change, confront the overwhelming majority of the people, the masses, who no longer accept capitalism as just or efficient and who demand that it be replaced by socialism. Since he believes that only the few who enjoy the privileges of the old order stand in the way of the necessary changes, he concludes that it is not only right but politically wise for Labor's leaders to demand a revolution by consent during the war. His analysis ignores the crucial fact, which Attlee and Morrison were constantly forced to remember, that about half of the citizens of Britain were opposed to the program of the Labor Party. This fact was clearly demonstrated by the results of

[27] See WDWG, pp. 157–58.   [28] MT, p. 25.
[29] *London, Washington, Moscow, Partners in Peace?*, p. 9.

the 1945 election in which Labor received less than fifty per cent
of the popular vote although it won an overwhelming majority in
the House of Commons. The fairly equal division between the supporters and opponents of the Labor Party in 1945 indicates the error
of Laski's assumption that there was an overwhelming popular demand for a wartime socialist transformation. Had the leaders of the
Labor Party followed his advice, they would have been condemned
by at least half of the English voters; if they had threatened to withdraw from the Coalition before the end of the war in Europe or, a
fortiori, if they had actually carried out this threat, they might well
have antagonized enough of the middle-class voters to give the Conservatives the victory in the general election of 1945. Labor won
power in 1945 only because a number of these voters, who were not
normally its supporters, switched from the Conservative to the Labor
Party.[30]

2. MARXISM AND LENINISM

We have seen that Laski's central thesis is that a fundamental contradiction exists between the essence of capitalism and the essence
of democracy. This antithesis, which was obscured during the nineteenth century by the economic successes of the capitalist system, has
been clearly revealed since 1919 in Europe and since 1929 in the
United States. The ruling class, having become convinced that the
operations of democracy constitute a danger to property and its
privileges, is prepared to abandon representative and constitutional
government. Laski has still not resolved the basic dilemma of his
position. When he is discussing the advances in popular welfare and
the limitations on the power of property that have been made by the
positive state, he insists that "business men will not return to their
mastery of the state upon their own terms for the simple reason that
no one has any longer confidence in them except themselves." [31] At

[30] See W. Ivor Jennings, *The British Constitution* (2d ed., Cambridge: Cambridge
University Press, 1947), p. 44.
[31] RR, p. 7.

the same time he argues that since the state is the instrument of the capitalist class its power cannot be used to advance the interests of other groups or to regulate the power of wealth. His only attempt to resolve the contradiction is the argument that the programs of twentieth-century progressive governments have at no point touched the "essentials" of capitalism. Since continued contraction of the economy cannot be prevented as long as capitalism is retained, the drift to Fascism at home and imperialism and aggression abroad is inevitable. The American situation is particularly dangerous since a totally outmoded individualism still holds sway there, and no socialist movement of any consequence exists. "There is little evidence to suggest that the American business man, or even the American Trade Unionist, has begun seriously to understand the degree to which capitalism and democracy are now the antithesis of each other in the United States." [32]

The existence of a strong labor movement does not, however, guarantee the preservation of democracy. The moment a socialist party moves to act on its principles it throws the ruling class into a panic. Even the actions of reform governments, such as the British Labor Government of 1929, the New Deal, or the Popular Front in France, arouse bitter opposition among businessmen. By withdrawing their "confidence," the holders of property are able to cripple or destroy the authority of such governments. A popular leader such as Roosevelt is forced to choose between reform and recovery. His hold over public opinion "depends, to a considerable degree, upon his power to obtain the conditions of economic revival; and this power, in its turn, depends upon his ability to secure that co-operation from business men which, by definition almost, his reform program repels." [33] The relatively mild measures of the New Deal have made American capitalism increasingly skeptical of the validity of democracy; he asserts that "by 1940, beneath the formal acceptance of democratic principles, the Fascist idea had penetrated deeply into the minds of American business men." [34] Laski's sweeping conclusion is that "at the historical stage we have reached, the will of the people is unable

[32] *London, Washington, Moscow, Partners in Peace?*, p. 15.
[33] *The American Presidency* (New York: Harper and Bros., 1940), pp. 62–63.
[34] RR, p. 148.

to use the institutions of capitalist democracy for democratic purposes." [35] The ruling class is highly dubious about the value of democratic procedures that facilitate assaults on its privileges, while the workers, embittered by the repeated failures of progressive governments to accomplish their goals, are becoming more and more cynical about democracy and more receptive to Communist arguments against democracy. As a result, he states, the Left has often been led to the rationalization "that, seen in its proper perspective, the Russian dictatorship was, in fact, democracy." [36] We have seen that this is a rationalization which Laski himself often comes perilously close to making.

The crucial problem that confronts socialists is whether the replacement of capitalism by socialism can be accomplished by peaceful and democratic means. We have seen that before the war Laski was virtually certain that a violent revolution was the only possible method of transition. Writing in 1939, he seems to reaffirm this position when he says: "I have been driven to the conclusion that no class voluntarily abdicates from the possession of power. I have come to learn that the private ownership of the means of production made it impossible for the democratic idea to transcend the barriers of class without the capture of the state power by the working class." [37] Explicitly rejecting the Fabian philosophy of gradualism, he insists that only "a central attack on the structure of capitalism" can save us from Fascism and a new iron age. During the 1946 libel trial he stated that he changed his 1934 view that violent revolution was inevitable as conditions changed.

I think the condition began to change with the advent of full employment during the war, with the emphasis on the victory of democracy at the close of the war, and, as a result of the victory of the Labour Party, its passage to the possession of the political power of the State and the acquiescence thus far of the Conservative Party and the privileged classes in the legislation of the Government of the day. . . .[38] I thought when the Coalition

---

[35] "Harold J. Laski," in Clifton Fadiman, ed., *I Believe: The Personal Philosophies of Certain Eminent Men and Women of Our Time* (New York: Simon and Schuster, 1939), pp. 146–47.

[36] RR, p. 141.

[37] "Harold J. Laski," in Clifton Fadiman, ed., *I Believe*, p. 144.

[38] *Laski v. Newark Advertiser Co., Ltd., and Parlby* (London: Daily Express, 1947), p. 108.

Government took office and Labour and Mr. Churchill joined forces, it gave a greater hope of the achievement of revolution by consent.[39]

Let us examine some of his wartime statements on this subject to see how much he actually changed his previous position that revolution was virtually inevitable. We have already noted that he believes that the heightened sense of common interests among all groups and the feeling of common danger offer an unprecedented opportunity of obtaining, during the war, general consent for the initiation of fundamental social changes. But repeatedly he warns that if this opportunity is not utilized, "the objective historical circumstances in which we live make violent readjustment certain." [40] If great changes are not begun before the end of hostilities and if the ruling class is unwilling to cooperate in eliminating the irrational inequalities and the vested privileges of the old order, the masses will move to a violent destruction of the system that contains these evils; in that case, "we shall drift rapidly to social revolution in this country." [41] In 1941 he writes: "I believe myself that the choice before our generation is, in fact, a choice between a revolution by consent and a revolution by violence; and I do not for one moment deny that to secure the first is as difficult and as rare an achievement as any in history." [42] He has even graver doubts of the possibility of making the necessary changes by consent "when the main psychological impulse to agreement no longer has the dramatic validity that common danger imposes." [43] His conclusion in *Reflections on the Revolution of Our Time* in 1943 is that

if we have failed, by the Armistice, to lay the foundations of a revolution by consent, we shall pass rapidly to a position where, because men no longer hold the great ends of life in common, they will be unable to agree

[39] *Ibid.*, pp. 145–46.

[40] WDWG, p. 166.

[41] "The Need for a European Revolution," in *Programme for Victory*, p. 25.

[42] SOF, p. 97. See also the statement: "I say with emphasis that we have got to begin now the organization of a revolution by consent or we shall drift, after the war, to a revolution by violence which will destroy the major ends for which we fight." "Democracy in War Time," in G. D. H. Cole *et al., Victory or Vested Interest?* (London: George Routledge and Sons, Ltd., 1942), p. 52.

[43] RR, p. 345. See also the comment that "the changes which we require we can make by consent in a period in which, as now, conditions make men remember their identities and not their differences. It is, at the very best, at least highly doubtful whether such a chance will again be available to us." *Ibid.*, p. 193.

upon the methods of social change. In that event, the reorganization of our basic principles will not be capable of accomplishment by peaceful means; and the final disposition of forces will be determined not by discussion but by violence.[44]

By 1943, however, he begins to argue that because of the failure of the Labor leaders to compel Churchill to inaugurate the necessary revolution by consent the postwar period will see the return, in intensified form, of all the contradictions and evils of the capitalism of the 1930's. The despair and bitterness that will be the consequence of serious unemployment and unused productive capacity will make it almost impossible to settle our differences peacefully. In addition, "the post-war society will be one in which the major ideological principle will be provided by the fact that the Russian Revolution . . . has, so to say, received its letters of credit from those masses in every country of the United Nations who know, even proudly know, how immense has been the contribution of the Soviet Union to victory." [45] The example of Russia—the constant expansion of its economy, its elimination of unemployment and the privileges of ownership, its elevation of the status of labor, and its overwhelming concern for world peace—will make the people of other countries unwilling to endure the evils of capitalist society. He warns: "We approach the final phase of the second world war. Either we read its lessons by the light of Marxism, with the hope that we may then grasp the historic mission that could be ours, or, once again we evade the obligation of that mission and watch an iron age slowly close down upon the world." [46] Since he has already stated that the Labor Party's leaders refuse to base their actions on the Marxist analysis, the clear implication is that the great opportunity has been missed and that our only alternatives are now Fascism and violent revolution and dictatorship. While stressing the need for a social revolution during the war, he adds: "It is unforgiveable that the very men who should be leading that revolution are devoting their main energies to preventing its accomplishment." [47]

During 1944 and 1945 he seems convinced that the unique opportunity of using the war years to begin the revolution has been irre-

[44] *Ibid.*, p. 385.
[45] *London, Washington, Moscow, Partners in Peace?*, p. 4.
[46] MT, p. 33.
[47] "An Age of Transition," *Political Quarterly*, XIV (April–June, 1943), 172.

trievably lost. Privilege will not abdicate without conflict when it is safe if it has not been asked to abdicate when it is in danger. The agreement between the two major parties to postpone until after the war the discussion of "controversial" issues "leaves the vested interests in possession of power at the very time when the dynamic of democracy is proportionate to the changes we ought to be discussing." [48] Outside of the Soviet Union, there is no assurance that the victory of the United Nations will be a victory for socialist democracy. If the forces of the old order triumph in the inevitable postwar conflict, we will have a Fascist dictatorship, and if the revolution results in the triumph of the popular forces, democratic institutions will have to be suspended for a long period.[49] In sum, it is Laski's position that we have only two possible choices, socialist revolution and Fascist counterrevolution; we can make the socialist revolution by consent if we act before the war ends, or we will have to make it later by violence. By the last year of the war he has become convinced that the latter alternative is overwhelmingly probable; and he states that if the transformation of capitalism into socialism is "effected and maintained by force . . . it is obvious from all historic experience that all those who resist the validity of the change will necessarily be excluded from any share in the organisation of power." [50] The conclusion that he draws from his analysis is "the necessity of a unified working-class party able either to win political power or, if it meets the challenge of Fascism, to emerge victorious from the conflict. The lesson of Germany and Italy is the clear one that division of the working class means its defeat." [51] This necessary unity of socialists and Communists can be achieved in England only by persuading the Communists that they are wrong in believing that social democracy is the principal enemy of the proletarian revolution. They will not abandon that belief until a British Labor Govern-

[48] *London, Washington, Moscow, Partners in Peace?*, p. 8.

[49] See "The Need for a European Revolution," in *Programme for Victory*, pp. 30–31. See also the statements that "a revolution by violence, even if it be successful, is bound to suspend the procedures of democracy" (RR, p. 178), and that "a planned society imposed by the state-power after society has been bitterly rent in pieces by civil war is not likely, for a long period, to admit the climate of freedom." *Ibid.*, p. 375.

[50] *Will Planning Restrict Freedom?* (Cheam, England: The Architectural Press, 1944), p. 28.

[51] "Harold J. Laski," in Clifton Fadiman, ed., *I Believe*, p. 146.

ment achieves "a genuine understanding" with the Soviet Union, which is "the central support upon which the future of working-class interests depends." [52]

When, towards the end of the war, Laski saw that none of the basic changes that he had advocated had been made, he reverted to his pre-1939 view that a peaceful transition to socialism was extremely unlikely and that we must anticipate a period of violent conflict and dictatorial rule before we reached the new society. When he stated during the trial in 1946 that the victory of the Labor Party in 1945 and the general acceptance of its right to govern by the Conservatives were important factors in changing his view that violence was inevitable, he was simply conceding the inaccuracy of his predictions from 1932 to 1945 that the old ruling class would not permit a Labor Government to carry out its socialist program and that England would move rapidly to revolution or counterrevolution. His analysis was not altered at any time until the 1945 election and the first years of the new Government proved that it was faulty. The wartime thesis that a revolution by consent might be possible was valid, in his view, only as long as the extraordinary psychological and political conditions engendered by the war continued. Right up to the 1945 election he maintained that with the end of hostilities and the removal of the Nazi threat to the existence of Britain there would be a return to the "normal" conditions of class war and that the drift to revolution would inevitably be resumed.

When Laski speaks of "a revolution by violence," does he mean a revolution by the oppressed masses or an uprising of the privileged class against a Labor Government? During the trial, in attempting to explain a statement which he made in a speech at Bournemouth on December 13, 1941,—"We have the choice of revolution by consent before it [the war] ends or revolution by violence after the war" [53]—he says, "I think that 'revolution by violence after the war,' means a general worsening of conditions and a conflict between classes and a drift to violence, the initiation of which [that is, by the Conservatives or by the Communists or socialists] I could not possibly predict, nor did I seek then to predict it." [54] Against this inter-

---

[52] "Russia and Labor Unity," *The Nation*, CLVII (Sept. 18, 1943), 318.
[53] Quoted in *Laski v. Newark Advertiser Co., Ltd., and Parlby*, p. 125.
[54] *Ibid.*

pretation, however, must be placed the normal usage of the term "revolution by violence," which clearly implies the forceful overthrow of existing institutions from below. In many of his statements he is obviously using the term in this sense; when he speaks of this violent revolution as the abolition of privilege and when he says that a successful revolution would necessarily entail the suspension of democratic procedures, he is certainly referring to a mass uprising, led by Marxists of some variety.

To these two positions—first, that he did not pretend to know who would initiate the revolution, and, second, that the workers would be the revolutionaries—there must be added yet a third argument. He states: "My view is the view I have consistently [*sic!*] affirmed, that a Labour Government would obtain the power, would be challenged and would have to suspend the constitution, that the outcome of its suspension would nevertheless be its successful Government, and by the successful Government it would operate the changes for which it was elected." [55] When he takes this view—and it is the position that he adopts most frequently—he is, of course, making a flat prediction that violence will be initiated by the Conservative forces, which will bear the responsibility for beginning the revolutionary conflict. One would hardly speak of the actions of a duly elected government to counter an overt challenge to its authority as "a revolution by violence." The argument that the forces of reaction will not permit a socialist party to achieve and maintain power in the normal fashion is essentially the position that he adopted at the time of the MacDonald crisis in 1931; he found further evidence of its truth in the rise of Fascism in Germany, in the failure of the Popular Front government in France, and in business hostility to the American New Deal. In opposition to the Fabian gradualism and the "naive" constitutionalism of the vast majority of the members of the Labor Party, he maintained this belief until the experiences of the initial years of the postwar Labor Government rendered it untenable. He thereby demonstrated that his analysis of social and political forces in Britain had led him to give the wrong answer to the central problem that confronts any labor party in a democratic society.

Laski constantly insists that ours is a dying civilization. Traditional

[55] *Ibid.*, p. 131.

values are in complete decay and no longer maintain their hold on
the minds of men. The collapse of capitalism means that men lose
their sense of security; insecurity robs them of their normal judgment and their ability to reason together. Caught in the grip of fear
and mutual hatred, they tend to be either blindly hostile to the great
reforms that are necessary if revolution is to be averted or sullen
and passive as they look out upon the world. The fear that is omnipresent arises because a growing proportion of the people feel that
the fundamental principles of our society are unjust. The "whole
predominant ethos" of capitalist society, he states, "is set in terms of
the fear of its rulers of what might happen to themselves if he [the
common man] were called to power in society." [56] By subordinating
every aspect of life to acquisitiveness, capitalism has "degraded the
dignity of human nature in the masses; and by the very fact of that
degradation it separated its successful men from its unsuccessful by
the abyss of fear." [57] The predominant characteristics of the period
between the two wars are the phenomena that always mark an age
of revolution—profound moral crisis, which exhibits itself in widespread disillusion, pessimism, and antirationalism, violence and growing contempt for law, the collapse of "normal" expectations and
"natural" patterns of social behavior, the absence of certainty about,
or confidence in, the future, and a general drive for "externalized"
pleasures. It is natural, he says, that a world "so haunted by fear and
insecurity . . . regarded the growing success of the Soviet experiment as a challenge." [58]

In *Faith, Reason, and Civilization,* Laski attempts to indicate how
this spirit of decay and disillusion is reflected in the prevailing nega-
tivism and cynicism of the leading literary artists and intellectuals
of our society.[59] This venture into literary criticism follows the pattern of the Marxist approach to literature in its most mechanical and
unimaginative form. Writers such as Henry James and T. S. Eliot
are attacked for not being "socially conscious" since they do not deal
with the pressing problems of the masses, while the works of the
early Dreiser or Howard Fast are praised as examples of truly "vital"
and "significant" literature. Our novelists and poets, he says, hate the

[56] RR, p. 136.   [57] *Ibid.,* p. 372.
[58] *London, Washington, Moscow, Partners in Peace?,* p. 17.
[59] See FRC, pp. 96–104.

present society and its values and realize that a great change is imminent; but, afraid of the uncharted future, they do not dare to give
us a positive, creative lead, and so they take refuge in a private world
of fantasy. They have failed to perform the function of the intellectual, which is "to find the means whereby he correlates the vague
aspirations of the masses into the coherence of a practical programme." [60] He insists that "the responsibility of the intellectual
who sees the drift of his time towards the abyss is to mitigate its
dangers by seeking, through the profundity of his alliance with the
masses, to make their dreams and hopes seem practicable and
legitimate." [61] The scholars and artists of our period, however, have
"with rare exceptions ignored the meaning of the world it was their
business to assist in changing in the hope that their claims to security
and comfort might be accepted by those in whose power they thought
it lay to dispense such satisfactions." [62]

Little needs to be said about Laski's criticisms of the activities of
artists and intellectuals in our society. His attack—and particularly
the charge that they have abandoned their proper function in the
expectation of being rewarded with prestige and material possessions
by the rulers of society—is the usual diatribe against those thinkers
who do not accept the true faith. His argument that it is the duty
of the intellectual to concentrate popular attention on the crucial
problems of the age completely begs the question of what those problems are. He believes that the destruction of capitalism and the creation of the socialist society are the central issues of our time; once
they are settled, most of the evils and difficulties in the world will
disappear. He does not have the right to insist that other thinkers
must accept his belief and propagate his gospel if they wish to avoid
the charge of intellectual treachery. A writer such as James believes
that moral problems are far more complex and deep-seated than
Laski's simple economic determinism makes them appear. James,
who is concerned with the problems of good and evil in the actions of
men and not with abstractions such as the wicked ruling class and the
good masses, locates moral responsibility in the individual rather

[60] *Ibid.*, p. 121. He says of Eliot's writings: "The note of disdain and contempt for
the masses is omnipresent; and I call this a betrayal of culture, a form of intellectual
treason, because it leaves those prisoners of the dark forces in society to whom it might
have sought to communicate their way to emancipation." *Ibid.*, p. 99.

[61] *Ibid.*, p. 122.   [62] *Ibid.*, p. 123.

than in the group. Because he sees ugliness and brutality in the actions of men of every social group, he cannot accept it as his function to make the aspirations of any given class seem practicable and legitimate. The duty of the writer and artist is to report what they see and feel, to criticize the reality they perceive in terms of their values, and to insist that morality resides in the choices made by individual men. They must resist any completely deterministic theory of human action, which destroys the very concept of morality in so far as it allows men to transfer the burden of responsibility for their actions to social groups or impersonal historical forces.

Laski's principal criticism of the intellectuals is that they have failed to move beyond cynicism and satire to the formulation of a new positive faith. We must find, he says, "a faith which elicits in time of peace the spirit which gave most Englishmen, during the Battle of Britain, the sense that they were truly soldiers in the war of human liberation." [63] His basic argument is that "the revival of faith in values among men means the creation of the conditions of expanding welfare. It means releasing the productive forces of society from the shackles by which they are now impeded." [64] The expansion of material well-being for all is the key to the re-emergence of an atmosphere of hope and of a common faith by which men can live. Only when the great ends of life are held in common will tolerance, respect for law, and the rule of reason over the minds of men be restored. During the years between the wars "the mental climate of moral disillusion and economic collapse was unavoidable" [65] because no statesman, outside of Russia, dared to launch a real attack on the forces of privilege. We need not look far for our salvation and for the outline of the new faith; "the Soviet Union has discovered the secret of vigour, and therein, the means to that common faith which binds men together in peace." [66] In particular, Laski urges that the British Labor movement needs a new and compelling faith, as well as a Marxist philosophy of action. The movement must "recover the faith and enthusiasm of its pioneers; it requires, also, the power to communicate them to an area of the population far wider than the ranks of the trade unions to whom it now predominantly appeals." [67]

[63] *Ibid.*, p. 72.   [64] RR, p. 203.   [65] FRC, p. 69.   [66] *Ibid.*, p. 154.
[67] RR, p. 224.

This new secular faith must be shared by the leaders as well as the rank and file, and it must be held with religious intensity. His enthusiasm for the Soviet Union is based on his belief that this faith of the future is there being transformed into a living reality. He asserts that

the basic idea of the Russian Revolution satisfies the conditions any new system of values must satisfy if it is to fill the void left by the wholesale decay of the old. It offers to the common man not only a rising standard of welfare; it enables him to see that his own productive effort is directly relevant to the standard achieved. And, as an idea, it has the immense social merit of making function and not status the basis of the individual's place in society.[68]

Like most men, Laski admires success, and, since Russia is the only important example of a state founded upon Marxist principles, he tends to equate the Soviet Union with the idea of the socialist society. The nobility and grandeur of the original socialist ideal are transferred to the Soviet reality, while any serious discrepancies are explained away as the results of peculiar historical circumstances that have had no effect on the "essence" of socialism. The fundamental error in all his discussions of the Soviet Union is his assumption that its leaders are creating, or are concerned to create, a socialist society that will embody the hopes and aspirations of the Western European socialist movement—an adequate standard of living for all men, justice, freedom, opportunities for personal development, and a high level of creative culture. He argues that Lenin and Stalin have begun a renovation of values among the citizens of Russia comparable to that accomplished by the leaders of the French Revolution, but he is unwilling to admit that the Bolshevik "renovation of values" has little in common with the generous hopes of socialism.

The Russian worker "feels that the present is his; given victory, he has a greater assurance than the citizen of any other society at present constituted, that, with the organization of an enduring peace, the future is his also." [69] In contrast to the fear and disillusion that haunt capitalist society, he stresses the optimism and exhilaration of the Russians. A whole people has faith in its future, and "that faith is the outcome of a great lesson learned from the unity of co-operation, a unity made all the more profound because it refuses to organize

[68] FRC, p. 44.   [69] RR, p. 399.

authority upon an antithesis between the worker by hand and the worker by brain." [70] Again we see that Laski is borrowing the slogans of the socialist movement in order to describe the structure of authority in Soviet society. He concludes his eulogy of the idea of the Russian Revolution by saying that it has insisted on the common man's

inherent dignity as a person. It has given to manual labour a higher status than it has ever elsewhere attained. It has refused to accept that separation of manual labour from the cultural heritage which has . . . characterized all past civilizations. . . . It has found the means of giving to a larger proportion of its working population a significance which arises out of the duties allotted to it than any comparable experiment has so far achieved. It has opened more widely a career to the talents than any previous régime.[71]

In spite of his admiration for the "socialist society" of the Soviet Union and his conviction that the principles of the Bolshevik Revolution constitute the only possible faith for the future, Laski cannot be dismissed as a mere apologist for Communism. He maintains that Lenin's decision to split the forces of the working class by creating the Third International and the various national Communist parties was disastrous because it "gave the status of rigid orthodoxy to a strategy of revolution the validity of which was built almost wholly on the assumption that the unique experience of Russia was a pattern for peoples with a century of quite different history behind them." [72] The Communists, he says, have been contemptuous of ordinary men and willing to use any means, even cooperation with the worst enemies of the working class, to destroy all socialist influence they cannot control. He strongly condemns the Nazi-Soviet Pact of 1939 as well as Moscow's efforts to force the non-Russian Communist parties to oppose the war against Hitler and to adopt the policy of revolutionary defeatism. He calls the Pact "a cynical manoeuvre which . . . became a shameless exhibition on Stalin's part, of complete indifference to the fate of the working-class outside the Soviet Union"; [73] the result of the events of 1939, for "all who are not vowed to the myth of Bolshevik infallibility has been to create the first

---

[70] FRC, p. 143.   [71] *Ibid.*, pp. 52–53.   [72] RR, p. 82.

[73] *Ibid.*, p. 87. He asserts: "Stalin transformed the national Communist parties into the defenders of Hitler for no other reason than his own need for peace . . . and his own requirements in strategic defence." *Ibid.*, pp. 66–67.

profound doubts since 1917 of the identity of Soviet interest with those of the world-proletariat." [74]

One of his sharpest blows at Stalinism is the statement that "the Soviet dictatorship, in Stalin's hands, carries on the Byzantine tradition of Czarism." [75] At the same time he is unwilling or unable to draw the conclusions that follow from these facts; while he admits that the actions of the Soviet Union in 1939 were designed to further the national interests of Russia rather than the interests of the world proletariat, he continues to regard the Soviet Union as the embodiment of the principles of socialism. In 1943 he states: "It is still the fact that whatever weakens the U.S.S.R. weakens the working class all over the world." [76] But this is precisely the argument of those who, in his phrase, are "vowed to the myth of Bolshevik infallibility."

In his strong condemnation of the Soviet invasion of Finland he notes: "Every item in the Soviet adventure in Finland coincided in character with that Fascist technique of aggression upon which, for six years, the Soviet government had been foremost in heaping execration." [77] But this judgment does not lead him to modify his general thesis that the Soviet system is, by its nature, incapable of aggression and that international peace has been the constant aim of the rulers of Russia since 1917. He is confident that if the Soviet Union is assured of security after the war, it will clearly demonstrate its will for peace, but in the next breath he refers to Stalin as "a Bolshevik whose Marxism has at least a tinge of Slavonic nationalism," [78] and complains that "one would like to be certain—and one cannot be certain—that Marshal Stalin draws his inspiration from Lenin and not from the war against Napoleon I." [79] It is incredible that the Nazi-Soviet Pact and Stalin's cynical exploitation of foreign Communist parties in 1939 and 1940 in the interest of Russia's strategic position were the first events that caused Laski to have doubts about the identity between Russian and proletarian interests. For he admits that, by about 1924, the Communist International "settled down into the position, increasingly emphasized, of a secondary de-

[74] *Ibid.*, p. 86.   [75] *Ibid.*, p. 89.

[76] "Russia and Labor Unity," *The Nation*, CLVII (Sept. 18, 1943), 317.

[77] RR, p. 23.

[78] *Will the Peace Last?*, Peace Aims Pamphlet No. 28 (London: National Peace Council, 1944), p. 3.

[79] *Ibid.*, p. 6.

partment of the Soviet Foreign Office," [80] which enabled the Soviet leaders "to control the national Communist parties in the interests of Soviet foreign policy." [81]

He demonstrates the same remarkable skill in keeping conflicting views in watertight compartments in his discussions of Soviet domestic policies. He concedes that a militaristic obedience is forced on all members of the Communist Party and that the people are governed by a stern dictatorship; but he defends the dictatorship of the Party leaders as "a necessary consequence of the conditions the Bolsheviks confronted. Without it, quite certainly, there would have been a return to capitalism" [82]—a fate, it is clear, far worse than terror or death. Although he admits that the Russian government "has been driven . . . to rely more and more upon holding the army, and using the secret police, as its essential instruments," [83] he explains that this terroristic rule is the necessary outcome of the decision to embark upon a program of rapid and widespread industrialization and to restrict sharply the production of consumption goods. That decision, in turn, is defended as a necessary consequence of the decision to build socialism in a single country in the face of the political isolation and economic strangulation imposed upon the Soviet Union by a hostile capitalist world. Laski constantly returns to the theme that the success of the Russian experiment has constituted a threat to the entire structure of world capitalism; capitalist countries have been profoundly hostile to the Soviet Union and anxious to engineer its downfall.[84] The Communist dictatorship in Russia is then defended on the ground that it is necessary as long as the process of forced industrialization, which is essential to the protection of the Soviet Union from foreign attacks, is continued. He states: "So long as there is a widespread conviction that the capitalist powers are prepared to attack the Soviet Union, so long the dictatorship will persist." [85]

---

[80] RR, p. 64.   [81] *Ibid*.   [82] *Ibid*., p. 68.   [83] *Ibid*., p. 60.

[84] See FRC, p. 145. See also his statement that it is fundamental to understand "that only security from without can break bureaucratic tyranny from within, and that this security cannot be achieved so long as the destruction of the U.S.S.R. is a main objective, direct or indirect, of the forces of privilege throughout the world." "Critic of Stalin," review of *Stalin's Russia and the Crisis in Socialism* by Max Eastman, *The New Statesman and Nation*, XX (Sept. 14, 1940), 263.

[85] RR, p. 77.

Only when the other great powers, by accepting socialism, eliminate from power the groups that are hostile to the Soviet Union will the grounds for Soviet suspicion of the West be removed; only then will the Russian leaders feel sufficiently secure to relax their ruthless dictatorship.[86] If Britain and America allay Soviet fears by transforming themselves into socialist societies, they can, thereby, "restore to the Russian Revolution that power to achieve the balance between individual liberty and social security which is the objective of all political effort." [87] Along with this chain of reasoning, which not only throws the main responsibility for the Soviet dictatorship on the hostility of the capitalist powers but assigns to them the task of creating the conditions that will make possible its abolition, Laski also elaborates a casuistical defense of the Soviet regime which states that it must be judged by different standards than those used to judge other governments. He argues that when "massive transvaluations" of all values of the kind that occurred in the French and Russian revolutions take place, "the criteria of the past must be adapted to the new principles if they are to be relevant. . . . The new society which Calvin's doctrines made possible did not seem less outrageous at Rome or Vienna or Madrid than the new society which the doctrines of Marx and Lenin helped to make seems outrageous in Lombard Street or Wall Street." [88]

His basic argument that the Soviet dictatorship is primarily the result of foreign hostility to Communism and that it will disappear when the fear of capitalist encirclement and attack is removed is refuted by an examination of Lenin's writings and his actions as leader of the Bolshevik Party in exile. Proletarian dictatorship, the dictatorship of the Communist Party, and control of the Party by its leaders were the principal elements in Communist theory even before the seizure of power in 1917. Laski casts doubt on his own thesis by his admission that "after the attempt on Lenin's life in 1918, the transformation of Soviet dictatorship into democracy was never, save, perhaps, for a brief moment in 1936, when the new constitution was promulgated, really seriously considered." [89] Above all, the Soviet attitude towards Britain after 1945 and the postwar relationships be-

[86] See *ibid.*, p. 301; FRC, p. 145; *The Economic Revolution*, p. 23; and WDWG, pp. 151–52.

[87] RR, p. 89.   [88] *Ibid.*, pp. 411–12.   [89] *Ibid.*, pp. 54–55.

tween Russia and Communist Yugoslavia and the satellite states strikingly demonstrate the futility of Laski's belief that the Russian leaders would feel secure in the presence of other socialist states. It is apparent that the rulers of Russia equate true socialism with complete willingness to serve what they believe to be the interests of the Soviet Union.

Twenty years earlier, before Laski had achieved his "realistic" insight into "the dynamics of power," he was aware, as he is not in the 1940's, that no group of absolute and irresponsible rulers will voluntarily surrender their power over a nation. Even now he has occasional suspicions that the fear of foreign intervention has been used by the rulers of Russia "to evoke a narrow and intense patriotism among the masses" and "as a weapon with which to attack the critic" [90] and that the result of this process has been "the growth of the secret police into something like a state within a state." [91] And he completely destroys his thesis that the Russian dictatorship will "wither away" as soon as the rest of the world accepts socialism when he concedes: "Certainly it is difficult not to feel that the range and intensity of the Soviet dictatorship has [*sic*] for its objective less the achievement of its socialist end than the maintenance of Stalin and his chosen associates in power at all costs." [92]

But he does not stay to elaborate these suspicions or to realize that his admissions make nonsense of his apology for the Russian dictatorship and of his thesis that the aims of the Soviet leaders are the well-being of their own people and peace and good will with other nations. Dramatic events such as the Nazi-Soviet Pact or the invasion of Finland may make him wonder for a moment whether the policy of the Russian leaders is not dictated by their desire to strengthen their own power at home and the international position of the Soviet Union. But he never relinquishes his central belief that Russia is the living example, even though not yet perfect, of his ideal of a socialist society. A socialist society cannot be aggressive or imperialistic; it must make the welfare of the people its first concern; it must offer the individual great opportunities for self-realization, as well as a profound sense of the dignity of his labor and the worth of his contribution to a great social purpose. The Soviet Union is a socialist society; *ergo,* these are the characteristics of the Soviet Union. If unpleasant doubts about

[90] *Ibid.*, p. 59.   [91] *Ibid.*   [92] *Ibid.*, pp. 70–71.

Byzantinism or Slavonic nationalism arise momentarily, they can always be submerged in flights of rhetoric about the new Soviet faith or the need to eliminate the contradictions that make capitalist society unjust, warlike, and incapable of economic expansion. No doubt, no criticism of the New Jerusalem can be allowed to obscure the central fact that "we can only understand the Russian Revolution in the degree that we recognize it as the first stage in a fundamental transformation of the social principles of Western civilization." [93]

[93] *Ibid.*, p. 39.

Part Five

1946-1950

13

The Last Years

1. INTRODUCTION

IT IS HARDLY surprising that during the last four years of his life Laski
wrote nothing indicating that he was developing new ideas or seriously revising his earlier views. Although his strength was obviously
failing during these years, he did not curtail his strenuous round of
activities as a teacher, lecturer, and Labor Party worker, and he produced five books and dozens of pamphlets and articles. Since he had
neither the time nor the energy to attempt any fundamental analysis
or serious reworking of his position, his discussions of the problems
of the postwar period have little relevance to contemporary realities.
His writings strike the reader as fundamentally anachronistic and
outdated. He continues to do battle with the capitalism of the era of
Coolidge and Hoover while retaining much of the enthusiasm for
"the Soviet experiment" displayed by a more innocent generation
during the 1930's. As Max Beloff has commented, "It is surely significant that Laski's last major work, *The American Democracy* (published in 1948) should have seemed above all, a very old-fashioned
book, as though appearing a quarter of a century after its time." [1]
By 1946 the destruction of the free individual and of his social groups
by totalitarian regimes had become, for ordinary men and women
as well as for specialists in political and cultural analysis, the crucial
problem of our time. After the experience of Nazism, Laski's insistence that capitalism was the principal enemy of human freedom
and dignity seemed so fantastically disproportionate that it was often
difficult to listen to the repetition of his analysis. And his emotional
commitment to the Soviet Union as the *fons et origo* of the new
socialist world made it impossible for him to treat realistically the

[1] Max Beloff, "The Age of Laski," *The Fortnightly,* n.s., CLXVII (June, 1950), 378.

problems of Russia's postwar imperialism and the persistence of tyranny within the Soviet Union. To read Laski in the late 1940's is to be reminded of the writings of the last days of the Greek city-states, in which outworn disputes are carried on, with little or no attention to the shadow of Macedon that was soon to extinguish the independence of all the Greek cities.

One of his greatest difficulties is the fact that the 1945 electoral victory of the Labor Party and its period in office constitute a serious, if not fatal, blow to his fundamental thesis—that the capitalist class will not allow the instruments of democracy to be used to effect a transformation of the property system. The failure of this prediction shatters the whole structure of his political thinking—his analysis of the class structure, his view of the nature of the state, his discussion of political parties, his concept of democracy, and his theory of social and political change. In consequence, his attitude towards the achievements of the Labor Government is ambivalent. On the one hand, he feels a tremendous pride in its victory and in its accomplishments; he insists that Britain was saved from social upheaval after 1945 only by "the fact that the government was in the hands of a political party built upon the strength of the organized workers and their allies." [2] On the other hand, he is loath to surrender his dogma that the ruling class will not permit a democratic society to move towards socialism. Writing in 1948, he says, "We are permitted by the mental climate of this country to hope—we cannot say more than hope—for success in our effort to build a socialist Britain by democratic means." [3] He insists that the power still concentrated in the hands of private ownership imposes drastic limits upon the area within which the Labor Government will be permitted to use the state power that it formally possesses.[4]

He now refers to those who aim to transform capitalist democracy into socialist democracy by peaceful means as "radical bourgeois." These optimists, who believe that the transformation can be made without revolution or dictatorship, differ "in degree, but not in kind,

[2] *Trade Unions in the New Society* (New York: The Viking Press, 1949), hereinafter cited as TU, p. 179.

[3] "Efficiency in Government," in Douglas P. T. Jay *et al., The Road to Recovery,* Fabian Society Lectures (London: Allan Wingate, Ltd., 1948), p. 49.

[4] See TU, p. 22.

from the conservative bourgeois." [5] Since democratic and constitutional socialism is here assigned to the "radical bourgeois," one wonders what position is left for Laski except that of the Communist. But, as we shall see,[6] he explicitly rejects the Communist theory that revolution and dictatorship are the inevitable path to socialism. In effect he abandons both the socialist and Communist positions on this issue, but fails to elaborate an alternative thesis or a synthesis of the rejected theories. After insisting that the condition of the successful operation of democratic socialism is the acceptance of its objective by management as well as the workers, he adds that no such agreement on a common objective exists in Great Britain. The normal alternation in power of Government and Opposition, which would mean Conservative repeal of at least a part of Labor's socialist program and then its re-enactment by a new Labor Government, would therefore be fatal to the stability and self-confidence that are necessary if the industrial system is to function successfully. Either objective—that of the Labor Party or that of the Conservatives—"requires a long term of power for the political party that promotes it, as well as genuine acquiescence in the objective by the Opposition party and its supporters." [7]

Since the sabotage of democracy that he had predicted did not occur when Labor assumed power in Britain, he endeavors to save his thesis by arguing that the threat to democracy will come if the forces of conservatism triumph at the next election, for "they seek to alter both the direction and the pace of social change." [8] Were he alive today, he would probably argue that the "real crisis" of democracy will come when a second Labor Government assumes office after the present interval of Conservative rule. Since he is less interested in the problems of a socialist government in power than in the struggle for power, he has relatively little to say about Britain during these years, and what he does say is marked by a general complacency about the adequacy of traditional political institutions to their new tasks.[9] In large measure he focuses his attention on the United States,

[5] *The Dilemma of Our Times* (London: George Allen and Unwin, Ltd., 1952), hereinafter cited as DOT, p. 65; see also pp. 66–67.
[6] See below, pp. 298–99.   [7] DOT, pp. 67–68.   [8] TU, p. 179.
[9] See *Reflections on the Constitution* (New York: The Viking Press, 1951), hereinafter cited as ROC, esp. pp. 37–74.

which still languishes in the capitalist dungeon, waiting for its socialist salvation. In effect, he transplants to America the analyses, the
predictions, and the dire warnings which, in the prewar period, he
had applied to England.

2. GENERAL CONCEPTS

Laski still proclaims his devotion to the principles of Marxism; he
argues that the materialist conception of history contains the major
clue to the causes of social change and that the record of history is
primarily the story of class struggle. "Few documents in the history
of mankind have stood up so remarkably to the test of verification
by the future," he asserts, "as the Communist Manifesto. A century
after its publication no one has been able seriously to controvert any
of its major positions." [10] He ignores the large number of the predictions made in the Manifesto which have been left unverified or
disproved by the events of the past century. What he himself calls the
central principle underlying the whole of the Manifesto—that those
who seek to build socialism will be successful only if the economic
conditions of the particular capitalist society in which they are operating are ripe for socialism—was clearly ignored by the architects of
the Russian Revolution. The Leninist abandonment of the basic tenet
of the Marxist analysis Laski regards as an adaptation of Marxism
to the special conditions of Russia; in this transformation the idea
of the dictatorship of the proletariat, which originally meant that
the authority of the state was to be transferred from the ruling class
to the workers, developed into something closely resembling the
Jacobin idea of a Committee of Public Safety.[11] Laski also grants
to ideas a far larger role in social and political change than the Marxist analysis allows. Rejecting the view that men are the blind instruments of a destiny beyond their control, he insists that "on the contrary, the ideas of men shape the purposes of the State power just
as the State power of [*sic*] any government wields shapes the pur-

[10] *Communist Manifesto; Socialist Landmark* (London: George Allen and Unwin,
Ltd., 1948), hereinafter cited as CM, p. 101.
[11] See *ibid.*, p. 96.

poses to which men lend the drive of their energy and emotion." [12]

He maintains that the British Labor Party is the greatest socialist party in Europe, and yet it "rejects the Marxian theory of a community which can only be made Socialist by a revolution to establish the dictatorship of the proletariat, which then, by repressing all opposition, passes into the classless society." [13] We note that he now omits his previous criticism of the Party's rejection of the Marxist theory of revolution and its adherence to the tradition of progress by constitutional consent. He underscores one of the most striking weaknesses in *The Communist Manifesto*'s predictions by noting that on no occasion has an important sector of the socialist movement in any country placed its loyalty to international socialism before loyalty to the nation-state. The socialist faith in the international solidarity of the working class, which is certainly the keystone of the Manifesto, has not been shown to be much more than a pious enunciation of hope. [14] Socialists, organized as parties and, still more, as governments, have demonstrated, he says, that they are nationalists first; in each country they have made their own conception of enlightened self-interest the first test of action. [15] In fact, the stronger the trade unionism of a given country, the more intensely nationalist it has been. In order to secure the greatest possible welfare for their members, unions have favored tariffs and restrictions on immigration and opposed the admission of refugees. [16]

He states that although he regards the economic factor as fundamental in social change, he recognizes the force of such noneconomic factors as nationalism, religion, color, race, and tradition. [17] But in analyzing political and social phenomena, he employs a simple eco-

[12] *The American Democracy* (New York: The Viking Press, 1948), hereinafter cited as AD, p. 557. But note the much more orthodox position taken in his last book: 1) the intellectual patterns of a society are shaped by its productive relations; the basis of the social philosophies for which men live and die is "the impact of an objective material reality and the relations of production which arise from it" (DOT, p. 149); 2) "overwhelmingly, our notions of good and bad, right and wrong, are conditioned, in a class-society, by the place we occupy in it." *Ibid.*, p. 211.

[13] "The First Fifty Years," *The Nation*, CLXX (Feb. 25, 1950), 174.

[14] See *Socialism as Internationalism*, Research Series No. 132 (London: Fabian International Bureau, 1949), pp. 3–4.

[15] See *ibid.*, p. 7.

[16] See *ibid.*, p. 8; he also notes the existence of "a special strain in the trade unions of zenophobia wherever the Jews are concerned." *Ibid.*, p. 9.

[17] See TU, p. 147.

nomic explanation, based on the Marxist view of the necessary course of development of the capitalist system. The fundamental reason for the world-wide revolutionary crisis, which lies at the root of the two wars, is the serious and growing disproportion between the forces of production and capitalist relations of production. The decline of capitalism imposes ever greater sacrifices upon the masses who live by the sale of their labor power. In order to still their protests, the state must unveil its full coercive power and reveal its central purpose—the protection of capitalist ownership of the means of production and the repression of all ideas and values that call that ownership into question. A tremendous volume of sheer coercion is now required to keep the capitalist system from total collapse; it is increasingly difficult to maintain either freedom or democracy, since private ownership continues to impede the "vertical expansion of production" that is necessary. More and more, business and the state power, or the vested interests and government, are becoming interchangeable terms. Hitler and Mussolini are simply the clearest examples of this one-to-one correlation between the coercive power of the state and the economic power of the capitalist class.[18] Although he admits that for the last eighty years the history of law has been very largely "the history of an importation into freedom of contract of limitations and conditions which are . . . the result of the intervention of society which uses the authority of the state-power to deprive the owner of property" [19] of his economic sovereignty, he does not seem to realize that this admission seriously weakens his Marxist analysis of the function of the state and the legal system.

Laski argues that since the Civil War majority rule in the United States has been a mask behind which a property-owning minority has operated a legal and political system designed to protect their interests.[20] The freedom of the citizen is limited to the right to vote, while the ruling class has seen to it that the vote is never used in such a manner as to threaten the fundamental laws of the market economy. In 1950 he still asserts that "private property in the means of production . . . is a sacred category so far never successfully challenged except at the price of revolution." [21] His conclusion is that, particularly in the present period of capitalist contraction, "political de-

18 See *ibid.*, p. 83.   19 DOT, p. 80.   20 See AD, p. 260.
21 TU, p. 150.

mocracy is not seldom a facade behind which the great corporations prepare a social order the character of which is not unlike that of the corporate state." [22] It is the function of the courts as of all the organs of the state to protect the property of the few against the will of the people. The right of the minority to hold the instruments of production as private property, backed by the full force of the state's power, "thus becomes the right to determine how and when both the natural resources and the current technological knowledge of our time shall be employed." [23] Laski insists that the individualistic economic philosophy of America, set by its businessmen, is the philosophy of an economic civilization in contraction. He makes the astounding charge that this philosophy, which is characterized by its suspicion of all state intervention in economic life except tariffs and subsidies, "differs in degree only, and not in principle, from the central ideas of the Nazi economy and of the quasi-feudal capitalism of Japan." [24] He reiterates his thesis that sabotage is the answer of capitalism to any government which persists in the effort to use the power of the state to control the basic habits of the system.[25]

In replying to his critics who emphasize the activities of the American government since 1933, he admits that the New Deal's achievements on behalf of labor were great and that much of its legislation represents an invasion of the sovereignty of American finance capitalism. He then dismisses these facts with the argument that these achievements have not fundamentally altered the characteristics of the state power and that there is serious doubt whether they constitute permanent gains.[26] Both ownership and control of property remain fundamentally in the same hands as before President Roosevelt's entry into the White House; as a result, the enterprise of America is founded on the theory of restriction and not of abundance.[27] To the criticism that the socialist governments of Britain, Australia, New Zealand, and Scandinavia indicate the inadequacy of his thesis that the government and the vested interests are, to an increasing degree, one and the same, he retorts that any "democratic socialist government . . . is always walking upon a razor's edge. Formally, the coercive power of the state is in its hands; actually, it knows perfectly well that it

[22] *Ibid.*, p. 83. [23] *Ibid.*, p. 70. [24] AD, p. 531.
[25] See *ibid.*, pp. 754–55. [26] See *ibid.*, p. 235; and TU, pp. 64–65.
[27] AD. pp. 178–79.

must not use it in such a way as to outrage the vested interests." [28]
He insists that in none of the countries where democratic socialism
has attained power has it "touched more than the outworks of the
capitalist fortress, or achieved more than large-scale, in some cases
even spectacular, social reforms of a kind that were always within
the compass of a bourgeois democracy based upon universal suffrage." [29]

Some of Laski's comments on the concept of sovereignty suggest
that he is moving back towards his original hostility towards the
sovereign state. For example, he says that sovereignty is always the
covering behind which the ties that bind the vested interests and the
government are concealed from the people.[30] But in his discussions
of the "new synthesis" that must be created, he maintains that the
builders of the socialist society must be able to employ "the sanction
of that ultimate ability to coerce which is embodied in the state power,
and in the state power alone." [31] While he expresses his "frank fear"
of the monistic state and of the concentration of power in a few hands,
his proposals for curbing centralized power are confined to a general
plea for effective decentralization by area and by function and for
a wider evocation of the citizen's interest and initiative in politics.[32]
At the root of our failure lies our inability to arouse the interest of the
ordinary citizen and worker by allowing him to "participate in some
activity which makes him significant in and to himself, and gives
him the desire for . . . spontaneous collaboration on the planes of
political and economic life." [33] Since democracy means participation,
the ability of each man to make his own experience articulate in the
shaping of the law by which he is ruled, the "oligarchical bureau-
cratization" of the trade unions, especially the large mixed unions
in Great Britain, is a serious threat to democracy.[34]

He is disturbed by the fact that large-scale nationalized enterprises
seem to show the same bureaucratic tendencies that are evident in

[28] TU, pp. 22 and 89–90.   [29] DOT, p. 104.

[30] See AD, p. 551; and TU, pp. 15–16 and 20.   [31] TU, p. 147.

[32] See *ibid.*, p. 42; but contrast RQC, pp. 46–50.

[33] "Efficiency in Government," in Jay *et al., The Road to Recovery,* p. 64.

[34] See TU, pp. 163–64 and 170. Nevertheless, he admits that most people are
wrapped up in their private affairs and "regard their leisure as a period in which
they are entitled to rest and be amused rather than driven into the discomfort of
thought." AD, p. 620.

the large privately owned corporations; so far there have been no "attempts at serious experiments in industrial democracy in any of the public corporations, and . . . there is little that is really exciting in the relations between management and men." [35] He repeats his earlier pleas for "constitutional government in industry" as a means of winning the consent of the workers' representatives in the larger, and of the workers themselves in the smaller, issues of policy and management, and he advocates the greatest possible use of territorial and functional decentralization in the management of the nationalized industries.[36] Most significant is his frank admission that we do not get rid of

an economic system in which ownership, by definition, becomes a method of exploiting men and women . . . merely by transferring ownership from private to public hands, and then seeking to plan the processes of production. The problem is the much more complicated one of planning the whole economy of the society in such a way that each worker is able, at the level of his effort, to co-operate in defining the end and the means of that part of the plan in which he is involved as producer, while as consumer and as citizen he can participate in judging the operation of the plan as he experiences its results upon himself.[37]

Laski makes the startling concession that the wholesale socialization of the means of production in Russia has not solved the problem of economic democracy any more than have the great technological advances in America.

Both leave the mass of workers instruments to be manipulated for ends in the definition of which they do not in any decisive way share. Both of them elevate the few at the price of leaving the many disciplined and insignificant because the routine they are told to follow evokes from them nothing of that initiative and spontaneity without whose evocation the quality of freedom in society is inevitably depressed.[38]

Laski continues to believe that decentralized machinery for consultation with both producers and consumers will lead us towards a society where men may "share in the shaping of the effort to produce in a way that evokes from them both the sense that what they are doing is worth doing, and that they can bring to their task an activity of reason that prevents the widespread conviction that they have been

[35] ROC, p. 201; see also TU, pp. 156–57.   [36] See TU, pp. 144 and 158–59.
[37] DOT, p. 89.   [38] *Ibid.,* pp. 88–89.

emptied of what makes life an adventure in responsibility." [39] But he makes no attempt to spell out these proposals for decentralization or to weigh their adequacy to accomplish the goals which he sets for them.

In Laski's view any effort to revitalize or socialize liberalism is completely futile. In the main, he regards liberalism as simply the expression of the interests and desires of the economically powerful, and he assumes that there is no middle way between liberalism and socialism. We are forced, that is, to choose between "institutions which assume that freedoms must be won by the few and institutions which assume that they must be planned by the many." [40] When he recognizes a wider meaning of liberalism, as he does in his discussion of William James, Dewey, and Whitehead, he dismisses their philosophy as an effort to persuade businessmen to cooperate in the accomplishment of social changes that will destroy their supremacy; this philosophy he calls "a simple optimism of which the outcome, in the end, is catastrophe." [41] Liberalism of this sort, which assumes the continuance of tolerance, fails to see that "tolerance is always the outcome of the social security of a ruling class aware that no amount of discussion can seriously disturb its authority." [42] He continues to insist that we must choose one of two alternatives—a new socialist society or the death of our civilization by violence and civil war. Democratic institutions are no longer compatible with private ownership of the means of production; the longer capitalism survives, the more likely is its violent death, even in Britain and the United States.

He now seems somewhat more confident than he was before 1945 about the possibilities of a peaceful and democratic transition to socialism. He maintains that the British Laborites have the right to believe that social democracy is better and more firmly established by the method of freedom than by its abandonment. He states that the Communists believe that even in a democracy the ruling class will resort to naked force to maintain their domination the moment the capitalist basis of the society is threatened.[43] This, we note, is precisely the thesis that Laski himself repeatedly defended before the Labor victory of 1945. He also labels as a Communist argument the

[39] *Ibid.*, p. 85.   [40] "Plan or Perish," *The Nation*, CLXI (Dec. 15, 1945), 651.
[41] AD, p. 391.   [42] DOT, p. 155.
[43] See *The Secret Battalion* (London: The Labour Party, 1946), p. 8.

view that a socialist government cannot use the state apparatus for socialist purposes and that, although it can secure important concessions and social reforms for the masses, it must, if it wishes to avoid a revolutionary challenge, leave untouched the foundations of capitalism.[44] Here again we observe that this "Communist" thesis was one of Laski's favorite pre-1945 arguments against the gradualist, Fabian views of the majority of the Labor Party. He now tends to emphasize the great authority which any labor government possesses when it endeavors to maintain the principles of constitutional democracy. In England a socialist government moves steadily forward by constitutional means to national ownership and control of the vital instruments of production. It would, therefore, be sheer folly to throw away the benefits of civil liberties, tolerance, and respect for the rule of law "in the name of a theory which would bring into swift jeopardy the chance Great Britain possesses of making its revolution no doubt with difficulty, but also by consent." [45]

The error of the Communist leaders is that they elevate the strategy that proved successful in Russia to a universal principle that must be followed by working-class parties in every country. Since they believe that the capitalist class will not abdicate unless compelled by violent revolution, they consider it essential to organize the party of the proletariat in such a way that it will be prepared for the onset of that revolution. The Communist theories of inevitable revolution and the dictatorship of the proletariat were developed by men who had no intimate experience of constitutional government or of a developed trade-union movement. The diagnosis and strategy of the Communists are completely inapplicable to the contemporary British situation, and it would require a long period of economic ruin, leading to the destruction of the popular faith in the institutions of parliamentary democracy, to create the conditions that Lenin regarded as essential for successful revolution.[46] But he warns the members of the Labor Party that they are not "entitled to complete and unbreakable confidence in constitutional methods as the road to a socialist society. . . . it is the duty of all sections of the Labour Movement to watch with vigilance for any tendency in those who live by privilege to maintain it by an attack on our parliamentary system." [47]

[44] See *ibid.*, pp. 7–8.   [45] *Ibid.*, p. 17.   [46] See *ibid.*, pp. 21 and 29.
[47] *Ibid.*, p. 23.

Laski insists that the primary condition of liberty is an expanding economy. Men can only be free when the satisfaction of their basic material wants is assured and when they have sufficient leisure to enable them "to reflect upon their situation . . . to recognize that they need not helplessly accept the routine in which, before, they seemed hopelessly immersed."[48] Fear, which is the inevitable consequence of economic contraction in a society, always breeds suspicion and the curtailment of freedom. He argues that today, as in all past epochs, the whole problem of liberty hinges upon the issue of property,[49] but he fails to explain the conspicuous absence of the fundamental freedoms in the Soviet Union in spite of its "solution" of the issue of property. Liberty now depends upon revolutionary reforms. The alternative is "a new dark age in which even the memory of freedom may be forgotten in the bitter struggle to survive."[50] In another passage, however, he places the problem of freedom in a much wider context than that of its relation to property. Since "liberty is always a function of power, the fewer the men who own or operate that power, the smaller the number of those to whom liberty has significance."[51] He uses this formulation to show that liberty has decreased in America with the increasing concentration of economic power and that with the crisis in American economic and cultural life the older sense of openness and expansion in American thinking has given way to pessimism and skepticism. He does not pursue this insight into the relationship between freedom and the diffusion of power to the point of realizing that the concentration of political power in the hands of a small minority can destroy the significance of freedom for the average citizen.

Although he retains in the new and "thoroughly revised" edition of *Liberty in the Modern State,* published in 1949, the definition of liberty as absence of restraint, he insists in his other publications that "freedom, in fact, is not the abstract negation that the bourgeois era urged that it was."[52] The benefits of bourgeois capitalism have been for the most part confined to the small minority who possess wealth and property, while the masses have been excluded from any real opportunity to enjoy freedom in any positive sense. In our age man's

[48] Introduction to the revised edition of *Liberty in the Modern State* (New York: The Viking Press, 1949), p. 7.

[49] See *ibid.,* p. 15.   [50] *Ibid.,* p. 21.   [51] AD, p. 449.

[52] DOT, p. 72.

search for the freedom that fulfills his nature is frustrated by social and economic conditions that enforce subordination upon him. He is driven, therefore, to seek escape from this frustration in the routine of his job, in hobbies or games, in the vicarious enjoyment of the success of another person or of an organization, or in the total surrender of his individuality to a leader such as Hitler. According to Laski, Lenin's great strength lay in his recognition that new relations of production had to be created if freedom was to be made meaningful to the masses. He saw that "to make freedom effective in the sense that an aristocracy or a successful bourgeois have defined freedom, he must first create the conditions in which ideal ends like freedom of the press or constitutional freedom should mean something real and vivid to those who could rarely read or write, and to whom the principles of constitutional government lay outside any experience with which they had become acquainted." [53] The Russia that he and his successors have created has succeeded in throwing "new light on the nature of that freedom which alone gives dignity to the human person." [54]

[53] *Ibid.*, pp. 174–75.   [54] *Ibid.*, pp. 59–60.

14

America and Russia

1. THE UNITED STATES

WE HAVE ALREADY noted that Laski now focuses his attention primarily on the United States as the last stronghold of the capitalist system and of its ideological expression, liberalism. His entire analysis of American life and thought rests on the assumption that "Americanism" can be equated with rugged individualism and the *laissez-faire* philosophy of free enterprise. America has no general perception of the need for a new social order, although the ideology of individualism lags at least thirty years behind the actual facts of social and economic life in the United States. Laski's writings abound in easy generalizations about the American spirit and the attitude of Americans; he tells us, for example, that "Americans insist that . . . the denial of 'free enterprise' is incompatible with the achievement of liberty." [1] He ignores the American passion for group action noted by Tocqueville and many other observers as well as the long tradition of positive action by government to aid and influence economic and social development. "Americanism," he insists, exhibits a constant tendency "to shrink . . . from collective action on the ground that because collective action must involve coercion, it destroys that power of self-regeneration in man without which no reform is ever fully achieved." [2]

Equally simple is his explanation of the reason for the persistence among Americans of this spirit of *laissez-faire* liberalism despite the overwhelming trend toward collectivism in social and economic organization. The American businessman, anxious to prevent the use of the power of government to keep him from doing what he will with his own, naturally assumes that the less government we have the

[1] Introduction to the revised edition of *Liberty in the Modern State* (New York: The Viking Press, 1949), p. 6.
[2] AD, p. 738.

better. Through his dominance over every sphere of American life and culture, the businessman has been able to impose upon the masses his own individualism and hostility to the state. "His function is so to organize American society that he has the freest possible run of profitable adventure. To do this he must organize the symbolism of that society so that there are no vital obstacles to the performance of his function." [3] Therefore, he must control education, the state power, the boundaries within which scientific discovery may be used, the churches, the press, and the moving pictures. This thesis that American civilization is shaped at every point by the needs and desires of "businessmen" is the single theme repeated *ad nauseam* through the 761 pages of *The American Democracy*. The great American philosophers, such as Peirce or William James, have sought, perhaps unconsciously, to construct a metaphysic to justify the businessman's claims; [4] and there has never been a time "when the character of the American state power has been shaped by a philosophy which the owning class has not been able to define." [5] He insists that the power of wealth controls higher education and scientific research in the United States. For example, "academic economists who showed signs of a disproportionate interest in alternative doctrines were hunted down in their colleges as angrily as theological unorthodoxy was attacked a century ago." [6]

The artist and writer are forced to accept the values of the businessman or to flee from American society by retiring to Europe as Henry James did or by resorting to satire as their ineffectual weapon of protest. Similarly, the churches of America have promoted not religion, but religiosity—the support of the folklore of a given social order by an institution claiming divine authority. The churches have generally supported the values which the relations of production have made it necessary to impose, either directly by urging devotion to the existing social order or indirectly by offering to the victims of that order the consolation of visions of another world. Above all, the

---

[3] *Ibid.*, p. 389.   [4] See *ibid.*, p. 166.

[5] *Ibid.*, p. 51. Laski here seems to be assuming that it is possible for a philosophy to shape the nature of the state power; this is strange Marxist doctrine. In any case, the Jacksonian era and the years of the New Deal are surely examples of periods in which the owning class was not able to define the philosophy that shaped the ends for which the power of the state was utilized.

[6] *Ibid.*, p. 193.

cinema, radio, theater, and virtually all of the press have become a branch of big business; they support the vested interests against the American democratic tradition. Discussing the role of the media of mass opinion, he asserts: "Private ownership in this realm shapes the battle to ends which sacrifice the need for the facts to be before the community for weighing to the need for preserving the power and privilege inherent in this ownership." [7] No matter what the subject of discussion is, Laski's analysis is, in a word, that the attitudes and values of Americans are for the most part similar, and that their ideas are those which the businessmen have impressed upon their minds by means of the churches, schools, publications, radio, moving pictures, and other instruments of capitalist domination.

His discussion of American institutions and of the great movements in American social, economic, and political life rests on the equally simple—and equally false—premise that American democracy is "divided into a very small number of enormously rich families and a vast multitude who, whatever their aspirations, have no hope of attaining wealth." [8] This is one of the assumptions which give to Laski's writings their strangely old-fashioned quality, as if he were describing and criticizing the America of the McKinley era—or at least, of the 1920's—rather than the America of 1948 or 1949. Ten years after the revolution in the role of the Supreme Court in American life, a decade during which the Court invalidated only two minor provisions of Federal law,[9] he states that the courts are "a third chamber of the legislature in the area of their operation; and it is difficult not to argue that in all major political matters they find it extremely difficult to avoid the temptation to substitute their own ideas of what is politically wise or reasonable for the conclusions at which the elected members of the legislature have arrived." [10]

Since Laski's analysis of American political parties never escapes from a simple economic determinism, it completely fails in its effort

[7] "Civil Liberties in the Soviet Union," *The New Republic,* CXV (Oct. 21, 1946), 508. But note the statement: "I am . . . doubtful whether the popular belief that the citizen is the prisoner of an environment made for him by vested interests through the propaganda at its [*sic*] command is more than a half-truth in any except the closed totalitarian society." AD, p. 623.

[8] AD, p. 172.

[9] Tot v. United States, 319 U.S. 463 (1943) and United States v. Lovett, 328 U.S. 303 (1946).

[10] AD, p. 20.

to describe or explain the workings of the party system. He maintains that "the party machine is the intermediary between the power of the state and the protection of owners from invasion by that power," [11] although this function is hardly necessary if, as he argues, the state power itself is a direct reflection of the interests of the owning group. He insists that genuine political parties must rest on an economic basis. Therefore, the two major American parties are only the two wings of a single conservative party, which is committed to an archaic individualism and to the outmoded concepts of "free enterprise." It is not surprising that these postulates lead Laski to the conclusion that in 1944 President Roosevelt abandoned the social advances of the New Deal in order to win the support of the great city machines, the bosses of which "are, for all practical purposes, simply the affiliates of Big Business, acting as their agents in municipal affairs." [12]

Laski repeatedly uses the facts of the 1930's to support sweeping conclusions about the America of 1948. For example, he estimates that the number of migratory farm workers and their families is five million and states that the percentage of American farms worked by tenants rose from 25 per cent in 1880 to 42 per cent in 1930.[13] He does not mention the fact that by 1945 the percentage of farms that were tenant-operated had fallen to about 32 per cent.[14] On the basis of these outdated facts he proceeds to the totally erroneous conclusion that the developments of the last decades have combined "either to drive the owner of a family farm off the land altogether, or to reduce him to the half-helpless condition of a tenant-farmer battling hard against remorseless debt and semi-starvation." [15]

The "disappearance" of the independent farmer during the last half-century is to Laski only one example of "proletarianization" and the general decline of the capitalist system in the United States. American capitalism has never really recovered from the fatal depression of the early 1930's. Before the war began economic disaster was averted only by vast programs of public works and public relief, while the full employment achieved during the war was possible only because millions of men were in the armed forces and millions

[11] *Ibid.*, p. 151.   [12] *Ibid.*, p. 120.   [13] *Ibid.*, pp. 238 and 487.
[14] See the figures given in U.S. Bureau of the Census, *Statistical Abstract of the United States: 1951* (72d edition, Washington, D.C.: Government Printing Office, 1951), p. 571.
[15] AD, p. 489.

more in war production. His explanation of this collapse of capitalism is that "the outstanding fact in the economic life of America is that the distribution of wealth does not make possible the use of its productive resources by American consumers." [16] On the basis of this hypothesis he predicts that in the postwar period American monopoly capitalism will, after a period of boom, move towards a new depression. Writing in the summer of 1949, he argues that this economic crisis will occur within a few years if the United States does not achieve a comprehensive understanding with the Soviet Union; this depression will bring about a major political crisis, since capitalism will endeavor to save itself by destroying the power of the organized workers. He says: "If the unions were able to hold their ground, business interests, rather than give up their sovereignty in the economic field, would safeguard their property by what would come to be a frontal attack upon democratic institutions." [17]

The contraction of American capitalism has already resulted in serious breaches in the democratic system. The struggle of a dying capitalism to maintain its power explains the growing doubt of the validity of democratic institutions, the decline in tolerance with respect to economic and political issues, the increasing attacks upon the trade-union movement, the drive against equality, and the growing skepticism about the possibilities of mass education. [18] The loyalty investigations and the actions of the House Committee on un-American Activities demonstrate that "the right to speak freely and to act upon that freedom, which Jefferson wrote of as the very heart of Americanism, has been transformed relentlessly into the very antithesis of Americanism." [19] As a result of the ever-deepening cleavage between classes in America, which is a necessary consequence of the growing contradiction between the capitalist economy and the productive power of industry, citizens no longer hold the great ends of life in common. What Laski calls "the unity of a culture" has collapsed. "There is no agreement about principles, no agreement about values, no central frame of reference within which the critics can find a common purpose. Only on the plane of action where, as in

---

[16] *Ibid.*, p. 180.
[17] See "America, Good and Bad," *The Nation*, CLXIX (July 2, 1949), 8.
[18] See AD, p. 257.   [19] DOT, p. 112; see also p. 53.

war, different philosophies are forgotten in the short-term struggle for victory does unity appear." [20]

In his examination of every phase of American capitalist civilization, he notes a pervasive "failure of nerve" that reminds him of the Hellenistic world; this pessimism and lack of confidence he attributes to the fear that has gripped the members of the ruling class, a fear which rises from their suspicion that if bourgeois democracy "is to keep its bourgeois character, it cannot remain democratic . . . that if it remains democratic, it cannot keep its bourgeois character." [21] He argues that this decline in the American sense of security and in the self-confidence of the ruling class is clearly evidenced in the "immense growth" of anti-Semitism and anti-Negro prejudice in the United States since 1918.[22] Since he regards anti-Semitism and oppression of the Negro as weapons which "a ruling class needs to keep in reserve either to divide its enemies or present them with a kind of scapegoat in the sacrifice of which their sense of failure can be sublimated," [23] it is not surprising that he believes that only the Soviet Union has really solved both the problem of racial relations and that of religious prejudice.[24]

Laski believes that the only hope for the preservation and extension of democracy and for the rebuilding of a common system of values in America lies in the creation of a labor party dedicated to the principles of socialism. Repeatedly he criticizes the American trade unions for their failure to build an independent political movement of this kind, as well as for their willingness to accept, for the present, the capitalist system as indestructible. The unions are motivated only by the pragmatic desire to win from that capitalist system the best possible terms for their members. The vital weakness in their approach to politics is that they have accepted the capitalists' theory of the state—the belief that "the American government, as the agent of the State power, is a neutral and mediating force among the different elements in society." [25] As a consequence the unions have restricted their exercise of political influence to the techniques of indirect action as a pressure group. They do not recognize that in

---

[20] AD, p. 430.
[22] See AD, pp. 187, 194, and 480–86.
[24] See *ibid.*, p. 453.

[21] DOT, p. 114.
[23] *Ibid.*, p. 486.
[25] *Ibid.*, p. 223.

a capitalist society which has reached the stage of monopoly, it is the business of the government to preserve the law and order that maintain the monopolists' property rights and their continued access to profits. They have not yet learned that the goals and methods of the trade unions compel the capitalists and the government to view them as a threat to law and order and that government action in any industrial dispute will therefore normally be to labor's disadvantage.[26]

Laski's conclusion is that "the occasions are exceptionally rare when the government, even if its composition is progressive, is able to use the state power it operates on behalf of the trade unions, except in a special crisis like that of war."[27] Despite his admission that the status of unions has generally improved since 1919, he urges the workers to realize, as the capitalists clearly do, that a permanent and irreconcilable conflict exists between employers and workers. The moment the American economy lapses into its next depression, the great corporations will insist that the power of the state be employed to force the unions to accept the strict "discipline" that businessmen sincerely believe to be essential. Only if the unions have built before that time a powerful independent labor party, capable of taking control of the government or, at least, of offering organized opposition to the capitalist rulers, will labor be able to prevent the smashing of the free trade-union movement, the destruction of democracy, and the defection to the Communists of large numbers of workers.

For Laski, the Republican Party is the spokesman of the corporation, while the Democratic Party depends upon a strange amalgam of the South, the big-city machines, and the Roman Catholic Church;[28] neither of the major parties is genuinely interested in the trade unions or in the well-being of the workers. He urges the American unions to create an independent labor party of their own, drawing into that party all the progressive forces in American life. American liberals must and will learn what the British Labor Party learned between 1900 and 1918—"that when the basic objectives of the two parties between which an electorate must choose are the same, the electorate has no real choice. Thus deprived of the power to choose, it cannot secure either the men or the measures which its situation requires. It is then driven to a realignment of parties

26 See TU, pp. 16, 18, 20, and 22.   27 *Ibid.*, p. 21.
28 See *ibid.*, p. 102.

so that the institutions of representative democracy may work with genuine effectiveness." [29] This party realignment, which can be effected only by the creation of an independent labor party, is essential if the irresponsibility of the American system of government and its inability to deal with vital domestic and international problems are to be overcome. Direct participation in politics by the trade unions would be the most effective means of drawing a large number of workers into an active role in the political process and in the business of government. The danger of totalitarianism in the United States would be greatly lessened if unions exercised responsible political power and trained their members to know how to use that power.[30]

Laski pays scant attention to the difficulties involved in attempting to build an American labor party that would have a chance of becoming one of the two major political parties; he ignores the complex geographical and social differences that render the problem of creating a disciplined and ideologically homogeneous party far more complex than it is in Britain. Nor does he attempt to answer the criticism that an American labor party that was avowedly the creature of the trade-union movement would, *ipso facto,* doom itself to the status of a minor party for the foreseeable future. From his Marxist premises he draws the dogmatic conclusion that the unions can attain their economic goals only when they are able to define the ends of the political system. Union power must be mobilized politically, not simply to attain certain specific goals of the labor movement, but "so that it can carry out the redefinition of the relations of production with the state power in its hands, and not in its opponents' hands." [31] As always, his analysis and his exhortations rest on the simple but erroneous hypothesis that "when the state power belongs to the owners of economic power—and it has always belonged to them— it will be used to define relations of production which benefit those owners." [32]

[29] "The American Political Scene," *The Nation,* CLXIII (Nov. 23, 1946), 584.
[30] See TU, pp. 41 and 96.   [31] *Ibid.,* p. 172.
[32] *Ibid.,* p. 173.

2. THE SOVIET UNION

Laski's analysis of Communism rests in large part on his conviction that the secret of its success lies in its deeply religious character. "No one who has watched the evolution of Russian Communism over the last thirty years," he maintains, "can avoid the conviction that all the phenomena it has revealed bear the closest resemblance to the phenomena of Christianity." [33] In pressing this analogy between Communism and religious movements, Laski ignores the very real differences between the phenomena being compared—above all, the difference between the intensity and range of the Party's control over the political, economic, and social, as well as the psychological and ideological, aspects of men's lives, and the extent of the power of the Church, even at its highest point. He uses the analogy in an effort to gloss over or explain away some of the more unpleasant features of the Communist regimes in the Soviet Union and in the satellite states. He was never able to arrive at a realistic attitude towards Communism, particularly in Russia, although his enthusiasm for the Soviet experiment receded from its wartime high, and he became somewhat disillusioned about the prospects of a relaxation of the Party's internal dictatorship and about the genuineness of Moscow's desire for international cooperation.

At no point is he successful in overcoming the crucial contradiction between his commitment to the values of Western liberalism—individual freedom, spontaneity, tolerance of diverse opinions and beliefs—and his feeling that he must defend or excuse many of the policies and actions of the Soviet leaders that are destructive of those values. For example, after summarizing the reasons for the Russian rulers' refusal to permit contacts between the Russian people and the Western world, he concedes that this attitude is repugnant to those who believe that men should be free to learn about beliefs and ways of life different from their own and to choose freely between the alternatives. But he immediately retreats from the full force of this principle lest it involve him in a fundamental criticism of the Communist position. He reminds us of "the historical fact" that "the number of those

[33] DOT, p. 206; see also p. 224.

in any period who would genuinely welcome tolerance of this order of magnitude has been in every society in every period pitifully small." [34] He thus blurs the fact that the Communists deny as a matter of principle the desirability of tolerance of other opinions and fails to distinguish between lapses from an ideal and its complete and overt rejection. Although he is critical of the one-party system and of the decision of the Russian leaders to achieve progress by coercion rather than persuasion,[35] he does not see that these defects are inherent in Bolshevik ideology and practice rather than accidental characteristics or merely temporary responses of the Soviet system to external situations.

Laski's discussion of the applicability of the term "democracy" to Russian institutions reveals much of the ambivalence and confusion in his attitude toward Soviet Communism. At times he admits that Russia is obviously not a democracy in the accepted sense of the term; it is a dictatorship of the party leaders, and the secret police, "under the Bolsheviks as under the Czar, set the perspective in which the Russian citizen lives." [36] But he soon proceeds to confuse the issue and to draw the sting from his criticism by saying: "I think Russia has achieved a remarkable social democracy; it has gone, in my judgment, farther toward an effective democracy in the realm of economic life than any other country I have seen." [37] He argues that against the background of years of civil war and international war and of "grave conspiracies against the state," it is "perfectly possible for anyone with common sense to understand why Generalissimo Stalin and his colleagues do not yet feel that the time has come for political democracy in Russia." [38] At other moments he reduces the entire discussion to a relatively insignificant question of semantics. "The debate on the presence or absence of democracy in Russia is, in one sense, no more than an unreal discussion about terms. We

[34] *Ibid.*, p. 265.

[35] See Introduction to the revised edition of *Liberty in the Modern State*, 1949, pp. 13–14.

[36] *The Secret Battalion* (London: The Labour Party, 1946), p. 13. See also his statement: "It seems to me dishonest, indeed, to deny that Russian political institutions may be regarded as maintaining the possibility of democratisation, but, unless words cease to have any real meaning, democratisation has not yet seriously begun." CM, pp. 95–96.

[37] "Why Does Russia Act That Way?," *The Nation*, CLXIV (March 1, 1947), 241.

[38] *Ibid.*

in the West emphasize certain things we regard as desirable, and call them democracy; the Russians emphasize other things to which, also, they give the name of democracy." [39]

Every time he refers to what he calls the "immense evils" in the Soviet record, he balances the account with a reference to the immense achievements of the Bolshevik regime and to the Soviet Union's significance as the source of "new and creative" values in our civilization; he warns that we must not apply to Soviet practices criteria derived from our own historical evolution. What the Bolshevik government has accomplished is, he insists,

certainly more revolutionary of the values of mankind than anything elsewhere accomplished since the French Revolution. It has ended the exploitation of the many in the interest of a few. It has given to manual labour a dignity and a recognition which, in the normal process of industrialisation, only a small oligarchy of highly skilled craftsmen have been able successfully to attain. It has organised opportunities for innumerable numbers of those who earn their living by manual toil to find in their leisure a self-respect and a fulfilment on a scale elsewhere unknown. . . . It has broken down all the major barriers of colour and of creed.[40]

The Russian citizen has important compensations for his inability to participate in the choice of his rulers or in the determination of their policies, as well as for the threat of the secret police which constantly menaces him. No other citizen can exercise power over him simply because of wealth or power [*sic!*]; nothing but his own capacity and character determines the extent to which he can improve himself; the values of his community are not set by the small group of the wealthy or well-born, and labor is regarded as honorable.[41] From these fantasies Laski advances to an even more fantastic conclusion:

Behind all the dogmas and the orthodoxies, the cruelties and the fanaticism, there is an elasticity, a power of sweeping adjustment, a capacity to admit error, an experimental audacity, which have in them something that is essential to freedom. There is a conscious effort to make man the master of his own fate, a deep respect for the cultural heritage, a recognition of the need for cultural diversity as the safeguard against the implications of technological uniformity.[42]

[39] "What Democracy Means in Russia," *The New Republic*, CXV (Oct. 28, 1946), 551.

[40] DOT, p. 169.   [41] See *ibid.*, p. 60.   [42] *Ibid.*, pp. 60–61.

Despite his repeated assertion that the absence of civil and political liberties in Russia must be viewed in the light of the fact that the Soviet citizen enjoys a large measure of freedom and significance in the vital nonpolitical spheres of action, he states, with no apparent sense of contradiction, that the Russian citizen is unable to express his opinion on any matter of policy in such a way that the government must take account of it.[43] He reduces to absurdity his laudatory comments about the "economic democracy" that exists in Russia when he admits that the Party is the vital factor in the process of decision-making in industry and agriculture, while "the ordinary worker has less chance of shaping his own destiny than a respected trade-union member in the average well-run workshop in Great Britain or the United States."[44] After indicating his agreement with the criticisms which Rosa Luxemburg made, before the Bolshevik Revolution, of Lenin's conception of the nature and functions of the Communist Party, he insists that her prophecy of the dangers of dictatorship and bureaucracy has been fulfilled in detail by the continuous increase in the power of the Russian Politburo since 1917, as well as by the development of Communist regimes in other countries.[45] These statements—together with the admission that "Lenin and Stalin have separated the two ideals that all socialists have sought to combine: the ideal of a people no longer exploited in their search for well-being, and the ideal of freedom"[46]—should have led Laski to recognize that dictatorship, the police state, and the destruction of individual freedom and autonomy are inevitable characteristics of Communist society and necessary consequences of Bolshevik doctrine, not simply temporary distortions or deformations of the model of a democratic socialist society. But he is unwilling to accept the consequences which follow from his own admissions; he clings to the belief that Communism in Russia must, in the last analysis, be viewed as an effort to realize the goals and values of Western European socialism.

The apparent failure of the Soviet regime to develop in accordance with this blueprint is then "explained" as the result of external factors for which the Russian leaders cannot be blamed, such as the

---

[43] See TU, p. 12.   [44] *Ibid.*, p. 162.

[45] See DOT, pp. 160–64; and "Reason and Russia," *The New Republic*, CXIX (Dec. 6, 1948), 22–24.

[46] "Reason and Russia," *The New Republic*, CXIX (Dec. 6, 1948), 24.

Allied intervention against the Bolsheviks, the world-wide campaign carried on for over thirty years by capitalist interests to crush the new values that had emerged in Russia in 1917, the willingness of the rulers of the capitalist democracies during the 1930's to sacrifice the Soviet Union to Hitler's thirst for power and aggrandizement, or the anti-Russian attitudes and actions of the United States and its allies at the close of the Second World War.[47] Alternatively, Laski explains the absolute dictatorship maintained by the Soviet leaders or the "immensity" of their blunders as necessary consequences of the rapid and forced industrialization of Russia, which had to be accomplished in the face of strong peasant opposition and which was essential if the Soviet Union was to be made secure against attacks from abroad.[48] The force of this apologetic argument is shattered by his own admission that even "when the foundations of Soviet industrialism had been firmly laid, there was no real relaxation of the dictatorship on its political side . . . and the leaders of the Communist Party were, so to say, convinced of the need to perpetuate their own authority as a dictatorship."[49]

Laski states that Stalin is aware that if Russia were to experience a period of peaceful development that would permit the easing of the hardships of the masses, the people would make demands for personal and political freedom that no government could deny. But he does not concede that this awareness that the tight dictatorship of the Party leaders could not survive a period of peaceful relations with other nations and improvement of the popular standard of living may be the fundamental reason for the efforts of Stalin and his successors to convince the masses that Russia's existence is endangered by the aggressive designs of the capitalist powers. He fails to draw this conclusion from the facts at hand because he continues to believe that Stalin is genuinely anxious to attain a *modus vivendi* with the West[50] and because he still has confidence in the "limitless idealism" of the Bolshevik leaders; "they have never failed to keep in view the idea of a great Russian civilisation leading in the great task of emancipating the workers of the world."[51]

[47] See TU, pp. 176–77; and DOT, pp. 191–92 and 246.
[48] See DOT, pp. 166–67.   [49] *Ibid.*, p. 190.
[50] See "My Impressions of Stalin," *The New Republic,* CXV (Oct. 14, 1946), 478–79.
[51] DOT, p. 164.

Laski is far more realistic in his analysis and evaluation of the policies of the Communist parties outside the Soviet Union than in his attitude towards Russian Communism. In *The Secret Battalion,* as well as in several of his other postwar publications, he sharply condemns the non-Russian Communist movements for their blind adherence to the orders of the Russian leaders, particularly in the 1939–1941 period. He warns Western socialists against any effort at unity with groups which "act without moral scruples, intrigue without any sense of shame, are utterly careless of truth, sacrifice, without any hesitation, the means they use to the ends they serve." [52] He notes that the members of each Communist party are expected to obey without question the commands of their leaders, no matter how sudden and unexpected the shifts in policy or the changes in leadership may be. Immediate advantage is the sole criterion used by the Communist parties to determine the methods which they will employ. As a result, "we have seen history falsified, documents forged, men and women . . . slandered and broken." [53] The real purpose behind Communist strategy outside Russia in the postwar period is "the organization of catastrophe"; this policy is "the straight road to the betrayal of civilisation." [54] In both France and Italy, Communist policy, instead of attempting to build a strong alliance of all Left groups and to create the conditions for economic recovery, aims to produce social and economic collapse, from which only the reactionary groups can benefit.[55] Laski thus explicitly accepts the view that the Communists are willing to do anything that will prevent Western Europe from achieving stability and prosperity with American aid; elsewhere, however, he completely rejects this estimate of Communist intentions, which he regards as the basis of American policies, such as the Truman Doctrine and the North Atlantic Pact. He notes that in the people's democracies of Eastern Europe, coalition governments including the Communists have invariably led to Communist domination of the coalition and finally to the emergence of the police state and the open dictatorship of the Communist Party. In both Western and Eastern Europe it is clear that the present object of the world Communist movement is the same as that of the

[52] *The Secret Battalion*, p. 15; see also pp. 10–13; and CM, p. 89.
[53] *The Secret Battalion*, p. 26.   [54] *Ibid.,* p. 28.
[55] See DOT, pp. 231–32; and *Russia and the West: Policy for Britain*, Peace Aims Pamphlet No. 43 (London: National Peace Council, n.d. [1948?]), p. 10.

Third International between the wars—the defense and promotion of the interests and achievements of Russia.

Laski is particularly vehement in his denunciations of the British Communist Party for its attacks on the Labor Party as "social-fascist" and for its unceasing attempts within the trade unions to hamper the efforts of the Labor Government to promote economic recovery. In contrast to his prewar attitude, he is now completely opposed to the Communists' request to be admitted to affiliation with the Labor Party. Since the Communists believe that all democratic parties of the Left are in essence only a shield for capitalist reaction, they must aim either to destroy the Labor Party while seeking an alliance with it, or to dominate the Party after joining it so that they can convert it into another instrument to further the goals of the Russian Communist Party.[56] He observes that in any non-Communist group or organization Communists "act like a secret battalion of paratroopers within the brigade whose discipline they have accepted."[57] If the British Communists are sincere in their desire for organic unity with Labor, let them disband their party and cease their attacks on the policies and principles of the Labor Party and its leaders. He also observes that acceptance of the Communist Party into the ranks of Labor would be a major strategic error, since it would strengthen the forces of reaction by persuading the voters that the Labor Party shared the Communists' conviction that the system of parliamentary democracy, which is accepted by the vast majority of the British people, is headed for inevitable disaster.[58]

At the same time he sharply criticizes trade-union leaders who seek the help of employers and the state in preventing Communist infiltration into their unions. In both Britain and the United States the relatively great influence of a small number of Communists in certain unions is largely the result of their greater zeal and devotion to their ideals, and the failure in the exercise of democratic leadership on the part of the non-Communists who head these unions. The only way to deal effectively with Communist attempts at infiltration is to make the union's organization and activities completely democratic; in this way the large majority of the members who are not

[56] *The Secret Battalion*, pp. 9, 11, 15, and 27–28.
[57] *Ibid.*, p. 12.   [58] See *ibid.*, p. 29.

Communists will be encouraged to participate actively in union affairs. He warns that an anti-Communist alliance of union leaders, organized employers, and the state is likely to result in a weakening of the unions' position vis-à-vis the employers and in a slowing down of the pace of social progress.[59]

[59] See TU, pp. 166–75.

15

The Cold War

IN THE POSTWAR PERIOD Laski, like most of us, gave increasing attention to the problems of international relations and, in particular, to the mounting tension between the United States and the Soviet Union. For Laski, who had been even more hopeful than most wartime observers about the peaceful intentions of the Russians and more confident that cooperation among the Allies would produce a new era of international peace after the collapse of Fascism, the rapid disintegration of the wartime coalition and the onset of the "cold war" constituted a catastrophe and a disillusionment of shattering proportions.[1] It is difficult not to feel that the rapid deterioration of relations between Russia and the West and the specter of a Third World War fought with atomic weapons contributed in no small measure to the enormous stress under which Laski was obviously laboring in 1948 and 1949 and to his sudden death in 1950. Far more than many observers of politics, he felt the cold war as a personal tragedy; after England, the United States and the Soviet Union were the two nations in which he was most interested and to which, for very different reasons, he was most attracted. He had lived and taught in America as a young man and had visited it frequently through the years. He numbered Americans among his closest friends and found much to admire in American life. Although the Soviet Union was less familiar to him personally, he had a long-standing emotional commitment to it as the great example of a socialist society in which, he believed, his hopes and dreams for a better world would be fulfilled. There is bitter irony in the fact that in the last years of his life he was compelled to face the prospect of a clash between these two coun-

[1] See his remark in 1948: "It seems fantastic that it should be as it is today after what we have been through together." "Let's Start Over," *The Nation*, CLXVII (Nov. 27, 1948), 602. In September, 1947, he wrote to Felix Frankfurter: "But I have the feeling that I am already a ghost in a play that is over." Quoted in Kingsley Martin, *Harold Laski* (New York: The Viking Press, 1953), p. 192.

tries he admired—a clash in which, inevitably, Britain would be involved.

From what has been said about his analyses of American and Russian political and economic institutions, it would not be difficult to deduce his attitude towards the struggle between the United States and the Soviet Union. Let us, however, examine directly some of his comments about that struggle and about the policies that should be adopted to diminish the danger of open war. His analysis of the contemporary situation is restricted by his firm adherence to the conviction that capitalism necessarily involves imperialist expansion and war. In any capitalist society, such as the United States, there is an increasing concentration of wealth and income, which results in a fatal disproportion between the power to produce and the power to consume. This contradiction can be temporarily resolved and full employment achieved only by imperialist policies that will drain off the excess goods and capital. In view of the vast increase in American productive capacity during the war, Laski is convinced that the United States must attain full employment by a drastic redistribution of wealth that will make the ability to consume roughly equal to the power to produce; or it must undertake a permanent program of public works on a scale that will make the New Deal experiments seem insignificant by comparison; or it will have to embark upon a policy of economic imperialism. This last choice, which is the one America is most likely to make, means that it will "export its unemployment with catastrophic results to the rest of the world," [2] and, finally, will plunge the world into a new war. Laski does not argue that Americans consciously desire to dominate the world economically or politically or to launch a new world conflict. But what Americans as individuals want or do not want is of small consequence; in his analysis, the determining forces are abstractions, such as "finance capitalism" and "capitalist imperialism." The power of the workers and even that of the government are overshadowed by the power of capital. With incredible naïvete, he advances the outmoded thesis that in the present stage of capitalism the initiative in industrial or agricultural strategy rests with the bankers who control the vital credit mechanism of the community. [3]

[2] Introduction to the revised edition of *Liberty in the Modern State* (New York: The Viking Press, 1949), p. 20.

[3] See TU, pp. 75–76.

In the sphere of international relations the essential weapon of finance capitalism is the principle of national sovereignty, a principle which is thoroughly outmoded in an age when the entire world is caught up in a network of economic interdependence. For Laski national sovereignty is necessary if governments are to defend the claims of the "vested interests" of capitalism which it is their function to protect. Yet in his discussions of the inadequacy of the United Nations Charter and of its provision for the exercise of the veto by any of the Great Powers, he concedes that at San Francisco the government of the Soviet Union, which presumably has no "vested interests" to protect, "was not less insistent than the United States that the principle of national sovereignty was the heart of the Charter and why, therefore, it insisted upon the veto as the instrument which would express that sovereignty in the operation of international decisions." [4] One is left to wonder how he can reconcile his assumptions that Russia is a socialist society and that national sovereignty is the expression of the needs of the capitalist state with his statement, which applies to all the Great Powers, that the United Nations is dependent "upon the sovereign wills of nation states which express, in all vital matters, the purposes of their ruling classes and subordinate to those purposes the interests of the common peoples." [5]

In Laski's view the most important reason for the cold war is the bitter opposition of the forces of reaction, which largely dominate American policy, to the Soviet Union, which is a socialist society embodying the antitheses of their bourgeois values and beliefs. The fundamental reason for hostility to Russia lies in the fact that American capitalism, unable to expand internally, is compelled in order to survive to engage in "outer horizontal expansion" in Asia, the Middle East, and Europe.[6] American foreign policy is seeking to impose the values of "an immensely wealthy and powerful middle-class civilisation . . . not only upon a Europe where those values are losing their hold, but upon a Middle East, a Russia and an Asia, where they are either already dead or have never existed." [7] His view of the Marshall Plan and of other American efforts to provide economic aid for Europe is that these programs represent the inevitable

---

[4] "The Crisis in Our Civilization," *Foreign Affairs*, XXVI (Oct., 1947), 46.
[5] *Ibid.*, p. 45.
[6] See "Is Europe Done For?," *The Nation*, CLXV (Nov. 22, 1947), 549.
[7] DOT, pp. 108–9.

policy of foreign expansion of a nation dominated by finance capitalism; also, they may well represent an effort to employ America's tremendous economic power to check the postwar trend towards socialism among the peoples of Europe.[8] Late in 1947 he warns that the terms on which American aid will be granted to Western Europe will be the reversal of the march to socialism and the preservation of the power and privileges of the discredited capitalist ruling class. These terms will encourage European capitalists to refuse to abdicate their positions of power in spite of the popular demands for socialism. As a result, counterrevolution and civil war will engulf Western Europe, while America itself will be compelled to choose between a capitalist dictatorship and a socialist democracy. By the end of 1948, however, he is urging President Truman to "keep Congress firmly behind the European Recovery Program," [9] since the life of Western Europe depends on it.

In the book which he was writing at the time of his death, he insists that since his speech at Fulton in March, 1947, Winston Churchill has been the real leader of the campaign for an anti-Russian bloc, although the details of the campaign have been executed by Truman and Bevin in the Truman Doctrine and the organization of NATO. He refers to these measures of American foreign policy as the "organisation of the Grand Alliance against Russia—*inadequately camouflaged as alliance against 'aggression.'*" [10] The argument that these measures are necessary to the defense of the West is dismissed with the comment: "Any calm and detached American observer will agree that the spread of Communism cannot be effectively stayed by force of arms." [11] He does not attempt to meet the obvious reply by this "detached American observer"—that the spread of Communism cannot be effectively stayed without the force of arms. He is convinced that the Atlantic Powers, under American leadership, are prepared to use Western Germany "as the basis of the attack by which they hope to destroy a way of life they know to be ultimately incompatible with their own." [12]

Laski's analysis of American foreign policy is straightforward and consistent, though seriously at variance with the facts. The United

[8] See AD, p. 512.
[9] "Truman's Task in Europe," *The New Republic*, CXIX (Dec. 20, 1948), 11.
[10] DOT, p. 200; italics mine.   [11] *Ibid.*
[12] *Ibid.*, p. 242.

States, inspired by Churchill's evil genius, has attempted "to drive Russia into a position where its natural desire for security against an *einkreisung* sponsored by American diplomacy should lead the world to the brink of a third World War." [13] His analysis and evaluation of Soviet foreign policy are far more complex and inconsistent. Sometimes, as in the last quotation, he seems to assume that Russia has no aggressive intentions and that its actions on the international scene are motivated only by a legitimate desire for security against America's hostile policy of encirclement. At one point he clearly states his view of the basic issues in the conflict between the United States and the Soviet Union in these terms; capitalist America is necessarily aggressive and imperialistic, while socialist Russia is inherently peaceloving and uninterested in dominating other nations. "The Russian way of life . . . seeks as clearly to prevent external economic exploitation as the American way of life inherently drives its business leaders at once to seek for that exploitation and to regard its critics as dangerous stumbling blocks in the way of the fulfilment of America's 'manifest destiny.' " [14] He categorically rejects "any view of Russian policy which attributes to it an expansionist character, whether on strategic or on economic grounds." [15] Russia's primary concern is security, and it neither desires a world war nor is capable of waging one.

At other moments he concedes that the Russian transformation of Poland, Hungary, Bulgaria, Czechoslovakia, and Yugoslavia into "something like satellite powers" is difficult to interpret as anything but "a series of steps in exactly the kind of power politics which preceded the Second World War." [16] He describes the course of Soviet diplomacy in terms that cannot be reconciled with his insistence that Russian policy has not been in any sense expansionist. Russia has destroyed all opposition parties, including socialist groups, in its satellite allies, "and it has turned all of them into police-states subordinate to its own purposes. It has shown hardly a sign of any willingness to give strength and direction to the United Nations." [17] It has done everything possible to prevent the success of the Marshall Plan "by using Communist parties in Western Europe to hamper

[13] ROC, p. 86.   [14] AD, p. 516.
[15] *Russia and the West: Policy for Britain,* Peace Aims Pamphlet No. 43 (London: National Peace Council, n.d. [1948?]), p. 13.
[16] AD, p. 512.   [17] DOT, p. 49.

the effort there at the economic rehabilitation which American aid sought to achieve [*sic!*]." [18] One is forced to ask how Laski can simultaneously hold these two contradictory views of Russian post-war foreign policy: first, that it has been a defensible, nonexpansionist policy of building up its own strength to meet the real dangers of capitalist encirclement and attack, and, second, that the Soviet Union has demonstrated a completely "ruthless" attitude toward the satellite states and that, since late in 1946, "the directive of the Politbureau in Moscow was mainly hostile to the kind of effort which would lead to any real *modus vivendi* between Russia and its allies, on the one hand, and to [*sic*] the United States and its allies, on the other." [19]

Laski's contradictory attitudes toward Soviet foreign policy are not to be explained simply by reference to his general ability to hold thoroughly inconsistent positions. In this case there is a more specific reason for his ambivalence; although he is unable to ignore completely the record of Russia's ruthlessness in its postwar dealings with other nations, he cannot, without abandoning his entire Marxist-Leninist analysis of the causes of imperialism and war, admit that Russia, which he insists is a socialist nation, is guilty of aggressive or imperialistic designs or actions. He is more interested in saving his general thesis than in making his theories conform to the facts at hand. Even more important, perhaps, as an explanation of the reasons for Laski's desperate anxiety to minimize the dangers of the Soviet threat to the West is his overpowering fear of a new world conflict that will completely shatter European civilization. He admits: "We think that Russia can be cruel and secretive, arrogant and obscurantist. But we want Europe to live. We think it has a civilization worth preserving. . . . We are not ashamed to admit that we are afraid. We are not ashamed to insist that we have a grim reason to be afraid." [20] This argument, which assumes that European civilization will be preserved in the event of Communist domination of the West, is similar to the arguments of the "appeasers" of the 1930's, who were criticized by Laski when they asserted that Hitler's demands must not be resisted in view of the calamitous effects of a general war.

All these factors lead Laski to return, after any criticism of a particular phase of Soviet policy, to the general conviction that the Rus-

[18] *Ibid.*, p. 51.   [19] *Ibid.*, p. 254.
[20] "Truman's Task in Europe," *The New Republic*, CXIX (Dec. 20, 1948), 12.

sian leaders obviously have no desire for war. The brutality and obstinacy that they display are manifestations of their deep sense of insecurity, which must be understood as a more or less legitimate reaction to the threat of American imperialism. In order to maintain these convictions he is compelled to ignore the facts that he has conceded, as well as their implications, if they do not support his thesis. Not only does he refuse to credit the official American explanations of such policies as the Truman Doctrine or the formation of NATO, but he consistently accepts the most unfavorable and sinister interpretations of American actions. But when he discusses Russian foreign policy, he conjures up elaborate excuses to justify the policies of the Soviet government and often accepts, quite uncritically, the official explanations of its actions. There is no evidence to suggest that Russia wants war or is capable of fighting a major war; indeed there is "no sufficient evidence to prove that Russia is bent upon imperialist expansion." [21] On the other hand, the Russians are justified in concluding that American interests center around the defense of capitalism. It is the leaders of the United States who "have created a mentality which makes it impossible to try to reach an understanding with Russia." [22] Laski concludes: "Every sin with which the US charges Russia can fairly be charged against itself. War talk, expansionism, bases, satellites, economic predominance, communism as a threat to world peace, encouragement of the most reactionary groups in Europe and even in China, reduction of Japan to a position of US vassal, witch-hunting crusades in the United States itself." [23]

Although he never totally accepts the Communist line on the cold war, he emerges as a fairly consistent apologist for the actions of the Soviet government at home and abroad. The pattern of his apologetic is remarkably constant. He begins by admitting the magnitude of the Communists' crimes and mistakes, but he always ends by insisting that their actions cannot be judged in terms of "a standardized ethic" [24] and that their errors must be seen against the background of their great accomplishments and high aspirations. Thus, for example, he concedes that the Soviet Union is

[21] "Getting on with Russia," *The Nation*, CLXVI (Jan. 10, 1948), 36.
[22] "A Socialist Looks at the Cold War," *The New Republic*, CXVII (Oct. 27, 1947), 10.
[23] *Ibid.*, p. 11.   [24] See DOT, p. 95.

a dictatorship. It is a hard regime. It has made vast mistakes and blunders that are difficult to distinguish from crime. *But whatever the temporary deformation,* its zeal for science, its enthusiasm for education, the great avenues of opportunity it has opened to its own people, the elevation of its subject nationalities, the new status it has given to women, *the suppression of anti-Semitism,* the absence of a color bar—all these seem to me proof that within the framework of the dictatorship there lies the purpose of building in Russia a democratic way of life. The stumbling-block is its leaders' sense of total insecurity on the international plane.[25]

Laski's favorite argument is that the continuance of the Soviet dictatorship together with the hostility and suspicion of other nations displayed by the Russian leaders are due to their deep fears that their country's security is menaced by the capitalist world. He is convinced that if those fears can be removed, the Russians will move towards democracy at home and friendly relations with other powers. He expresses "profound confidence that there can be full reliance on the purposes of Russia once we convince its leaders that we are as eager as they are to make its international security effective and will take steps to see that any attempt to revive Fascism is broken into pieces at its birth." [26] He always assigns to the Western Powers, and particularly to the United States and Britain, the responsibility for creating the conditions that will persuade the Russians to relax their suspicions and fears. Russia has, for example, the right to insist that the governments of Eastern Europe should not be hostile to her. The United States and Britain must, by accepting without question the new "people's democracies" that have replaced the previous corrupt and undemocratic regimes in this area, assure the Russians that they have no intention of creating a rift between the Soviet Union and the countries of Eastern Europe.[27] He never urges the Soviet Union to make a serious effort to demonstrate by its actions that it desires friendly relations with the West, or that the fears of the United States and the other democracies are unwarranted, although he demonstrates that they have some grounds for their fears when he admits that "Soviet Russia not only spends a larger proportion of its national income upon defense than any other country in the world,

[25] "Getting on with Russia," *The Nation,* CLXVI (Jan. 10, 1948), 37; italics mine.
[26] "Why Does Russia Act That Way?," *The Nation,* CLXIV (March 1, 1947), 242.
[27] See *Russia and the West,* pp. 8–9.

but holds under arms a larger standing army than the total force of all other European states, if we omit the armies of the countries allied to it in Eastern Europe." [28]

He applies to only one of the conflicting powers his thesis that a government will behave peacefully once other nations begin to act in a manner calculated to strengthen its sense of national security. But even if the thesis were applied equally to both the United States and Russia, it would have no real value or significance. In so far as it states that a government will not be aggressive or hostile if it is assured that its national security is not threatened by other powers, the argument is virtually tautological. The real problem arises when we ask: What are the conditions which the Soviet Union, for example, regards as essential to its sense of security? What would the United States or Britain have to do to convince the Soviet leaders that they can with safety relax their suspicions and hostilities? The example of Yugoslavia indicates that even the existence of a Communist regime in a country is not a guarantee to the Russians of the trustworthiness and *bona fides* of its government. Would the rulers of Russia feel secure if all Europe and Asia were in the hands of Communist governments that were completely submissive to the will of Moscow? Possibly, although even then they might argue that they were still threatened by the great power of a hostile capitalist regime in the United States. And what effect would such a total surrender of Western Europe and Asia to Communism have on the American government's sense of national security? In any case, it is plain that the postwar policies of the West cannot be held responsible for the entire catalogue of Russia's hostile actions and attitudes that Laski admits—its intense nationalism and deep xenophobia, its ruthless attitude toward its "allies," its return to the policy of denouncing socialists as "social fascists," its obvious effort to transform the Eastern Zone of Germany into another of its dependencies, the endless obstructions and delays it has created to block international agreements.[29]

In the last year or so of his life, Laski seems to have become somewhat weary of his never-ending task of explaining and attempting

[28] TU, p. 11.

[29] See *Socialism as Internationalism,* Research Series No. 132 (London: Fabian International Bureau, 1949), p. 7; *Russia and the West,* pp. 4–5; and DOT, pp. 255–57.

to justify the actions of the Soviet government. While his interpretations of Russian foreign policy are still far more charitable than his analyses of American policies, he admits that after Molotov's refusal even to discuss the Marshall Plan proposals, each step of Soviet policy "had the ugly look of a conscious effort to block the hope of that recovery [of Europe] by splitting the European continent into two camps." [30] Increasingly he insists that both antagonists in the cold war are equally guilty and equally responsible for the current international tension. "A heavy responsibility and heavy blame rest upon both sides. Both have been crude and Machiavellian, arrogant and ill-mannered, secretive and dishonest. The barbaric ruthlessness of the Russian leaders has been at least as evil as the immaturity and incoherence with which America has displayed its overwhelming power." [31] Even in this attempt at evenhanded condemnation of both sides, his bias appears in the charge that American "immaturity and incoherence" are just as evil as "the barbaric ruthlessness" of the Soviet rulers.

In his last book he returns to this theme that Russia and the West are equally responsible for the cold war.

I do not think anything is gained by the attempt to measure the degree of responsibility for its inception which all the great Powers have incurred; it is as foolish to blame Russian Communism and its devotees in other countries, for the cleavage from which we suffer as it is to insist that America and Great Britain are seeking by different ways to arrest, and, ultimately, to destroy, the communist idea in the interest of the privileged classes which are fighting to retain their traditional authority.[32]

He does not mention that his own analysis of United States foreign policy in the postwar period is, in general, based on the argument that he here describes as foolish. In similar vein he argues that just as the rulers of Russia denounce and persecute anyone who presumes to question any item of the Communist orthodoxy, so "the rulers of the United States are driven by a wild hysteria to denounce and to persecute those among their citizens who think that there may be something of social import in the dogmas to which Soviet Russia pins its faith." [33] He admits, however, that it would be ridiculous to sug-

[30] DOT, p. 256.
[31] "Let's Start Over," *The Nation*, CLXVII (Nov. 27, 1948), 604.
[32] DOT, pp. 94–95.   [33] *Ibid.*, p. 37.

gest that "witch-hunting" in the United States even begins to approximate the scale upon which it is practiced in the Soviet Union; he notes the differences between the trials of Hiss and Remington, of whose innocence he is completely convinced, and the trials of those accused of actions hostile to the state in Russia or the satellite countries.[34]

In the light of his analysis of the underlying reasons for the cold war and his evaluation of Soviet and American foreign policies, it is not surprising that his positive suggestions for dealing with the problems of international relations can be reduced to the simple formula: we have all made mistakes, but now we must "find terms of common understanding and not allow ourselves to drift to ever graver differences." [35] He gives no advice on how to achieve this common understanding in the face of the dreary record of Soviet obstruction, veto, and inability—or unwillingness—to compromise. And it is difficult to see how he can deduce the possibility of discovering terms of agreement from his major premise—the complete antithesis that exists between the American and Russian economic and social systems and fundamental ideas and values. At no point does he offer the framers of British or American policy a realistic suggestion for lessening the tensions of the cold war, while his discussions of American policies are completely lacking in that responsible criticism that the United States needs from its friends abroad. His general support of an international order based on the principles of functional federalism, as opposed to world government or European or Atlantic Union, has little if any concrete significance. His proposals for supranational planning in such fields as electric power, transport, or coal and steel assume that each of the participating nations has already accepted socialism; had he lived, he probably would have joined many other European socialists in denouncing schemes for "functional federalism," such as the Schuman Plan, which are not based on this premise that all the participating governments must be socialist. His positive suggestions are applicable only to a nonexistent world of socialist states. He has nothing to say about the problems of international relations in the real world, made up of Communist, socialist, capitalist, socio-capitalist, quasi-fascist, and feudal societies.

[34] See *ibid.*, pp. 267–68.
[35] "Information Please, Mr. Molotov," *The Nation*, CLXII (June 15, 1946), 711.

His only advice to his own government is to avoid alliance with or dependence upon either Washington or Moscow. In 1947 he insists that a common front between London and Washington on matters of international politics would be a major mistake. Britain should not only pledge itself not to join any Western bloc that threatens Russia's security, but should continue to work for close friendship with the Soviet Union.[36] During the last year or so of his life, Laski tends to be less hopeful about the possibilities of close Anglo-Russian co-operation; his attitude shifts in the direction of a vague neutralism, which is evident in his denunciations of both American and Soviet policies. After reviewing the Communists' renewed attacks on the Labor Party, he notes: "So far from the advance of socialism in Great Britain having assisted closer Anglo-Russian relations, it seems, as far as Moscow is concerned, to have assisted in their deterioration." [37] In view of Russia's unwillingness to work toward better relations with the Labor Government, he has nothing to suggest but an effort by England to avoid close cooperation with the United States and to pursue an independent foreign policy. He does not attempt to demonstrate how Britain can hope to cut herself off from both the American and the Russian blocs and, at the same time, deal successfully with the pressing economic and financial problems that she must now solve with little or no help from her empire or from the Dominions.

At the time of his death, Laski's major fear was that a Conservative Government might be returned to power in Britain; with "capitalist" regimes in both London and Washington, there would be a great drive for the political and economic integration of Western Europe, including Western Germany. This new pattern of union "could not avoid becoming the apparatus for defending middle-class supremacy in America and maintaining it against the challenge of socialism in Western Europe; and it could not avoid becoming the patron of the opposition to Russia and its allies in Eastern Europe, and of the old order both in the Middle East and in Asia." [38] Since this union would inevitably become the active weapon of the forces of counterrevolution, it would lead finally to a Third World War.

[36] See *Russia and the West*, pp. 11–14.
[37] DOT, p. 258.   [38] *Ibid.*, p. 111.

Part Six

CONCLUSION

16

Unfulfilled Promise

OUR SUMMARY and analysis of Laski's writings demonstrate that he
never achieved the distinction as a political theorist or as a scholar
in the field of political philosophy that was promised by the erudition
and brilliance of his early essays. It would be difficult to deny that
his originality and intellectual vigor began to decline after 1930; in
the last decade of his life his published works were repetitious and
rhetorical to the point of bombast. His style became increasingly
labored. The accents were those of a man who, although exhausted,
was making a desperate effort to go on talking, in the belief that
sheer repetition and volume of words would convince his audience
of the truth and the importance of his message. His intellectual deterioration in this last phase is so striking that one is tempted to
conclude that just as he had attained intellectual maturity at an
unusually early age, so he became tired and old at the comparatively
early age of fifty. But the peculiar characteristics of his pattern of
maturation and decline, together with the great pressure under which
he worked and lived for so long, while they may help to explain his
weaknesses as a political analyst in the final years, do not provide
answers to the central questions—Why did his early talents as a
historian and a legal and political theorist fail to mature, and why
did he never produce a major contribution to historical scholarship
or to philosophic construction?

To answer these questions adequately would require an intimate
knowledge of Laski's life and his personality, as well as a careful
consideration of the social and political factors that seem to have
made the last thirty years so uncongenial to philosophical creativity.
On the basis of our examination of his writings, we can venture only
to outline some of the elements that contributed to the frustration of
his native talents. The most obvious reason for his failure to produce
a work of scholarly profundity and intellectual power is that he always spread his intellectual energies too thin. In less than thirty-five

years he published about thirty books and over sixty pamphlets and chapters in books, as well as hundreds of articles for scholarly and popular periodicals and for newspapers. This fantastically rapid rate of production compelled him to write hurriedly, with no time to revise or reflect upon what he had written. As a result, his longer works tend to be repetitious and poorly organized; these faults, which are obvious in as early a volume as *A Grammar of Politics,* become particularly marked in a late work such as *The American Democracy.*

Laski not only wrote far too much, but he attempted to deal with too wide a range of subjects. His early studies of religious movements and of conflicts between state and church and the articles on the history of legal institutions that he wrote during the same period are, in a sense, his most careful and scholarly pieces. After 1920 even his serious works show that he made little effort to focus his attention on a particular set of theoretical problems or on a given historical period. He was willing to write about anything that had any connection with modern politics; his subjects ranged from English political institutions to the American presidency, from economics to international relations. He was not willing to confine himself to legal history and philosophy, a field in which he might have become a worthy successor to Maitland, and he never found time to write the history of French political thought in the seventeenth century for which he had been collecting pamphlets and making notes for many years. It may seem ungenerous to criticize Laski for the breadth of his interests, especially in a period when many scholars have been successful in building a reputation by restricting their attention to a minute corner of a field or to a brief period of history. But obviously there is a middle ground between overspecialization in the trivial and refusing to recognize any limitations to the range of one's scholarly activities. Laski's unwillingness to limit himself in any way compelled him to sacrifice depth of insight and careful scholarship to variety of theme and the illusion of omnicompetence. After 1930 his tendency to write too much about too many subjects was aggravated by the relentless pressures upon him to produce for the Labor movement or some other popular audience books or articles on themes of current interest. Even if he knew comparatively little about the subject, he could always produce a manuscript in short order. By dexterously manipulating a few Marxian categories and then imposing them upon the facts, he was able to write a long essay that pleased many of his readers and outraged only the scholars who were experts in the field.

When we consider the range of his activities, quite apart from his teaching or his scholarly and popular writing, it is not difficult to understand why he never found the time or the energy to undertake sustained philosophic reflection. A continuous round of speeches, conferences, meetings, and electioneering during a busy teacher's "free time" scarcely provides an atmosphere conducive to the growth of theoretical insight or philosophic poise. His failure as a theorist, however, is not simply due to his overwriting or to the pressure of nonacademic responsibilities. His greatest virtues as a speaker and a writer—an extraordinary memory, an unbelievable faculty for rapidly reading and comprehending the works of others, the ability to write and speak with great ease and fluency—were also the greatest dangers to his growth as a serious thinker. His verbal facility and rhetorical skill often allowed him to glide nimbly over the surface of a problem whose difficulty might have compelled a less articulate person to stop and ponder until he had worked out a more satisfactory conclusion. Rarely do Laski's writings give the reader the sense that the author is struggling with an idea. There is virtually no sense of friction, no feeling that one is witnessing a clash between a complex and refractory subject and a powerful mind that is resolved to pursue the analysis to the limit of its powers and perhaps a step beyond them.

Throughout his career he seems to have been unwilling to stop the flow of words long enough to wrestle with fundamental problems or to probe into the philosophical foundations of his assumptions and values or of the concepts and definitions that he was employing. We have seen that even in his early writings he was careless about the terms and the premises upon which he based his analysis and that he borrowed definitions and theories from a variety of different philosophic systems—idealism, empiricism, and instrumentalism. In this period his uncritical eclecticism might have been excused on the ground that he was still a young man, who would, as he matured, develop a more coherent and consistent theoretical structure. Actually, his later writings show little evidence of increasing philosophical maturity and consistency; in the 1930's when he finally adopted Marxism as his basic creed he made no real effort to dig beneath the surface of the clichés that he took as his fundamental premises. But the commitment to Marxism eliminated any possibility that he might finally undertake a serious evaluation of his assumptions.

Another important deterrent to Laski's development as a political philosopher was that, after his return to England in 1920, he became increasingly more interested in prophecy and preaching, in molding the opinions of the people and of their leaders, than in the role of the philosopher or the analyst of the political scene. Particularly after 1930 his books and articles shifted more and more from serious discussion to propaganda for a particular political movement. His articles were usually journalistic pieces with a marked editorial bias, while his books were tracts in which, from a variety of standpoints, he preached the value as well as the necessity of socialism and the evils of a moribund capitalism. Above all, Laski was seduced by the idea that he was, or might become, a "Gray Eminence," who, without holding political office, could influence a great political movement and its leaders by offering advice in private conversations, letters, and meetings.[1] This desire to wield influence and power behind the scenes is, perhaps, a natural temptation to the intellectual concerned with politics; in Laski's case, the temptation was unusually grave because he took great delight in being known as the friend and confidant of famous men and in being able to relate stories about what Asquith had said to Haldane about Curzon. There seems to be little doubt that he vastly overestimated the extent of his influence upon the leaders of the Labor Party and other great figures in British and American politics. As a result he wasted in the preparation of letters and memoranda many hours that might more profitably have been devoted to scholarly pursuits. His almost pathetic eagerness to be close to the source of power and his belief that he could, from this

---

[1] In April, 1920, writing to Holmes to explain his decision to leave Harvard and accept the post at the London School of Economics, he says: "It brings (I dare to hope) some very real political influence within my grasp." *Holmes-Laski Letters, 1916–1935,* ed. by Mark DeWolfe Howe (2 vols., Cambridge: Harvard University Press), I, 257 (April 2, 1920). In this connection it is interesting to note a later comment by Laski: "And I read with pleasure Villard's *American Portraits,* liking especially the one on Colonel House, probably because there are few political types I dislike so completely as *eminences grises." Ibid.,* II, 1083 (Aug. 4, 1928).

vantage point, exercise an important influence on political decisions were the principal reasons why he delayed until February, 1949, his often-threatened resignation from the burdensome post on the Executive Committee of the Labor Party.

Through his writings, especially his articles in popular journals and newspapers, and by speeches to Party groups, labor unions, and other popular audiences in all parts of England, Laski also attempted to direct the thinking and the activities of the rank-and-file members of the Labor Party into the channels that he believed to be desirable and necessary. These efforts to guide public opinion became especially important in the period after the 1931 crisis in the Party caused by MacDonald's defection. Throughout the 1930's, while Arthur Henderson, Attlee, Cripps, and Morrison were endeavoring to rebuild the Party after its shattering defeat in the 1931 election, Laski sought to convert the members of the trade unions and the constituency parties to the doctrines of Marxist socialism. The era of the Left Book Club, directed by Victor Gollancz, John Strachey, and Laski, marks the high point of his success as a propagandist for socialism. But even after the war began, he continued to travel around the country, speaking to members of the Party, military personnel, and trade unionists in an effort to keep alive during the war years the Party's organization and its socialist message.

A consideration of Laski's activities as a "Gray Eminence" and as a political propagandist and party worker raises complex problems about the relationship between intellectual interest in political questions and involvement in partisan political activity. Laski always insisted that his role as a political activist did not interfere with his work as a scholar and a teacher. Indeed he argued that no one could be fully successful as a political scientist or political philosopher unless he had firsthand knowledge of the workings of political parties, elections, and the various branches of the government. It is difficult to give a satisfactory general answer to the question, can or should the political philosopher also be a partisan advocate of a particular party or movement? Much of the literature of political philosophy has been produced by men who were defending a particular point of view and a specific political group or party; the works collected in the *Libelli de lite,* dealing with the struggles between medieval Popes and Emperors, the pamphlets produced by various groups dur-

ing the period of the Puritan Revolution in England, and the mon-
archomach writings in sixteenth-century France are only a few examples of this phenomenon.

Even when one considers the more substantial works in political
theory—the writings of Plato, Augustine, Aquinas, Machiavelli,
Hobbes, Locke, or Rousseau—it is clear that political philosophers
have usually been vitally interested in the political issues of their
times and have rarely adopted a neutral or impartial attitude toward
contemporary political controversies. But the great figures in the
history of political thought have never been simply political pam-
phleteers for a given group or partisan propagandists for a particular
movement. In the midst of battles over details and concrete issues,
they have been able to see the underlying problems of political life
and to set forth ideas that men of later centuries, facing radically different concrete political situations, still find interesting and instruc-
tive. Plato's *Republic* is not simply a tract supporting the Athenian
aristocracy against the democratic party; as his royalist critics clearly
realized, Hobbes's *Leviathan* is far more than an attack on those who
rebelled against the Stuarts. Partisan feelings may constitute an important element in the motivation of the author of a significant work
in political theory, but by themselves they do not lead to the production of a major philosophical treatise or to the formulation of a
broad and deep view of the problems of man and the state. Laski
was not particularly successful in this effort to penetrate either to
the perennial problems behind contemporary controversies or to the
fundamental new questions that arise in any period. And, as we have
seen, his partisan activities extended far beyond the writing of books
and pamphlets. He was actively engaged in the details of party
organization and electioneering and in efforts to influence both the
leaders and the ordinary members. His career suggests that no one
can hope to make significant contributions to scholarship if he is
caught up to any great extent in the work of organizing, mobilizing,
and influencing a modern mass political party.

Another major handicap to Laski's efforts to produce a significant
political theory was his tendency throughout his life to seek and to
discover a simple formula that would provide the answers to a wide
range of complex political, economic, and social problems. This
Utopian strain in his make-up, his passion for a quick panacea that

would, once for all, abolish evil and enthrone good, is evident in his early pluralist period as well as in the Marxist phase of the 1930's and 1940's. He was always convinced that most of the evils in the world could be eliminated and a new and better world created if only men would accept his simple prescriptions and practice his precepts. The prescription varied at different stages of his career. At first he urged that the solution to modern political and social problems lay in transferring many of the functions of the state and of industrial management to decentralized and specialized groups and institutions. Later, abandoning this formula, he argued that the way to salvation was the gradual extension of governmental supervision and ownership in order to control private economic power and to insure approximate economic and social equality among the members of the society. Finally, he shifted away from this Fabian approach and insisted that only the acceptance of the principles of Marxism could lead men to the New Jerusalem where there would be no classes and no coercive state. The fundamental pattern of his thought, however, never varied. Always he was certain that all would be well if only the particular formula that he was advancing at the moment were accepted; he was equally confident that chaos and violence would inevitably result if his warnings went unheeded.

Laski's desire to find a simple formula for creating a new society and abolishing human poverty, ignorance, and cruelty is most clearly evident in his Marxist period. We have noted that he never thoroughly digested Marxism or assimilated it to his earlier stress on individual freedom and spontaneity. During the period of the capitalist crisis in the 1930's he seized upon a simple set of Marxist phrases and categories; these he used as his explanatory principles in every field and as the bases for his predictions about the inevitable trends in social evolution. His Marxism enabled him to give glib answers to any problem about which he was asked to write or speak, and the answers fell into a monotonously simple pattern. No matter what the issue might be—unemployment, foreign trade, the danger of war, Fascism, anti-Semitism, the decline in morality, the crisis in religion, or the sad state of literature and the arts—the reply was always that the difficulty was merely another example of the decay of capitalism and of the fatal disharmony between the forces of production and the relations of production. And the solution to any one of these problems was always the same; we must transcend this disharmony by instituting a new set of socialist relations of production. Only then would economic difficulties disappear, dictatorships and imperialism vanish, and "faith, reason, and civilization" flourish with renewed vigor.

When the world refused to behave in accordance with the precepts of Laski's Utopian optimism, his only recourse was to preach a sermon about the certain wrath and destruction to follow. When capitalist governments would not deal with economic depression by the "inevitable" deflationary remedies, he simply added to his previous explanation a footnote in which he dismissed such deviation as no more than a temporary and futile expedient to postpone disaster. We have seen that his simple view that the world was divided between capitalism, the source of all evil, and socialism, the basis for everything good, left him unable to deal with the forces that emerged in the form of Fascism. He was driven to accept a "devil" theory of history, which explained Fascism as the product of a capitalist conspiracy to destroy both socialism and democracy. His discussions of Fascism became increasingly more unrealistic, because the categories with which he was operating did not permit him to give adequate recognition to the historical, political, and socio-psychological factors that played so large a part in the rise of Hitler and Mussolini.

Throughout his life the ultimate ideals that Laski cherished remained the same, and he pursued them with great zeal and unusual selflessness. He wanted to see human suffering, ignorance, and poverty alleviated; he wanted every man to have the opportunity to develop his potentialities in his own way; and he hoped for the growth of a spirit of sympathy and understanding in men's relationships with their fellows. His fundamental goals were the principles of the French Revolution—liberty, equality, and fraternity. For him the essence of religion was the "search for a fraternal relation with all who suffer and all who are broken by the tragedy of a pain they cannot face." [2] In his personal life he remained faithful to these ideals. He spent himself unceasingly in efforts to help and encourage those who were laboring under serious handicaps in beginning their careers, or those to whom life had brought suffering and despair. In his public career as a writer and a speaker, he sought to extend this same

[2] AD, p. 320.

help to the unknown millions in every country whose lives were warped by bitter poverty and who had never known freedom and equality, the essential conditions of human development. To this desire to ease the pain of the world, Laski added the Utopian and chiliastic strain to which we have referred; he was always confident that evil could be eliminated from society if only a few simple but sweeping changes were made in human institutions. As a result he was unduly optimistic about the glories of the new age that would follow the great transformation and gave little sense of being aware of the elements of tragedy and suffering that are inherent in the human situation.

Even more fatal to his stature as a philosopher was the fact that the power of his emotions and his sympathies was not matched by his intellectual depth and acuity. As a consequence his statements and judgments were often irresponsible, and he was led to ignore the moral demands imposed upon the serious writer. His failure to think with clarity and with depth led him to defend methods of attaining his ideals which, in practice, would have led to consequences radically different from the goals he espoused. So fiercely did he resent the suffering, injustice, and compulsion which he saw in the society around him that he was willing to rush headlong into far worse evils. In the later phases of his career, he was forced into the position of supporting, as immediate aims, policies that involved restrictions on fundamental human liberties, as well as fatal injury to the spirit of reason and fraternity in human relations. We have seen how far he was willing to close his eyes to violations of his basic values as he attempted to defend many of the actions of the rulers of the Soviet Union. In his view much had to be forgiven them because they alone were seeking to create the new society of which he dreamed; in order to accomplish so great a good, they must be allowed to do some evil.

In addition to these personal limitations and excesses which played a large part in Laski's failure as a political philosopher, there are some general cultural factors that must be taken into account. The twentieth century has, so far, produced no political or social philosophy of the first rank and, indeed, no striking departures in political thought. For the most part, intellectuals have continued to be preoccupied with nineteenth-century doctrines, Marxism and the liberalism of John Stuart Mill, while Roman Catholic thinkers still operate within the framework set by St. Thomas Aquinas and his followers. Even today, Marxism, liberalism, and Catholicism are the major ideological forces in the politics of Western Europe. Since Catholic writers support a wide variety of political, social, and economic doctrines, ranging from dictatorship and the corporate state to democracy and Christian socialism, it is difficult to see that there is any necessary connection between Thomism and any specific social and political philosophy.

Marxism and classical liberalism are philosophies poorly equipped to deal with the central political issues of our times. Both are fundamentally concerned with the society and the economy rather than the polity. For classical liberalism the state is merely an instrument to preserve order and protect the antecedent personal and property rights of individuals against encroachment by others. Marxism shares this nineteenth-century view that the real center of power lies outside the realm of politics. Ultimately, the Marxist envisions a stateless society in which all power relationships have been dissolved into harmonious social and economic relationships. Immediately, he views the political process as no more than a pale reflection of the really vital changes that are taking place in the economic order. Both doctrines are seriously inadequate as analytic or predictive instruments in a period when, in one country after another, the power of the state, and especially that of the executive, to control individuals and to regulate economic and social affairs has grown tremendously in response to a series of domestic and external crises.

So-called "positive liberalism" has not been successful in filling this theoretical vacuum. In England and the United States there have been political programs that have attempted to merge the values of liberalism with the need for extensive state action, but such programs have proceeded by pragmatic trial and error rather than on the basis of a consistent political philosophy. Two world wars, an economic depression of unprecedented proportions, and, finally, a world struggle between Communism and democracy have not provided a favorable environment for political and social theory. The relentless pressure of immediate events has induced many intellectuals, as well as men of action, to concentrate their energies on formulating *ad hoc* measures to deal with a succession of specific economic and political difficulties. At the same time the specters of Fascism and Communism have produced a revulsion, even among thinkers, against any attempt at a major reconstruction of ideas or institutions. Increasingly the temper of our times makes us willing to bear evils that we know rather than to venture to move towards dangers that we know not. As we become more and more defensive about established institutions and values, we tend to restrict our criticisms to relatively minor elements of the existing social and political order.

This failure to develop a philosophy of positive liberalism in this century can also be viewed as the consequence of certain intellectual trends. The triumph of logical positivism has meant a widespread reaction against traditional philosophy, especially against ethics and political philosophy. The positivists have attempted to eliminate a large number of traditional philosophic problems by insisting that only those propositions are meaningful which can be stated in the rigorous language of mathematics and the exact sciences. Ethics and political philosophy have been placed far beyond the pale, both because of the vagueness of the terms they employ and the value-laden nature of their materials. For almost forty years, therefore, the subjects of morals and politics have, in large measure, been left to the Marxists and the theologians. Apart from the great figures in the pragmatist tradition, whose influence has been greatest in the United States, most philosophers have concentrated their attention on the refinements of linguistic analysis or the complexities of symbolic logic. The utterances of this new philosophy have been virtually unintelligible to all but the professional logicians, who have sedulously avoided the problems of metaphysics, epistemology, ethics, aesthetics, and politics—all the questions that concern men most deeply. Since the philosophers offered them little guidance or enlightenment, men have been left to the tender mercies of publicists, propagandists, and purveyors of various political and moral nostrums. In the period between the wars many students, in particular, felt that Marxism was the only systematic political and social theory offered for their consideration that had any real title to intellectual respectability. In the minds of many of the best students of an entire generation, therefore, Marxism won an easy victory. As Laski's career makes clear, its victory was too easy, since no significant theories existed as alternatives or as a critical opposition to force the Marxist to clarify and to reformulate his arguments. Collingwood has commented: "In order to criticize a gloves-off philosophy like that of Marx, you must be at

least enough of a gloves-off philosopher to think gloves-off philoso-
phizing legitimate." [3]

Collingwood's bitter reflections on the attitudes created among
students by the skeptical teachings of the Oxford "realists" may not
be without applicability to the effects of the doctrines of their successors, the logical positivists.

> The pupils, whether or not they expected a philosophy that should give
> them, as that of Green's school had given their fathers, ideals to live for
> and principles to live by, did not get it; and were told that no philosopher
> (except of course a bogus philosopher) would even try to give it. The in-
> ference which any pupil could draw for himself was that for guidance in
> the problems of life, since one must not seek it from thinkers or from
> thinking, from ideals or from principles, one must look to people who
> were not thinkers (but fools), to processes that were not thinking (but
> passion), to aims that were not ideals (but caprices), and to rules that were
> not principles (but rules of expediency). If the realists had wanted to train
> up a generation of Englishmen and Englishwomen expressly as the poten-
> tial dupes of every adventurer in morals or politics, commerce or religion,
> who should appeal to their emotions and promise them private gains
> which he neither could procure them nor even meant to procure them, no
> better way of doing it could have been discovered. [4]

When philosophy becomes largely a highly refined technique of
linguistic and logical analysis, which is a complete mystery to all but
a narrow circle of skilled professionals, and when it proclaims its
inapplicability to most of men's central problems, even the reasonably
well-educated members of the society are deprived of an important
defense against the assaults of conscious manipulation, blind irrationalism, and cults and fads of every description. Alexandrianism
at the upper levels of a society seems always to be matched by widespread popular superstition, anti-intellectualism, and irrationalism.

Laski's political teachings were not of major philosophic significance or profundity; in the years between the wars he too often substituted emotion and rhetoric for intellectual rigor and discipline. But
when we are tempted to dismiss him simply as a propagandist and
a partisan orator, we should remember that in that period some of
the ablest young minds in England and America were profoundly in-

---

[3] R. G. Collingwood, *An Autobiography* (London: Oxford University Press, 1951),
p. 153.

[4] *Ibid.*, pp. 48–49.

fluenced by him. These young men and women were neither fools nor dupes. They were acutely conscious of the social, economic, and political problems of their age and sensitive to the suffering they saw around them. They wanted passionately to understand the world in which they lived, so that they could discover how they might use their talents to help build a better world. Most of the social scientists of the period offered them pure description of institutions or volumes of statistical data, while the philosophers invited them to join their pleasant game of manipulating symbols and transforming propositions. Is it surprising that Laski was one of the few teachers who stimulated their thoughts, fired their imaginations, and won their hearts? Later, they might discover his weaknesses and his inadequacies. At the moment they knew only that he spoke to them about the questions that were uppermost in their own minds, that he talked in language that was intelligible to them, that he was willing to communicate to them the meaning that he had found in life, and that he was confident that men could create a better society if they determined to do so. Above all they knew that he believed that thinking was not merely an amusing and interesting pastime, but the most significant activity that a man can undertake.

Bibliography

THE FOLLOWING list is not intended as a complete bibliography either of Laski's writings or of works dealing with his contributions or the themes with which he was concerned. I have included only books and articles which I have read. Section I, "Works by Laski," includes all the separately published books, pamphlets, and speeches that are listed in the catalogues of the Library of Congress, the British Museum, the Library of the London School of Economics and Political Science, and the Library of Columbia University, but lists only those periodical articles which I have cited in the notes to this work. A much more extensive list of his contributions to periodicals can be obtained from the volumes of the *Reader's Guide to Periodical Literature* and the *International Index to Periodicals* for the years from 1910 to 1951. In Section II, I have noted a number of works which Laski edited, translated, or for which he wrote introductions or prefaces. Section III includes a number of books and articles in which Laski and his works are given extended treatment. Since this list includes only those items that have come to my attention, it is undoubtedly far from complete. In Section IV are listed all the other books and articles to which I have made references in this work.

I. WORKS BY LASKI

"An Age of Transition," *Political Quarterly,* XIV (April–June, 1943), 164–72.

"America, Good and Bad," *The Nation,* CLXIX (July 2, 1949), 8–10.

The American Democracy. New York: The Viking Press, 1948; London: George Allen and Unwin, Ltd., 1949.

"The American Myth and the Peace," *The Nation,* CLVIII (Feb. 12, 1944), 180–84.

"The American Political Scene," *The Nation,* CLXIII (Nov. 23, 1946), 582–84.

The American Presidency. New York: Harper and Bros., 1940; London: George Allen and Unwin, Ltd., 1940.

"The Apotheosis of the State," *The New Republic,* VII (July 22, 1916), 302–4.

Authority in the Modern State. New Haven: Yale University Press, 1919; London: Humphrey Milford, Oxford University Press, 1919. Contains "Authority in the Modern State," "Bonald," "Lamennais," "The Political Theory of Royer-Collard," and "Administrative Syndicalism in France."

The British Cabinet; a Study of Its Personnel, 1801–1924. Fabian Tract No. 223. London: The Fabian Society, 1928.

"British Democracy and Mr. Kennedy," *Harper's Magazine,* CLXXXII (April, 1941), 464–70.

"British Labor Reconstruction Proposals and the American Labor Attitude," *Proceedings of the Academy of Political Science,* VIII (Feb., 1919), 59–63.

"The Challenge of Our Times," *The American Scholar,* VIII (Autumn, 1939), 387–99.

"China and Democracy," in Ernest R. Hughes, ed., China, Body and Soul. London: Secker and Warburg, 1938.

"Choosing the Planners," in G. D. H. Cole *et al.,* Plan for Britain. London: George Routledge and Sons, Ltd., 1943.

"Civil Liberties in the Soviet Union," *The New Republic,* CXV (Oct. 21, 1946), 507–8.

"The Civil Service and Parliament," in The Development of the Civil Service; Lectures Delivered Before the Society of Civil Servants, 1920–1921. London: P. S. King and Son, Ltd., 1922.

"The Committee System in Local Government," in H. J. Laski, W. Ivor Jennings, and William A. Robson, eds., A Century of Municipal Progress. London: Allen, 1935.

Communism. Home University Library of Modern Knowledge, No. 123. New York: Henry Holt and Co., 1927; London: Williams and Norgate, Ltd., 1927.

"Communism as a World Force," *International Affairs,* X (Jan., 1931), 21–30.

"Communism Faces the Wrath to Come," *The New Republic,* LXXXIV (Oct. 30, 1935), 339.

Communist Manifesto; Socialist Landmark. London: George Allen and Unwin, Ltd., 1948.

The Crisis and the Constitution: 1931 and After. Day to Day Pamphlet No. 9. London: L. and V. Woolf at the Hogarth Press, 1932.

"The Crisis in Our Civilization," *Foreign Affairs,* XXVI (Oct., 1947), 36–51.

"The Crisis in the Theory of the State," in Vol. II of Law: A Century of Progress, 1835–1935. Published by the New York University School of Law. New York: New York University Press, 1937. (This also appears as the introductory chapter to the 4th ed. of A Grammar of Politics, London: George Allen and Unwin, Ltd., 1938.)

"Critic of Stalin," *The New Statesman and Nation,* XX (Sept. 14, 1940), 263.

The Danger of Being a Gentleman and Other Essays. New York: The Viking Press, 1940; London: George Allen and Unwin, Ltd., 1939. Contains "The Danger of Being a Gentleman," "On the Study of Politics," "Law and Justice in Soviet Russia," "The Judicial Function," "The English Constitution and French Public Opinion, 1789–1794," "The Committee System in English Local Government," "Nationalism and the Future of Civilization," and "Mr. Justice Holmes: For His Eighty-ninth Birthday."

The Dangers of Obedience and Other Essays. New York: Harper and Bros., 1930. Contains "The Dangers of Obedience," "The American Political System," "The Recovery of Citizenship," "Teacher and Student," "The Academic Mind," "Foundations, Universities and Research," "A Portrait of Jean Jacques Rousseau," "A Plea for Equality," "Machiavelli and the Present Time," and "Can Business Be Civilized?"

The Decline of Liberalism. L. T. Hobhouse Memorial Trust Lecture No. 10. London: Oxford University Press, 1940.

The Decline of Parliamentary Government. With Josef Redlich. Foreign Policy Association Pamphlet No. 74. New York: Foreign Policy Association, 1931.

"Democracy at the Crossroads," *Yale Review,* n.s., IX (July, 1920), 788–803.

Democracy in Crisis. Chapel Hill: University of North Carolina Press, 1933; London: George Allen and Unwin, Ltd., 1933.

"Democracy in War Time," in G. D. H. Cole *et al.,* Victory or Vested Interest? London: George Routledge and Sons, Ltd., 1942.

The Dilemma of Our Times. London: George Allen and Unwin, Ltd., 1952.

"Does Capitalism Cause War?," in Henry Brinton, ed.; Does Capitalism Cause War? London, 1935.

"The Economic Foundations of Fascism," *The New Statesman and Nation,* XXV (March 27, 1943), 212.

"The Economic Foundations of Peace," in Leonard S. Woolf, ed., The Intelligent Man's Way to Prevent War. London, 1933.

The Economic Revolution. With Wilfred Wellock and P. W. Martin. Peace Aims Pamphlet No. 5. London: National Peace Council, 1941.

Edmund Burke. Address Delivered to College Historical Society, Trinity College, University of Dublin, March 14, 1947. Dublin: Falconer, 1947.

"Efficiency in Government," in Douglas P. T. Jay *et al.,* The Road to Recovery. Fabian Society Lectures. London: Allan Wingate, Ltd., 1948.

"England Confronts a New World," in S. D. Schmalhausen, ed., Recovery through Revolution. New York: Covici Friede, 1933.

"English Politics Today," *The New Republic,* XLIII (July 8, 1925), 171–74.

"Fabian Socialism," in British Broadcasting Corporation, Ideas and Beliefs of the Victorians. London: Sylvan Press, 1949.

"The Fabian Way," *Current History,* XLI (Oct., 1934), 33–38.

Faith, Reason, and Civilization. New York: The Viking Press, 1944; London: Victor Gollancz, Ltd., 1944.

"The First Fifty Years," *The Nation,* CLXX (Feb. 25, 1950), 171–74.

The Foundations of Sovereignty and Other Essays. New York: Harcourt, Brace and Co., 1921; London: George Allen and Unwin, Ltd., 1922; New Haven: Yale University Press, 1931. Contains "The Foundations of Sovereignty," "The Problem of Administrative Areas," "The Responsibility of the State in England," "The Personality of Associations," "The Early History of the Corporation in England," "The Theory of Popular Sovereignty," "The Pluralistic State," "The Basis of Vicarious Liability," and "The Political Ideas of James I."

Freedom of the Press in Wartime. London: National Council for Civil Liberties, 1941.

The Germans—Are They Human? London: Victor Gollancz, Ltd., 1941.

"Getting on with Russia," *The Nation,* CLXVI (Jan. 10, 1948), 34–37.

"Government in Wartime," in H. J. Laski *et al.,* Where Stands Democracy? London: Macmillan and Co., Ltd., 1940.

A Grammar of Politics. London: George Allen and Unwin, Ltd., 1925; 2d ed., 1930; 3d ed., 1934; 4th ed., 1938; New Haven: Yale University Press, 1925, 1931, 1938.

"Harold J. Laski," in Clifton Fadiman, ed., I Believe: The Personal Philosophies of Certain Eminent Men and Women of Our Time. New York: Simon and Schuster, 1939.

I Speak to You as a Socialist. Alabaster, Passmore and Sons, Ltd., n.d. (1941?).

"Information Please, Mr. Molotov," *The Nation,* CLXII (June 15, 1946), 710–11.

An Introduction to Politics. London: George Allen and Unwin, Ltd., 1931. The American edition has the title Politics (*see also* that title).

"Is Europe Done For?," *The Nation,* CLXV (Nov. 22, 1947), 548–50.

Is This an Imperialist War? London: The Labour Party, 1940.

Karl Marx: An Essay. London: The Fabian Society and George Allen and Unwin, Ltd., 1922; New York: League for Industrial Democracy, 1933.

"A Key to Communism," *The New Statesman and Nation,* X (July 20, 1935), 102.

The Labour Party and the Constitution. Socialist Programme Series No. 2. London: The Socialist League, 1933.

The Labour Party, the War, and the Future. London: The Labour Party, 1939.

Labour's Aims in War and Peace. With Clement Richard Attlee *et al.* London, 1940.

Law and Justice in Soviet Russia. Day to Day Pamphlet No. 23. London: L. and V. Woolf at the Hogarth Press, 1935.

"The Leaders of Collectivist Thought," in British Broadcasting Corporation, Ideas and Beliefs of the Victorians. London: Sylvan Press, 1949.

"Lenin and Mussolini," *Foreign Affairs,* II (Sept., 1923), 43–54.

"A Leningrad Letter: I," *The Nation,* CXXXIX (July 18, 1934), 69–71.

"A Leningrad Letter: II," *The Nation,* CXXXIX (July 25, 1934), 100–101.

"Let's Start Over," *The Nation,* CLXVII (Nov. 27, 1948), 602–4.

Liberty in the Modern State. New York: Harper and Bros., 1930; London: Faber, 1930; Pelican ed., Harmondsworth, England: Penguin Books, Ltd., 1937; revised ed., London: George Allen and Unwin, Ltd., 1948, and New York: The Viking Press, 1949.

The Limitations of the Expert. Fabian Tract No. 235. London: The Fabian Society, 1931.

"The Literature of Politics," *The New Republic,* XIII (Nov. 17, 1917), Supplement, 6–8.

"The Literature of Reconstruction," *The Bookman,* XLVIII (Oct., 1918), 215–20.

"A London Diary," *The New Statesman and Nation,* XI (June 20, 1936), 958–59.

London, Washington, Moscow, Partners in Peace? Peace Aims Pamphlet No. 22. London: National Peace Council, 1943.

Marx and Today. Fabian Society Research Series No. 73. London: Victor Gollancz, Ltd., and The Fabian Society, 1943.

"Marxism after Fifty Years," *Current History,* XXXVII (March, 1933), 691–96.

"The Means and the End," *The New Republic,* IV (Sept. 4, 1915), 133.

"M. Duguit's Conception of the State," in Arthur L. Goodhart *et al.,* Modern Theories of Law. London: Oxford University Press, 1933.

"The Mother of Parliaments," *Foreign Affairs,* IX (July, 1931), 569–79.

"My Day in Court," *Atlantic Monthly,* CXC (Nov., 1952), 65–68.

"My Impressions of Stalin," *The New Republic,* CXV (Oct. 14, 1946), 478–79.

Nationalism and the Future of Civilisation. Conway Memorial Lecture, 1932. London: Watts and Co., 1932.

"The Need for a European Revolution," in Programme for Victory. London: The Fabian Society and George Routledge and Sons, Ltd., 1941.

"The New Test for British Labor," *Foreign Affairs,* VIII (Oct., 1929), 69–83.

"The Obsolescence of Federalism," *The New Republic,* XCVIII (May 3, 1939), 367–69.

On the Correlation of Fertility with Social Value. With Ethel M. Eiderton, Amy Barrington, *et al.* London: Dulau and Co., Ltd., 1913.

On the Study of Politics. Inaugural Lecture Delivered at the London School of Economics, University of London. London: Humphrey Milford, Oxford University Press, 1926.

"The Outlook for Civil Liberties," in Bertrand Russell, Vernon Bartlett, G. D. H. Cole, *et al.,* Dare We Look Ahead? London: George Allen and Unwin, Ltd., 1938.

"Palestine: The Economic Aspect," in Joseph B. Hobman, ed., Palestine's Economic Future. London, 1946.

"Parliament and Revolution," *The New Republic,* XXII (May 19, 1920), 384.

Parliamentary Government in England. New York: The Viking Press, 1938; London: George Allen and Unwin, Ltd., 1938.

"The Personality of the State," *The Nation,* CI (July 22, 1915), 115–17.

"A Philosophy Embattled," *The Dial,* LXII (Feb. 8, 1917), 96–98.

The Place of the Scientist in Post-War Administration. Lecture Delivered to the British Association of Chemists, Feb. 14, 1945. London, 1945.

"Plan or Perish," *The Nation,* CLXI (Dec. 15, 1945), 650–52.

Political Offences and the Death Penalty. 6th Roy Calvert Memorial Lecture. London: E. G. Dunstan and Co., 1940.

"Political Science in Great Britain," *American Political Science Review,* XIX (Feb., 1925), 96–99.

"Political Theory and the Social Sciences," in The Social Sciences: Proceedings of a Conference under the Auspices of the Institute of Sociology and the International Student Service, British Committee. London: Le Play House Press, 1936.

"Political Theory in the Later Middle Ages," in J. B. Bury, ed., Cambridge Medieval History, Vol. VIII, 1936. Cambridge: Cambridge University Press.

Political Thought in England: From Locke to Bentham. Home University Library of Modern Knowledge, No. 103. New York: Henry Holt and Co., 1920; London: Williams and Norgate, Ltd., 1920; new ed., London: Oxford University Press, 1950.

Politics. The Hour Library. Philadelphia: J. B. Lippincott Co., 1931. The English edition has the title An Introduction to Politics (*see also* that title).

"The Position and Prospects of Communism," *Foreign Affairs,* XI (Oct., 1932), 93–106.

The Position of Parties and the Right of Dissolution. Fabian Tract No. 210. London: The Fabian Society, 1924.

"The Present Evolution of the Parliamentary System," in H. J. Laski, Ch. Borgeaud, *et al.,* The Development of the Representative System in Our Times. Lausanne: Payot et Cie., 1928.

"The Present Position of Representative Democracy," in H. J. Laski *et al.,* Where Stands Socialism Today? London, 1933.

The Problem of a Second Chamber. Fabian Tract No. 213. London: The Fabian Society, 1925.

The Problem of Administrative Areas. Smith College Studies in History, Vol. IV, No. 1. Northampton, Mass.: Smith College, 1918.

"The Prospects of Constitutional Government," *Political Quarterly,* I (July–Sept., 1930), 307–25.

The Prospects of Democratic Government. *Bulletin of The College of William and Mary in Virginia,* Vol. XXXIII (April, 1939). Williamsburg, Va.: College of William and Mary, 1939.

"The Prospects of Peace in Europe," in Benjamin S. Rowntree *et al.,* Wharton Assembly: Addresses, 1938. Philadelphia: University of Pennsylvania Press, 1938.

"The Public Papers and Addresses of Franklin D. Roosevelt," *University of Chicago Law Review,* VI (Dec., 1938), 29.

"Reason and Russia," *The New Republic,* CXIX (Dec. 6, 1948), 22–24.

The Recovery of Citizenship. Self and Society Booklet No. 4. London: Ernest Benn, Ltd., 1928.

Reflections on the Constitution. New York: The Viking Press, 1951; Manchester: Manchester University Press, 1951.

Reflections on the Revolution of Our Time. New York: The Viking Press, 1943; London: George Allen and Unwin, Ltd., 1943.

The Relation of Justice to Law. Horace Seal Memorial Lectures, No. 2. London: Ethical Union, 1930.

The Rights of Man. Macmillan War Pamphlets, No. 8. London: Macmillan and Co., Ltd., 1940.

The Rise of European Liberalism. London: George Allen and Unwin, Ltd., 1936. The American edition (New York: Harper and Bros., 1936) has the title The Rise of Liberalism.

"The Roosevelt Experiment," *The Atlantic Monthly,* CLIII (Feb., 1934), 143–53. In England this appears as Socialist League, Capitalism in Crisis, Forum Series, 1933–4, No. 1. London: Socialist League, 1933.

"Russia and Labor Unity," *The Nation,* CLVII (Sept. 18, 1943), 315–18.

Russia and the West: Policy for Britain. Peace Aims Pamphlet No. 43. London: National Peace Council, n.d. (1948?).

The Secret Battalion. London: The Labour Party, 1946.

Socialism and Freedom. Fabian Tract No. 216. London: The Fabian Society, 1925.

Socialism as Internationalism. Research Series No. 132. London: Fabian International Bureau, 1949.

"A Socialist Looks at the Cold War," *The New Republic,* CXVII (Oct. 27, 1947), 10–11.

The Socialist Tradition in the French Revolution. London: The Fabian Society, 1930.

"Some Implications of the Crisis," *Political Quarterly,* II (Oct.–Dec., 1931), 466–69.

Speeches in Commemoration of William Morris. With John Drinkwater *et al.* Walthamstow, England, 1934.

The Spirit of Co-operation. 1936 Hodgson Pratt Memorial Lecture. Manchester: The Co-operative Union, Ltd., n.d. (1936?).

"Stafford Cripps, Socialist Leader," *The Nation,* CXLIV (Jan. 23, 1937), 92–93.

The State in the New Social Order. Fabian Tract No. 200. London: The Fabian Society, 1922.

The State in Theory and Practice. New York: The Viking Press, 1935; London: George Allen and Unwin, Ltd., 1935.

"State, Worker, and Technician," in Georges Gurvitch, ed., Industrialisation et technocratie. Paris: Librairie Armand Colin, 1949.

The Strategy of Freedom. New York: Harper and Bros., 1941; London: George Allen and Unwin, Ltd., 1942.

Studies in Law and Politics. New Haven: Yale University Press, 1932; London: George Allen and Unwin, Ltd., 1932. Contains "The Age of Reason," "Diderot," "The Socialist Tradition in the French Revolution," "The Problem of a Second Chamber," "The State in the New Social Order," "The Political Philosophy of Mr. Justice Holmes," "The Technique of Judicial Appointment," "The Personnel of the

British Cabinet, 1801–1924," "Judicial Review of Social Policy," "Procedure for Constructive Contempt," "Law and the State," and "Justice and the Law" (separately published as The Relation of Justice to Law; *see also* that title).

Studies in the Problem of Sovereignty. New Haven: Yale University Press, 1917; London: Humphrey Milford, Oxford University Press, 1917. Contains "The Sovereignty of the State," "The Political Theory of the Disruption," "The Political Theory of the Oxford Movement," "The Political Theory of the Catholic Revival," "De Maistre and Bismarck," "Sovereignty and Federalism," and "Sovereignty and Centralisation."

"The Temper of the Present Time," *The New Republic,* XXI (Feb. 18, 1920), 335–38.

"The Theory of an International Society," in Geneva Institute of International Relations, Problems of Peace, Sixth Series. Lectures of August, 1931. London: George Allen and Unwin, Ltd., 1932.

"Towards a Universal Declaration of Human Rights," in UNESCO, Human Rights. New York: Columbia University Press, 1949.

The Trade Disputes and Trade Unions Bill. With Ernest J. P. Benn. Present Day Papers, No. 12. London: P. S. King and Son, 1927.

Trade Unions in the New Society. New York: The Viking Press, 1949; London: George Allen and Unwin, Ltd., 1950.

"Trotsky," in Men of Turmoil. New York: Minton, Balch, and Co., 1935.

"Truman's Task in Europe," *The New Republic,* CXIX (Dec. 20, 1948), 10–13.

"The Value and Defects of the Marxist Philosophy," *Current History,* XXIX (Oct., 1928), 23–29.

The Webbs and Soviet Communism. Webb Memorial Lecture No. 3. London: Fabian Publications, Ltd., 1947.

"What Democracy Means in Russia," *The New Republic,* CXV (Oct. 28, 1946), 551–52.

What Is Democracy? With Alexander D. Lindsay and S. de Madariaga. Peace Aims Pamphlet No. 38. London: National Peace Council, 1946.

"What Is Vital in Democracy?," *Survey Graphic,* XXIV (April, 1935), 179–80 and 204–5.

Where Do We Go from Here? New York: The Viking Press, 1940; Harmondsworth, England: Penguin Books, Ltd., 1940.

Will Planning Restrict Freedom? Cheam, England: The Architectural Press, 1944.

Will the Peace Last? Peace Aims Pamphlet No. 28. London: National Peace Council, 1944.

"Why Does Russia Act That Way?," *The Nation,* CLXIV (March 1, 1947), 239–42.

II. LASKI AS EDITOR, TRANSLATOR, OR INTRODUCER

Burke, Edmund. Letters of Edmund Burke: A Selection. The World's Classics, No. 237. Edited with an Introduction by H. J. Laski. London: Humphrey Milford, Oxford University Press, 1922.

Duguit, Léon. Law in the Modern State. Translated by Frida and Harold Laski. New York: B. W. Huebsch, 1919.

Gooch, George P. English Democratic Ideas in the Seventeenth Century. 2d ed., with Supplementary Notes and Appendices by Prof. H. J. Laski. Cambridge: Cambridge University Press, 1927.

Haldane, Richard B. H., 1st Viscount Haldane. The Problem of Nationalization. Introduction by R. H. Tawney and H. J. Laski. London: George Allen and Unwin, Ltd., Labour Publishing Co., Ltd., May, 1921.

Holmes, Oliver Wendell. Collected Legal Papers. Compiled by Harold J. Laski. New York: Harcourt, Brace, and Co., 1920.

Languet, Hubert (Junius Brutus). A Defence of Liberty against Tyrants. A translation of the Vindiciae contra tyrannos. Introduction by H. J. Laski. London: G. Bell and Sons, Ltd., 1924.

Lévy, Louis. France Is a Democracy. Introduction by H. J. Laski. London: Victor Gollancz, Ltd., 1943.

The Library of European Political Thought. Edited by H. J. Laski. London: Ernest Benn, Ltd., 1926–28. Includes M. Roustan, Pioneers of the French Revolution, translated by Frederic Whyte, 1926; Rev. R. H. Murray, The Political Consequences of the Reformation, 1926; Bede Jarrett, Social Theories of the Middle Ages, 1200–1500, 1926; A. Aulard, Christianity and the French Revolution, translated by Lady Frazer, 1927; and Emile Faguet, Politicians and Moralists of the Nineteenth Century, translated by Dorothy Galton, 1928.

Mill, John Stuart. Autobiography. The World's Classics, No. 262. Preface by H. J. Laski. London: Humphrey Milford, Oxford University Press, 1924.

Neep, Edward J. C. Seditious Offences. Introductory Note by H. J. Laski. Fabian Tract No. 220. London: The Fabian Society, 1926.

Robinson, Edward. Just Murder. Preface by H. J. Laski. London: Lincolns-Prager, 1947.

Say, Jean Baptiste. Letters to Thomas Robert Malthus on Political Economy and Stagnation of Commerce. Historical Preface by H. J. Laski. London: George Harding's Bookshop, Ltd., 1936.

Taylor, Sir Henry. The Statesman. Introductory Essay by H. J. Laski. Cambridge: W. Heffer and Sons, Ltd., 1927.

Woolf, Leonard S. Foreign Policy. Research Series No. 121. Foreword by H. J. Laski. London: The Fabian Society, 1947.

III. BOOKS AND ARTICLES ABOUT LASKI

Beloff, Max. "The Age of Laski," *The Fortnightly,* n.s., CLXVII (June, 1950), 378–84.

Catlin, George. "The Man Who Lost the British Election," *Commonweal,* XLII (July 27, 1945), 353–54. ·

——— The Story of the Political Philosophers. New York: Tudor Publishing Co., 1947, chap. XX.

Cook, T. I. "In Memoriam," *American Political Science Review,* XLIV (Sept., 1950), 738–41.

Elliott, Wm. Y. "Pragmatic Politics of Mr. H. J. Laski," *American Political Science Review,* XVIII (May, 1924), 251–75.

——— The Pragmatic Revolt in Politics. New York: Macmillan Co., 1928, chap. V.

Faÿ, Bernard. "D'une doctrine sociale à Harvard; le fédéralisme social de Laski," *Correspondant,* nouvelle série, tome 242, pp. 128–40.

Fourest, Michel. Les théories du Professeur Harold J. Laski; le declin de l'état moniste et l'avènement de l'état pluraliste. Paris: Recueil Sirey, 1943.

Fox, Ralph. A Defence of Communism; in Reply to H. J. Laski. London: Communist Party of Great Britain, 1927.

Griffiths, Thomas Hughes. Politischer Pluralismus in der zeitgenössichen Philosophie Englands. Giessen, 1933.

Hastings, Sir Patrick. Cases in Court. London: William Heinemann, Ltd., 1949. ("The Laski Case," pp. 55–71.)

Hawkins, Carroll. "Harold J. Laski: A Preliminary Analysis," *Political Science Quarterly,* LXV (Sept., 1950), 376–92.

Hoog, Armand. "Les théories d'Harold Laski et le pluralisme démocratique," *Archives de philosophie du droit et de sociologie juridique,* Année 7 (1937), pp. 140–65.

Howe, Mark DeWolfe, ed. Holmes-Laski Letters, 1916–1935. 2 vols. Cambridge: Harvard University Press, 1953.

Kampelman, M. M. "Harold J. Laski: A Current Analysis," *Journal of Politics,* X (Feb., 1948), 131–54.

Kirchwey, Freda. "Harold Laski," *The Nation,* CLXX (April 1, 1950), 291–92.

Laski v. Newark Advertiser Co., Ltd., and Parlby. London: Daily Express, 1947.

Magid, Henry Meyer. English Political Pluralism. Columbia Studies in Philosophy, No. 2. New York: Columbia University Press, 1941.

Martin, Kingsley. Harold Laski. New York: The Viking Press, 1953; London: Victor Gollancz, Ltd., 1953.

—— "Harold Laski, Socialist," *The Nation,* CLXX (April 29, 1950), 400–401.

Petersen, Arnold. Karl Marx and Marxism, a Universal Genius: His Discoveries, His Traducers. New York: New York Labor News Company, 1934.

Ray, N. C. B. "Laski, the Sociologist," *Indian Journal of Political Science,* XI (Oct.–Dec., 1950), 146–51.

Rees, J. C. "La teoria politica di Harold Laski," *Politico,* XVI (Dec., 1951), 285–305.

Sarma, G. N. "Harold J. Laski," *Indian Journal of Political Science,* XI (Oct.–Dec., 1950), 133–45.

Soltau, Roger. "Professor Laski and Political Science," *Political Quarterly,* XXI (July, 1950), 301–10.

Strachey, John. "Laski's Struggle for Certainty," *New Statesman and Nation,* XXXIX (April 8, 1950), 395.

Watkins, J. W. N. "Laski on Conscience and Counter-Revolution," *Nineteenth Century and After,* CXLV (March, 1949), 173–79.

Zerby, Lewis. "Normative, Descriptive and Ideological Elements in the Writings of Laski," *Philosophy of Science,* XII (April, 1945), 134–45.

IV. OTHER BOOKS AND ARTICLES CITED IN THE FOOTNOTES

Austin, John. Lectures on Jurisprudence. 2d ed. London: John Murray, 1861.

Barker, Ernest. "The Discredited State," *Political Quarterly,* No. 5 (Feb., 1915), pp. 101–21.

Coker, Francis W. "Pluralistic Theories and the Attack upon State Sovereignty," in Charles E. Merriam and H. E. Barnes, eds., A History of Political Theories—Recent Times. New York: Macmillan Co., 1924.

Cole, G. D. H. Guild Socialism Re-stated. London: L. Parsons, 1920.

———, and Raymond Postgate. The British People, 1746–1946. New York: Alfred A. Knopf, 1947.

Collingwood, R. G. An Autobiography. London: Oxford University Press, 1951.

Dangerfield, George. The Strange Death of Liberal England. New York: Harrison Smith and Robert Haas, 1935.

de Neuman, A. M. Consumers' Representation in the Public Sector of Industry. London, 1950.

Figgis, J. N. Churches in the Modern State. London: Longmans, Green, and Co., 1914.

——— The Divine Right of Kings, 2d ed. Cambridge: Cambridge University Press, 1914.

——— Studies of Political Thought from Gerson to Grotius. 2d ed. Cambridge: Cambridge University Press, 1916.

Fischer, Ruth. Stalin and German Communism. Cambridge: Harvard University Press, 1948.

Fisher, H. A. L., ed., The Collected Papers of Frederic William Maitland. 3 vols. Cambridge: Cambridge University Press, 1911.

Friedmann, W. Legal Theory. 2d ed. London: Stevens and Sons, Ltd., 1949.

Gierke, Otto von. Das deutsche Genossenschaftsrecht. 3 vols. Berlin: Weidmann, 1868–1913.

——— Political Theories of the Middle Age. Translated by F. W. Maitland. Cambridge: Cambridge University Press, 1900.

Hutchison, Keith. The Decline and Fall of British Capitalism. New York: Charles Scribner's Sons, 1950.

Jennings, W. Ivor. The British Constitution. 2d ed. Cambridge: Cambridge University Press, 1947.

——— Cabinet Government. 2d ed. Cambridge: Cambridge University Press, 1951.

Lange, Oskar, and Fred M. Taylor. On the Economic Theory of Socialism. Minneapolis: University of Minnesota Press, 1938.

Lorwin, Lewis L. Advisory Economic Councils. Brookings Institution Pamphlet Series No. 9. Washington: The Brookings Institution, 1931.

MacIver, Robert M., ed., Conflict of Loyalties. New York: Harper and Bros., 1952.

—— The Modern State. London: Oxford University Press, 1926.

—— The Web of Government. New York: Macmillan Co., 1947.

Marx, Karl, and Friedrich Engels. The Communist Manifesto. New York: International Publishers, 1932.

Neumann, Franz L. European Trade Unionism and Politics. New York: League for Industrial Democracy, 1936.

Orwell, George. "Such, Such Were the Joys," *Partisan Review,* XIX (Sept.–Oct., 1952), 505–45.

Plamenatz, John. German Marxism and Russian Communism. London: Longmans, Green and Co., 1954.

Reich, Nathan. Labour Relations in Republican Germany. New York: Oxford University Press, 1938.

Russell, Bertrand. The Practice and Theory of Bolshevism. 2d ed. London: George Allen and Unwin, Ltd., 1949.

Schumpeter, Joseph A. Capitalism, Socialism and Democracy. 2d ed. New York: Harper and Bros., 1947.

Sweezy, Paul M. The Theory of Capitalist Development. New York: Oxford University Press, 1942.

U.S. Bureau of the Census. Historical Statistics of the United States, 1789–1945. Washington, D.C.: Government Printing Office, 1949.

—— Statistical Abstract of the United States: 1951. 72d ed. Washington, D.C.: Government Printing Office, 1951.

Wunderlich, Frieda. German Labor Courts. Chapel Hill: University of North Carolina Press, 1946.

Index

Imperialism (*Continued*)
88; and Fascism, 161; contrast between Great Britain and Nazi Germany, 230; necessary consequence of capitalist contradiction, 319 f., 322
Import duties (British), 146
Incitement to Disaffection Act of 1934, 182
Income, minimum, *see* Minimum income
Income taxes, 112
Individual, rights of, *see* Rights (individual)
Individuality, *see* Personality
Individuals, responsibility of, 38 f.; importance of, 39; Laski's reliance upon moral judgments of, 40; political importance of, 87; nature of, 105; Laski's contradictory attitudes toward freedom of conscience, 244 f.
Industrial councils, 31, 63 f., 95, 119 f., 122, 126; *see also* National federation of industrial councils
"Industrial democracy," Laski's meaning, 56
Industrial government, 122 f.
Industry, nationalization, 59 f., 124 f.; government control, 124 ff.; private, 127; impracticality of equal rewards, 189
Inequality, *see* Equality
Inevitabilities, recognition of, 256
Inheritance taxes, 112
Intellectuals, Laski's criticism of, 277 f.
Intelligence, *see* Knowledge
Intolerance, *see* Tolerance

James, Henry, 276, 277, 303
James, William, 298, 303; quoted, 21
Judges (British), 159
Judicial control, 51 f.

Kerry, Frida, 5

Keynes, John Maynard, 177, 191
Knowledge, man's road to salvation, 140 f.

Labor, nonmanual, 112 f.
Labor and laboring classes, France, 55; Great Britain, 57 ff.; hours of labor, 126
Labor government (British), responsibilities of, 205
Labor party, proposed for the United States, 308
Labor Party (British), 58, 82, 85 f., 121, 128 ff., 150, 195; influence on Laski's political thought, 103 f.; 1931 defeat, 146; movement toward the left, 148; philosophy of gradualism, 203; Laski's criticism of, 207, 211; difficulties facing, 210; need for religious enthusiasm, 218; Laski's shifting roles, 221; duties as an opposition party, 221 f.; role in the wartime Coalition Government, 222 ff.; essential principles frustrated by wartime Coalition, 224 f.; Laski's attack on leaders of, 225; Laski's criticism of, 227 f.; failure to adopt Marxism, 240; conformity within, 244; central wartime thesis, 263; opposed by half the citizens of Great Britain, 267 f.; advisability of achieving an understanding with the Soviet Union, 273 f.; need for renewed faith and enthusiasm, 278 f.; success of its postwar government a blow to Laski's thesis, 290; Laski's ambivalent attitude toward, 290; Laski's commitment to, 293; vigilance enjoined against privileged classes, 299; Communist efforts to control, 316; Soviet Union's hostility to, 329
Labor unions, *see* Trade unions
Laissez-faire, Laski's polemic against, 253

National federation of industrial councils, Laski's advocacy of, 64 ff.; later rejection of, 119 f.

Nationalism, commitment of socialists to, 293

Nationalization of industry, *see* Industry, nationalization

NATO, 321, 324

Natural rights, 117 f.; Laski's list, 50; *see also* Rights (individual)

Natural rights theories, Laski's sympathy with, 48 ff.; difficulties of, 50

Nazi-Soviet Pact of 1939, 231; Laski's condemnation of, 280

Negroes, failure of Bill of Rights to protect, 51; prejudice against in the United States, 307

Nevinson, H. W., 5

New Age, The, 58

Newark *Advertiser,* 202

New Deal, 177, 197 ff., 269, 295

Nisei, failure of Bill of Rights to protect, 51

Nonmanual labor, *see* Labor, nonmanual

Nonrational behavior, 131 f.

Obedience (political), 34 ff., 172 ff.; danger of Laski's theory, 39 ff.; Laski's analysis of, 100 ff.; qualifications of earlier defense of disobedience, 104; Laski's wartime analysis of, 247 ff.

Order, Laski's early attitude toward, 42 f.

Orwell, George, quoted, 6

Osborne case, 30

Ownership, socialized, *see* Socialized ownership

Parliamentary government (British), threats to, 147 ff.

Parties, political, *see* Political parties

Paternalism, Laski's antagonism to, 57

Peace, aim of Soviet rulers, 281

Pearson, Karl, 5

Peirce, Charles Sanders, 303

People's Convention Movement, 229

Personality, social aspects of, 106

Philosophes, 141

"Planned society," *see* Socialist society

Plato, 338

Pluralism, pragmatic character of, 21 f.; essential features, 23 f.; Laski's scheme of advisory councils not pluralism, 96; rejected by Laski, 153 f.

Political apathy, 57, 58

Political parties, 149, 304 f.; homage to the democratic idea in Great Britain, 226; in the United States, 304 f.

Politics, relationship to economics, 53 ff., 119 ff., 192 ff., 261 ff.; as a means of self-expression, 63

Polyarchism, Laski's theory of, 25

Positive liberalism, *see* Liberalism

Power (economic), predominance of, 18 f.

Power (political), 77 ff.; Laski's distrust of, 17; decentralization of, 30 f.; dangers of, 89 f.; coercive, 156 f.; influence over economic life in the United States, 168 f.; Laski's depreciation of importance of, 168; Laski's ambivalent attitude toward, 169; danger of inequalities in, 188 f.; dependence upon economic power, 192; based on popular will, 226; socialist use of, 242; unwillingness of dictators to surrender absolute power, 284; Laski's interest in the struggle for, 291

Press, subservience to business interests in the United States, 304

Private ownership, abolition essential for removal of economic inequalities, 190

Production, state's obligation toward, 156; restriction by capitalists, 177,